D0983777

WITHDRAWN

The poems of John Keats have traditionally been regarded as most resistant of all Romantic poetry to the concerns of history and politics. But recent critical trends have begun to overturn this assumption. *Keats and History* brings together exciting new work by British and American scholars, in thirteen essays which respond to recent interest in the historical dimensions of Keats's poems and letters, and open fresh perspectives on his achievement. The invigorating qualities of contemporary Romantic studies are fully represented in the essays, as are the strengths of more traditional disciplines of close reading, textual analysis, and manuscript study. Keats's writings are approached through politics, social history, feminism, economics, historiography, stylistics, aesthetics, and mathematical theory. The editor's introduction places the volume in relation to nineteenth- and earlier twentieth-century readings of the poet. *Keats and History* represents the latest research in contemporary studies of Romantic literature, and will be an important marker in modern under-standing of Keats. It will be welcomed by students of English literature, and by all those interested in English Romanticism.

KEATS AND HISTORY

The Peterloo Massacre, artist unknown. Published by Richard Carlile,
1 October, 1819

Keats and History

EDITED BY

NICHOLAS ROE

Reader in English Literature, School of English,
University of St Andrews

Published by the Press Syndicate of the University of Cambridge
The Pitt Building, Trumpington Street, Cambridge CB2 1RP
40 West 20th Street, New York, NY 10011–4211, USA
10 Stamford Road, Oakleigh, Melbourne 3166, Australia

© Cambridge University Press 1995

First published 1995

Printed in Great Britain at the University Press, Cambridge

A catalogue record for this book is available from the British Library

Library of Congress cataloguing in publication data

Keats and history / edited by Nicholas Roe.
p.   cm.
Includes index.
ISBN 0 521 44245 1 (hardback)
1. Keats, John, 1795–1821 – Knowledge – History. 2. Literature and history – England –
History – 19th century. 3. Historical poetry, English – History and criticism. 4. Romanticism –
England. I. Roe, Nicholas.
PR4838.H5K4 1995
821'.7 – dc20
94–12095 CIP

ISBN 0 521 44245 1 hardback

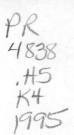

PR
4838
.H5
K4
1995

040996-5720X8

There is a great degree of reality about all that Keats writes: and there must be many allusions to particular Circumstances, in his poems: which would add to their beauty & Interest, if properly understood. – To arrest some few of these circumstances, & bring them to view in connexion with the poetic notice of them, is one of the objects of this collection –

Richard Woodhouse

Note in the Morgan Library 'Scrapbook of Richard Woodhouse', transcribed in Stuart M. Sperry, 'Richard Woodhouse's Interleaved and Annotated Copy of Keats's Poems (1817)', E. Rothstein and T. K. Dunseath (eds.), *Literary Monographs* (Madison, Milwaukee, and London, 1967), 106.

Contents

Illustrations

Notes on contributors

Martin Aske taught for several years at the University of Hong Kong and is now Field Chair of English Studies at Cheltenham and Gloucester College of Higher Education. He is the author of *Keats and Hellenism: An Essay* (1985) and is currently completing an edition of Romantic art criticism and a book on Romantic *ressentiment*.

John Barnard, Professor of English Literature at the University of Leeds, has published on seventeenth, eighteenth century and Romantic topics, and is General Editor of Longman Annotated English Poets. He edited *John Keats: The Complete Poems* (1973) and published *John Keats* in 1987.

Kelvin Everest is A. C. Bradley Professor of Modern Literature at the University of Liverpool. He has written *Coleridge's Secret Ministry* (1979) and *English Romantic Poetry* (1990), edited and contributed to several volumes of essays on Romantic literature, and is currently editing Shelley's poems in the Longman Annotated English Poets series.

Terence Allan Hoagwood is Professor of English and Fellow of the Interdisciplinary Group for Historical Literary Study at Texas A & M University. He is the author of *Prophecy and the Philosophy of Mind: Traditions of Blake and Shelley* (1985), *Skepticism and Ideology: Shelley's Political Prose and its Philosophical Context from Bacon to Marx* (1988), and *Byron's Dialectic: Skepticism and the Critique of Culture* (1993). He has also published editions of Sir William Drummond's *Academical Questions* (1984) and *Philosophical Sketches of the Principles of Society and Government* (1986); Joseph Priestley's *Doctrines of Heathen Philosophy Compared with those of Revelation* (1988); Mary Hays's *The Victim of Prejudice* (1990); and Charlotte Smith's *Beachy Head* (1993).

Theresa M. Kelley is author of *Wordsworth's Revisionary Aesthetics* (1988) and essays on Romantic aesthetics and poetics, the sister arts, Kant, Wordsworth, Keats, Robert Browning, Romantic allegory, and the history of rhetoric. Her current work is *Reinventing Allegory*, a study of allegory's contestatory survival in early modern and modern English culture. She teaches at the University of Texas at Austin.

John Kerrigan is a Fellow of St John's College, Cambridge and University Lecturer in English. He is the author of numerous essays on textual bibliography, literary history, Renaissance poetry and drama. Among the works he has edited are *Motives of Woe: Shakespeare and 'Female Complaint'. A Critical Anthology* (1991) and (with Michael Cordner and Peter Holland) *English Comedy* (1994).

Greg Kucich is Associate Professor of English at the University of Notre Dame. He is the author of *Keats, Shelley, and Romantic Spenserianism* (1991). His recent essays on Romanticism and tradition have appeared in the *Keats–Shelley Journal*, the *Keats–Shelley Review*, and the *Wordsworth Circle*. He is currently writing a book on Romantic inventions of the past, and is co-editor of *Nineteenth-Century Contexts*.

Vincent Newey is Professor of English at the University of Leicester. He is the author of *Cowper's Poetry: A Critical Study and Reassessment* (1982), and joint editor of *Byron and the Limits of Fiction* (1988) and *Literature and Nationalism* (1991). His other publications include a range of articles on Puritan writers, Victorian fiction, and, especially, the Romantic poets. He was a founding editor of the *Bulletin of the British Association for Romantic Studies* and is currently an editor of the *Byron Journal*. He is preparing a volume on Wordsworth for the Longman Critical Readers series.

Michael O'Neill is Reader in English at the University of Durham. His most recent book is the Longman Critical Reader *Shelley* (1993). He is editing *The Defence of Poetry Fair Copies* for Garland's *The Bodleian Shelley Manuscripts* series.

Nicholas Roe is Reader in English Literature in the School of English, University of St Andrews, Scotland. He is the author of *Wordsworth and Coleridge. The Radical Years* (1988) and *The Politics of Nature* (1992). He co-edited *Coleridge's Imagination. Essays in Memory of*

Peter Laver (1985) and has edited and introduced *William Wordsworth. Selected Poetry* for the Penguin Poetry Library (1992), and *Selected Poems of John Keats* for the Everyman Library (1995).

Nicola Trott is a Fellow by Special Election at St Catherine's College, Oxford. She has a Postdoctoral Research Fellowship from the British Academy, which she gratefully acknowledges. Her monograph, *Wordsworth's Second Sight*, will be published by Oxford University Press.

Daniel P. Watkins is Professor of English at Duquesne University in Pittsburgh, Pennsylvania. He is the author of *Social Relations in Byron's Eastern Tales* (1987), *Keats's Poetry and the Politics of the Imagination* (1989), and *A Materialist Critique of English Romantic Drama* (1993). His most recent book is entitled *Romantic Texts and Sadeian Logic*.

Susan J. Wolfson is Professor of English Literature at Princeton University and the author of several essays and articles on English Romantic writing, as well as *The Questioning Presence: Wordsworth, Keats, and the Interrogative Mode in Romantic Poetry* (1986).

Preface and editor's acknowledgements

In recent years, historical readings of Keats's poetry have formed one of the most rewarding aspects of Romantic criticism and scholarship. The thirteen essays brought together in *Keats and History* respond to and develop this fresh concern for the historical dimensions of Keats's achievement and reputation, employing critical and theoretical methods that reflect the full diversity of contemporary Romantic studies. Materialist, feminist, and gender-based criticisms are represented in the book, alongside essays that focus on Keats's writings through more traditional approaches of close textual analysis and the transcription of hitherto unpublished manuscript material. The essays also display a wealth of different interests, considering Keats's poems and letters in relation to his early intellectual background, political and social history, historical narratives, literary criticism, feminist issues, economics, historiography, stylistics, aesthetics, and mathematical theory. The object of all contributions to this book is expressed by the epigraph from Keats's admirable friend and perceptive critic, Richard Woodhouse.

Keats and History would not have been possible without the interest and commitment of the contributors, who over the three years that the book was in preparation cheerfully met deadlines and coped with editorial correspondence. The editor's work was assisted by research support from the School of English, St Andrews University, by staff at the University Library, and by Helen Kay's word-processing skills. At the Keats Memorial Library, Hampstead, Christina Gee and Roberta Davis helped in locating material for the introduction. John Barnard and David Fairer of the School of English, Leeds University, have been encouraging presences throughout the evolution of this book. For valuable advice and suggestions I am indebted to Jane Stabler, Department of English Literature, Glasgow University. Finally, Josie Dixon at Cambridge University Press supported this book from the outset, and she has guided it through the various stages of production with great care. To all, my thanks.

Nicholas Roe

Abbreviations and a note on texts

AP	Miriam Allott, *The Poems of John Keats*. Longman's Annotated English Poets Series (London and New York, 1970)
D.NB	*Dictionary of National Biography*
EinC	*Essays in Criticism*
ELH	*Journal of English Literary History*
HW	P. P. Howe (ed.), *The Complete Works of William Hazlitt* (21 vols., London, 1930–4)
JEGP	*Journal of English and Germanic Philology*
KC	Hyder E. Rollins (ed.), *The Keats Circle. Letters and Papers 1816–1878 and More Letters and Poems 1814–1879* (2nd edn, 2 vols., Cambridge, Mass., 1965)
KCH	Geoffrey Matthews (ed.), *Keats. The Critical Heritage* (London, 1971)
KHM	Jerome McGann, 'Keats and the Historical Method in Literary Criticism', *Modern Language Notes* 94 (1979); rpt. *The Beauty of Inflections. Literary Investigations in Historical Method and Theory* (Oxford, 1985), 17–65
KL	Marjorie Levinson, *Keats's Life of Allegory. The Origins of a Style* (Oxford and New York, 1988)
KP	Susan Wolfson (ed.), 'Keats and Politics: A Forum', *SIR* 25 (Summer 1986)
KPP	Daniel P. Watkins, *Keats's Poetry and the Politics of the Imagination* (London and Toronto, 1989)
K–SJ	*Keats–Shelley Journal*
L&L	Richard Monckton Milnes, *Life, Letters, and Literary Remains, of John Keats* (2 vols., London, 1848)
Letters	Hyder E. Rollins (ed.), *The Letters of John Keats, 1814–1821* (2 vols., Cambridge, Mass., 1958)
MHRA	Modern Humanities Research Association

PJK	Jack Stillinger (ed.), *The Poems of John Keats* (Cambridge, Mass., and London, 1978)
PMLA	*Publications of the Modern Language Association of America*
PQ	*Philological Quarterly*
SEL	*Studies in English Literature*
SIR	*Studies in Romanticism*

A note on texts

Unless indicated otherwise, quotations from Keats's poems are from *PJK*, and quotations from Keats's correspondence are from *Letters*. Angle brackets denote cancellations; square brackets supply letters or words missing in the original manuscript source.

CHAPTER I

Introduction

Nicholas Roe

KEATS AND HISTORY: THE CRITICAL BACKGROUND

Keats's first biographer Richard Monckton Milnes announced his subject as 'one whose whole story may be summed up in the composition of three small volumes of verse, some earnest friendships, one passion, and a premature death' (*L&L*, i. 2). In his *Life, Letters, and Literary Remains, of John Keats* (1848), Milnes filled two volumes, and almost six hundred pages, with these bare circumstances. Yet, although Keats's life, works, and times have been minutely documented in subsequent biographies and studies, the idea of his minimal worldly presence was accepted throughout the nineteenth century and has continued to influence critical approaches to Keats and his poems for the greater part of the twentieth.[1]

A late but representative expression of Keats's unworldliness emerges from Paul de Man's conjecture that, because of the 'unfavorable circumstances of his birth', Keats 'lived almost always oriented toward the future':

The pathos, of course, is that he never reached these days, but he was no longer able to write by the time he realized this. In reading Keats, we are therefore reading the work of a man whose experience is mainly literary. The growing insight that underlies the remarkably swift development of his talent was gained primarily from the act of writing. In this case, we are on very safe ground when we derive our understanding primarily from the work itself.[2]

The point is tactfully argued. Although de Man does not banish context entirely, he avoids discussion of Keats's illness and death by heading for the comparatively 'safe ground' of a life understood to have been 'mainly literary'. Here de Man would be further reassured by many precedents for this idea of Keats's wholly literary existence. Ernest de Selincourt, for example, wrote in 1905 that 'Keats was

educated almost exclusively by the English poets. His studies, and he
was a deep and earnest student, were concentrated upon their works,
and the friendships which encouraged his genius were sealed in a
common enthusiasm for them.' The historical corollary appeared two
years later in Stopford A. Brooke's extraordinary account of Keats as
the apathetic sublime. For Brooke Keats was a poet who had no
regard whatsoever for humanity or 'the excitement [and] the turmoil'
of contemporary events: 'He has, in spite of a few passages and till
quite the end of his career, no vital interest in the present, none in man
as a whole, none in the political movement of human thought, none in
the future of mankind, none in liberty, equality, or fraternity, no
interest in anything but beauty.'[3]

All three critics – de Man, de Selincourt, and Brooke – were
echoing a strong tradition of nineteenth-century commentators who
presented a totally de-historicised Keats. One such was William
Howitt (1847): 'On this world and its concerns [Keats] could take no
hold, and they could take none on him. The worldly and the worldly
wise could not comprehend him, could not sympathize with him' –
and another was David Masson (1860): 'In short, [Keats] kept aloof
from opinion, doctrine, controversy, as by a natural instinct; he was
most at home in the world of sense and imagery, where it was his
pleasure to weave forth phantasies.'[4] Readily dismissing 'opinion,
doctrine, controversy' from Keats's 'world of sense and imagery',
Masson's account came to be typical in offering a sentimental image
of a poet who was 'by a natural instinct' unfitted for intellectual life,
and aloof from the tumultuous goings-on of the contemporary world.
In this way the poet of sensual imagery and pleasing phantasies was
taken out of history into a supposedly separate world of the aesthetic.
In his *Life of John Keats* (1887) William Michael Rossetti agreed with
Masson in doubting whether Keats 'felt very strongly upon any
matters of intellectual or general concern other than poetic ones'.
According to Rossetti, Keats took 'but very faint interest' in 'political
matters': his early death 'doomed [him] to be the poet of youthfulness'
and 'by being the poet of youthfulness he was privileged to become
and remain enduringly the poet of rapt expectation and passionate
delight'.[5] That last phrase indicates how closely Keats was made to
agree with the abiding beauty of his own Grecian Urn, without
recognising that the urn is actually a 'high-sorrowful' historian (albeit
a 'Sylvan' one) that tells of desolation, old age, and the passing of
generations. That this image of Keats has endured to the end of the

twentieth century is indicated by a recent account of the revolutionary context of Keats's times, in which he is presented as 'the most apolitical of the great Romantic poets': 'Poetry was Keats's life – but like all the Romantics he suspected that there were times when poetry was not enough.'[6] Here, as in the other passages quoted above, Keats's dedication to poetry is represented as a timeless enthralment that somehow isolated him from the movements of contemporary life.

The myth of Keats's unworldliness originated during the poet's lifetime, in the critical argument surrounding his three collections of verse, *Poems* (1817), *Endymion* (1818), and *Lamia, Isabella, The Eve of St. Agnes, and Other Poems* (1820). As is well known, this controversy divided according to political opinion. For the Tory critic John Lockhart, Keats's association with Leigh Hunt and his imitation of Hunt's 'loose, nerveless versification' was sufficient to explain how the cockney 'bantling' had learned to 'lisp sedition' in his own verses. In the fourth of his 'Cockney School' essays in *Blackwood's Edinburgh Magazine* (August 1818), Lockhart set out to discredit Keats's literary achievements through ridiculing his youth, social background, and radical political sympathies. By enforcing a stereotype of childishness, naivety, and immaturity, Lockhart sought to explode the upstart 'Johnny Keats' and his associates in order to secure received cultural and political values against the Cockneys' challenge. In Lockhart's view of Keats, there was no discrimination of the aesthetic and the political; quite the contrary. For him Keats's poetic language was itself reprobate, an insolent challenge to the establishment. After quoting some 'very pretty raving' from *Sleep and Poetry*, Lockhart observed that 'our youthful poet passes very naturally into a long strain of foaming abuse against a certain class of English Poets, whom, with Pope at their head, it is much the fashion with the ignorant unsettled pretenders of the present time to undervalue'. Compared with Keats, the one-time Jacobin 'pretender' Wordsworth appeared in Lockhart's pantheon alongside Pope as 'the purest, the loftiest, and . . . the most classical of living English poets'.[7]

In the present collection, Martin Aske's essay 'Keats, the critics, and the politics of envy' shows how the *ressentiment* that greeted Keats's earlier poems was assimilated, in *Isabella* and *Lamia*, as imaginative strength and humane understanding. The longer perspective of Keats's evolving reputation discloses that his response to critical hostility was frequently misrepresented as evidence of personal weakness. During the poet's lifetime, his friends endeavoured to defend him by emphasising his distance from political and cultural controversy. Writing in the *Alfred, West of England Journal and General Advertiser* (6 October 1818), John Hamilton Reynolds argued that a true appreciation of Keats's 'singular feeling, force, and pathos' depended upon comparative insulation from the literary and political establishment: 'We have the highest hopes of this young Poet', he wrote,

We are obscure men, it is true . . . We live far from the world of letters, – out of the pale of fashionable criticism, – aloof from the atmosphere of a Court; but we are surrounded by a beautiful country, and love Poetry, which we read out of doors, as well as in. We think we see glimpses of a high mind in this young man, and surely the feeling is better that urges us to nourish its strength, than that which prompts the Quarterly reviewer to crush it in its youth, and for ever.[8]

At the start of the nineteenth century, therefore, the idea of Keats's youthful isolation was already forming: 'obscure . . . far from the world of letters . . . aloof from the atmosphere of a Court'. As this was developed and elaborated in subsequent years, it worked to obscure the genuinely challenging qualities of his poetry that had originally unsettled Lockhart, Croker, and others.

Reynolds's vindication of Keats was reprinted by Leigh Hunt in the *Examiner*, 11 October 1818, where it would have been noticed by another 'young poet' of the day, Shelley. Some two years later, on hearing of Keats's death at Rome, 23 February 1821, Shelley set about composing his elegy *Adonais*, prefacing his poem with an attack on Croker's 'savage criticism' of Keats in the *Quarterly Review*. The theme of Keats's vulnerability, which had been latent in Reynolds's article, now emerged as a significant factor in the evolving myth of Keats's untimely demise: 'The genius of the lamented person to whose memory I have dedicated these unworthy verses, was not less delicate and fragile than it was beautiful; and where cankerworms abound, what wonder if its young flower was blighted in the bud?'[9] In her essay 'Keats enters history: autopsy, *Adonais*, and the fame of Keats', Susan Wolfson presents ample documentary evidence recording how, for succeeding generations, Shelley's memorial established a potent myth that determined Keats's reception in terms of gender, the politics of poetry, canons of taste, and as a focus for sentimental Romanticism. *Adonais* fixed Keats as the poet of delicate and fragile genius who had been destroyed by unfavourable criticism, or, to adopt David Masson's terms, by his contact with 'opinion, doctrine, controversy'. For many years 'Adonais' supplanted the reality of Keats's life and, until very lately, this enduring myth of Keats's achievement and death reinforced the prejudice against historical approaches to, and understandings of, his poetry. Indeed, this neglect may explain why Keats has formed an important and rewarding focus for the newly-invigorated historical criticism of Romantic poetry that has flourished since the 1980s. In 1979 Jerome McGann rightly claimed that Keats was a poet 'for whom historical analysis – by the virtually unanimous decision of western literary critics – has no relevance whatsoever' (*KHM*, 26). His essay 'Keats and the Historical Method' argued for poetry's 'complete, social particularity', reasserting the centrality of history to critical analysis against 'the great commonplace of twentieth-century literary criticism: that a poem is fundamentally a word-construct, a special arrangement of linguistic units, or – as we now like to say – a "text"' (*KHM*, 18, 22, 62). In terms of Romantic studies more especially, McGann's analyses of some Keats poems reminded his readers how an historically oriented criticism might open a range of contextual literary matters such as the social, political, and gendered inflections of poetic style, the bibliographical histories of publication and reception, and biographical and socio-historical frames of reference.

McGann's essay has encouraged a diversity of critical and theoretical approaches to Keats, all of which share a preoccupation signalled by the title of this book: *Keats and History*. Essays in the present volume by Theresa Kelley, Michael O'Neill, Vincent Newey, and Nicholas Roe, variously answer, develop, or redirect McGann's argument. They treat broad questions of the relation between writing and history, as well as the ways in which Keats's texts 'inevitably operate under – though they may also reformulate, react against, even provisionally transcend – the impress, socio-structural, historical, discursive, of the world [Keats] inhabits' (Vincent Newey). In her consideration of aesthetic form and the mediation of history, 'Keats, ekphrasis, and history', Theresa Kelley answers McGann's materialist approach by showing how the ekphrastic claims of *Ode on a Grecian Urn* belong to a 'compelling . . . argument about history and art that permeates Keats's poetic career'. *To Autumn* provides a focus for Michael O'Neill's close reading of the ways in which Keats's poems debate 'in [their] own terms the relationship between art and history', suggesting how, 'though a poem emerges from a life it takes on a life of its own' which cannot be entirely accommodated and explained by materialist criticism. Both Vincent Newey and I respond to the charge that *To Autumn* is a lyrical 'escape' from political crisis. Newey's 'Keats, history, and the poets' emphasises the poem's 'positive transhistorical value', at once 'local *and* universal, geographically specified *and* unspecific, of its time *and* timeless'. My own essay, 'Keats's commonwealth', presents a detailed reading of *To Autumn* alongside contemporary discourses of 'conspiracy' generated by Peterloo, to suggest how the poem answers and redresses crisis rather than seeking an aesthetic 'escape' from the world.

The changing climate of Keats studies during the 1980s was registered in Marilyn Butler's *Romantics, Rebels, and Reactionaries* (1981), which drew upon the poet's discussion of social progress and revolution in his journal letter to the George Keatses of 17–27 September 1819 (*Letters*, ii. 193–4) to argue that 'Keats's larger intention in both "Hyperions" . . . is broadly to represent historical change as the liberal habitually sees it: continuous, inevitable, and on the most universal level grand, for it is Progress – the survival of the fittest, the best, the most beautiful and the quintessentially human'. This evidence was sufficient to suggest that, with other poets of 1817–20, Keats was not 'in any important sense evasive' of history.[10] Although subsequent readings of Keats's Hyperion poems have been more sceptical about his belief in meliorative progress (see below), Butler's concern with the ways in which his poems responded to and negotiated with contemporary events is broadly representative of current approaches to his poetry and letters.

The diversity of these new readings was apparent in 'Keats and Politics: A Forum', edited by Susan Wolfson and published in *Studies in Romanticism* (Summer 1986). The forum as a whole made 'permanently incredible the choice between Keats and politics' (David Bromwich's words)[11] although the contributors did not unite in a consensus on the subject. Paul H. Fry resisted any socially determined interpretation of *To Autumn* as 'a fallacy of misplaced concreteness'. Yet, by asserting that the poem's concerns may be limited to 'the ontology of the lyric moment', Fry indicated how the matter of Keats and history had already moved from the margins of literary study to become a focus of wider debate about literary-critical methods and interpretive strategies. Keats's lively, perceptive interest in his own times was fully accepted, however, although the evidence of imagination in the poems elicited diverging interpretations. Morris Dickstein followed Jerome McGann in contending that Keats's poetry was a 'kind of evasive action' that evoked a 'refreshing alternative' to historical tensions, an 'aesthetic creation that . . . aims at a renewal of both self and society'. By contrast Bromwich showed why Keats's contemporaries would have perceived him as a radical, pointing out that Lockhart had recognised the 'ennervatingly luxurious' poetry of the 1817 volume and *Endymion* as 'transparently political'. His recovery of Keats's presence for his first readers significantly required the dispersal of received or 'standard' readings of the poems which had accumulated over the years. In a further demonstration of this approach, William Keach explored the political and cultural meanings of the animosity directed at Keats's 'cockney couplets', arguing more broadly (and *contra* Fry) that 'acts of writing and reading may be subject to historical and political circumstances quite remote from a poem's immediate field of reference'. One case in point is the concluding essay in the forum, in which Alan J. Bewell elucidated the politics of *Hyperion* by considering the historical meanings of the Titans' representation as Egyptian, rather than Greek sculptures. Instead of depicting history as enlightened progress (from Egyptian aesthetics to Greek; from Titans to Olympians; from Milton to Wordsworth) Bewell contended that in *Hyperion* Keats's valuation of 'the "sorrow" of Egyptian sculpture' expressed history as 'a continuous process of displacement' in which the poet's sympathies are with victims and outsiders.[12] In this account, Keats's idea of history in *Hyperion* was the reflex of the poet's own self-image as politically and culturally disenfranchised – a point to which I shall return in a moment.

Two recent full-length studies bear on some of the essays in this volume: Marjorie Levinson's *Keats's Life of Allegory. The Origins of a Style* (1988) and Daniel Watkins's *Keats's Poetry and the Politics of the Imagination* (1989). Both adopted a materialist approach to history, arguing vigorously for the social–political conditioning of Keats's poetry against earlier literary, aesthetic, metaphysical, and psycho-logical studies. Levinson glossed Keats's 'life of allegory' in terms of his social class and literary ambitions. In these factors, she contended, one might find an explanation for Keats's 'badness' as a poet: the vulgar, overwrought qualities of some of his poems that were ridiculed in journals of the day. A lower-class poet, who felt himself excluded from literary culture, Levinson's Keats was *literally* on the make: aggressive to the point of creating a parodic *anti*-literature.[13]

Where Levinson's approach was social–stylistic, Watkins placed

Keats's career more broadly in relation to an age of anxiety: the post-Napoleonic period when Wordsworth's 'blissful dawn' of revolutionary optimism had finally yielded to a period that threatened a 'return to an older, conservative, potentially oppressive and violent political situation'.[14] In this volume, Watkins's essay 'History, self, and gender in *Ode to Psyche*' reads the ode as an expression of Keats's desire to shape meaning from an age of social instability and transition; he draws out the 'bourgeois character of gender relations' in the poem and develops this in terms of a sadistic 'need for violence against feminine existence'. Kelvin Everest also pursues feminist critical issues to reveal how the opposition of the lovers and the two brothers, which forms the 'palpable design' of *Isabella*, is complicated by a 'deep connectedness' between Isabella's and Lorenzo's code of sexual behaviour and the economic interests of her brothers – those murderous 'ledger-men'. A similar complicity between economics and Keats's imagination is traced by Terence Hoagwood. December 1818 saw no less than four trials in London for the forgery of bank notes – a capital crime that intensified an existing crisis of confidence in paper money.[15] Hoagwood's 'Keats, fictionality, and finance: *The Fall of Hyperion*' argues that the speculative, 'fictional' value of paper money offers a pattern for structures of surrogation in *The Fall of Hyperion*, such that Keats's poem may be said to have been situated in a 'symbolic economy' peculiarly appropriate to the post-Waterloo period. Here, as in other essays in this collection, the literary texture of Keats's poetry is shown to have emerged from and to have acknowledged the manifold pressures of contemporary history. Indeed the forcefully proleptic imagination, which de Man associated with Keats's orphaned childhood, may also be understood as an expression of wider historical processes.

IN PROGRESS AGAIN? KEATS'S HISTORY

In his journal letter of 17–27 September 1819, Keats announced that he would write 'a little politics'. What followed in his letter, however, was a liberal account of history as progressive enlightenment, 'a continual change for the better':

Look at this Country at present and remember it when it was even though[t] impious to doubt the justice of a trial by Combat – From that time there has been a gradual change – Three great changes have been in progress – First for the better, next for the worse, and a third time for the better once more. The first was the gradual annihilation of the tyranny of the nobles, when kings found it their interest to conciliate the common people, elevate them and be just to them. Just when baronial Power ceased and before standing armies were so dangerous, Taxes were few. [K]ings were lifted by the people over the heads of their nobles, and those people held a rod over kings. The change for the worse in Europe was again this. The obligation of kings to the Multitude began to be forgotten – Custom had made noblemen the humble servants of kings – Then kings turned to the Nobles as the adorners of the[i]r power, the slaves of it, and from the people as creatures continually endeavouring to check them. Then in every kingdom therre was a long struggle of kings to destroy all popular privileges. The english were the only people in europe who made a grand kick at this. They were slaves to Henry 8th but were freemen under William 3rd at the time the french were abject slaves under Lewis 14th. The example of England, and the liberal writers of france and england sowed the seed of opposition to this Tyranny – and it was swelling in the ground till it burst out in the french revolution – That has had an unlucky termination. It put a stop to the rapid progress of free sentiments in England; and gave our Court hopes of turning back to the despotism of the 16 century. They have made a handle of this event in every way to undermine our freedom. They spread a horrid superstition against all inovation and improvement – The present struggle in England of the people is to destroy this superstition. What has rous'd them to do it is their distresses – Perpaps on this account the pres'ent distresses of this nation are a fortunate thing – tho so horrid in the[i]r experience. You will see I mean that the french Revolution put a temporry stop to this third change, the change for the better – Now it is in progress again and I thing in an effectual one. This is no contest beetween whig and tory – but between right and wrong.[16]

Keats began this letter one month after the Peterloo Massacre on 16 August 1819, when political tension was acute throughout England. The passage reveals him interpreting English (and European) history from the middle ages as a 'gradual enlightenment' in the relationships between the aristocracy (king, nobles, court) and the people ('popular privileges'). He touches on matters of justice, tyranny, commonwealth, military power, and taxation. In concluding, however, he approaches the more recent phenomenon of the French Revolution stressing in particular its consequences for England. As Greg Kucich shows in 'Keats's literary tradition and the politics of historiographical invention', the poet's idea that the revolution arose from the liberal enlightenment of the preceding century was a widespread feature of eighteenth-century historiography. Yet Keats's account of the revolution's failure, its 'unlucky termination', surrenders the progress of humankind to the rules of chance which from the

1790s had 'undermined' freedom and returned England to the tyranny of former times. In his essay 'Writing numbers: Keats, Hopkins, and the history of chance' John Kerrigan argues that an 'inspired randomness', hospitable to the chanciness of life and rhyme, was integral to Keats. This appears in the numerical wittiness of his poetry and letters, and it is markedly different from Gerard Manley Hopkins's attraction to mathematics as 'scientific' evidence of divine providential order, an antidote to later nineteenth-century 'theories of atomistic "chance" and fateful statistics'. By glossing the French Terror and Napoleon's imperial career as 'unlucky' developments, Keats avoided inquiry into the causes of revolutionary defeat that had preoccupied an earlier generation of poets and radicals. In so doing, he escaped the 'prison house of history' which Nicola Trott brings forward as a prominent motif in Keats's writing: the suffocating, serpentine opposite of the 'camelion' poet's unrestricted capabilities. He was correspondingly at liberty to dwell on the 'present distresses' of the nation as the motive for a renewed 'change for the better' – the outcome of which might yet turn out to be a 'happy lot'.

At a critical moment in recent history, Keats identified the resurgence of 'effectual progress' with vigorous contemporary opposition to the government and renewed calls for a parliamentary reform. His letter is striking in its optimistic outlook, and for the long historical perspective in which he sought to understand recent events. As Keats knew, David Hume's *History of England* presented a similar interpretation of historical cycles, or 'great changes . . . in progress', although with a less auspicious gloss on the prospects for cumulative betterment: 'There is an ultimate point of depression', Hume had written, 'as well as of exaltation, from which human affairs naturally return in a contrary progress, and beyond which they seldom pass either in advancement or decline.'[17]

William Robertson had discussed this passage from Hume in his *History of the Reign of the Emperor Charles V*, which Keats read at Enfield School.[18] Hume interpreted history as an unameliorative movement between extremes of 'depression' and 'exaltation'. For Robertson, however, history displayed a cumulative progress in the improvement of society, offering a pattern for Keats's broadly optimistic letter of September 1819 – a 'hard-driving' whig tradition that Newey also associates with William Cowper. Keats's thinking about history, like his liberal politics, was initiated by his reading at Enfield School and discussions with his tutor and mentor Charles Cowden Clarke. John

Barnard's transcription and analysis of entries from 'Charles Cowden Clarke's "Cockney" commonplace book' adds much to our understanding of the liberal cultural milieu of Keats's early years at Enfield and Edmonton. The hitherto unpublished material from Clarke's notebook contains passages of literary, political, and historical interest, and – as Barnard shows – Clarke's recurrent themes are echoed in Keats's letter of September 1819: the constitutional liberties of England, religious toleration, the tyranny of the Stuarts, admiration for seventeenth-century libertarians, opposition to war and violence, and – above all – a belief in liberty. Here, then, is a specific documentary source for Keats's thinking about the nature of history. Yet, given this generous and liberal background, it is striking that in some of Keats's poems history and the imagination coincide in a distinctly militant vision of progressive humanity.

The Scottish theologian and historian William Robertson was 'an avowed optimist of the eighteenth-century type' (*DNB*). Charles Cowden Clarke recalled that Keats had also read Robertson's *History of Scotland* and *The History of America*.[19] In all three histories, and as Greg Kucich shows in his essay, Robertson was concerned to demonstrate universal progress in the fields of politics, society, commerce, science, and the arts. Like other liberals of his generation, Robertson welcomed the American Revolution as a promise of the 'future condition' of the world that commanded the 'attention and expectation of mankind': 'a new order of things must arise in North America', he wrote, 'and its affairs will assume another aspect'.[20] In all these respects Robertson's books would have complemented Keats's wider reading in the liberal and republican texts that were representative of the intellectual environment at Enfield School. Barnard and Kucich provide fresh evidence relating to this formative milieu in Keats's intellectual and imaginative life, suggesting how it may have contributed to the poet's ideas of a 'gradual enlightenment' in human affairs. As one might expect, though, Keats's later expressions of those ideas in his poems and letters were not always consistent.

Oceanus's explanation of the law of progress in *Hyperion*,

> 'So on our heels a fresh perfection treads,
> A power more strong in beauty, born of us
> And fated to excel us'　　　　　　　　(II. 212–14)

is in some respects an epitome of the liberal historical theory characteristic of Robertson. The poem is distinctive, however, in its emphasis upon the competitive power of imagination and 'the eternal law/ That first in beauty should be first in might' (II. 228–9). Here, ideal beauty determines the advance of history in successive acts of conquest and usurpation, an imperial progress in the course of which Neptune triumphs over Oceanus:

> 'Have ye beheld the young God of the Seas,
> My dispossessor? Have ye seen his face?
> Have ye beheld his chariot, foam'd along
> By noble winged creatures he hath made?
> I saw him on the calmed waters scud,
> With such a glow of beauty in his eyes,
> That it enforc'd me to bid sad farewell
> To all my empire: farewell sad I took . . .'   (II. 232–9)

According to the same eternal law, beautiful Apollo will enforce his succession to Hyperion as god of music, poetry, and medicine. In each case the 'transcendental cosmopolitics' of *Hyperion*, remarked by Leigh Hunt, are defined by a militant quest for ideal beauty.[21]

In *The Fall of Hyperion* this imperious vision is qualified by Moneta's admonition that the poet should 'think of the earth' (I. 169); think, that is, of the distresses of human beings, but also of the 'unlucky' excesses to which extreme idealism might lead. In this last respect, Keats's schooling in the benevolent and vicious potentials of the imagination resembled the experiences of Coleridge and Wordsworth during the 1790s, for whom Robespierre's Terror projected the lethal effects of imagination's 'horrible misapplication'.[22] To Keats at Enfield School, Robertson's *History of America* presented a compelling narrative of the Spanish conquests in the new worlds of the Caribbean and South America. As is well known, these passages from Robertson's book constitute the invigorating and chastening historical matter that shadows the golden realms of Keats's early sonnet *On First Looking into Chapman's Homer*. The sonnet encompasses poetry and history, in that Keats's first reading of Chapman's Homer is said to have 'felt . . . like' Herschel's and Cortez's momentous discoveries (9). The felt kinship between poetic imagination and the revelation of new worlds (across the Atlantic, beyond the Pacific, at the edge of the solar system) is one of marvellous, unutterable possibility: 'a wild surmise –/ Silent' (13–14). In the aspiration to 'goodly states and kingdoms' (2), Keats suggests that political history and poetic imagination coincide.[23]

In his recent account of William Robertson's importance to the sonnet, Daniel Watkins elucidates parallels between the poem and the discovery-narratives of Cortez and Balboa in the *History of America*, suggesting that Keats aspires to unite poetry and history as 'a single enterprise', although in fact his sonnet may be achieved 'at the expense of history itself'.[24] Robertson's description of the 'visionary ideas' of the explorers has not yet been discussed in this context, so far as I am aware. It offers a compelling analogue to the 'realms of gold' of Keats's imagining, and may permit a reintegration of history and imagination under the sign of imperial militarism – the 'conquest and command' that Vincent Newey's essay notices as the 'latent concern in Keats's sonnet'. Here is the relevant passage from Robertson's *History of America*:

The Spaniards, at that period, were engaged in a career of activity which gave a romantic turn to their imagination, and daily presented to them strange and marvellous objects. A New World was opened to their view. They visited islands and continents, of whose existence mankind in former ages had no conception. In those delightful countries, nature seemed to assume another form; every tree and plant and animal was different from those of the ancient hemisphere. They seemed to be transported into ancient ground; and, after the wonders they had seen, nothing, in the warmth and novelty of their admiration, appeared to them so extraordinary as to be beyond belief. If the rapid succession of new and striking scenes made such an impression even upon the sound understanding of Columbus, that he boasted of having found the seat of Paradise, it will not appear strange that Ponce de Leon should dream of discovering the fountain of youth.[25]

Along with this 'romantic' account of discovery, in which reality and the imaginative power of 'admiration' were at one, Robertson also describes (and deplores) the Spaniards' violent exploitation of human beings in the gold mines of Hispaniola: 'the consumption of the human species [was] no less amazing than rapid'.[26] Keats's sonnet omits the human cost of Spanish activities in the new world, and celebrates Cortez (all struggles past) gazing over the Pacific in a moment of solitary personal triumph. Yet in so doing the sonnet has located imperial aggressiveness as a prerogative of the imagination 'Which bards in fealty to Apollo hold' (4). Thus, Homer appropriated 'one wide expanse' which he 'ruled as his demesne' (5, 6). And so the conqueror's 'eagle eyes ... star'd at the Pacific', as an expression of the poet's own ambitions (11). Imagination and imperial power coincide in the appropriation of strange and marvellous new worlds – 'realms of gold', 'a new planet' (10), 'the seat of Paradise', or 'the fountain of youth'.

As Keats knew, Cortez had claimed his new world for the king of Spain. In a comparable gesture of courtesy, Herschel had named his new planet *Georgium Sidus* in honour of his monarch George III. For the poet such 'dim-conceived glories' were the measure of his own ambitions as a writer, although his aspiration was fortunately tempered by a compassionate humanity and a sense of his own limitations as a person:

> My spirit is too weak – mortality
> Weighs heavily on me like unwilling sleep,
> And each imagined pinnacle and steep
> Of godlike hardship tells me I must die
> Like a sick eagle looking at the sky.
>
> (*On Seeing the Elgin Marbles*, 1–5)

From his schooldays, Keats's understanding and imagining of history comprehended a humane, liberal, and progressive tradition, as well as the thrusting, competitive imperialism of European activities in South America. Alongside these histories may be placed Keats's lived experience of 'the agonies, the strife/ Of human hearts' (*Sleep and Poetry*, 124–5), appropriately represented by the 'sick eagle' of weak mortality. A comparable, universal wisdom is bestowed upon Apollo at the climactic moment of his deification in Book III of *Hyperion*:

> 'Knowledge enormous makes a God of me.
> Names, deeds, gray legends, dire events, rebellions,
> Majesties, sovran voices, agonies,
> Creations and destroyings, all at once
> Pour into the wide hollows of my brain,
> And deify me . . .'
>
> (III. 113–18)

In the lines immediately following, leading up to the point where Keats abandoned his poem, Hyperion's ultimate knowledge is likened to

> '. . . the struggle at the gate of death;
> Or liker still to one who should take leave
> Of pale immortal death, and with a pang
> As hot as death's is chill, with fierce convulse
> Die into life . . .'
>
> (III. 126–30)

For Keats himself, the invigorating power of knowledge that he held necessary to poetic immortality passed into oblivion before the fact of his own drawn-out sickness and progressive decline. As he wrote to Charles Brown from Rome, 30 November 1820: 'I am afraid to encounter the proing and conning of any thing interesting to me in England. I have an habitual feeling of my real life having past, and that I am leading a posthumous existence' (*Letters*, ii. 359). Some four days after Keats's death Joseph Severn, who had nursed him throughout, rallied himself sufficiently to write to Keats's friend: 'My dear Brown, He is gone – he died with the most perfect ease – he seemed to go to sleep.' This was one of many letters in which Severn described in painful detail the poet's last days – 'The Doctors could not conceive by what means he had lived these two months' – although, as Severn admitted, he had not marked the exact moment of Keats's passing: 'he gradually sunk into death – so quiet – that I still thought he slept.'[27] With no final, 'fierce convulse', and as Keats himself uncannily suspected, there was no distinct boundary between the extinction of his physical life and the quickening of his 'posthumous existence' in elegy, memorials, reminiscences, and biographies. As Keats was entering history, he was already the property of myth.

NOTES

1 Significant work that does consider Keats in relation to historical matters includes H. W. Garrod, *John Keats* (Oxford, 1926); Herbert G. Wright, 'Keats and Politics', *Essays and Studies* (Oxford, 1933), 7–23; Clarence De Witt Thorpe, 'Keats's Interest in Politics and World Affairs', *PMLA* 46 (1931), 1228–45; Kenneth Muir, 'The Meaning of *Hyperion*', in K. Muir (ed.), *John Keats. A Reassessment* (Liverpool, 1969), 103–23; June Q. Koch, 'Politics in Keats's Poetry', *JEGP* 71 (1972), 491–501.

2 'The Negative Road', in *Selected Poetry of John Keats* (New York, 1966); rpt. Harold Bloom (ed.), *John Keats*, Modern Critical Views Series (New York, 1985).

3 De Selincourt (ed.), *The Poems of John Keats* (London, 1905), xx. Brooke, 'Keats', in *Studies in Poetry* (London, 1907), 204.

4 Howitt, *Homes and Haunts of the Most Eminent British Poets*, extracted in *KCH*, 311–13; Masson, 'The Life and Poetry of Keats', *Macmillan's Magazine* (Nov. 1860), extracted in *KCH*, 368–83.

5 pp. 130, 148, 209.

6 P. M. S. Dawson, 'Poetry in an Age of Revolution', in Stuart Curran (ed.), *The Cambridge Companion to British Romanticism* (Cambridge, 1993), 49. Dawson cites as examples of Keats's political poetry *Written on the Day That Mr. Leigh Hunt Left Prison*, *To Kosciusko*, and *The Jealousies*, although it is clear from the context that these poems are held to be uncharacteristic of Keats's interests and creativity.

7 'Cockney School of Poetry. No. IV', in *KCH*, 97–110.

8 See *KCH*, 117–22.

9 See D. Reiman and S. Powers (eds.), *Shelley's Poetry and Prose* (New York and London, 1977), 390–2.

10 *Romantics, Rebels, and Reactionaries. English Literature and its Background 1760–1830* (Oxford and New York, 1981), 151–4.

11 'Keats's Radicalism', *KP*, 197.

12 Fry, 'History, Existence, and "To Autumn"', *KP*, 217. Dickstein, 'Keats and Politics', *KP*, 177, 181. Bromwich, 'Keats's Radicalism', *KP*, 197, 199, 202. Keach, 'Cockney Couplets: Keats and the Politics of Style', *KP*, 196. Bewell, 'The Political Implication of Keats's Classicist Aesthetics', *KP*, 227–9.

13 *KL*, 2–38, and, for particular examples, 200, 230, 232–5.

14 *KPP*, 189.

15 See Thomas Love Peacock's letter to Shelley, 15 Dec. 1818, in F. L. Jones (ed.), *The Letters of Percy Bysshe Shelley* (2 vols., Oxford, 1964) ii. 70 fn.

16 *Letters*, ii. 193–4, with minor alterations to punctuation.

17 *The History of England, from the Invasion of Julius Caesar to the Accession of Henry VII* (6 vols., London, 1762) ii. 441.

18 (3 vols., London, 1769) i. 21. For Keats's reading, see 'Recollections of John Keats', in Charles and Mary Cowden Clarke, *Recollections of Writers* (London, 1878), 124.

19 Clarke, *Recollections of Writers*, 124.

20 *The History of America* (6th edn, 3 vols., London, 1792) i. v.

21 *The Autobiography of Leigh Hunt* (3 vols., London, 1850) ii. 202.

22 For Robespierre and imagination see Coleridge's 'Introductory Address' to *Conciones ad Populum* and his 'Lecture on the Slave Trade', in Lewis Patton and Peter Mann (eds.), *Lectures 1795 on Politics and Religion*, Bollingen Collected Coleridge Series Vol. 1 (London, 1971), 35, 235–6. See also the discussion in Nicholas Roe, *Wordsworth and Coleridge. The Radical Years* (Oxford, 1988), 210–23.

23 For the aspiring, speculative qualities of Keats's sonnet, contrasted with the 'ontic' settlement of Wordsworth's sonnets, see John Kerrigan, 'Wordsworth and the Sonnet: Building, Dwelling, Thinking', *EinC* 35 (1985), 45–75, esp. 59–65.

24 *KPP*, 26–31.

25 i. 282–3.

26 *The History of America*, i. 262–3.

27 *KC*, ii. 94. For a discussion of the 'extraordinary mix-up' about the time and date of Keats's death see *KC*, i. 225–7 n.

CHAPTER 2

Keats enters history: autopsy, Adonais, and the fame of Keats

Susan J. Wolfson

> Once the poem passes entirely beyond the purposive control of the author, it leaves the pole of its origin and establishes the first phase of its later dialectical life (what we call its critical history) . . . The moving pole of its receptive life . . . dates from the first responses and reviews it receives.
>
> Jerome McGann, *KHM*, 24

> Virtually the whole course of Keats criticism, directly until the 1840s and indirectly until about 1900, was determined by two exceptional circumstances: his supposed death at the hands of the reviewers, and the early age at which he died . . . it was not possible to discuss Keats's work without prejudice.
>
> G. M. Matthews, *KCH*, 1

> Thanks be to thee, Jack Keats; our thanks for the dactyl and spondee; Pestleman Jack, who, according to Shelley, the Quarterly murdered with a critique as fell as one of his own patent medicines.
>
> 'An Idyll of the Battle', *Blackwood's Edinburgh Magazine* (July 1823), 67

> This is a mere matter of the moment – I think I shall be among the English Poets after my death . . . Even as a Matter of present interest the attempt to crush me in the . . . Quarterly has only brought me more into notice . . .
>
> John Keats, 14 October 1818, *Letters*, i. 394

KEATS'S FAME

In Spring 1819, having suffered the abuse of *Blackwood's*, the *Quarterly*, and the *British Critic* for *Endymion*, and meditating on the vagaries of public reception and the debasements of courting its favour, Keats wrote a sonnet, *On Fame*, which he, at least, never proffered to the fame of publication:

Fame, like a wayward girl, will still be coy
　　To those who woo her with too slavish knees,
But makes surrender to some thoughtless boy,
　　And dotes the more upon a heart at ease;
She is a gipsey, will not speak to those
　　Who have not learnt to be content without her;
A jilt, whose ear was never whisper'd close,
　　Who thinks they scandal her who talk about her;
A very gipsey is she, Nilus born,
　　Sister-in-law to jealous Potiphar;
Ye love-sick bards, repay her scorn for scorn;
　　Ye artists lovelorn, madmen that ye are!
Make your best bow to her and bid adieu;
Then, if she likes it, she will follow you.

The gendered scheming of this address is animated by Keats's irritation at the power he imagines female readers hold over his fame in the market-place.[1] The urbane tone and pose of jaded sophistication with which the sonneteer cajoles a masculine rhetorical culture mark a self-possessed counter-courtship: here is a poet in ironic regard of all the 'love-sick bards', 'artists lovelorn', and 'madmen' who compromise their autonomy and integrity in suits of desire. It is one of the historical ironies of Keats's posthumous fame that this piece of 'masculine' discourse would be published first in *Ladies' Companion* and *Ladies' Pocket Magazine*, reaching a culture of female readers all too prone to dote on the vulnerable 'boy'.[2]

Something more than this irony constitutes the historical sense of the sonnet, however; it is Keats's weirdly prophetic intuition that the most effective bow and adieu to fame, the final exit of death, would win the notice he affected to disdain. This prophecy was fulfilled within months of his death in early 1821, by Shelley's great 'Elegy on the death of John Keats', *Adonais* – a text that immediately achieved canonical status in the story, and critical history, of Keats. Until the late 1840s he was more widely known in Shelley's figure than by his own works.[3] Shelley was not deliberately puerilising Keats nor conveying him to explicitly female regard. These were side-effects of a primary myth designed to cancel the entire culture in which fame is courted – 'the world's slow stain' (XL) – by removing the poet to a higher sphere of influence, and releasing him thereby from 'the dream of life' (XXXIX) in which reviewers hold ephemeral but poisonous sway.[4] Yet, however idealising in intent, Shelley's mythology would prove as promiscuous in its own cultural afterlife as anything Keats ever imputed to wayward 'Fame'.

The *Metropolitan Magazine*, quoting stanzas XXXIX and XL in 1835, said that Shelley had 'given life' to Keats.[5] He *had* immortalised Keats – not in the way he claimed, with a fame transcendent of worldly ills and vindicated by 'the Eternal', but with an all too perdurable infamy in worldly reception. Even as Shelley's elegist proclaimed Adonais's welcome into 'Heaven' by poets 'whose names on Earth are dark/ But whose transmitted effluence cannot die/ So long as fire outlives the parent spark' (XLVI), the cultural transmission of *Adonais* was keeping alive Keats's name on earth as a type unable to suffer the slings and arrows of critical fortune. Keats may have been killed by consumption, but the 'Keats' of the cultural legend Shelley was instrumental in fashioning had surely been consumed by reviews. Two decades later, Elizabeth Barrett could refer to 'the common tale' of 'Poor Keats! . . . slain outright & ingloriously by the Quarterly Reviewer's tomahawk'.[6] And a century later, F. R. Leavis casually affirmed the critical corollary: 'Keats has become a symbolic figure, the type of poetic genius, a hero and martyr of poetry, with claims to greatness such as can hardly at any time have, for the devout, invested the symbolic Chatterton; and there is a general consensus that the greatness is a matter of promise and potentiality rather than achievement.'[7] Struggling at the gate of death, Keats dies into symbolic life.

In this essay, I address 'Keats and History' as 'Keats' *in* a particular history, one in which his agency is slight at best, surpassed by a 'Keats' summoned for definitions of gender, the politics of poetry, the canon of fame, and, not the least, as the evocative focus, even at the risk of parody, of a peculiarly sentimental and melodramatic romanticism. Indeed, the cultural processing of 'the death of John Keats' was one of the main routes by which the 'romance' of 'Romanticism' emerged in the nineteenth century – and it was a construction from which the author of *Adonais* would also benefit.

A FAMOUS STORY

It wasn't, of course, reviews *per se* that were noted in Keats's autopsy; it was establishment reviews, or, more specifically, and as Shelley's Preface advertised, the 'savage criticism of his Endymion, which appeared in the Quarterly Review'.[8] The first cut had been inflicted in August 1818 by *Blackwood's* '*Z*', who aligned Keats with the 'Cockney School of Politics, as well as the Cockney School of Poetry', condemning him for his praise of Hunt – in Z's view 'the meanest, the filthiest, and the most vulgar of Cockney poetasters'. The political labelling, implicit in any naming of Hunt, appears late in the review, and attaches to one of Keats's few overtly political texts, the attack in *Endymion* on the 'gilded masks' of vain and rapacious 'regalities' (III. 1–22) – proof enough that Keats had 'learned to lisp sedition'. Three years later the publication of *Adonais*, with Hunt in its train of mourners (**XXXV**), allowed *Blackwood's* to reopen its campaign, which now extended to Shelley. *Adonais* affirmed Shelley's consanguinity with Keats: directed 'against the *death-dealing* Quarterly Review, which has made such havoc in the Empire of Cockaigne', *Adonais* was a 'merely malignant, mean, and peevishly personal' call to 'correspondents throughout the realm'.[9]

Blackwood's was joined in its assault by the *Literary Gazette*, a Tory confederate whose response to the death of Keats, a 'radically presumptuous profligate', resorted to the same armoury. Announcing that 'the treacherous puffing of his cockney fellow gossips' was really the cause of his suffering, they could not resist flaying him all over again, and, like *Blackwood's*, saving some choice lashes for Shelley: 'For what is the praise of the cockneys but disgrace, or what honourable inscription can be placed over the dead by the hands of notorious libellers, exiled adulterers, and avowed atheists'. Describing *Adonais* as 'the refuse of a school-boy's commonplace book, full of the vulgarisms of pastoral . . . of this stuff is Keats's wretched Elegy compiled', it pretended to mere literary judgement, but the mobilising of 'cockney' as the cover term for vulgarity, radicalism, profligacy, political subversion, 'licentiousness and profaneness', declared the political and cultural stakes.[10] Keats was a convenient battleground and Shelley's lament one more clarion call.

Shelley's attack on the *Quarterly* in his Preface to *Adonais* was launched from an already well-constructed story of 'poor Keats', the victim of a bad press. Richard Woodhouse outlined it to Keats himself, 21 October 1818, in a long impassioned letter meant to help him weather 'that malicious, but weak & silly article on Endymion in the last Quarterly Review'. 'Weak & silly' notwithstanding, the narrative he presents for Keats entails the fatal outcome that Shelley's elegy would formalise: this is a country, after all, 'which let Chatterton

& K. White die of . . . unkindness & neglect' (*KC*, i. 46–52). The reference goes beyond the fact that Keats had inscribed *Endymion* 'to the memory of Thomas Chatterton', for both Chatterton (d. 1770, at seventeen) and Henry Kirke White (d. 1806, at twenty-one) had legendary status as young geniuses killed by neglect and despair – Chatterton by his own hand; White (eulogised in Byron's *English Bards*: 'Unhappy WHITE!/Oh! what a noble heart was here undone') by overwork and consumption. Keats and his friends may have begun to fear this fate for him as well, in consequence of the sore throat he had been unable to shake off after the past summer's tour of Scotland with Charles Brown, perhaps the first symptom of the consumption that was already wasting his brother Tom. A few days after writing to Keats, Woodhouse gave the literary genealogy to a cousin, Mary Frogley, along with a copy of *Endymion* which he hoped she would pass around to her friends in London: 'So said the Monthly of Kirke White – So said Horace Walpole of Chatterton. And how are such Critics now execrated <by> for their cruel injustice.'[11]

In the public domain of execration, a letter to the editor of the *Morning Chronicle* (3 October 1818) explicitly associated Keats and White with the political warfare carried on in the journals. The signatory, 'J.S.' writes to expose the 'article in the last Number of *The Quarterly Review*, professing to be a Critique on "The Poems of John Keats"' as an act 'of malice and gross injustice' motivated by a 'war' with Hunt.[12] Keats's friend and fellow-poet John Hamilton Reynolds also took this case to the public in the *Alfred* (albeit anonymously). The opening sentence is not about Keats's merits, but about his detractor's Toryism: 'We have met with a singular instance, in the last number of the *Quarterly Review*, of that unfeeling arrogance, and cold ignorance, which so strangely marked the minds and hearts of Government sycophants and Government writers.' Sarcastically opining that only a 'Government Pensioner' could have been responsible, Reynolds then summons the icon of White: 'The Monthly Reviewers . . . endeavoured . . . to crush the rising heart of young Kirk White; and indeed they in part generated that melancholy which ultimately destroyed him.' Hunt reprinted this article a few days later in the *Examiner*, prefacing it with his own gibe at the *Quarterly*.[13] The role-call of martyrs had become so routine by the mid-1830s that *Metropolitan* could invoke it ritualistically, unquestioningly associating Keats with Shelley's mythology: 'There was Chatterton . . . There was Kirke White . . . and lastly, there was "Adonais", the sensitive

Keats, who might have prospered, though his birth was humble, and his means straitened, had not an enmity, as gratuitous as it was wanton, as cruel in act as it was malignant in spirit, met, tore, and trampled him to the earth!'[14]

It was not only the Tory reviewers who cast Keats in this role; it was also the script of the Keats circle itself, who sensed in his 'story' an outlet for sentimentality as well as politics. 'We commence our article this month with but a melancholy subject – *the death of Mr. John Keats* –', writes *London Magazine*'s 'L.' announcing that 'we could not reconcile ourselves to the idea of letting a poet's death pass by in the common obituary.'[15] The 'death of Mr. John Keats' was no ephemeral phenomenon, but the stuff of a literary genre, 'a poet's death', replete with identifying tags – neglect or scorn in life, torture by morbid internalisation, vindication in the hereafter: 'Mr. Keats was, in the truest sense of the word, A POET . . . he had a fine ear, a tender heart, . . . and notwithstanding all this, he has been suffered to rise and pass away almost without a notice, . . . and has at last died, solitary and in sorrow, in a foreign land.' Climaxing in Keats's prescriptive epitaph – 'said he, "let it be – *Here lies the body of one whose name was writ in water!*"' – the story is one that 'L.' finds 'most painfully affecting; indeed the whole story of his later days is well calculated to make a deep impression'.

With the cue for action borne by his own terms – *affecting, impression, story*, and especially *calculated* – 'L.' depicts the genre that supplants common obituary:

The public is fond of patronizing poets: they are considered in the light of an almost helpless race: they are bright as stars, but like meteors

Short-lived and self-consuming.

We do not claim the *patronage* of the public for Mr. Keats, but we hope that it will now cast aside every little and unworthy prejudice, and do justice to the high memory of a young but undoubted poet.

Dying, it turns out for Keats's fame, was a good career move. His death evoked genuine compassion, and it also produced a text 'calculated' for rhetorical, political, and ideological uses. L.'s proto-literary 'story' was quickly reproduced – in *Imperial Magazine* the same year, in *Time's Telescope for 1822*, and in several American journals. The *New Monthly*'s obituary not only retold the story of the epitaph and, like *London*, printed it in italics, it also reinforced the packaging of the master-narrative: 'There is something very impressive

about the death of genius, and particularly of youthful genius.'
Keats's death was gaining an 'impressive' afterlife indeed, a modern
myth of 'the Poet' cast as a figure necessarily doomed by a wretched
world unable to appreciate him, and calling for revival by a coterie of
more refined sensibility.[16]

The most devoted imprimatur, clearly, would be that of another
poet. 'Does Shelley go on telling strange Stories of the Death of kings?'
Keats asked Hunt on 10 May 1817, adding ironically: 'Tell him there
are strange Stories of the death of Poets – some have died before they
were conceived' (*Letters*, i. 139–40). A complex investment of personal grievance and cultural polemic would be Shelley's manifold
inspiration for 'such an elegy as poet might be expected to write upon
poet' (so Hunt advertised it in 1822) – and the terms of his deep
impression on the history of Keats.[17]

THE FRAME OF *ADONAIS*

The single most influential text on Keats's nineteenth-century
reception was Shelley's highly contentious and polemical defence in
Adonais. Shelley genuinely admired Keats's talent (especially the
promise of the *Hyperion* fragment in the 1820 volume), but it was a
desire to do combat with the reviews that framed the deeper
motivation of *Adonais*. Before he knew any details, he had already
decided that Keats was killed by political animosity. Telling his
publisher Charles Ollier, 8 June 1821, to advertise 'a poem entitled
"Adonais" . . . a lament on the death of poor Keats, with some
interposed stabs on the assassins of his peace and of his fame', Shelley
then asks him to inquire 'of some of the friends and relations of Keats
respecting the circumstances of his death, and . . . transmit me any
information you may be able to collect, and especially as to the degree
in which, *as I am assured*, the brutal attack in the *Quarterly Review*
excited the disease by which he perished'. This request may arise from
Shelley's 'characteristic attention to historical detail' (so Stephen C.
Behrendt argues), but it also reflects something else: an appetite for a
history already conceived.[18] It mattered that this was a history the
outlines of which applied to Shelley as well, for the *Quarterly* had also
taken aim at his poetry and character. Redeeming Keats was a
political project whose self-interest could be vented in a rhetoric of
generous disinterest.[19]

This project began well before *Adonais*. After the *Quarterly* had commenced hostilities, Shelley drafted a public letter 'To William Gifford, Editor of *The Quarterly Review*' (it wasn't sent, but when Mary Shelley published it in 1840, it joined the bibliography of defence).[20] Shelley opens with a slightly disingenuous disclaimer: 'Sir/ Should you cast your eye on the signature of this letter before you read the contents you might imagine that they related to a slanderous paper which appeared in your review . . . *I* certainly bear you no ill will for having edited the abuse.' This protest takes up about a quarter of the letter, before Shelley turns to his ostensible, 'unfortunate subject . . . the Author of Endymion'. Shelley projects Keats as the abject other, the helpless victim requiring his defence:

Poor Keats was thrown into a dreadful state of mind by this review . . . embittering his existence & inducing a disease from which there are now but faint hopes of his recovery. – The first effects are described to me to have resembled insanity, & it was by assiduous watching that he was restrained from effecting purposes of suicide. The agony of his suffering at length produced the rupture of a blood vessel in the lungs, and the usual process of consumption appears to have begun.

This early defence summons a 'Poor Keats' that was already codified.[21] Indeed, the notation 'described' shows that the tale had gone through considerable processing. Robert Finch, learning the details from his friend Joseph Severn (who nursed Keats in Rome), sent an account to John Gisborne, who promptly sent it on to the Shelleys. On the day of receipt, 16 June 1821, Shelley reported the gist of Finch's letter to Claire Clairmont as 'a most melancholy account of the last illness of poor Keats' (virtually a title in itself), and wrote to Gisborne to acknowledge 'the heart rending account of the closing scene of the great genius whom envy & ingratitude scourged out of the world'. Before sending *Adonais* off 'to the press at Pisa', he incorporated some of Finch's details and phrasing into his Preface:

The circumstances of the closing scene of poor Keats's life were not made known to me until the Elegy was ready for the press. I am given to understand that the wound which his sensitive spirit had received from the criticism of Endymion, was exasperated by the bitter sense of unrequited benefits; the poor fellow seems to have been hooted from the stage of life. (5)

Deriving 'poor Keats's life' and 'poor fellow' from the already existing tales, Shelley conceives a 'scene' to serve the polemical agenda of the elegy.[22]

Managing this literary genre, a kind of pathetic sublime, depended on distance from Keats himself: 'I do not think that if I had seen [Finch's letter] . . . I could have composed my poem', Shelley tells Gisborne: 'the enthusiasm of the imagination would have been overpowered by sentiment.' His power required an independence of imagination, or, put another way, a control of the narrative for self-composition. It is thus with a statement on the authority of his 'criticism' as the arbiter of anyone's 'claims . . . to be classed among the writers of the highest genius who have adorned our age' that Shelley opens his Preface, not naming the 'lamented object', 'Keats', until the second paragraph – and then only by the date, the place of his death, and the location of burial. His real role is to front a charge at the reviews and, among other elements, this script required a Keats of extreme vulnerability – a fictive vessel for the supposedly tough-minded, masculine Shelley, even as it bears his grievance. When the Preface says the reviewers 'scatter their insults and their slanders without heed as to whether the poisoned shaft light on a heart made callous by many blows, or one, like Keats's composed of more penetrable stuff' (4), the syntactic slot produces Shelley's heart as the one of sterner stuff. The allusion to Hamlet's sneer at Gertrude (whether her heart is 'brazed . . . against sense' or 'made of penetrable stuff', 3.4.35–8) does Keats no good, either, for the effect is to cast him in the form of ideal female sensitivity (which Hamlet accuses Gertrude of lacking). This is also the effect of Shelley's charge, 'Nor shall it be your excuse, that, murderer as you are, you have spoken daggers, but used none' (5), for Hamlet's spoken daggers (3.2.387) were aimed at Gertrude. When Byron (who wondered at Keats's '*yielding* sensitiveness') used the first allusion in *English Bards*, it was to warn Scotch Reviewers of possible retaliation: 'they too are "penetrable stuff"' (1050). In the last instalment of his 'Memoir of Shelley' for the 1832 *Athenaeum*, Thomas Medwin invokes this figure to cast a Shelley 'brazed' for battle in defence of helpless Keats: 'that Shelley could wield a lash of bronze for others, he proved in Adonais, . . . perhaps the stanzas on Keats's Reviewer cut nearer to the bone than any in our language'.[23] Indeed, these stanzas (XXXVI–XXXVIII) were as impressive as anything in the poem; Hunt quotes them in full in his review of *Adonais* for the *Examiner*, and Milnes's *Life* gives them equal notice along with Shelley's letter to Gifford – even though the intent was not to confirm Shelley's narrative but to show his capacity to 'bend for others that pride which ever remained erect for himself'. *Blackwood's* thought the first lines of XXXVII a case of '*Absurdity*', but

Hunt contended that these stanzas would not be '"unintelligible" to the dullest *Quarterly* peruser, who had read the review of Mr. Keats's *Endymion*'.[24]

The most effective strategies for Shelley's polemics entangled the history of Keats's reception with questions of gender.[25] Heroic self-fashioning was helped by a 'Keats' defined in codes of feminine delicacy. The Preface thus laments a 'genius . . . not less delicate and fragile than it was beautiful', a 'young flower . . . blighted in the bud' (4), and the elegy itself recounts the perishing of this 'youngest, dearest . . . nursling' of the muse, one

. . . who grew,
Like a pale flower by some sad maiden cherished,
And fed with true love tears, instead of dew;
. . . .
[Her] extreme hope, the loveliest and the last,
The bloom, whose petals, nipt before they blew
Died on the promise of the fruit, is waste;
The broken lily lies – the storm is overpast.   (VI)

At best, Keats is a son pathetically abandoned: 'Where wert thou mighty Mother, when he lay,/ When thy Son lay, pierced by the shaft which flies/ In darkness?' (II) – lines that H. B. Forman would place on the obverse of the title page in his edition of Keats's letters to Fanny Brawne.[26] Or he is a son finally restored to, and by, those female forces that had forsaken him:

He is made one with Nature: there is heard
His voice in all her music, from the moan
Of thunder, to the song of night's sweet bird . . .   (XLII)

Charles Brown found this 'language so soothing and poetical' that he used it and part of the next stanza as the epigraph of his 'Life of John Keats' (written in a sympathetically 'fevered and nervous' state). He begins this 'Life' endorsing Shelley: 'When "Adonais" was sent to me from Italy, I recognized . . . my own every day, involuntary, inevitable reflections.' His last paragraphs resume its myth: 'my belief continues to be that [Keats] was destroyed by hirelings, under the imposing name of Reviewers . . . Could he have been less sensitive . . . he might have <been alive> existed at this moment.'[27]

An article in the *Olio* tendered not only Shelley's story but its very language: 'A certain crew among critics did their best to nip his genius in the bud, and it is but justice to them to say they succeeded . . . those canker-worms of literature.' Regretting that he did not defend Keats

more vigorously, Hunt retails Shelley's terms in his review of *Adonais*
for the *Examiner* (7 July 1822), calling Keats 'the nursling of the Muse'
and in *Lord Byron* (1828) broadcasting Shelley's larger mythology: 'I
little suspected at the time, as I did afterward, that the hunters had
struck him; that a delicate organization, which already anticipated a
premature death, made him feel his ambition thwarted by these
fellows.'[28] Even as the poem's rhetoric translated Adonais into
'Nature' or a 'Power . . . Which has withdrawn his being into its own'
(XLII), the social and cultural text of *Adonais* reified this power in the
nature of reading Keats. Shelley's myth proved so potent that Keats's
actual history reorganised itself around it. A mid-century biography
of Benjamin Robert Haydon reports him saying that after *Blackwood's*
attack, Keats 'became morbid and silent'. An account from the same
era painted a scene of Fanny Brawne and Fanny Keats often finding
him 'with [the *Quarterly's*] review in his hand, reading as if he would
devour it – completely absorbed – absent, and drinking it in like
mortal poison'. The scene is patent fiction, but that it could be
reported as fact in 1857 shows how entrenched the story had
become.[29] In his lifetime Keats was already being represented as
killed by and killing himself with the reviews, a connoisseur of his own
wound. As Elizabeth Barrett's fuller rendition of the common tale
goes, 'he suffered himself to be slain'.[30] If it is bad medical pathology
and a distortion of Keats to say that he was snuffed out by an article,
in terms of cultural discourse it was a truth universally acknowledged.
When one twentieth-century scholar states that on the 'historical
level' *Adonais* 'concerns the death of John Keats as a result of the
vicious attack made upon his *Endymion* in the *Quarterly Review*', we see
the degree to which Shelley's construction became an accepted
reading of history.[31]

In the immediate politics of the reviews, it was inevitable that
defences of Keats issued from others who were Tory targets; one such
was Hazlitt, who, like Shelley, found a resource for pathos in
feminising his subject. Repeating Shelley's image of 'the serpent' press
in *Table-Talk*, he stages their disdain with a cluster of quotations that
are all – inadvertently – damaging in their effects:

he had no pedigree to show them . . . he could only offer them 'the fairest
flowers of the season, carnations and streaked gilliflowers', – 'rue for
remembrance and pansies for thoughts' – they recked not of his gift, but tore
him with hideous shouts and laughter,

'Nor could the Muse protect her son!'[32]

Hazlitt invokes the language of flowers as a compliment to Keats's poetic gifts but the Shakespearean contexts work beyond this design, to install Keats in a gallery of maids: his poems are the 'bastard' flowers disdained by Perdita, or a bouquet for mad, pitied Ophelia. Nor does gendering the reviewers as hysterical bacchantes (by virtue of Milton) redeem Keats's masculinity, for it supplements Shelley's trope of Urania's absence with a similarly vulnerable son, a slight misquotation too aptly converting Milton's *defend* to a more flutteringly maternal *protect*.[33]

While Keats was still alive, *Blackwood's* uttered a mock apology, with a tenderness of regard that was snidely effeminising:

We are informed that he is in a very bad state of health, and that his friends attribute a great deal of it to the pain he has suffered from the critical castigation his Endymion drew down on him in this magazine. If it be so, we are most heartily sorry . . . had we suspected that young author, of being so delicately nerved, we should have administered our reproof in a much more lenient shape and style.[34]

Frailty, thy name is Keats. The *New Monthly* and the *Alfred* failed to deflect the charge when, in a liberal spirit, they likened the *Quarterly*'s 'laborious attempt to torture and ruin Mr. Keats' to its attack on Lady Morgan – subject, in the *Monthly*'s words, to 'one of the coarsest insults ever offered in print by man to woman'. Reynolds (in the *Alfred*) called the *Quarterly*'s language 'lower than man would dare to utter to female ears', and surmised that 'a woman is the best prey for its malignity, because it is the gentlest and the most undefended', adding that honourable criticism ought to 'chuse its objects from the vain, the dangerous, and the powerful, and not from the young and the unprotected'.[35] Despite his ensuing characterisation of Keats as a 'young and powerful writer' whose poems display 'solitary vigour' and a 'sinewy quality' of thought, the effect of linking Keats's plight with Lady Morgan's was to make him seem the victim of ungallant male behaviour towards women deserving kinder, gentler treatment.

The excesses of defence courted parody. While Keats's friends were bonding in sympathy, another circuit was forming, bonded by ridicule. Byron wrote to Murray, the *Quarterly*'s publisher, 'He who would die of an article in a review – would probably have died of something else equally trivial.'[36] Asking him if he is 'aware that Shelley has written an elegy on Keats – and accuses the Quarterly of killing him', he preempts it with his own:

Who killed John Keats?
  I, says the Quarterly
So savage & Tartarly
    < Martyrly >
'Twas one of my feats –
Who < drew the [pen?] > shot the arrow?[37]

In similar tones, the *Literary Gazette* converted pathos to bathos: 'Solemn as the subject is, (for in truth we must grieve for the early death of any youth of literary ambition,) it is hardly possible to help laughing at the mock solemnity with which Shelley charges the Quarterly Review for having murdered his friend with — a critique!'; if criticism were so successful, 'Shelley would not have been alive to write [his] Elegy'.[38]

Woodhouse's intuition of Keats's place in literary history had unwittingly entailed 'martyrly' reviews as a parodiable prerequisite to the justice of fame. No wonder, then, that Shelley's myth bore poison fruit: a 'Keats' without 'masculine' resilience. Byron was frankly incredulous when Shelley told him that 'Young Keats . . . died lately at Rome from the consequences of breaking a blood-vessel, in paroxysms of despair at the contemptuous attack on his book in the *Quarterly Review*', 16 [17] April 1821: 'is it *actually* true? I did not think criticism had been so killing . . . in this world of bustle and broil, and especially in the career of writing, a man should calculate upon his powers of *resistance* before he goes into the arena.' When he was assured that it was all 'too true', Byron became one of the first to rewrite the literary assassination as a farce.[39] The elegy he issued in 1823 acquired an influence that was equal to, if not greater than, Shelley's:

John Keats, who was killed off by one critique,
  Just as he really promised something great,
. . . .
  Poor fellow! His was an untoward fate: –
'Tis strange the mind, that very fiery particle,
Should let itself be snuffed out by an Article.

(XI. 60)

Byron first wrote 'weakly Mind' in the couplet of this notorious stanza of *Don Juan* before cancelling the redundancy and allowing a pointedly feminine rhyme to tune the flippancy. The wit was potent, and the poem's popularity guaranteed notice and repetition. In his essay on Keats in *Lord Byron*, even Hunt refreshed its publicity as he

expressed regret for its very existence: 'A good rhyme about *particle*
and *article* was not to be given up. I told [Byron] he was mistaken in
attributing Mr. Keats's death to the critics, though they had perhaps
hastened, and certainly embittered it; and he promised to alter the
passage: but a joke and rhyme together!'[40]

Byron's scoff had attained a wide currency. Interrupting Medwin's
'Memoir of Shelley' – which dared to intimate that *Endymion* was a
work of 'sickly affectation' and 'perverse and limited' principles – the
editor of the *Athenaeum* was moved to interpolate a column-length
note in defence of Keats: 'Lord Byron's opinion, that he was killed by
the reviewers, is wholly ridiculous; though his epitaph . . . might seem
to countenance it.' But the very fact of this defence, with its almost
wholly gratuitous application to a very tangential provocation,
attests to the force of Byron's formulation on public opinion.[41] Four
years previously Carlyle observed that Dr Johnson 'was no man to be
killed by a review'. And on the other side of the world, Poe began one
of his fantastic tales with laconic authority, 'Keats fell by a criticism'.
Even when applied to a different subject, 'snuffed out by an Article'
might be intoned with a wink, as in *Blackwood's* review of Alexander
Smith in 1854. Byron's story of Keats had become a standard reference.[42]

This story, which Shelley tried so hard to manage, would also affect
posthumous estimates of Shelley himself in ways that he could not
have anticipated. W. M. Rossetti felt it advisable in his edition to
annotate the 'one frail Form' among the poem's mourners (**XXXI**)
with a concession that 'some readers may think that Shelley insists
upon this aspect of his character to a degree rather excessive, and
dangerously near the confines of feminine sensibility, rather than
virile fortitude'.[43] The *Cornhill* was blunter: *Adonais* is 'unmanly
wailing' and 'Byron's contempt . . . more to the purpose'; deriding
'the soul which let itself be snuffed out by an article', the *Cornhill*
sneered that this elegy could be 'justified' only 'on the theory that
poetry and manliness are incompatible, that a poet is and ought to be
a fragile being, ready to ["]Die of a rose in aromatic pain"'. Hazlitt
had used this phrase from Pope's *Essay on Man* to limn 'Effeminacy of
Character' in an essay whose summary example, with echoes of
Shelley's terms, was Keats: 'I cannot help thinking that the fault of
Mr. Keats's poems was a deficiency in masculine energy of style. He
had beauty, tenderness, delicacy, in an uncommon degree, but there
was a want of strength and substance.' Even George Gilfillan, with his
habitually affectionate regard of this 'boy', speculates that his 'great

defect' was the 'want . . . of a man-like constitution'. And Hazlitt, again with an unwitting subversion by allusiveness, takes up this theme in another *Table-Talk* essay, 'On Living to one's-self', which describes 'poor Keats' as one for whom abuse

proved too much . . . and struck like a barbed arrow in his heart . . . What was sport to the town was death to him. Young, sensitive, delicate, he was like

> 'A bud bit by an envious worm,
> Ere he could spread his sweet leaves to the air,
> Or dedicate his beauty to the sun' –

and unable to endure the miscreant cry and idiot laugh, withdrew to sigh his last breath in foreign climes.

Bringing in the voice of Romeo's father on his lovesick son amplifies the deficiency, for Romeo is famously unmanned by love.[44]

The reciprocal was Keats's adoration by female readers, for whom the *Adonais* myth was intrinsic to Keats's biography. Routinely rehearsed in periodicals such as the *Ladies' Companion* was the story of the poet who 'burst a blood vessel on reading a savage attack on his "Endymion" published in the London Quarterly Review, and died in Rome as a consequence'.[45] It was a fetish for Keats's female biographers. Mrs F. M. Owen crowned her study of Keats with this stanza:

> He is a portion of the loveliness
> Which once he made more lovely: he doth bear
> His part, while the one spirit's plastic stress
> Sweeps through the dull dense world, compelling there,
> All new successions to the forms they wear;
> Torturing th'unwilling dross that checks its flight
> To its own likeness, as each mass may bear;
> And bursting in its beauty and its might
> From trees and beasts and men into the Heaven's light.[46]

A half century on, in 1937, Dorothy Hewlett titled her biographical offering *Adonais: A Life of John Keats*.

'Poor Keats' in Tory journals such as *Blackwood's* conveyed contempt or mock pity – and only slightly more sympathy in Byron's letters; the epithet bore pity mixed with judgement for Hazlitt, and was a polemical bond for Keats's male allies.[47] In female voices, however, 'poor Keats' figured in a phantasy adoption of the role of the 'mighty Mother' whose absence was lamented in *Adonais*. For example, *Victorian Magazine* concludes its essay on Keats, 'the Daintiest of Poets', in a voice of outrage: 'What shall we say of the malicious, the utterly brutal criticism, the hand of the cloddish boy tearing the myriad-hued fragile butterfly to fragments! No words can express the loathing every honest educated Englishman must feel for the ruffian tasks which inaugurated a long career of prosperity for the two Quarterlies.' In this scenario, the feminine gender of the victim emerges as a reflexive otherness from the masculine figures: cloddish boys, Quarterly ruffians, and Englishmen called to defence. Keats does not survive as a man. This 'poor young poet . . . savagely used by the censors of literature', laments Mrs Oliphant, echoing Shelley's indictment of 'the savage criticism on his Endymion' and finding the 'fluctuations of this bitter drama . . . heart-rending. . . . the poor sick lad'. Keats's most famous female biographer, Amy Lowell, is wrenched to exclaim, 'Poor little shaver, so pitiably unable to cope with his first great sorrow', and vilify the reviewers as 'first-class cads', 'ruffians at heart without a spark of decent feeling'.[48]

Supplementing and in some ways contending with this feminising attention, however, was the culturally prestigious theme of geniuses alienated from an uncomprehending world but mutually supportive of each other. Co-ordinated with the emerging grammar of 'the English Romantic Movement' as an ethos of 'resistance . . . to the material world itself', this was 'a culture of lyrical feeling' that *Adonais* meant to define and endorse as a fraternal trust of poets.[49]

THE FAME OF *ADONAIS*

It is telling of this emerging fraternity that even the conservative *European Magazine and London Review* opened its notice on *Adonais*, in tones only faintly sarcastic:

Hardly ever does the poet appear in a more amiable point of view, than when his magic hand is employed in twining laurels round the brow of a brother minstrel, especially if that brow has been darkened by the shadow of death . . . *all* sympathize . . . as if his gifted existence had supplied the charm of their own, or had been so interwoven with it, that his termination fell on their enjoyments as a mortal blow.[50]

Shelley's strategy in *Adonais* was to reverse the mortal blow with a polemic on the poet's life in the politics of popular reception, indeed to elevate the poet as moral authority, acknowledged legislator. The rankling motive is spelled out in the letter he sent to Severn, 29 November 1821, accompanying one of the Pisan printings of the poem:

I send you the Elegy on poor Keats – . . .

In spite of his transcendant [*sic*] genius Keats never was nor ever will be a popular poet; & the total neglect & obscurity in which the astonishing remnants of his mind still lie, was hardly to be dissipated by a writer, who, however he may differ from Keats in more important qualities, at least resembles him in that accidental one, a want of popularity. I have little hope, therefore, that the poem I send you will excite any attention.

Little hopes aside, Shelley meant to excite attention. He pressed bookseller Ollier, 11 January 1822, for reports to feed an appetite 'more than commonly interested in the success of "Adonais", – I do not mean the sale, but the effect produced'.[51] Defiantly warning Ollier that *Adonais* was 'little adapted for popularity',[52] Shelley courted effect with a deliberate resistance to popularity: erudite references, and conspicuously untranslated Greek texts on the title page (Plato) and at the top of the Preface (Moschus). This resistance is, in fact, continuous with the poem's politics: if in the mythology of Adonais Keats dies out of this world to live in another, in the ideological code of Shelley's aesthetics, he dies out of popular scorn to be reconstituted for elite consumption. The text performs a political statement with a grammar of aesthetics. *Adonais* 'is a highly-wrought *piece of art*, perhaps better in point of composition than any thing I have written', he tells the Gisbornes, 5 June 1821, and boasts to another friend, 'I have lately been composing a poem on Keats: it is better than any thing that I have yet written, & worthy both of him & of me', 8 June 1821 – 'worthy' not in the measure of sales that would interest Ollier, but in gathering an elite fraternity round Keats and his vindicator.[53]

Hunt grasped Shelley's politicised aesthetic right away and advertised it, with a Keatsian supplement, to the *Examiner*'s readers:

It is not a poem calculated to be popular; . . . it is of too abstract and subtle a nature for that purpose; but it will delight the few, to whom Mr. Shelley is accustomed to address himself. Spenser would be pleased with it if he were living. A mere town reader and a Quarterly Reviewer will find it *caviare* . . . The author has had before him his recollections of Lycidas, of Moschus and Bion, and of the doctrines of Plato; and in the stanza of the most poetical of poets, Spenser, has brought his own genius, in all its etherial beauty.[54]

When the first English edition of *Adonais* appeared in 1829, the

Athenaeum's notice stressed Shelley's status as a poet not for the 'mob' or 'crowd' seeking the 'lazy relaxation' of 'modern vulgar literature', but as one whose 'effort of the imagination requires a corresponding effort in the reader', a 'labor of thought'.[55] Elite reading, as Shelley's highly wrought framing had prophesied, was being exercised as liberal art, a bond of sympathy against mob prejudice, the 'Quarterly Reviewer', and the 'mere town reader'.

Perhaps the most daring of Shelley's resistances to popularity is his rhetorical pose of the blaspheming prophet, one who can adopt religious authority at one moment and outrage propriety at the next. 'It may be said, that these wretched men know not what they do', he writes in his Preface, casting the *Quarterly*'s 'cankerworms' with the tormentors of Christ. When he tells John Gisborne, 16 June 1821, 'I have dipped my pen in consuming fire for his destroyers', the rhetoric is not of political debate but of divine retribution and a stage of cosmic vengeance.[56] Vindication mattered not just for Keats, but also for Shelley – or more so, given the repeated damning in the reviews of all aspects of his life – domestic, intellectual, and political. Shelley produces the figure of a tortured visionary in the parade of mourners, spinning out four stanzas (**XXXI–XXXIV**) that make Keats's trials by the reviews seem a mere irritation by comparison:

> Midst others of less note, came one frail Form,
> A phantom among men; companionless
> As the last cloud of an expiring storm . . .   (XXXI)

'Not the least valuable part of that Idyll is the picture he has drawn of himself, in the two well-known stanzas beginning "'Mid [*sic*] others of less note"', reports Medwin's 'Memoir' in the *Athenaeum*; 'How well do those expressions, "a pard-like spirit, beautiful and swift!" – "a love in desolation marked" [*sic*] – "a power girt round with weakness" – designate him.'[57] Shelley's self-portrait had exceeded the pathos of Keats's demise.

Refusing Shelley's game, but alert to the agenda, the *Literary Gazette* noted these lines as '*Nonsense – personal*', remarkingly coyly, 'We have some idea that this fragment of character is intended for Mr. Shelley himself.' It read the sense of the climactic stanza XXXIV only too well, announcing it as a 'memorable and ferocious blasphemy', an insult to 'the common order of society', and '*contemptible*' poetry to boot:

'He with a sudden hand
Made bare his branded and ensanguin'd brow,
Which was like Cain's or CHRIST's'!!!

What can be said to the wretched person capable of this daring
profanation. The name of the first murderer – the accurst of God – brought
into the same aspect image with that of the Saviour of the World! We are
scarcely satisfied that even to quote such passages may not be criminal.

In a similar ideological bundle of politics, social order, and religion,
Blackwood's featured the same lines and accused Shelley of trying for
fame 'on the stilts of blasphemy': 'He is the only verseman of the day,
who has dared, in a Christian country, to work out for himself the
character of direct ATHEISM!'[58] When a friend urged a revision of the
pairing Christ and Cain, fearing it would convey irreverence or
sarcasm, Shelley was adamant. No small part of his performance of
sympathy for Keats was staging his own martyrdom ('well knew that
gentle band/ Who in another's fate now wept his own' [XXXIV]).
Although he was persuaded to excise from the Preface sentences to the
effect that 'never upon one head was heaped calumny in so profuse a
measure as upon mine', what remained made it easy enough to grant
the claim.[59] *Metropolitan* was one of many in the 1830s to note that he,
like 'poor Keats', had been 'assailed by reviewers', and William
Howitt privileged this bond with a slight tilt of the heroic scales to
Shelley: 'Keats was the martyr of poetry, but Shelley was the martyr
of opinion.'[60]

Blackwood's cartoon of Shelley's self-elevation was apt, for the fame
of *Adonais* would imprint the life of Keats for years afterwards.
Cowden Clarke concluded his 'Recollections of Keats' with its last
three lines. And Milnes, despite his sense of the damage wrought by its
myth, closed his *Life* of Keats with the genesis of *Adonais* – quoting four
stanzas and the letter to Severn – but literally giving Shelley yet
another last word. Tendering a 'lesson' on the inevitability of
misunderstood genius, his *Life* ends:

And therefore men

'Are cradled into poetry by wrong:
They learn in suffering what they teach in song.'[61]

This quotation attests not just to Shelley's overwhelming force on the
history of Keats by mid-century, but also to Milnes's sense that Keats
stood to gain by the association: 'Contrary to the expectation',

Shelley expressed to Severn (that 'a critical notice of [Keats's] writings' would not 'find a single reader'), Milnes notes that the fame of both has 'ascended, and now they rest together . . . twin-stars'.[62] The metaphor is more than celebrity cliché, for the final stanza of *Adonais* had already drawn the elegist to 'the soul of Adonais, like a star', beaconing and beckoning from the abode of the Eternal. And, of course, by the time Milnes was summoning an earlier stanza (XL) to contemplate Keats in this abode, Shelley had arrived there, too, drowned a little over a year after packing *Adonais* off to the press.

Indeed, one of the posthumous fates of *Adonais* itself was its retrospective (or uncannily prophetic) application to Shelley. The *Literary Register* opened its remarks in September 1822 with a sympathetic linking of the fates of poet and subject: 'The following lines which nearly conclude Adonais [LIII, 'Why linger, why turn back, why shrink, my Heart?'], cannot be read without an awful association of ideas. It would almost seem that the Disposer of events had listened and attended to the poet's mournful wish.' Medwin's 'Memoir' affirmed this melancholy bond with personal testimony:

I have never been able to read . . . his tribute to the memory of Keats, without, under the name of Adonais, impersonating the companion of my youth. There was, unhappily, too much similarity in the destinies of Keats and Shelley: both were victims to persecution – both were marked out for the envenomed shafts of invidious critics – and both now sleep together in a foreign land.[63]

Hunt had already tightened the bond of destiny by publicising Trelawny's account of the role of Keats's last volume in the identification of Shelley's corpse, then adding his own note on the society of corpses bound by *Adonais*:

Mr. Shelley's remains were taken to Rome, and deposited in the protestant burial-ground, near those of . . . Mr. Keats. It is the cemetery he speaks of in the preface to his Elegy on the death of his young friend, as calculated to 'make one in love with death, to think that one should be buried in so sweet a place'. A like tenderness of patience, in one who possessed a like energy, made Mr. Keats say on his death-bed, that he 'seemed to feel the daisies growing over him'. These are the feelings that servile critics ridicule, and that all other human beings respect.[64]

By a peculiar force, it seems, it took Shelley's own death to give his sympathy for Keats's a better reception. Opening with a quotation of the Preface to *Adonais*, an essay on Keats for the *Nation* in the mid-1840s elaborates the fraternal twinning:

Thus wrote SHELLEY . . . When one recollects the contempt of neglect with which the first outpourings of these young and noble hearts were received – how delicate their organisation – how impressible their nature – how sensitive their feelings – one is almost reconciled to the fate which consigned them both an early grave, beneath the blue sky of the Eternal City, where –

> Envy and calumny, and hate, and pain,
> And that unrest, which men miscall delight,
> Can touch them not, and torture not again!

In their case, however, there has been a sort of retributive justice. These two young men . . . have exercised, since their deaths, a most remarkable influence over English literature. If they did not guide it during their lives, 'they rule it from their urns'.[65]

Under the aspect of common justice, however, the twinning of 'these young and noble hearts' was gradually being qualified by a literary assessment of distinct and different poetic sensibilities. One effect for Shelley was that the self-investment of *Adonais* became more legible as devoted followers claimed the elegy for him alone. The most emphatic gesture was Mary Shelley's, whose 'Note on Poems of 1821' declared:

There is much in the Adonais which seems now more applicable to Shelley, than to the young and gifted poet whom he mourned. The poetic view he takes of death, and the lofty scorn he displays towards his calumniators, are as a prophecy on his own destiny, when received among immortal names, and the poisonous breath of critics has vanished into emptiness before the fame he inherits.

The close of her final note affirms this transfer: '– who but will regard as a prophecy the last stanza of the "Adonais"?' Supplementing this metaphorical link, a ghoulishly literal application to Shelley came to light after Mary's own death, when his actual heart, redeemed from cremation, 'was found in her desk, dried to dust, and wrapped in a copy of *Adonais*'.[66]

By the mid-nineteenth century, Shelley, the poet who had wrapped Keats in a self-invested version of his history, was now the sole centre of the fiction he had created. Keats, meanwhile, was emerging from *Adonais* to fame by force of his own writing and gaining independent cultural (and cult) status. By 1861, Severn reports, his grave had become a 'shrine' whose 'Pilgrims' were so avid for mementos that its *Custode* complained 'that notwithstanding all his pains in sowing and planting, he cannot "meet the great consumption"'.[67]

NOTES

Thanks to Ronald Levao for his usual careful reading and good advice.

1 Keats may have repeated this trope from his friend John Hamilton Reynolds's rally against the *Quarterly*'s review. See *Alfred, West of England Journal and General Advertiser* (6 Oct. 1818), rpt. *KCH*, especially 119–20. For the publication of *On Fame*, see *PJK*, 648–9.

2 For further discussion see Sonia Hofkosh, 'The Writer's Ravishment: Women and the Romantic Author – The Example of Byron', in Anne K. Mellor (ed.), *Romanticism and Feminism* (Bloomington and Indianapolis, 1988), 93–114; Margaret Homans, 'Keats Reading Women, Women Reading Keats', *SIR* 29 (1990), 341–70; and my 'Feminizing Keats', in H. de Almeida (ed.), *Critical Essays on John Keats* (Boston, 1990), 317–57.

3 Although Shelley's publisher Charles Ollier did not sell out copies of *Adonais* Shelley sent from Italy, the poem reached many readers through an extensive reprint in the *Literary Chronicle and Weekly Review* 133 (1 Dec. 1821), 751–4. For publication details see F. L. Jones (ed.), *The Letters of Percy Bysshe Shelley* (2 vols., Oxford, 1964) ii. 294 n., 372 n. and Anthony Knerr, *Shelley's 'Adonais': A Critical Edition* (New York, 1984), 12–13, 257–8 n. 24. After Galignani's *Poetical Works of Coleridge, Shelley, and Keats, Complete in One Volume* (1829), there was no further edition of Keats's works until 1840, and this was remaindered; see Sidney Colvin, *John Keats: His Life and Poetry, His Friends, Critics, and After-Fame* (London and New York, 1917), 528. In 1845, Keats's publisher John Taylor could command only £50 from Moxon for his copyrights and rights to unpublished Keats manuscripts; see *KC*, ii. 115–16, 128–9.

4 Quotations follow *Adonais* (Pisa, 1821; facsimile rpt. New York, 1927). Page references are denoted by arabic numbers, stanzas by roman numerals.

5 W. G. T., 'The Poems of Percy Bysshe Shelley', 14 (Sept. 1835), 53–66.

6 Letter to Mary Russell Mitford, 26 Oct. 1841 in P. Kelley and R. Hudson (eds.), *The Brownings' Correspondence* (10 vols., Winfield, Kansas, 1984–92) v. 158, possibly recalling a letter to the *Morning Chronicle* in protest at the *Quarterly*'s political agenda: 'hence Mr K. is doomed to feel the merciless tomahawk of the Reviewers, termed Quarterly, I presume from the modus operandi' (3 Oct. 1818; *KCH*, 115). For Elizabeth Barrett's further references to Keats's death, see *Brownings' Correspondence*, vi. 126 and x. 52.

7 'Keats', *Revaluation: Tradition and Development in English Poetry* (1936; New York, 1947), 241.

8 *Adonais*, 4. The unsigned review by John Wilson Croker, dated April 1818, did not appear until September; see D. H. Reiman (ed.), *The Romantics Reviewed: Contemporary Reviews of British Romantic Writers, Part C: Shelley, Keats, and London Radical Writers* (New York and London, 1972), 767, and *KCH*, 110–16. The *Quarterly*'s influence and establishment voice

made it the target of choice for Keats's advocates: 'Croker's article made a better myth, because the official literary voice of the Establishment could be said to have jeered a good poet out of existence by pretending, for political reasons, that he was a bad one' (*KCH*, 19).

9 John Lockhart, 'Cockney School of Poetry. No IV', *Blackwood's Edinburgh Magazine* 3 (Aug. 1818), 524, 520; *KCH*, 99, 109. 'Remarks on Shelley's Adonais, *An Elegy on the Death of JOHN KEATS, Author of Endymion, &c.*', *Blackwood's* 10 (Dec. 1821), 696–700; Reiman identifies the reviewer as George Croly, 'trying to make his reputation by surpassing "Z" in satire', *Romantics Reviewed*, 147. See also Nicholas Roe, 'Keats's Lisping Sedition', *EinC* 42 (1992), 36–55.

10 'Adonais', *Literary Gazette, and Journal of the Belles Lettres* (8 Dec. 1821), 772–3.

11 Quotations from Byron's poetry are from J. J. McGann (ed.), *Lord Byron: The Complete Poetical Works* (7 vols., Oxford, 1980–93). White is noticed in a full stanza of *English Bards* (831–48), and in a pathetic footnote. Byron repeatedly praised White as a figure of 'Poesy & Genius', associating his 'Genius' with Chatterton's; see L. Marchand (ed.), *Byron's Letters and Journals* (12 vols., Cambridge, Mass., 1973–82) ii. 76, 82, iv. 332. For Woodhouse to Mary Frogley, 23 Oct. 1818, see *KC*, i. 55.

12 *KCH*, 115–16. Generally accepted is Colvin's identification of 'J. S.' as John Scott, 'editor of the *London Magazine*, and soon afterwards killed by a friend of Lockhart's in a duel arising out of these very Blackwood brawls'; *Keats* (London and New York, 1887), 124. Joseph Severn annexed this event to his own story of Keats's death as 'another scene of the tragedy'; see 'On the Vicissitudes of Keats's Fame', *Atlantic Monthly* 11 (Apr. 1863), 401–7.

13 *Examiner* (11 Oct. 1818), 648–9, and *KCH*, 117.

14 14 (Sept. 1835), 61. See also George Gilfillan, 'John Keats', *First and Second Galleries of Literary Portraits* (Edinburgh, 1854), 253–62.

15 'Town Conversation. No. IV', Baldwin's *London Magazine* (Apr. 1821), 426–7. 'L.' is 'Barry Cornwall' (Bryan Waller Procter). All quotations follow *KCH*, 241–2, where details of subsequent publication also appear.

16 *New Monthly Magazine and Literary Journal* 3 (1 May 1821), 256–7. Shelley incorporated the epitaph as first line of a stanza possibly written for *Adonais*, later published by Mary Shelley as a 'Fragment' under the title 'On Keats, WHO DESIRED THAT ON HIS TOMB SHOULD BE INSCRIBED–: "Here lieth One whose name was writ on water!"' See *The Poetical Works of Percy Bysshe Shelley* (4 vols., London, 1839) iv. 183. Keats's grave was also managed to articulate the myth. Severn determined that 'poor Keats's Grave' would incorporate a narrative:

Our Keats Tomb is simply this – a Greek Lyre in Basso relievo – with only half the Strings. – to show his Classical Genius cut off by death before its maturity. – the Inscription is this 'This Grave contains all that was Mortal of a Young English poet – who on his death-bed – in the bitterness of his heart – at the malicious power of his enemies – desired these words to be engraven on his Tomb Stone'/ 'Here lies one whose name was writ in Water' (1 June 1823; *KC*, i. 273)

The 'name' literally vanishes into a symbolic type, 'a Young English Poet', and an emblematic narrative.

17 Hunt's unsigned review, 'Letters to the Readers of the Examiner, No. 6 – On Mr. Shelley's New Poem, Entitled *Adonais*', appeared in *Examiner* 754 (7 July 1822), 419–21; rpt. Newman Ivey White, *The Unextinguished Hearth: Shelley and his Contemporary Critics* (1938; rpt. New York, 1972), 298–303.

18 Jones, *Letters of Shelley*, ii. 297, my emphasis. Behrendt, *Shelley and his Audiences* (Lincoln, Neb., and London, 1989), 250. Knerr observes that, even before publication of *Adonais*, 'Shelley became the major publicist for the belief that Keats had been killed by the reviews', *Shelley's 'Adonais'*, 251, n. 26.

19 For *Adonais* as intentionally 'elegy and a polemic' see Richard Holmes, *Shelley: The Pursuit* (1974; rpt. London, 1987), 656. For the turns of this polemic and the fictionalising of Keats it entailed, see James Heffernan, '*Adonais*: Shelley's Consumption of Keats', *SIR* 23 (1984), 295–315. The *Quarterly*'s review of Hunt's *Foliage* (Jan. 1818, 324–5) gave a damning account of Shelley's character and assaulted *The Revolt of Islam* (Apr. 1819, 460–71) in language similar to that with which it had attacked Keats. The reviewer, whose identity obsessed Shelley, also described the poem as mischievous 'poison', a word that Shelley turned back upon the *Quarterly* in a letter of 15 Oct. 1819 (Jones, *Letters of Shelley*, ii. 126) and repeated in his allusion to the murderous journal in *Adonais*: 'Our Adonais has drunk poison' (XXXVI). Mary Shelley invokes the term in her own remarks about the application of *Adonais* to Shelley: 'the poisonous breath of critics has vanished into emptiness before the fame he inherits'; 'Note on Poems of 1821', *Poetical Works*, iv. 150.

20 Jones, *Letters of Shelley*, ii. 251–3 and n. and *Essays, Letters from Abroad, Translations and Fragments by Percy Bysshe Shelley* (2 vols., London, 1840) ii. 197–9. Milnes reprinted the letter by way of refuting Shelley's myth-making; *L&L*, i. 208–11.

21 Cf. Hunt: 'Poor Keats!', he writes to Shelley, 'They send word from Rome that he is dying' (1 Mar. 1821); D. H. Reiman (ed.), *Shelley and His Circle 1773–1822*, vols. v–viii (Cambridge, Mass., 1973) v. 418. Cf. Charles Cowden Clarke, 'Recollections of Keats', *Atlantic Monthly* (Jan. 1861); rpt. *KCH*, 396, where further publication details are given. See also n. 47 below.

22 Finch's account was sent in Gisborne's letter of 13 June; see Jones, *Letters of Shelley*, ii. 299–302. Shelley uses Finch's term 'closing scene', paraphrases, and directly (mis)quotes some of his text. Severn's essay 'On the Vicissitudes' also reiterates 'closing scene', giving it his own elaborate staging (407). See also Thomas Medwin's account of *Adonais*, 'Memoir of Shelley': 'Poor Keats died . . . and much of the remainder of that year . . .

was occupied on "Adonais"', *Athenaeum* 250 (11 Aug. 1832), 522–4.

23 Shelley said to Byron, 16 July 1821, that if he had 'erred' in *Adonais*, it was only 'in defence of the weak – not in conjunction with the powerful'; Jones, *Letters of Shelley*, ii. 309. Peter Manning suggests that Shelley's Preface, in conscious conversation with Byron, is echoing *English Bards*; see 'Byron's "English Bards" and Shelley's "Adonais": A Note', *Notes and Queries* 215 (Oct. 1970), 380–1. Shelley attempts to coopt Byron's ridicule by placing him among the mourners in *Adonais*, with a pointed reminder that his 'fame' (unlike Keats's) 'Over his living head like Heaven is bent/ An early but enduring monument' (XXX). The story of Keats certainly put Byron in mind of the genesis of *English Bards*: see Marchand, *Byron's Letters and Journals*, viii. 173. For Medwin, see *Athenaeum* 252 (25 Aug. 1832), 554.

24 For Hunt on these stanzas, see White, *Unextinguished Hearth*, 302; see also *L&L*, i. 208–12, and 'Adonais', *Blackwood's* 10 (Dec. 1821), 699.

25 In 'Feminizing Keats' I consider the nineteenth-century discussion of Keats's gender, with preliminary attention to the force of *Adonais*; see especially pp. 322–4.

26 See H. B. Forman (ed.), *Letters of John Keats to Fanny Brawne* (New York, 1878).

27 *KC*, ii. 51–3, 96.

28 'Recollections of Books and their Authors. – No. 6. John Keats, The Poet', *Olio* (28 June 1828), 391–4, extracted in *KCH*, 256–8, which notes J. R. MacGillivray's suggestion that 'Barry Cornwall' is the author. For Hunt see White, *Unextinguished Hearth*, 300, and 'Mr. Keats', in *Lord Byron and Some of His Contemporaries* (London and Philadelphia, 1828), 213–31.

29 See Tom Taylor (ed.), *Life of Benjamin Robert Haydon* (2 edn, 3 vols., London, 1853) and *The Life of Gerald Griffin* (2nd edn, Dublin, 1857), in *KCH*, 17. At the time of the *Quarterly*'s review, Fanny Keats did not know Fanny Brawne, nor could she have 'often found' her brother reading the review since she was not living in the same house and her visits were restricted.

30 Letter to Mary Russell Mitford, 26 Oct. 1841, Kelley and Hudson, *Brownings' Correspondence*, v. 158.

31 The legend was all but canonised by mid-century in *Chambers's Cyclopedia* (1858) where the entry on Keats opened with a long account of the fatal reviews. See also Ross Grieg Woodman, *The Apocalyptic Vision in the Poetry of Shelley* (Toronto, 1966), 159. Heffernan, 'Shelley's Consumption', 295–6, makes a similar observation to Woodman's, and notes that Earl Wasserman, *Shelley: A Critical Reading* (Baltimore, 1971) also translates Shelley's myth into facts of 'biography'.

32 'On the Aristocracy of Letters', *Table-Talk; or, Original Essays* (1821–2), in *HW*, viii. 205–14.

33 Hazlitt quotes *The Winter's Tale*, 4.4.81–2; *Hamlet*, 4.5.173–80, and *Paradise Lost*, 7.37–8.

34 'Prometheus Unbound', 7 (Sept. 1820), 679–87.

35 'Modern Periodical Literature', *New Monthly Magazine* 14 (Sept. 1820), 306. *Alfred* (6 Oct. 1818), in *KCH*, 118, 121, 122.

36 He recalls to Murray, 30 July 1821, 'the same thing nearly happened to Kirke White – who afterwards died of consumption' (as if Keats had not) and more tactfully muses to Shelley, 30–31? July 1821, that 'Kirke White was nearly extinguished in the same way – by a paragraph or two'; see Marchand, *Byron's Letters and Journals*, viii. 163.

37 Marchand, *Byron's Letters and Journals*, viii. 162–3. Though not published in Byron's lifetime, the jingle appeared soon enough in *The Works of Lord Byron: With His Letters and Journals, and His Life, By Thomas Moore, Esq.* (14 vols., London, 1832), 212. It is telling that 'Who killed John Keats?' and the stanza about Keats's death from *Don Juan* (XI. 60) are routinely reprinted in critical editions of *Adonais*, from Rossetti's in 1891 to Knerr's in 1984; see Knerr, *Shelley's 'Adonais'*, 251 n. 26.

38 'Adonais' (8 Dec. 1821), 773.

39 Jones, *Letters of Shelley*, ii. 284; Byron to Shelley, 26 Apr. 1821, Marchand, *Byron's Letters and Journals*, viii. 103. Shelley's reassurances and repetition of his narrative are given to Byron in a letter of 4 May 1821, *Letters of Shelley*, ii. 289–90.

40 'Mr. Keats', *Lord Byron*, 229. Keats's epitaph was also the subject of a joke. Severn reports that after the 'gravestone was placed', a host of 'scoffers' often repeated 'a silly jest: "Here lies one whose name was writ in water, and *his works in milk and water*" . . . this I was condemned to hear for years repeated', 'On the Vicissitudes', 403, in *KCH*, 412.

41 Medwin, *Athenaeum* 249 (4 Aug. 1832), 502–4; the editor was Keats's friend Charles Dilke; *KC*, ii. 95 n. 77. The durability of Shelley's myth and its parodic summation in Byron's epitaph appears from the long line of refutations: Masson insisted that the 'story of [Keats's] having been killed by the savage article in the *Quarterly* is proved to have been wholly untrue', 'The Life and Poetry of Keats', *Macmillan's Magazine* (Nov. 1860), 7; extracted in *KCH*, 371. Charles Cowden Clarke: '"Snuffed out by an article", indeed!', 'Recollections of Keats', in *KCH*, 401. Colvin, too, refuted the 'false impression' that Keats was 'a weakling to whom the breath of detraction had been poison' (*John Keats*, 209–10). Matthew Arnold admired the Preface to *Endymion* as the voice of 'a strong man, not of a weakling avid of praise, and meant to be "snuff'd out by an article"'; Keats had 'flint and iron in him . . . he had character' and was no 'sensuous weakling'; see 'John Keats', in R. H. Super (ed.), *The Complete Prose Works of Matthew Arnold* (11 vols., Ann Arbor, 1960–77) ix. 205–16.

42 Thomas Carlyle, 'Burns' (review of Lockhart's *Life of Robert Burns*) *Edinburgh Review* 48 (1828); rpt. *Critical and Miscellaneous Essays* (5 vols., New York, 1969) i. 258–319. Poe, 'The Duc de L'Omelette', *The Works of Edgar Allan Poe* (6 vols., New York, 1840) iii. 199–204. 'Alexander Smith's Poems', *Blackwood's* 75 (Mar. 1854), 345–51.

43 *Shelley/ Adonais* (Oxford, 1891), 126. Wasserman sustains this impression: the 'self-portrait . . . has almost always proved unpleasant reading because it seems sadly marred by extravagant self-pity and unmanliness', *Shelley*, 499.

44 'Thoughts on Criticism, by a Critic', *Cornhill Magazine* 34 (1876), 556–69. Hazlitt, 'On Effeminacy of Character', in *HW*, viii. 248–55. Gilfillan, 'John Keats', *Literary Portraits*, 261–2. Hazlitt, in *HW*, viii. 90–100, quoting slightly inaccurately *Romeo and Juliet*, 1.1.149–51; a Romeo unmanned by love is evident enough in his cry, 'O sweet Juliet,/ Thy beauty hath made me effeminate/ And in my temper soften'd valour's steel' (3.1.115–17).

45 *Ladies' Companion* (Aug. 1837), 186. The narrative, J. R. MacGillivray remarks, coincided with 'the popular Victorian and feminine ideal of the unhappy and beautiful youth of genius', *Keats: A Bibliography and Reference Guide with an Essay on Keats' Reputation* (Toronto, 1949), xiii.

46 See her version of *Adonais* XLIII in F[rances] M[ary] Owen, *John Keats: A Study* (London, 1880), 183.

47 See Marchand, *Byron's Letters and Journals*, viii. 102, 172. Shelley's Preface to *Adonais* sounds more evidently sympathetic: 'poor Keats's life . . . the poor fellow' (5). 'Mr Keats fell a victim to his too great susceptibility . . . poor Keats was of too gentle a disposition for severity', echoed the *Literary Chronicle*, in its own preface to a reprinting of *Adonais* (see n. 3 above). Milnes printed Severn's letters from Rome which, lavishly detailing Keats's demise, repeated the phrase as a routine epithet: see in particular *L&L*, ii. 85–98. Severn's own essay on Keats keeps up the theme; see 'On the Vicissitudes', 402.

48 'The Daintiest of Poets – Keats', *Victoria Magazine* 15 (May 1870), 55–67. Mrs [Margaret] Oliphant, 'John Keats', *The Literary History of England in the End of the Eighteenth and Beginning of the Nineteenth Century* (3 vols., London, 1882) iii. 133–55. Lowell, *John Keats* (2 vols., Cambridge, Mass., 1925) i. 14, ii. 80, 82. Heffernan demonstrates how Shelley recast the Adonis myth to make Adonais 'not so much a hunter as a defenseless . . . weak and immature child', 'Shelley's Consumption', 305–6.

49 Mark Kipperman, 'Absorbing a Revolution: Shelley Becomes a Romantic, 1889–1903', *Nineteenth-Century Literature* (1992), 197. Hunt explicitly managed Shelley's story for this end, evoking the mythology of *Adonais*:

When I heard of the catastrophe that overtook him, it seemed as if this spirit, not sufficiently constituted like the rest of the world, to obtain their sympathy, yet gifted with a double portion of love for all living things, had been found dead in a solitary corner of the earth, its wings stiffened, its warm heart cold; the relics of a misunderstood nature, slain by the ungenial elements. ('Mr. Shelley', *Lord Byron*, 157)

Mary Shelley also contended that Shelley was 'like a spirit from another sphere, too delicately organised for the rough treatment man uses toward man, especially in the season of youth', *Poetical Works*, i. 97.

50 Review of *Adonais* and *Hellas*, 87/4 (Apr. 1825), 345–7.

51 Jones, *Letters of Shelley*, ii. 366, 372. Shelley was avid to hear news about the reception of *Adonais*: see, for example, *Letters of Shelley*, ii. 357, 363, 365, 382, 387–8, 396.

52 To Ollier, 11 June 1821, Jones, *Letters of Shelley*, ii. 399.

53 Jones, *Letters of Shelley*, ii. 294, 296. Shelley closely supervised the Pisan printing in order, he told Ollier, to give him a clean copy for his pressmen that will avoid such 'errors as *assist* the obscurity of *Prometheus*' (ibid., ii. 297). Behrendt remarks that the elaborate literariness of *Adonais* is the device by which Shelley claims his place in the great tradition (*Shelley and his Audiences*, 246). Ronald Tetreault proposes a radical literary agency: 'The poetic persona of *Adonais* is less a free, creative subjectivity than a construct of the poem's highly deterministic discourse, as if the institutions of myth and genre had usurped the role of the poet ... Language seems to write itself'; *The Poetry of Life: Shelley and Literary Form* (Toronto, 1987), 226–7.

54 *Examiner* (7 July 1822); White, *Unextinguished Hearth*, 298. *Caviare* recalls Keats's signature on *La Belle Dame* in Hunt's *Indicator* (May 1820); in a rueful in-joke about his reviews, Keats was alluding to Hamlet's admiration for a play that 'pleased not the million, 'twas caviare to the general' (2.2.432–3).

55 'Shelley', 96 (2 Sept. 1829), 544–6. The extent to which Shelley's performance had overwhelmed its lamentable subject is evident in the fact that the name 'Keats' appears nowhere in this notice.

56 Jones, *Letters of Shelley*, ii. 300. For Shelley and blasphemy, see also n. 59 below.

57 250 (11 Aug. 1832), 523.

58 *Literary Gazette* (8 Dec. 1821), 773, and 'Adonais', *Blackwood's* 10 (Dec. 1821), 699.

59 Quoting from Knerr's transcription of Shelley's Notebook e.20, fol. 14r, *Shelley's 'Adonais'*, 199. The friend was John Taaffe: Shelley thanked him for his 'strictures on Adonais', saying that he was cancelling from the Preface 'the whole passage relating to my private wrongs', but would retain 'Cain's or Christ's' (4 July 1821, Jones, *Letters of Shelley*, ii. 306). When Hallam and Milnes sought a publisher for their reprinting in 1829, this passage posed a problem; see H. B. Forman (ed.), *The Poetical Works of Percy Bysshe Shelley* (4 vols., London, 1876) iii. 5n.

60 'The Poems of Percy Bysshe Shelley', *Metropolitan* 13 (Aug. 1835), 370–82; Howitt, 'Shelley', *Homes and Haunts of the Most Eminent British Poets* (London, 1847; London, 1857), 301–21.

61 *L&L*, ii. 99–108; the stanzas of *Adonais* quoted are XL, XLIX, L, LI. The couplet from *Julian and Maddalo* closing the *Life* was so well known as not to need annotation; the grammatical ambiguity of this couplet (do poets teach what they have already suffered? suffer as they teach? learn

by suffering what they've only sung about heretofore?) coincides aptly with the anachronism by which Shelley is read by his song on Keats. William Keach attends to this 'indeterminate grammar' in *Shelley's Style* (London and New York, 1984), 201–2.

62 Shelley to Severn, Jones, *Letters of Shelley*, ii. 366; *L&L*, ii. 105–6.
63 Review of *Adonais*, *Literary Register* 13 (28 Sept. 1822), 193–4; Medwin, *Athenaeum* 252 (25 Aug. 1832), 555.
64 Trelawny writes: 'Mr. Keats's last volume of "Lamia", "Isabella", &c. being open in the jacket pocket, confirmed [Shelley's body] beyond a doubt', Edward John Trelawny, 'Mr. Trelawney's [*sic*] Narrative of the Loss of the Boat Containing Mr. Shelley and Mr. Williams, on the 8th July, 1822, off the Coast of Italy (Now First Published)'; see Hunt, 'Mr. Shelley', *Lord Byron*, 172–4 and for Hunt's note, 177. The next essay in *Lord Byron*, on 'Mr. Keats', concludes noting his interment 'in the English burying-ground at Rome . . . where his friend and poetical mourner, Mr. Shelley, was shortly to join him'; ibid., 231.
65 'Recent English Poets No. IV. – John Keats', 3, 157 (11 Oct. 1845), 858–9.
66 Mary Shelley, 'Note on Poems of 1821', *Poetical Works*, iv. 150, and 'Note on Poems of 1822', iv. 235–6. Howitt also joins Shelley to *Adonais*, quoting the last stanza 'as a prophesy' of his own death, 'Shelley', *Homes and Haunts*, 321. For Shelley's heart, see Newman Ivey White, *Shelley* (2 vols., New York, 1940) ii. 635n.
67 'On the Vicissitudes', 406–7.

CHAPTER 3

Keats, the critics, and the politics of envy

Martin Aske

It is doubtful whether there is anybody left in the world of Keats scholarship who would subscribe to the belief that the author of *Endymion* was harried to an early grave – 'hooted from the stage of life', as Shelley put it – by attacks in the Tory press.[1] We are reluctant to sentimentalise the poet's early death, and a recent critic's surmise, that the ailing Keats 'felt that the hostile reviews confirmed the failure and futility of his poetic career, and allowed them to deepen the depression of his last months' is about as much as our scepticism will permit.[2] Nevertheless, it may be worth revisiting this myth. Here, for example, is Benjamin Robert Haydon's lament for 'poor Keats': 'He began life full of hopes! fiery, impetuous, & ungovernable, expecting the World at once to fall beneath his powers! Alas, his genius had no sooner began to bud, than Envy & hatred spat their poison on its leaves, & tender, sensitive, & young, it shrivelled beneath their putrid effusions.'[3] Haydon's imagery may have been a recollection of a passage in act one of *Romeo and Juliet*, which Hazlitt also used on more than one occasion to describe the young poet's untimely demise:

> A bud bit by an envious worm,
> Ere he could spread his sweet leaves to the air,
> Or dedicate his beauty to the sun . . .[4]

In *Adonais* Shelley represents the departed poet as triumphantly secure from all the 'envy and calumny and hate and pain' (XL) which had conspired to torture him to death. In each case Keats is portrayed as hapless victim of 'the envy of the community' (the phrase is Hazlitt's)[5] – the envy, specifically, of the malevolent *critical* community. It is this common emphasis on envy which I want to isolate from the myth of 'poor Keats', and which will provide the necessary point of departure for this essay.

The suspicion that criticism might be motivated by envy had

46

already become a commonplace in the Romantic period; in its historical context Hazlitt's contention that 'taste is often envy in disguise' is less scandalous than it sounds.[6] Coleridge devotes a substantial part of *Biographia Literaria* to analysis of the role of envy in modern criticism, while Wordsworth's sensitivity to 'the envy and malevolence . . . which always stand in the way of a work of any merit from a living Poet' testifies to the problematic relations between writer and critic at a time when the opportunities for criticism – particularly in the form of periodical literature – seemed to be usurping the place of the 'creative artist'.[7] But there are specific nuances to Keats's defence against the envy of the community. Leigh Hunt claimed that Keats's 'powerful mind' had been weakened by the 'critical malignity' and 'unhappy envy' of the Tory press, yet poems such as *Isabella* and *Lamia* reveal a lucid and robust awareness of envy's disconcerting presence in human affairs (*KCH*, 173). Keats knows as well as Hazlitt that envy is one of the 'natural secretions of the human heart', an ineluctable fact of emotional life which cannot be hidden simply because it is defined, in René Girard's phrase, by an 'astringent and unpopular word'.[8]

Indeed, I take the poet's interest in envy to be comparable to his concern with embarrassment, which Christopher Ricks has shown to be particularly intelligent and liberating. Of course there are differences. Keats's great insight, which Ricks was the first properly to acknowledge, was that embarrassment has a special kind of potential in everyday life, and that it was part of Keats's 'special goodness as a man and as a poet' that he could voice that potential in his letters and verse.[9] By comparison, envy is obdurate and unyielding; its very nature is to be without potential, to deny itself the power or the possibility to change for the better. 'Almost every other crime', wrote Samuel Johnson, 'is practised by the help of some quality which might have produced esteem or love, if it had been well employed; but envy is mere unmixed and genuine evil.'[10] Yet Keats challenges us to recognise envy as being as central to human experience as embarrassment; he is as sensitive to the paralysing impotence of the one as he is to the liberating possibilities of the other.

In his acute understanding of envy Keats could be seen to belong to the great Romantic tradition of thinking on *ressentiment*, which includes Blake and culminates in Nietzsche. This is not the place to explore the general proposition that 'the romantic state of mind is pervaded by "*ressentiment*"'.[11] But I should wish to argue that contemporary critical reaction to Keats's poetry (that is, the hostile, negative, nay-saying reaction), combined with the poet's tactics in dealing with that reaction, constitutes a significant moment in the history of modern *ressentiment*. To suggest that Keats's verse celebrates a Nietzschean life-affirming 'yes', which then calls forth the reactive 'no' of critical *ressentiment*, might be too facile a summary of this complex cultural moment.[12] Yet the collective emphasis on envy in Haydon, Shelley, and Hazlitt, as a means of explaining the fate of 'poor Keats', may well tell us something about a culture where 'literary warfare' mirrored broader social and political tensions.[13]

Shortly after the mauling received by *Endymion* in *Blackwood's Edinburgh Magazine* and the *Quarterly Review*, Keats received an encouraging letter from his friend John Hamilton Reynolds who advised Keats to publish his more recent narrative poem, *Isabella* (completed April 1818), as soon as possible, because 'its completeness will be a full answer to all the ignorant malevolence of cold lying Scotchmen and stupid Englishmen'. After the 'slipshod Endymion', the 'simplicity and quiet pathos' of *Isabella* would surely provide 'the best of all answers' with which 'to annul the Quarterly Review'. Reynolds goes on to suggest that Keats 'look [the poem] over with that eye to the *littlenesses* which the world are so fond of excepting to' (14 October 1818, *Letters*, i. 376-7).

What Reynolds's advice emphasises is the extent to which Keats is compelled to write 'with [an] eye' to the public domain, to write within the 'gaze' of an ever vigilant readership. The poet has to watch himself because he knows he is being watched by a potentially hostile public. As one reviewer put it, 'in this *poetizing age* we are led to look with an eye of suspicion on every work savouring of rhyme' (*KCH*, 79). It is the construction of this 'eye of suspicion' that I want to analyse here. In a letter to Haydon, Wordsworth claimed that

I naturally shrink from solicitation of public notice. I never publish any thing without great violence to my own disposition which is to shun, rather than court, regard. In this respect we Poets are much more happily situated than our Brother Labourers of the Pencil; who cannot, unless they be born to a Fortune, proceed in their employments without public countenance.[14]

The ambiguities of Wordsworth's language are typically unobtrusive. The 'regard' which he professes 'to shun, rather than court' incorporates not only the sense of 'esteem' but also the fundamental idea of a *look* –

the public's estimation depends, precisely, on how it 'views' the writer. This underlying notion of 'looking' is already present, of course, in 'notice', and returns in 'countenance', a richly nuanced word in this context since it implies not only patronage or support but also the 'face' or 'regard' which the public bends upon the artist.

As it stands, of course, Wordsworth's argument is rather tenuous, and probably tells us more about his condescending attitude to Haydon than about the relative positions of writer and painter vis-à-vis the public in 1816. A similar declaration from Keats sounds much more like a gesture of defiance: 'I never wrote one single Line of Poetry with the least Shadow of public thought' (*Letters*, i. 267). This statement appears in a letter to Reynolds (9 April 1818), where Keats agrees to the publication of *Endymion* without the poem's original preface. The letter is notable for its expressions of contempt for the public; yet its sheer insistence upon this arouses a suspicion that Keats's aggressive rhetoric is little more than a symptom of what John Scott perceptively identified as 'the bravado style of many of his sentiments', a 'swagger' which is designed to mask a contrary truth (*KCH*, 226). The depth of Keats's sensitiveness to the power of 'public thought' is evident in the revised preface to *Endymion*, where he voices a desire 'to conciliate men who are competent to look, and who do look with a zealous eye, to the honour of English literature' (*PJK*, 102). As in Wordsworth's letter to Haydon, the language of looking here shades into complex possibilities of meaning. Keats's syntax seems clear enough: the poet seeks 'to conciliate men who are competent to look . . . to the honour of English literature'; the intervening clause – 'and who do look with a zealous eye' – is intended to lend extra weight to the proposition. But perhaps the structure of the whole sentence allows a pause half-way, and thereby a different inflection of meaning: 'This is not written with the least atom of purpose to forestall criticisms of course, but from the desire I have to conciliate men who are competent to look'. Might 'competent to look' mean here 'able to *read*'? The poet is not concerned to 'forestall criticisms', but he *is* anxious that such 'criticisms' should issue from readers who are qualified – 'competent' – to deliver them. But then this sense of 'looking' modulates into a kind of vigilance signified by the 'zealous eye' of those self-appointed guardians of public taste whose job is to protect 'the honour of English literature'. The structure of Keats's sentence thus uncovers a logic from which the poet cannot, apparently, escape: those 'men' who are 'competent to

look' – that is, who possess a genuine capacity to read and criticise –
need to be propitiated because they are also the guardians who
defend 'the honour of English literature'. The writer is 'looked at' –
read, and criticised – and this critical 'look' is simultaneously bound
up with the necessity of looking to see whether the writer enhances or
violates 'the honour of English literature'.

Given the subsequent critical reaction to *Endymion*, the preface's
avowed commitment to 'the honour of English literature' sounds
ironically prescient. In the eyes of its most hostile reviewers, Keats's
poem had indeed tarnished the reputation – the 'honour' – of English
literature (just as Keats himself feared, at the end of the preface, that
he had 'in too late a day touched the beautiful mythology of Greece,
and dulled its brightness'; *PJK*, 103). Issuing in particular from his
association with Leigh Hunt are 'uncleannesses' which, Keats is
advised, he must 'cast off' if he is 'to make his way to the truest strain
of poetry' (*KCH*, 73). The infamous 'Z', taking exception to the
juxtaposition of Wordsworth and Hunt in the sonnet 'Great spirits
now on earth are sojourning', indignantly contrasts the 'purest' of
living poets with the 'filthiest, and the most vulgar of Cockney
poetasters'. Thus the young poet finds those 'men' whom he had been
eager to 'conciliate' conspiring to defend the 'honour' of literature
against what they perceive to be the importunate 'Johnny Keats'. As
though they were defending the honour of a woman, these 'men' seek
to protect literature from the upstart purveyor of 'prurient and vulgar
lines', who 'touches' only that he might 'profane' and 'vulgarise'
(*KCH*, 99, 100, 102, 104). Their 'zealous eye' makes them *jealous* of the
'honour' which they are given to defend. Indeed, when Richard
Woodhouse appropriates the same phrase from the preface (in a letter
which, like the one from Reynolds, was intended to buoy Keats up in
the face of so much critical adversity), he misquotes it as 'a jealous eye
[to] the honor of English literature' (21 October 1818; *Letters*, i. 379).
What makes a 'zealous eye' jealous? The eye which zealously
safeguards the honour of literature becomes jealously possessive of
that honour; it looks askance at any attempt to break through the
cordon sanitaire which separates the 'pure' from the 'filthy', the 'clean'
from the 'unclean'. Thus can a 'zealous eye' turn into the 'venomous
eye of *ressentiment*', the hardened, resentful gaze which communicates
a silent but steadfast 'no' to any external force threatening to violate
the 'honour' over which it watches.[15]

Reynolds had already signalled his support for Keats in the *Alfred, West of England Journal and General Advertiser* (6 October 1818). His article defends Keats against the 'unfeeling arrogance' and 'cold ignorance' of the *Quarterly*, and recalls how another young poet, Henry Kirke White, had been threatened with comparable hostility from the *Monthly Review* – before 'the world saw the cruelty [and] hailed the genius which malignity would have repressed' (*KCH*, 117). As a more recent instance of such critical 'malignity' Reynolds goes on to cite the 'brutality' of the treatment meted out by the *Quarterly* to Lady Morgan's *France* (1817), and he concludes that 'a woman is the best prey for its malignity, because it is the gentlest and the most undefended' (*KCH*, 118).

The juxtaposition of these two cases would seem to imply that the situation of the young male poet is comparable to that of a woman writer, insofar as both occupy positions of extreme vulnerability vis-à-vis the press and the machinations of its 'Government critics' (*KCH*, 118). Indeed, Reynolds's belief that the situation of the woman writer is somehow paradigmatic ('a woman is the *best* prey', emphasis added) suggests that the young poet's position is already gendered; the very fact of his youthfulness makes him – in the eyes of those 'men' who look to the honour of English literature – less than a 'man', as it were, and therefore forces him into the same subject-position as that occupied by the woman writer. In their shared subjection both become 'prey' to the critics' malignity, the male violence committed through 'ignorant malevolence'.

The portrait of the young male poet as an 'undefended' woman becomes more visible later in the article when Reynolds calls poetry 'the coyest creature that ever was wooed by man: she has something of the coquette in her; for she flirts with many, and seldom loves one' (*KCH*, 120). Here, the image of violated honour has been reversed. It is no longer a question of the purity of English literature being soiled by the adolescent fumblings of young 'Johnny Keats', but rather a case of the poet's 'feminine' innocence (enhanced by having 'something of the coquette') being violated at the hands of a malevolently masculine press. Richard Woodhouse (in the same letter quoted earlier) describes the *Quarterly* reviewer of *Endymion* as having 'laid his finger of contempt upon passages of such beauty, that no one with a spark of poetic feeling can read them without a desire to know more of the poem' (*Letters*, i. 379). The suggestion of profanation, in the image of the critic's 'finger of contempt' prying among 'passages of such beauty', is taken up in a letter which Keats wrote to Haydon two months later, where – again in defiant mood – he declares: 'I admire Human Nature but I do not like *Men* – I should like to compose things honourable to Man – but not fingerable over by *Men*.' The fact that he speaks disparagingly in the next sentence of 'Men's and Women's admiration' scarcely lessens the disconcerting force of 'not fingerable over by *Men*', a phrase which evokes the image of a female muse harassed and molested, her 'body' vulnerable to being pawed, fingered, fondled by the contemptuous hands of her male critics (22 December 1818; *Letters*, i. 415).[16]

Crucially, the gaze which the hostile critic fixes upon the young ('feminine') poet is an invidious one; it is the evil eye of *envy*. But why should the men who look to the honour of English literature be represented as 'envious' and 'malignant' as well as 'undiscerning' in their treatment of 'Johnny Keats' (21 October 1818; *Letters*, i. 381)? In *Paradise Lost* it is the 'Sight hateful, sight tormenting' of Adam and Eve 'Imparadised in one another's arms' which forces Satan to turn aside 'for envy' and 'with jealous leer malign' to eye the happy couple 'askance' (IV. 502–6). What Satan envies is a perfect happiness which appears all the more intolerable because it borders on the excessive – the 'happier Eden . . ./ Of bliss on bliss' (IV. 507–8). Keats's poetry – particularly the early verse – makes exorbitant claims for the possibility of imagining states of happiness. '['T]is with full happiness that I/ Will trace the story of Endymion' (I. 34–5), announces the young poet, with a blithe confidence which the unsympathetic reader might find galling (what right has this young Cockney to be so cocky?). Moreover, the 'full happiness' sought by the poet is often imagined as a narcissistic pleasure, where the body is 'Blissfully haven'd' (*The Eve of St. Agnes*, 240) in 'Some flowery spot, sequester'd, wild, romantic' (*To George Felton Mathew*, 37), or 'pillow'd on a bed of flowers' (*To My Brother George*, 123). It is this imagery of self-contentment – the poet 'lost in pleasant smotherings' (*I stood tip-toe upon a little hill*, 132), the mutual absorption of Milton's Adam and Eve – which is calculated to arouse envy in the onlooker: 'It is as if we envied them for maintaining a blissful state of mind – an unassailable libidinal position which we ourselves have since abandoned'.[17] True envy, says Lacan, 'makes the subject pale before the image of a completeness closed upon itself'.[18] The 'critical malignity' and 'unhappy envy' which Leigh Hunt discerned in the Tory press's reaction to Keats betray an inability to accept the 'luxuries' imagined in Keats's verse, the dreams of happiness which it so wilfully insists upon. The otherwise sympathetic Francis Jeffrey accused the author of *Endymion* of being 'too constantly rapt into an extramundane Elysium' (*KCH*, 205). But perhaps this is Keats's most unsettling challenge, a sign of the radical impulse behind his 'bravado style'. Indeed, Scott invokes the term 'insolent' in his endeavour to characterise the specific quality in Keats which 'provokes opposition' (*KCH*, 226). The insolent young poet provokes opposition and envy because he disconcerts and *saddens* his critics with his unabashed visions of pleasure.[19] The image of a 'completed form of all completeness' – which is how Endymion sums up his first glimpse of Cynthia (I. 606) – might thus be applied to the 'body' of the poet's verse. Rapt in its own 'happier Eden', it antagonises the onlooker precisely because it seems to *vaunt* its own sense of 'completeness', to celebrate the potency of its narcissistic pleasures too happily, 'in full-throated ease' (*Ode to a Nightingale*, 10).

If the invidious eye looks with particular hatred on images of 'completeness', then Reynolds's belief that the 'completeness' of *Isabella* would provide a 'full answer' acquires a salient irony. Far from pacifying the critics, Keats's new poem might only antagonise them further. And the riskiness of Keats's 'full answer' is increased by the crucial fact that envy now becomes incorporated as a vital *theme* within the poem's story. *Isabella* internalises the young poet's anxieties over his standing with the men who look to the honour of English literature. The awkwardly flirtatious relationship of the poet's coy muse to her potentially malevolent critics becomes dramatised as a Nietzschean contest between happy sentiment and unhappy *ressentiment*.

The 'happier Eden' of erotic fulfilment which is then destroyed by envy – Milton's story in Book IV of *Paradise Lost* – offers an illuminating perspective on Keats's narrative of thwarted desire. So too, of course, does *Romeo and Juliet* – a play shot through, according to Hazlitt, with the 'buoyant spirit of youth', where 'passion, the love and expectation of pleasure, is infinite, extravagant, inexhaustible, till experience comes to check and kill it'.[20] (In these terms, the play's theme could be summed up in the image Hazlitt applies to Keats: 'A bud bit by an envious worm'.) It is hardly surprising that Keats should portray the lovers as completely engrossed in each other, but this erotic 'primal scene' has the very specific function of arousing envy. Isabella and Lorenzo unite to form an image of narcissistic

'completeness' which the heroine's brothers will find increasingly
intolerable:

> They could not sit at meals but feel how well
>   It soothed each to be the other by;
> They could not, sure, beneath the same roof sleep
>   But to each other dream, and nightly weep.   (5-8)

The famously audacious description of their first kiss, where Lorenzo's
lips 'poesied with hers in dewy rhyme' (70), suggests how the
'completeness' of erotic pleasure ('bliss on bliss', lips on lips) mirrors –
rhymes with – the satisfactions of poesy (the 'full happiness' that
comes with tracing stories, making rhymes).[21] The poem continues to
play with the idea of the lovers' 'rhyming' relationship:

> Parting they seem'd to tread upon the air,
>   Twin roses by the zephyr blown apart
> Only to meet again more close, and share
>   The inward fragrance of each other's heart.   (73-6)

Leigh Hunt observed that 'these pictures of their intercourse terribly
aggravate the gloom of what follows' (*KCH*, 171). What needs to be
emphasised, however, is that it is also these narcissistic 'pictures' of the
two rapt lovers – they meet together 'Close in a bower of hyacinth and
musk' (85) – which aggravate the gloom of Isabella's brothers. Their
unhappy envy is fired by the sight of the lovers' happiness. By
reducing the number of brothers from three to two Keats reworks
Boccaccio's tale in terms of a basic opposition between the happily
rhyming dyad of the lovers, on the one hand, and the Florentine
brothers' fearful symmetry on the other –

>   . . . as self-retired
>   In hungry pride and gainful cowardice,
> As two close Hebrews in that land inspired,
>   Paled in and vineyarded from beggar-spies . . .   (129-32)

Secluded in their 'coverts of cowardice',[22] the brothers are represented
as a grotesque parody – a distorted mirror-image – of the lovers'
'closeness': 'And many a jealous conference had they,/ And many
times they bit their lips alone' (169-70). Like Nietzsche's 'cellar
rodents full of vengefulness and hatred', they spy on Isabella with a
'vision covetous and sly' (141), with the 'venomous eye of *ressentiment*'.[23]
They nurse 'bitter thoughts'; each is 'well nigh mad' (164), not only
on account of Lorenzo's social difference – he is 'the servant of their

trade designs' (165) – but also because he 'Should in their sister's love be blithe and glad' (166). Like Keats's nightingale, Lorenzo embodies a promise of happiness which dismays and saddens the onlooker. John Barnard notes that as 'commercial imperialists' Isabella's brothers are 'jealous and fearful of the joys and mutuality of love, and its threat to their own advancement'. This perspective, where the 'opposition between commercialism and love' is seen in terms of 'social envy', is one to which Keats will return in *Lamia*.[24] The later narrative may be more sophisticated in its handling of *ressentiment*; and we know, of course, that Keats himself came to regard *Isabella* as 'too smokeable' and 'mawkish' (22 and 19 September 1819; *Letters*, ii. 174, 162). Yet some of the initial critical reactions provoked by *Isabella* suggest that as a narrative of envy it is more disconcerting, more embarrassingly transgressive than *Lamia*.

For example, the reviewer in the *Edinburgh Magazine* found the 'terms' which Keats 'inflicts upon the brothers of Isabella' to be 'in bad taste': 'He calls them "money-bags", "ledger-men", &c. which injures, in some respect, this delightful story' (*KCH*, 213). (Here again there is a hint of the young poet staining the honour of literature.) Writing in Baldwin's *London Magazine*, John Scott takes up the same point, and develops it into an argument that foregrounds many of the doubts concerning 'taste' and 'sensibility' which Keats inspired in his critics. Scott accuses Keats of upsetting 'the larger philosophy' and 'fine keeping' of Boccaccio's tale by caricaturing the brothers as 'money-bags', 'Baalites of pelf', and 'ledger-men'. The poem's 'school-boy vituperation of trade and traders' is a symptom of Keats's 'boyish petulance', 'insulting bravado', 'dissenting, and altercating prejudices and opinions', which are far removed from Boccaccio's 'more genial spirit' (*KCH*, 220, 222). Citing another early example of Keatsian invective (the rhodomontade against neo-classical poetics in *Sleep and Poetry*) Josiah Conder maintained that it was typical of the 'tetchy aspirant after fame' to 'vent his rancour in the satire of envy' (*KCH*, 69, 70). By 'satire of envy' Conder presumably means that the poet's satire is a consequence of his bitterness at not being recognised, his envy of others' success. And this would also seem to be Scott's point. The poem's undisciplined hostility to the Florentines' 'hungry pride and gainful cowardice' betrays the immaturity of the 'tetchy aspirant after fame', his lack of knowledge of worldly affairs. Without Boccaccio's cool, mature judgement, Keats's perspective on the story becomes skewed; instead of 'looking fairly into the face of human nature', he brings to his subject an eye distorted by envy. But perhaps the real scandal of *Isabella* – an offensiveness which the decorous Scott is unable to bring himself to acknowledge – is that the 'tetchy' poet violates the 'delicacy' of Boccaccio's tale ('venturing syllables', as Keats himself puts it, 'that ill beseem/ The quiet glooms of such a piteous theme', 151–2) by turning the brothers into such glaringly obvious figures of envy (the presence of which, crucially, is not even hinted at in the original story).

Keats's 'bad taste', then, is not just to have changed the spirit of Boccaccio's story into something less 'genial'; it is that he has sullied the purity of the 'old prose' by treating an emotion which Hazlitt describes as 'one of the most tormenting and odious of the passions' – envy, that 'timid and shamefaced passion' which, according to La Rochefoucauld, 'we never dare acknowledge'.[25] To caricature 'trade' as the manifestation of greed and envy is bad enough (Scott cites Lamb's *Elia* essay, 'The South-Sea House', as 'an elegant reproof of such short-sighted views of character; such idle hostilities against the realities of life'); but to represent envy, with such 'bravado' and lack of misgiving, as a powerful emotional and social force, is even more offensive. Scott claims that he is 'loath to see [Keats] irrevocably committed to a flippant and false system of reasoning on human nature; – because to his picturesque imagination, we wish that he would add a more pliable, and, at the same time, a more magnanimous sensibility' (*KCH*, 222, 223). Yet this interpretation of the poet's avowed departure from his original model is perhaps too convenient and facile; the more radical possibility which Scott refuses to consider is that envy is not the cause but rather the *object* of Keats's critique. In which case the poem's 'reasoning on human nature' is less 'flippant' and more searching and serious than Scott would care to admit. The author of *Isabella* shares with Stendhal an instinctive awareness that envy is one of the supremely 'modern' emotions.[26] What Boccaccio had treated as a delicate matter of honour, Keats rewrites in terms of vanity, hatred, and envy. In destroying – as Scott saw it – the 'fine keeping' of Boccaccio's story, Keats had not only broken the rules of poetic decorum. He had also perpetrated a social scandal, laying bare the mechanisms of an emotion which in polite society dares not speak its name.

The Florentines' envy translates itself into a double action: the killing of Lorenzo, followed by the theft of the pot of basil. In a curious way the fate of Isabella's 'sweet basil' – with its 'perfumed leafits' spreading 'as by magic touch' (432, 459) – echoes the image from *Romeo and Juliet* which Hazlitt uses to characterise the fate of 'poor Keats': 'A bud bit by an envious worm'. Just as the pot of basil grows into another sign of 'completeness' which the brothers cannot tolerate or understand (their incomprehension exacerbated, of course, by the fact that Isabella 'withers' as the plant flourishes, 447), so the young budding 'body' of Keats's verse – not yet fully 'open', like Shelley's 'rose embowered/ In its own green leaves' ('To a Skylark') – is defiled ('deflowered', to continue Shelley's metaphor) by the envy of the critical community. It is a body of writing which, with scandalous disregard for the proprieties, refuses to deny itself the pleasure of imagining a 'promised happiness'.[27] Like Romeo and Juliet, like Isabella and Lorenzo, it celebrates 'the love and expectation of pleasure' – until 'experience comes to check and kill it'. In *Isabella* the 'envious worm' of experience takes the form of the two brothers. In *Lamia* it is embodied in the figure of Apollonius.

The 'bald-head philosopher' (*Lamia*, II. 245) is indeed Keats's most forbidding portrait of *ressentiment*. Upholding the laws of 'cold philosophy' (II. 230), Apollonius is akin not only to Nietzsche's ascetic priest – the specifically *modern* thinker who manifests to an extreme degree the 'peculiar philosophers' irritation at and rancor against sensuality' – but also to the Benthamites, excoriated by Hazlitt as 'sour pedagogues' who 'hate and envy and would put an end to whatever gives others pleasure'.[28] But is important to recognise that as a narrative of *ressentiment Lamia* does not merely repeat the structure of *Isabella*. In the earlier poem the lovers are portrayed as innocent victims of the brothers' envy; Lorenzo and Isabella are themselves without envy. Thus the narrative depends, as I have suggested, on a relatively simple opposition between the lovers' desire for happiness and the brothers' 'unhappy envy'. In *Lamia* the situation becomes more complex. Perhaps it is evidence of the greater 'finesse' which Keats declared he would 'use . . . with the Public' that he represents his hero no longer as an innocent 'youngster' (*Isabella*, 172) but as someone already touched by envy (22 September 1819; *Letters*, ii. 174). Lamia's first sight of 'the young Corinthian Lycius' discovers him 'Charioting foremost in the envious race' (I. 216–17). I would argue that this initial image becomes a metaphor of Corinthian society as a whole. After all, it is, in Marjorie Levinson's words, 'Lycius's appetite for the envy of his neighbors' which compels him to make his 'erotic idyll' public:[29]

'What mortal hath a prize, that other men
May be confounded and abash'd withal,
But lets it sometimes pace abroad majestical,
And triumph, as in thee I should rejoice
Amid the hoarse alarm of Corinth's voice.
Let my foes choke, and my friends shout afar,
While through the thronged streets your bridal car
Wheels round its dazzling spokes.'   (II. 57–64)

Quoting these lines – although, curiously, he chooses to omit the
central couplet – John Barnard says that 'the motivation is as crude as
it is unconvincing (quite apart from the fact that there is no sign that
Lycius has any enemies)'.[30] But, if Corinth is a place of competition
and rivalry, taking its character from the dominant metaphor of the
'envious race' (I. 217), it would be entirely logical (and convincing)
for Lycius to think in terms of 'foes' and 'friends'. A clue to the kind of
milieu which Lycius inhabits can be found in a phrase which Barnard
chooses to omit: 'the hoarse alarm of Corinth's voice'. What, exactly,
is this 'hoarse alarm'? During one of his many meditations on the
psychology of *ressentiment*, Hazlitt observed that 'as selfishness is the
vice of unlettered periods and nations, envy is the bane of more
refined and intellectual ones', where men who were 'formerly ready
to cut one another's throats about the gross means of subsistence' are
now 'ready to do it about reputation'.[31] Perhaps, then, we are invited
to see Corinth as a 'refined', indeed, as a *modern* city, a Babel of
competing voices where the importance of 'reputation' means that
'everything seems to be a subject of litigation'.[32] Thus the mutterings
heard in the city's 'populous streets' (I. 352–3) could be the language
of malicious gossip, slander, envy – the same language of 'calumny
and falsehood' which turned London into 'a City of Assassinations'
for William Blake.[33]

As a 'young Corinthian' Lycius is a product of the city's competitive
ethos. Sensitive as he is to his reputation within the 'noisy world' (II.
33), it is not surprising that he should be tempted, eventually, to
solicit the envy of friends and foes alike by flaunting his new-found
'wealth'. Thus Lycius shows himself to be a peculiarly modern lover,
an example of the Romantic *vaniteux* whom Girard finds in Stendhal.
The *vaniteux*, says Girard, 'will desire any object so long as he is
convinced that it is already desired by another person whom he
admires'.[34] *Lamia* offers a variation on this basic structure of 'triangular
desire': Lycius wants to confound and abash 'other men' by making

them envy him and desire his 'prize' (II. 57). It is as though he can only 'prize' Lamia properly if he knows that she is desired by others. By showing Lycius eager to expose the 'secret bowers' of their 'sweet sin' to 'common eyes' (II. 31, 149), *Lamia* reveals the same psychological truth which Girard discovers in Stendhal – namely, that desire is never purely 'spontaneous' but always somehow *mediated*. The pure self-absorption of Lorenzo and Isabella has given way to a more complex mediation where desire is linked to social envy.

Lamia resigns herself to her lover's 'mad pompousness' (II. 114) and acts accordingly, conjuring up a 'fit magnificence' (II. 116) designed to set the wedding guests 'wondering/ Whence all this mighty cost and blaze of wealth could spring' (II. 197–8). In the account of the story in Burton's *Anatomy of Melancholy*, which provides the source of Keats's poem, Lamia's 'furniture' is described as 'no substance but mere illusions' (*PJK*, 475). Its 'lustre' and 'brilliance' (II. 173–4) cannot hide the fact that this 'furniture' is indeed mere *kitsch*, the glitzy opulence of the *parvenu* which is nevertheless perfectly calculated to excite the envy of the Corinthian 'herd' (II. 150). Nowhere, it seems to me, does Keats mark his distance from the perceived 'mawkishness' of *Isabella* more deliberately than in his ironic awareness of the social pressures which mediate Lycius's desire. The 'finesse' which *Lamia* uses 'with the Public' (*Letters*, ii. 174) manifests itself in a more sophisticated grasp of how the public sphere invades private experience, how the structure of desire can never attain the self-enveloping 'completeness' of Lorenzo and Isabella, but is always already mediated – and therefore inevitably *flawed* – by the importunate presence of other less 'pure' emotions such as envy. The highly ambiguous reference to 'Love' as having 'jealous grown of so complete a pair' (II. 12) suggests the presence of a psychological fault line absent in *Isabella*; it hints that the 'completeness' of desire represented by the lovers is *inherently* vulnerable in a way that it had not been in the earlier poem.

Thus it is that the structure of *ressentiment* which underpins the narrative in *Lamia* is more complicated than the disarmingly simple conflict of happiness and envy in *Isabella*. Apollonius is, undoubtedly, the high priest of *ressentiment* – his 'wrinkled countenance' (II. 244) signifying not only the furrows of thoughtful old age but also the distortions caused by the 'eye severe' (II. 157) which bends its baleful gaze on Lamia, 'Brow-beating her fair form' (II. 248). Yet he inhabits a social reality ('wide Corinth', II. 93) which is penetrated by a degree of envy to which Lycius himself is not immune. How, then, are we to explain the confrontation between old sage and young lover, if both are already caught up in the vicious circle of envy? At one level *Lamia* announces its modernity by demonstrating how individual desire is mediated by social envy. At another level the poem introduces Apollonius as a figure of *ressentiment* who is, quite clearly, the enemy of desire. From this perspective it could be argued that Apollonius performs the same function as the brothers in *Isabella*: he brings the 'experience' which will come to check and kill the love and expectation of pleasure. And yet the simple binary opposition which structures the earlier poem breaks down in *Lamia*, since Lycius, unlike Lorenzo, already shows a capacity for envy – as though he were already, as the pupil of Apollonius, on the way to learning the *ressentiment* of his master. What does this shift in accent signify? If the official story of *Isabella* masks another story – the young poet's fear of the hostility of those men who look to the honour of English literature – then *Lamia* could be seen to mark a further stage in this secondary narrative. One radical consequence of Keats heeding his friend's advice by casting a critical eye over his own work is a loss of innocence: the poet is forced to look at himself as the critic looks at him. It is a fall from happy unselfconsciousness into the 'envious race' of literature itself. Lycius, then, represents the fallen poet, the 'youngster' (Lorenzo, Endymion) who has died into the life of 'men'.

The presence of Apollonius bears witness to the profound change that has occurred between *Isabella* and *Lamia*. He appears as Lycius's conscience, a powerful superego absent in *Isabella* and which now intervenes to restrain desire and censor the imagination. In his role as 'trusty guide' and 'good instructor' (I. 375–6) to young Lycius, Apollonius embodies patriarchal law; he is akin to the 'Elders' representing 'the horrible dominion of the Scotch kirk', whom Keats had met on his Northern tour and who had 'done Scotland harm' by banishing 'puns and laughing and kissing' (7 July 1818; *Letters*, i. 319). In an ironical echo of the conciliatory preface to *Endymion*, Lycius fails in his attempt 'With reconciling words and courteous mien' to turn 'the sophist's spleen' into 'sweet milk' (II. 171–2), as Apollonius fixes his eye 'without a twinkle or stir/ Full on the alarmed beauty of the bride' (II. 246–7). His remorseless gaze blights Lamia's brightness, and elicits the following appeal from Lycius:

'Shut, shut those juggling eyes, thou ruthless man!
Turn them aside, wretch! or the righteous ban
Of all the Gods, whose dreadful images
Here represent their shadowy presences,
May pierce them on the sudden with the thorn
Of painful blindness; . . .
Corinthians! look upon that gray-beard wretch!
Mark how, possess'd, his lashless eyelids stretch
Around his demon eyes! Corinthians, see!
My sweet bride withers at their potency.'

(II. 277–82; 287–90)

Suggesting that the repeated address to his audience as 'Corinthians' may allude to Paul's First Epistle to the Corinthians, with its explicit rejection of the claims of the body, Marilyn Butler reads Lycius's speech as 'a call on behalf of the pagan and against the Christian approach to the life of the senses'. I would go further, and say that the speech is not only a 'challenge to Christian ascetism'[35] but also an appeal which can be traced back to the preface to *Endymion*: it becomes Keats's most eloquent protest against the 'cold philosophy' of *ressentiment*, against the withering potency of the critical community's 'jealous leer malign'. It is a protest by the young poet on behalf of his 'harassed muse' against the zealous guardians of literature with their 'proud-heart sophistries' and 'enticing lies' (II. 285–6). Yet Lamia, as the reincarnation of the female muse (Reynolds's 'coyest creature', *KCH*, 120), is finally caught – trapped between the importunate poet–lover who has now entered the 'envious race' (I. 217) of literature, and the potency of the sophist's eye, the malevolent shaft of criticism which goes through her, 'Keen, cruel, perceant, stinging' (II. 301). We know that the serpent's eye has the power to *fascinate*. Does Apollonius fix his eye on Lamia because he is fascinated by her? And is the only way in which he can overcome that fascination to engage her in a kind of looking contest, bending his 'demon eyes' on her until he stares her out of countenance? This is precisely how the 'venomous eye of *ressentiment*' wreaks its revenge. Indeed, the final scene of *Lamia* echoes, somewhat uncannily, Samuel Johnson's description of envious men as those who 'propose no advantage to themselves but the satisfaction of *poisoning the banquet which they cannot taste*, and blasting the harvest which they have no right to reap'.[36] And the whole psychic drama is epitomised with startling clarity in the late poem *To Fanny*: 'Who now, with greedy looks, eats up my feast?/ What stare outfaces now my silver moon!' (17–18).

'From the moment', says Hazlitt, 'that the eye fixes on another as
the object of envy, we cannot take it off.' The 'jealous leer malign'
might not dare 'to look that which provokes it in the face' (Satan, we
recall, eyed Adam and Eve 'askance'), yet it 'cannot keep its eyes from
it, and gloats over and becomes as it were enamoured of the very
object of its loathing and deadly hate'.[37] Perhaps this helps to explain
the motivation behind Apollonius's baleful gaze. And perhaps it
elucidates, further, the nature of the critical envy which greeted
young 'Johnny Keats'. Does the envy of the community betray a
profound fascination with this cultural phenomenon which bears the
name 'Keats'? Envy, Lacan reminds us, is 'usually aroused by the
possession of goods which would be of no use to the person who is
envious of them, and about the true nature of which he does not have
the least idea'.[38] The peculiar nature of Keats's 'goods' – the poetic
'luxuries' with which he seeks to win over the men jealous of the
honour of English literature – makes them somehow threatening, a
risk within the market of taste. If John Bayley is right to maintain that
there is something 'socially new' – and therefore disturbing – in 'the
world of Keatsian "beauties"', then the producer of that 'world'
becomes an object of envy because he cannot be understood or 'read'
as a social and aesthetic sign.[39] Professing himself to be bewildered by
the preface to *Endymion* – 'we really do not know what he means' –
John Wilson Croker in the *Quarterly Review* mischievously concludes
that, like Lycius, the young poet 'is of an age and temper which
imperiously require mental discipline' (*KCH*, 110, 111). His verse
falling outside the dominant order of poetic discourse, Keats comes to
be seen as a kind of literary and social *delinquent* – in Foucault's terms,
'a biographical unity, a kernel of danger, representing a type of
anomaly'.[40] In this sense both *Isabella* and *Lamia* provide a commentary
on the poet's own 'life of Allegory' (19 February 1819; *Letters*, ii. 67) –
a story of the displacements suffered by the modern muse, as she seeks
to outmanoeuvre the 'jealous leer malign' of criticism and its institutions.

NOTES

1 Preface to *Adonais*, in D. Reiman and S. Powers (eds.), *Shelley's Poetry and Prose* (New York and London, 1977), 390–2.
2 Kelvin Everest, *English Romantic Poetry* (Milton Keynes, 1990), 85.
3 W. B. Pope (ed.), *The Diary of Benjamin Robert Haydon* (5 vols., Cambridge, Mass., 1960–3) ii. 317, entry for 29 Mar. 1821.

4 *HW*,viii. 99; xi. 118. Hazlitt quotes, slightly inaccurately, 1.1.149–151.

5 *HW*, viii. 210.

6 *HW*, xx. 331.

7 See in particular chaps. 2, 3, and 21 of *Biographia Literaria* (1817), in J. Engell and W. J. Bate (eds.), *The Collected Works of Samuel Taylor Coleridge* (2 vols., Princeton and London, 1983) i. 30–62, ii. 107–12; E. de Selincourt (ed.), *The Letters of William and Dorothy Wordsworth*, ii, *The Middle Years*, Part 1 1806–1811, 2nd edn, rev. Mary Moorman (Oxford, 1969), 145 (letter to Lady Beaumont, 21 May 1807).

8 *HN*, xx. 322. Girard, *A Theater of Envy: William Shakespeare* (New York and Oxford, 1991), 4.

9 *Keats and Embarrassment* (Oxford, 1974; paperback edn, London, Oxford, and New York, 1976), 1.

10 *Rambler*, No. 183 (17 Dec. 1751), in W. J. Bate and A. B. Strauss (eds.), *The Yale Edition of the Works of Samuel Johnson*, Vols. 3–5 (New Haven and London, 1969) v. 200.

11 René Girard, *Deceit, Desire, and the Novel*, trans. Yvonne Freccero (paperback edn, Baltimore and London, 1976), 14.

12 See Friedrich Nietzsche, *On the Genealogy of Morals* (1887), in *Basic Writings of Nietzsche*, trans. Walter Kaufmann (New York, 1968), 472 and *passim*.

13 'Literary Warfare' is the title Leigh Hunt gives to the chapter in his *Autobiography* (1850) in which he describes the growing hostilities between himself and the Tory press. See *The Autobiography of Leigh Hunt* (3 vols., London, 1850) ii. 83–113.

14 E. de Selincourt (ed.), *The Letters of William and Dorothy Wordsworth*, iii, *The Middle Years*, Part 2 1812–1820, 2nd edn, rev. Mary Moorman and Alan G. Hill (Oxford, 1970), 273 (13 Jan. 1816).

15 Nietzsche, *Basic Writings*, 476.

16 On the image of the 'harassed' muse in *La Belle Dame sans Merci*, see Karen Swann, 'Harassing the Muse', in Anne K. Mellor (ed.), *Romanticism and Feminism* (Bloomington and Indianapolis, 1988), 81–92.

17 Sigmund Freud, 'On Narcissism: An Introduction' (1914), *On Metapsychology*, trans. James Strachey, Pelican Freud Library (Harmondsworth, 1984) xi. 83.

18 *The Four Fundamental Concepts of Psycho-Analysis*, trans. Alan Sheridan (Harmondsworth, 1986), 116.

19 On the relation of sadness to envy, see Spinoza's *Ethics*, trans. Andrew Boyle (London, 1967), 121–2.

20 *HW*, iv. 248, 249.

21 See Ricks's inspired commentary on this image in *Keats and Embarrassment*, 97–9.

22 'The cold malignity of envy may be exerted in a torpid and quiescent state, amidst the gloom of stupidity, in the coverts of cowardice'; Samuel Johnson, *Rambler*, No. 183, in *The Yale Edition of the Works*, v. 198.

23 Nietzsche, *Basic Writings*, 476, 484.
24 *John Keats* (Cambridge, 1987), 81. 'Social envy' is a term which Marjorie Levinson brings into her discussion of *Lamia*, in *KL*, 278.
25 *HW*, xx. 312; La Rochefoucauld, *Maxims*, trans. Leonard Tancock (Harmondsworth, 1988), 40.
26 Girard, *Deceit, Desire*, 14.
27 *HW*, iv. 249.
28 Nietzsche, *Basic Writings*, 542; *HW*, xx. 256.
29 *KL*, 276, 274.
30 *John Keats*, 125.
31 *HW*, xii. 87.
32 *HW*, xvii. 317.
33 Geoffrey Keynes (ed.), *Poetry and Prose of William Blake* (London, 1975), 894 (letter to William Hayley, 24 May 1804).
34 *Deceit, Desire*, 7.
35 *Romantics, Rebels, and Reactionaries. English Literature and its Background 1760–1830* (Oxford and New York, 1981), 135.
36 *Rambler*, No. 183, *The Yale Edition of the Works*, v. 197 (italics mine).
37 *HW*, xx. 312.
38 *The Four Fundamental Concepts*, 116.
39 *The Uses of Division: Unity and Disharmony in Literature* (London, 1976), 146.
40 Michel Foucault, *Discipline and Punish: The Birth of the Prison* (1975), trans. Alan Sheridan (Harmondsworth, 1979), 254.

CHAPTER 4

Charles Cowden Clarke's 'Cockney' commonplace book

John Barnard

Keats will remain (just) off-stage throughout this essay. But while the evidence presented is only obliquely related to his mature poetry, it documents the specific cultural matrix which shaped the young man who began writing poetry in 1814. The commonplace book which Charles Cowden Clarke kept in his last years at Enfield School is an important example of 'Cockney' intellectual, political, and literary attitudes which deserves wider attention than it has yet received. Most of the entries were made between 1810 and 1814, exactly the period when Clarke's influence on the young Keats was at its strongest. Keats certainly knew at least one of the poems copied into Clarke's book, and Leigh Hunt borrowed and made use of it in 1816. Clarke's notes from his reading have a double significance. They illuminate the interests of a representative reader of the *Examiner*, and give a sharper picture of Clarke's own ambitions and interests in these years than is otherwise available. Clarke's later memories of Keats's time at Enfield School and at Hammond's Edmonton surgery are the essential evidence for all biographers' accounts of the poet's early education, reading, and liberal political beliefs. In his *Recollections of Writers*, published nearly sixty years after Keats's death, Clarke's admiring report of the early manifestation of Keats's genius subordinates his own character so that he seems inordinately bland and benign.[1] The commonplace book, and in particular Clarke's own but infrequent observations, show that between the ages of twenty-three and twenty-seven Keats's schoolteacher and friend had intensely held libertarian political views which formed a continuum with his literary beliefs. It helps us to understand why Keats was attracted to Clarke. It also reveals that in these years Clarke, six years older than Keats and three years younger than Hunt, had ambitions of his own as a poet. Clarke's example, like that of John Hamilton Reynolds, shows how unsurprising it was for someone of Keats's class, background, and education to have aspirations as a writer. The commonplace book gives a record of Clarke's reading and views at a time when he was seeing Keats regularly, and provides a picture of the literary taste and political stance of a 'Cockney' reader.

A previous account of the commonplace book was published by Joan Coldwell in 1980.[2] Although she notes Clarke's interest in history and politics, Coldwell's main interest is in the poems quoted by Clarke which might have influenced Keats, and in showing that two of Clarke's poems may be echoed in *To Autumn* and *Ode to a Nightingale*. What she does not record in any detail are the recurrent themes evident in the passages copied by Clarke – the constitutional liberties of England (citing Selden, Locke, Bolingbroke, and Sir Francis Burdett), religious toleration, the tyranny of the Stuarts, admiration for seventeenth-century radical heroes (Milton, Hampden, Russell, and Penn) and for Bishop Burnet, an opposition to war and violence, and belief in liberty. These passages from earlier writers offer an implicit comment on early nineteenth-century politics: the satires in the commonplace book, the pseudonymous 'A New Catechism', Byron's 'Windsor Poetics', and 'The Prophecy' (then attributed to Chatterton) are all fiercely oppositional.

One important modification needs to be made to Coldwell's account. The chronology of Clarke's entries can be more closely established than she allows – the commonplace book was nearly filled well before the final entry was made in 1818. The proof of this depends on the physical evidence supplied by the manuscript itself.

Cowden Clarke's commonplace book is a substantial quarto of 185 leaves (not pages, as Coldwell reports) bound in leather. Although the binding is now scuffed and the spine covering detached, a decorative border, once gilt, is stamped round the front and back cover, and 'Common Place Book' is stamped on the spine. On its title page (fol. 2a) is written 'Common Place Book' in decorative upper- and lower-case delicately inked in blue and purple, with curlicues above and below: the first leaf is signed and dated 'Charles Cowden Clarke 1810'. The main body of the volume is paginated 1–342 (fol. 3a–173b), and there is a careful author and subject index (fol. 174a–85b). The latter is neatly thumb-indexed, each alphabetical letter carefully written in a strong black ink quite unlike the brown ink used by Clarke in the body of the text. This together with the evidence of the binding indicates that Clarke probably bought a professionally prepared commonplace book complete with a blank index section. The number of pages Clarke could fill was, obviously enough, predetermined. Clarke's writing is throughout clear, large, regular, and (with one exception) evenly lineated. He worked carefully and systematically, and seems to have kept up the index as he copied in excerpts.

Coldwell correctly says 'The first page bears the date 1810 and the latest dated entry is marked "October, 1818"' (p. 83). This, however, conceals the fact that the commonplace book was close to being full as early as March 1814. Clarke copied extracts into his manuscript book sequentially, but he carried forward very long passages, most notably the three series of extracts from Sir Joshua Reynolds's *Discourses on Art* (1769–90), the first running from pages 206 to 215, the second from pages 316 to 342 (the last page before the index begins) while the third extract goes back to page 288 and ends on page 309. He also intermittently left some pages blank for later entries. As a result, the volume's sequence looks random, but Clarke gives enough dates to establish his progress through the volume. In determining the period in which Clarke was most actively using the manuscript the most important dates are those he gave when copying out his own poems.[3] His translation of Horace's *Ode* I. xi is dated 'March 1814' and occurs on page 276. Most of the remaining 66 pages of text are taken up with the continuation of the series of extracts from Reynolds's *Discourses* started earlier, so that in March 1814 Clarke only had 20 blank pages left for text out of the 342 originally available to him.[4] Many of these remaining blank pages were subsequently filled in with Clarke's own work, including a sonnet on his sister's birthday on 27 February 1816. The poem dated 'Oct.r 1818' referred to by Coldwell as the *terminus ad quem* was clearly written later into three pages left blank in 1814 since there was not enough space to fit in the verses without cramping the lineation (see item 51 in the analysis below). Consequently the commonplace book was for the most part filled in between 1810 and early 1814, exactly at the time when Clarke's influence on Keats was most powerful. Keats left school in the summer of 1810 or 1811.[5] He carried on seeing Clarke frequently at Enfield School after being apprenticed to Hammond in Edmonton before leaving for London in 1815.

There is no firm proof that Keats had access to the commonplace book in these years, but a little more is known about its subsequent use which suggests that he did. On 17 October 1816 Leigh Hunt wrote from Hampstead thanking Clarke for the loan of his 'copy books',

saying 'I hope to stock them all with poetry such as you will relish, &
then I know that I shall be turning them to such account as both you
& myself like best.'[6] In 1816 the commonplace book was close to being
full, although Hunt's use of the plural indicates that Clarke had at
least one other commonplace book (covering the years 1814 to 1816?)
and possibly more. Hunt's access to the extant commonplace book is
the probable source of the text of the long political satire by 'Richard
Porson' which he was to print in the *Examiner* in 1818 (see item 14).

Keats too knew work copied into Clarke's commonplace book.
When he wrote to Clarke on 9 October 1816, eagerly looking forward
to being introduced to Hunt and showing him a 'sheet or two of
Verses', he said he was 'anxious too to see the Author of the Sonnet to
the Sun . . .' (*Letters*, i. 113), that is, Charles Ollier, whose 'Sonnet on
Sunset', dated August 1813, is copied out in the commonplace book
(see item 45).[7] Keats's knowledge of Ollier's sonnet means either that
he had seen a manuscript copy or the transcription in the commonplace
book.[8] If Keats did echo phrases from Clarke's 'Sunset' and 'The
Nightingale' the same also applies. The circumstantial evidence,
particularly Clarke's loan of his 'copy books' to Hunt, makes it hard
to believe that Keats was not allowed to see the commonplace books.[9]

By far the larger part of Clarke's extant commonplace book, then,
was mostly completed early 1814 – just before the first known poems
by Keats were written (*Imitation of Spenser* and *On Peace*, for example).
Keats started writing in the middle of the years (1812 to 1816, judging
by the commonplace book) in which Clarke was more than
half-thinking of a poetic career for himself.

Coldwell's focus in her account of the manuscript is on its
relationship to, and possible effect on, Keats's poetry. The following
excerpts and paraphrases augment Coldwell's description of the
literary contents of the commonplace book, concentrating largely on
Clarke's interest in history and politics from the sixteenth century to
his own time since art and literature, history and politics, are
interrelated in Clarke's (and Keats's) mind. However, rather than
concentrate exclusively on the historical and political, this supple-
mentary calendar includes an outline of Clarke's poetic ambitions as
they are represented in the commonplace book, and most of Clarke's
own observations.[10] These are mainly a political reading of history,
but since his rare and brief remarks on women and sex exhibit the
same kind of embarrassment found in Keats, they too have been
included (see items 2 and 5).

THE COMMONPLACE BOOK

The following extracts and summaries from Charles Cowden Clarke's commonplace book have been numbered for ease of reference. The italicised sub-headings present a framework of dates for the entries, and pagination of the entries in the original volume has also been provided in bold type. Observations by Cowden Clarke are cited as C.C.C. Throughout the following transcription, square brackets indicate editorial matter.

Date: after 1810

(1.) '... Ambition *catches* the unwary by Power, Titles, Dignities, and Preferments. And false Religion, under a darling outside of mysterious Sanctity, and pompous Ceremonies, conceals a *Net Work* of Priest-Craft and Superstition from which it will be still more Difficult to extricate yourselves. Ibid.' [i.e., Thomas Percival, Father's Instructions] (**p. 3**)

(2.) C.C.C.: 'The greatest Consolation to me upon a Death Bed (after having made Peace with my Maker) would be that: I had never been guilty of Conjugal Infidelity.' (**p. 5**)

(3.) 'The Principle of a Despotic Government is *Fear*. – [Voltaire,] Philosoph. Hist.' (**p. 5**)

(4.) 'There is no Friendship without Virtue. – M. Wollstonecraft.' (**p. 5**)

(5.) C.C.C.: 'Women of ordinary Features have generally the best furnished Understandings; because possessing nothing whereby they may recommend themselves they naturally resort to that which in the long-run is sure to prove useful and attractive. – Religion is never so punctually attended to as in Adversity or so much neglected as in Prosperity.' (**p. 5**) [A double pencil line in the margin draws attention to the first of these statements.]

(6.) A passage from Montesquieu on the 'droll Spectacle' of England's efforts towards 'the Establishment of Democracy' in the seventeenth century in which ambition and faction destroyed the attempt 'to erect a Commonwealth' and led to a return of 'the very Government which they had so wantonly proscribed'. (**pp. 9–10**)

(7.) A long quotation from a 'Sermon by M.ʳˢ Barbauld for a Fast Day in 1794' translating 'the word *War* into Language more intelligible to us . . . let us set down – so much for killing, so much for maiming, so much for making Widows and Orphans . . . so much for letting loose the Daemons Fury, Rapine, & Lust . . .' (**pp. 12–14**)

(8.) Clarke's translation of Virgil, *Aeneid*, iv. 522–32, earlier sent to Charles Ollier on 28 October 1812.[11] (**p. 19**)

(9.) 'The following lines by the Rev.ᵈ William Crowe, public Orator of the University of Oxford were suppressed . . . by the Vice-Chancellor on account of the Sentiments contained in them.' (**pp. 34–6**) The lines by Crowe (1745–1829), 'ultra-whig and almost republican', were meant for the installation of the Duke of Portland, and were praised by Rogers and Moore (see *DNB*). Crowe's verses vigorously attack war and violence, and regret that poets have bent 'low to lawless Power,' corrupting the 'Aonian fount' with 'Blood-stain'd Ambition'.

(10.) C.C.C.: 'It is asserted that "*all* have sinked and come short of the Kingdom of Heaven." It is likewise asserted that our Saviour came on Earth to *save Sinners*: then if the omniscient Judge be impartial; all will be pardoned at the great Day of Accounts.' (**p. 37**)

(11.) Unattributed passage, perhaps by Clarke himself despite the lack of the paragraph mark he uses to indicate his own writings: 'The inventions of Men have been many, and ingenious; every Art has been improved, every Science has been extended, by the industry and Application of Mankind. Yet have we not learned to confine the Energies of dangerous Individuals, without cutting them off from Existence. Is the industry of Man so occupied in other Pursuits in sharpening the Steel of the Soldier, or spreading the Sails for the merchants; in forming Schemes for Monopoly, Luxury, and Murder; that he has no Leisure to build Prisons for those whose nature is yet wild, but who through Discipline and Care may be made useful to that World they have injured by Error or by Crime?' (**p. 38**)

(12.) 'A numerous Nobility causeth poverty and inconvenience in a State because it is a surcharge of Expense. – Bacon's Essays – Nobility.' Followed by further quotations on the roles of Nobility and Princes. (**pp. 79–81**)

(13.) A letter from Sir Francis Burdett to his constituents asserting his intention to maintain the 'Laws and Liberties of the Land' as Westminster's elected M.P. (**pp. 82–4**) See *The Address of Sir Francis Burdett dated March 23, to his constituents, in a letter, denying the power of the House of Commons to imprison the people of England* [1810].

Date: *1811*

(14.) 'A New Catechism for the use of the Natives of Hampshire: Necessary to be had in all Sties . . . . by Rich.ᵈ Porson'. (**pp. 86–105**) Coldwell (85) believes that Clarke copied this satire from the *Examiner*. However, Clarke adds a note to Porson's footnote mentioning 20,000 soldiers (*'hogs in Armour'*) which reads, 'And aided by nearly the same number of *Bears* imported from Germany. – *Porson might now have added. 1811 –*' (**p. 100**). This savage satire, which portrays the British people as hogs who are systematically exploited by the monarchy, parliament, state, church, law, and army, dates from the 1790s. Its starting point is Burke's description in *Reflections on the Revolution in France* (1790) of the people of England as 'a swinish multitude', as the following section of the 'Catechism' makes clear: 'God made me Man in his own image; the *Right Honourable Sublime and Beautiful* made me a *Swine*. (* Reflections, p. 117 ed. 1)'. Porson makes a further reference to Burke ('Reflections p. 17. ed. 1') glossing his description of 'the King of Great Britain' as the *'chief hog-driver'*, who wears a 'brass Helmet on his head, and an iron poker in his hand', and who holds his office 'In contempt of the choice of the hogs' (**p. 88**).[12] The source of Clarke's text has not been identified. It belongs with the pamphlet attacks on Burke's *Reflections*, but is not to be found in the three volumes of *Pig's Meat; or, Lessons for the Swinish Multitude Published in Weekly Penny Numbers* (1793–6) or in Daniel Isaac Eaton's *Politics for the People: or a Salmagundy for Swine* (1793–5).[13] The satire, which takes up twenty-nine pages, was copied by Clarke in 1811. The text which Hunt printed in the *Examiner* (30 August 1818), 248–50 follows that in Clarke's commonplace book with only minor editorial changes, omitting Clarke's topical note referring to 1811. Clarke is almost certainly Hunt's source. If the commonplace book was one of Clarke's 'copy books' seen by Hunt in October 1816[14] he may have copied it out then, or remembered it in summer 1818 and asked for a copy. The satire, as applicable to England in 1818 as it had been in the 1790s or in 1811, struck an immediate chord. William Hone's

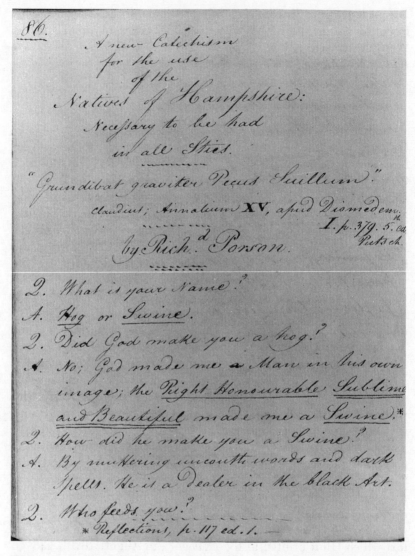

Figure 4.1   *A New Catechism for the use of the Natives of Hampshire: Necessary to be had
in all Sties*

three trials in 1817 for publishing satirical political parodies of the
litany, creed, and catechism, were followed with interest by Keats
(see his letters to George and Tom Keats of 21, 27 December 1817 and
5 January 1818, *Letters*, i. 191, 199) while Shelley subscribed five

guineas towards Hone's defence. Not surprisingly, Richard Carlile immediately reprinted it as an eight-page octavo, *'From the Examiner'*, and Walter Edwin Peck, who reprints the satire from the text in the *Examiner*, claims it to be one of the major sources for Shelley's *Oedipus Tyrannus; or, Swellfoot the Tyrant* (1820).[15] Clarke's reading and recording of a subversive satire in 1811 is clear evidence of his liberal politics at a period when he was in close contact with Keats, while its subsequent textual history indicates the strength of the satire's appeal.

(15.) A passage on the *'real Patriot'* and how the patriot should put his beliefs in effect 'to the good of his country' from Bolingbroke's *Letters on the Spirit of Patriotism: On the Idea of Patriot King* [1749]. (**pp. 106–7**) Bolingbroke is important here because of his place in Burke's demonology of liberal 'men of letters'.

(16.) Further passages from Bolingbroke (**pp. 108–13**) (i) on the *'Spirit of liberty'* and how a *'Patriot King, [is] the most uncommon of all phenomenon in the physical or moral World'* (**pp. 108–9**); (ii) 'Reverence for government' should not obscure that its source is *'national* not *personal'* – 'As well might one say that a ship is built, and loaded, and manned, for the sake of any particular pilot, instead of acknowledging that the pilot is made for the sake of the ship, her lading, and her crew, *who are always the* owners *in the political vessel, as to say that Kingdoms were instituted for Kings, not Kings for Kingdoms*. In short to carry our allusion higher, *majesty is not an inherent but a reflected right'* (**pp. 110–11**); (iii) *'Nothing can be more absurd . . .* than a *hereditary right in any mortal to govern other men*; and *yet in practice* nothing can be more absurd, than to have a King to chuse at every vacancy of a throne' (**p. 111**); (iv) kings are not 'the final cause for which societies were formed', since the 'ultimate end of all government is the *good* of the *people, for whose sake* they were made; and *without whose consent*, they could not have been made . . .' (**p. 111**); (v) weak kings wrongly imagine 'the King and the people in free governments' to be *'rival powers'* (**p. 113**).

Date: After March 1811

(17.) 'Axioms in favor of Religious Liberty & Toleration.' Twenty-one axioms dated 'Nov.ʳ 1810' taken from 'Monthly Mag.' March 1811 by 'Common Sense' (written over 'Sir Rich.ᵈ Philips qu[aer]e' which is crossed out). (**pp. 113–18**)

(18.) A long ironical passage taken from 'Edin. Review. No. 34. Feby. 1811' on how the reform of 'Borough-mongering' has been attacked by raising 'the old cry of – *Innovation!*', despite the need for constitutional reform. (**pp. 118–23**)

(19.) Further passages from Bolingbroke's *Patriot King*: (i) 'A *Patriot King* is the most powerful of all *Reformers . . .*' (**p. 123**); (ii) the need to prolong good governments (**pp. 123–4**); (iii) the Patriot King will not side with factions but 'will put himself at the head of *his people*' (**p. 124**).

(20.) A passage attacking commercial values from 'Trotter's *Memoirs of Fox* [1811] pp. 135–136.' (**pp. 124–5**): 'Commercial pride, is, perhaps, the most odious and tyrannical of any other . . . A base devotion, to Gain, stifles every germ of *Bravery, Genius*, and *Independence*'. The passage represents an attitude common to Hunt and Keats, and one shared by Clarke.

(21.) A passage on the freedom of the press (**pp. 125–6**). '*Johnson* in his life of *Milton*; when upon the Subject of the *liberty* of the *press*; says with his usual malignity when writing of that g[r]eat and good Man: "It seems not more reasonable, to leave the right of printing unrestrained, because writers may be afterwards censured, than it would be to sleep with doors unbolted, because by our laws we can hang a Thief." – To which Hayley has answered "This is vile sophistry; The writer's illustration of a thief may be turned against himself. To suffer no Book to be published without a licence, is tyranny as absurd as it would be to suffer no Traveller to pass along the highway without producing a certificate that he is not a Robber." *Hayley's* Life of Milton [1794].'

Date: After 17 November 1811

(22.) A long passage on religious toleration 'Extracted from "The News' of Novr 17.th 1811.' (**pp. 129–35**) It begins: 'I introduce the following extract from the Bishop of Norwich's speech upon the Catholic emancipation because it is a "rara avis in terris", – a phenomenon, to see a protestant Church dignitary expressing himself in the mild spirit of tolerance towards Sectarians . . .' Names Bishops Tillotson, Burnet, Hoadley, Watson, and Bathurst as exceptions who have prevented 'the whole from stinking in the nostrils of thinking Men, and Men of liberality' (**pp. 129–30**).

(23.) Quotations from Selden's *Table Talk*. (**pp. 136–43**) Covers various topics including the 'People' – 'in all the laws you make, have a special eye to the good of the people . . . .' (**p. 139**)

(24.) 'Ann. 1626.' A passage from 'Mrs Macaulay's History of Charles I.st' (**pp. 147–8**). An account of Charles I's unconstitutional confinement of the Earl of Arundel in the Tower, and the House of Lords' successful freeing of the Earl by an appeal to their privileges. Catharine Macaulay (1731–91) was the celebrated Whig historian. Her *History of England* (1763–83) condemned the Stuart tyranny, and was widely admired by contemporary readers in America and France.

A four-page note (**pp. 148–52**) follows, signed with the paragraph mark which Clarke uses to indicate his own writings. The main points are – 'This Circumstance alone gives us a clear Idea of the erroneous Opinion Charles had imbibed of the english Constitution & of the unwarrantable Strides he made towards arbitrary Powers. The Piety of his mind and the upright intentions of his Heart cannot be alleged, while this Incident is upon record.' Clarke quotes from one of Parliament's Remonstrances against Charles (**p. 149**), and then gives an account of Charles's betrayal of the Protestant citizens of La Rochelle (**pp. 149–51**): '. . . Charles like a stewart made a peace with the french Court and forgot his poor deluded Allies the Rochellers in the Treaty; who were consigned over to those human blood-hounds the Papists. They should have remembered the Advice of Psalmist "Put not your trust in Princes!!"! for it is a Melancholy but notorious fact, that few human Beings are less regardless of their promises than the misnomered Vicegerents of the Almighty. This is an irrasable blot in the Character of the Stewart' (**p. 151**).

(25.) A passage from '[Mrs.] Macaulay['s *History*] Vol. 2. P. 95' describing Archbishop Laud's persecution of two clergymen is followed by C.C.C.: 'Any comments upon these atrocities are needless. They speak for themselves. The rapid accumulation of them prepared that formidable Besom which swept the wicked high-Priest and his blind obstinate Master & Coadjutor to destruction. – Sic pecant omnis inimici Libertatis! – For the more dreadful Treatment of *Leighton* see the same Vol. P. 96. – It would have degraded any Dey of Algiers.' (**p. 152**)

(26.) Clarke explains Raleigh's imprisonment as follows: 'I have heard that the impure villain James never could forgive Raleigh for an indiscreet Expression he had been heard to let drop. This might be the Case. – Raleigh was a Man of the World, and knew more of Men and Manners than, perhaps any One at Court.' (**pp. 154–5**)

(27.) A two-page proto-essay by Clarke, signed with a paragraph mark (**pp. 156–8**), but not included in the index. The topic is fame. Clarke says that Alfred the Great's fame needed no eulogist, only the evidence of his acts; he appeals to 'every impartial reader' to confess that '[Lord] Russell's conduct', as described by Burnet is affecting: 'I am not comparing Jesus Christ to Socrates or Russell, but had the Saviour been a mere Man, we should have (I was agoing to say *equally*) venerated his Character from the account transmitted to us of him. – He needs no Eulogy. – Socrates needs none. – Russell needs none. – It has been the Fashion to cry down the incomparable History of Burnett by a Set of interested narrow minded individuals; by Courtiers because he has told too many Truths; by place-Hunters because they know, in endeavouring to crush him, he will become an excellent stepping Stool to preferment – and many have succeeded . . . . Burnett was so fine a Scholar and so great a Man' (**p. 157**).

(28.) 'Sonnet To the Memory of John Hampden', 'Extracted from [Thomas] Hollis. Mem. Vol. 2 P. 784' (**p. 158**) It concludes –

> Thy grateful country shall its Praise convey
> From age to age, and, long as Britain's free
> Britons shall boast in Hampden's glorious name.

Date: 25 October 1812

(29.) 'Extract from the Examiner 5 Oct.ʳ 1812. p. 683 left hand Column at the Top.' (**p. 158**) A single sentence: 'The *great* William Penn the Quaker appeared on the Hustings at Guildford, and addressed the Electors in support of his *friend Algernon Sydney*!'

(30.) Selections from three poems by Chatterton (**pp. 159–70**). (i) 'Ode to Freedom', first line 'Whanne Freedome dreste in blodde-steyned veste', ends 'Tenne bloddie arrowes in hys strayninge Fyste.' The heading, 'Ode to Freedom', seems to be Clarke's own title for the 'Chorus' which concludes the Rowley tragedy *Goddwyn*. Clarke's text derives from *Poems, supposed to have been written at Bristol by Thomas*

Rowley . . . (1777), or from the three volume edition of *The Works* by Southey and Coleridge (1803). The text in Taylor and Hoover's modern edition varies in detail, but not substantially, and it is clear that Clarke (and no doubt Keats) read Chatterton's incomplete tragedy of Harold's defeat by William the Conqueror as a patriotic work.[16] The visionary presentation of Peace imaged in militaristic terms overcoming England's oppressors provided a hopeful prophecy for early nineteenth-century liberals; (ii) selections from Chatterton's 'Elegy to the Memory of Mr. Thomas Philips, of Fairford' (**pp. 161–2**). The verses are chosen for their sentiment. Clarke runs the lines together in a single sequence (ll. 33–40, 53–6, 93–100);[17] (iii) 'The Prophecy' (**pp. 162–70**), a visionary satiric poem strongly opposed to the political structure of late Georgian England: it is no longer attributed to Chatterton. Its attack on corruption, commerce, George III and his ministers, along with the refrain –

> Look up, ye Britons! cease to sigh,
> For your redemption draweth nigh. –

explains Clarke's interest in the poem.[18] Chatterton's politics seem to have been as important for Clarke as his persecution and tragically early death.

This item is followed by a series of literary selections. Clarke copied out substantial quotations from William Browne's *Britannia's Pastorals* (1613–16) (**pp. 171–6, 238–40, 250–1**), a poem which Coldwell (86–7) and others have noted influenced Keats. Clarke also copied out 'Robin Goodfellow' (**pp. 176–8, 233–6**, not noted by Coldwell) from Percy's *Reliques* (1765).[19] These selections are followed by a long passage of theatrical criticism by Richard Cumberland taken from the *London Review* (No. 3, 1 August 1809) (**pp. 179–202**) which Coldwell (90) rightly relates to Clarke's future career as a reviewer.

(31.) A passage on the derivation of the term 'Whig' from 'Burnett's Hist. Vol. 1.ˢᵗ Page 43' (**p. 203**).

(32.) A passage from 'Locke on Government P. 296' (**pp. 204–6**). '... the community perpetually retain a supreme Power of saving themselves from the attempts and Designs of any Body even their Legislators whenever they shall be so foolish or so wicked as to lay and carry on Designs against the Liberties and properties of the Subject ....'

(33.) The first of three long quotations from Reynolds's *Discourses* which occupies, with breaks, a substantial portion of the volume. (**pp. 206–15, 316–42, 288–309**) Clarke worked through the fifteen Discourses in sequence. His first extract is from the second, his final one from the last. Important topics are 'ideal Beauty' (**pp. 207–11**), the 'Beauty and Simplicity of the antique' (**pp. 319, 329**), 'Genius' or the 'Man of Genius' (**pp. 295–6, 298–9, 333–4**), 'Beauty' and 'Genius' (**p. 317**), and Reynolds's claim that Beauty and Nature are only different modes (**pp. 339–40**). Raphael, Michelangelo, Rubens, Correggio, and the Dutch School are all mentioned. Poussin's intense empathy with the antique world and its ceremonies is noted (**pp. 327–8**). In a passage on Michelangelo, Reynolds says there is 'nothing in the air of [his works'] Actions or their Attitudes . . . . that reminds of their belonging to our Species' (**p. 317**), where 'attitude' is used in the same technical sense as in the *Ode on a Grecian Urn* (41).

(34.) A long passage from 'Hughes Letters Vol. 2.nd from page 61 to 64'. (**pp. 216–25**) An account of the persecution of the Hewling family by Judge Jeffreys during the reign of James II, which concludes 'Such were the City Patriots of those Times.'

Date: After October 1813

(35.) A passage from 'Edinburgh Rev. No. 43 [i.e., vol. 22, October 1813]. P. 215. Article/Mad.^{me} De Stael – De l'Allemagne.' (**pp. 225–6**) The passage notes that Klopstock was 'inflamed by the perusal of *Milton* and Young', and goes on to analyse the weakness of Young's poetry when set against Milton's. It is literature not politics which led Clarke to copy out this passage (*pace* Coldwell, 89).

(36.) Untitled poem by 'Lord Byron' (**p. 246**). This is written beneath the final stanza of Clarke's selection from James Beattie's *The Minstrel* (1770–4; i. 9, 20–2, 29, 38–9, 53; ii. 1, 16–17, 44). (**pp. 234–46**) Coldwell (89) notes that Clarke copied out a 'political' poem by Byron, but does not identify it as his 'Windsor Poetics', a savage attack on the Prince Regent, written in early April 1813 but not published until 1818 in Galignani's Paris edition of *English Bards and Scotch Reviewers . . . etc. Suppressed Poems*. In *Lord Byron: The Complete Poetical Works* Jerome McGann prints three versions of the poem which, by tradition, is entitled 'Lines, composed on the occasion of

H.R.H. the P[rinc]e R[e]g[en]t being seen standing betwixt the coffins of Henry 8th and Charles 1st, in the royal vault at Windsor'. All three versions circulated widely with Byron's encouragement.[20] The text in Clarke's commonplace book is of Version A, that printed by Galignani; since Clarke's text has minor variants it is worth giving in full:

> Fam'd for contemptuous breach of sacred ties,
> By *headless Charles* see *heartless Henry* lies;
> Between them stands another sceptr'd thing, –
> It moves, – it reigns, – in all but name a King.
> *Charles* to his *People, Henry* to his *Wife,*
> In him the *double Tyrant* starts to life.
> Justice and death, have mixed their dust in vain,
> The royal Vampires join to breathe again.
> What now shall tombs avail since they disgorge
> The blood and dust of both to mould a George.[21]

Clarke probably obtained the text on one of his visits to see Hunt in Surrey Jail which began at some time prior to 13 July 1813; Byron had begun visiting Hunt in May.[22] Hunt had been imprisoned for libelling the Prince Regent, and would have had a particular interest in Byron's poem, which obviously could only circulate in manuscript.

(37.) 'Modern Greece and Death exquisitely compared', a passage from 'The Giaour by Lord Byron 3.rd Edit. [1813]'. (**pp. 247–8**) Noted by Coldwell (89). The title is Clarke's. The quotation (ll. 67–102) provides a powerful metaphor for the effects of Ottoman tyranny on the democratic freedom of ancient Greece. Clarke's interest is not in the 'romantic' and melancholic Byron celebrated in Keats's sonnet *To Lord Byron* (written a year later in December 1814), but in Byron as a defender of freedom and hater of cant.

(38.) 'On my Birth Day 15.th Decr 1812'. (**pp. 258–61**) Unpublished poem by Clarke, copied into the commonplace book a year or so after its composition. It is important as a statement of intention on Clarke's twenty-fifth birthday.

> Time has roll'd o'er this thoughtless head
> Full five and twenty rapid years –
> Those years are gone; –
> For ever gone! –
> Gone to that gen'ral Magazine

Of lumber, heap'd beyond the flood: –
. . . .
Descend some winged Sprite! – descend,
  And fill my Mind
  With heavenly lore
And wisdom from that sacred fount,
. . . .
That pour'd so full and grand a tide
Majestic on the soul of him
  Who sung of arms,
  With 'battle proud',
Wag'd by the 'rebel-angel rout',
Upon the argent fields of God.
  O lead me forth
  Celestial Guide,
To ev'ry spring that flows adown
Parnassus' hill, and let me quaff
  In extacy
  Of ev'ry wave . . . .
Then shall another brilliant wreath
  Entwine thy brow
  Seraphic Bard! . . . .
  Nor would I fail
  To deck thy lyre,
Delightful Author of the Task!
But ever will I sing of HIM
. . . .
For this is his prime, his choicest Gift
  Vouchsaf'd to Man –
  Sweet LIBERTY! –

(39.) 'Sonnet'. (**p. 262**) Note at bottom, 'Left upon Milton's tomb Westminster abbey.'

  . . . who nobly emulous of fame
  . . . .
Of rebel Angels sung, and taught our sires
How best foul earth-born tyranny to tame.

Date: 30 April 1813

(40.) 'Sonnet' by Charles Ollier. (**p. 264**) Dated 'April 30.th 1813.' Begins, 'When wilt thou visit me my friend Cha.ˢ Clarke?' Describes Ollier's 'chiefest joys' as 'Couch'd in the books of noble Poets' which are also Clarke's 'best felicity'.

(41.) Three sonnets by Wordsworth. (**pp. 265–7**) 'Milton! thou shouldst be living at this Hour' ('London, 1802'), 'Great men have been among us! hands that penn'd', and 'It is not to be thought of, that the flood'. Taken from the second part of *Poems in Two Volumes* (1807) headed 'Sonnets Dedicated to Liberty'. Significantly, these are the only poems by which Wordsworth is represented in the commonplace book.

(42.) 'Translated from a Greek Epigram.' (**pp. 268–9**) Five epigrams, presumably translated by Clarke.

Date: 26 June 1813

(43.) 'Sunset. an irregular effusion', by Clarke. (**pp. 269–70**) Published in *Carmina Minima* (London, 1859), 3–4, where it is dated '1805'. Dated '26.th June 1813' in commonplace book. Discussed and printed by Richard Altick, *The Cowden Clarkes* (Oxford, 1948), 20–1; Coldwell (91–2) points out its influence on *To Autumn*.

Date: 28 June 1813

(44.) 'The Nightingale' by Clarke. (**p. 271**) Published in *Carmina Minima* (1859), 4–5, where it is dated '1807'. The commonplace book gives the date '28.th June 1813.' Printed by Altick (21–2); Coldwell (92) points to possible echoes in Keats's *Ode to a Nightingale*.

Date: August 1813

(45.) 'Sonnet on Sunset' by Charles Ollier. (**p. 272**) Dated 'Aug.ᵗ 1813.' A pencilled note identifies Ollier as 'Box Keeper. Cov. G. Theatre'. Discussed by Coldwell (89–90). Referred to by Keats in his letter of 9 October 1816 (see p. 68 above).

> Blest Sun! – whether across the eastern height
>   Thou rushest forth this nether world to cheer, –
>   Whether enthron'd, thou hold'st thy mid career
> And hotly, proudly, pour'st thy glowing light
> O'er hill and plain, – Still shall thy godlike might
>   By Man be hail'd; – but most to me thou'rt dear
>   When on eve's bosom nurs'd, thou dost appear
> Midst golden clouds, in tranquil beauteous plight.

Then not the Painter's hand, nor Poet's lyre
Can e'er express the wild fantastic dreams
That rise attendant on that dulcet hour! –
The Sylphs, the hymn on high, the domes of fire,
And glimmering shapes, which fly not till the beams
Softly decay, and light resigns its pow'r. –

Date: January 1814

(46.) 'Sonnet on Liberty' by Clarke. (**p. 273**) Dated 'Jany. 1814.'
Unpublished.

Oh thou! to whom the wretched toil-worn slave
In anguish groans his daily prayer for aid: –
Thou in whose shrine of adamant are laid
The spoils, and hard-gain'd trophies of the brave
Who tug for freedom. Spirit of Bliss! Oh save
Those favour'd ones, that have so long obey'd
Thy mandates. And although they now have stray'd
From thee; yet visit them again I crave. –

But come not Goddess as thou wont'st of yore,
In crimson war-car and with flaming brand;
With bick'ring spear and poignard steep'd in gore;
In dreadful Justice visiting each land:
But here in pity change thy wrathful hand: –
Goddess! no more of blood! – Oh, blood no more! –

(47.) 'Stanzas on the Death of General Moreau' over Leigh Hunt's
name. (**p. 274**) Coldwell (89) mentions this poem but not that it
appeared in the *Examiner* on 5 December 1813 (779), and was not
subsequently reprinted by Hunt. The *Examiner* had reported Moreau's
death on 12 September. Moreau 'was banished from France . . . on
the score of a real or pretended conspiracy against BONAPARTE'
and had retired to America. He returned to fight on the Allied side
against France, but was mortally wounded in the Battle of Dresden
on 27 August 1813 and died on 2 September. The *Examiner* (19
September 1813), 595–6, gave an account of how both his legs were
shot away as he was speaking to the Tsar, and of his subsequent
sufferings. It reported his death on 3 October 1813 (635), printing his
last letter to his wife, accompanied by one from his aide. Clarke
copied the poem from a version differing slightly from that in the

Examiner, whose printed text gives the poem a subtitle, 'SET TO MUSIC BY WEBBE, JUN.' (that is, Samuel Webbe, the younger (1770?–1843), teacher and composer).[23] The *Examiner* also dates the composition as '*October* 30, 1813.' Clarke evidently copied the stanzas in January 1814 from a version provided earlier by Hunt himself:

> No, not a Sigh: – let not a vulgar Woe
> Shake our free Bosoms for the dead Moreau:
> He died as freeman should,
> Unfetter'd, undisgrac'd, plain hearted, good:
> And if there's anguish in his Story,
> 'Twas but with deeper Fires to crown his Glory.
>
> Far from his Home & from his wedded Heart
> Patient he lay, to finish his great Part;
> But not bereft of all; –
> Monarchs were there, wondring their Tears should fall.
> And the pale Friend, with lost Endeavour,
> Which Monarchs rarely know, & Tyrants never.
>
> Say not, that Loss of Patriot worth was his;
> There is no Country where no Freedom is[.]
> He, with his honest Sword,
> His earthly Country might have yet restor'd,
> But Heav'n his higher Lot was casting,
> And now he's gone to Freedom everlasting.

Date: 4 January 1814

(48.) 'Sonnet' by Clarke. (**p. 275**) Dated '4.th Jan[y]. 1814.' First line, 'Sir Charles! my worthy friend, when shall we meet?' Printed by Coldwell (93–4) with a brief commentary, though she omits to note that the recipient was obviously Charles Ollier since it is in the same idiom as the latter's sonnet to Clarke (item 40).

Date: March 1814

(49.) Translation of 'Horace. 11th Ode I. Book. [ll. 1–end]' by Clarke. (**p. 276**) Dated 'March 1814.' Unpublished. First line, 'I advise my dear friend that you never demand.'

(50.) 'On my Venerable Grandmother's attaining her 85.th Year 28.th Jan.[y] 1814' by Clarke. (**pp. 277–8**) Unpublished.

(51.) 'On visiting a beautiful little dell near Margate called "Nash"'' by Clarke. (**pp. 280–2**) Dated 'Oct.ʳ 1818': this poem was in fact copied into the commonplace book after the next item, which was written in 1816. After item 50 Clarke left four blank pages before writing out 53. The handwriting of this poem (51) is more angular, and the lineation on **pp. 281–2** is more compressed in order to fit the lines into the available space. Published in Leigh Hunt's *Literary Pocket-Book* (London, 1820), and *Carmina Minima*, where it is dated '1818'.

(52.) 'Sonnet on the 27 Febʸ 1816 my elder Sister's Birthday' by Clarke. (**p. 283**) Printed in the *Champion*, 21 April 1816 (Clarke's first published poem and hitherto unrecorded), and in *Carmina Minima*, 6, where it is dated '1816'.

(53.) 'Prologue to a School Play' by Clarke. (**pp. 284–6**) Printed in *Carmina Minima*, 1–3, where it is dated '1806'. Discussed and printed in part by Coldwell (90–1).

(54.) 'The burial of a Soldier' by Clarke. (**pp. 309–13**) Printed in *Carmina Minima*, 28–32, where it is dated '1816'. The version in the commonplace book looks like a draft. It lacks the last five and a half lines, has some pencil and ink alterations, is less carefully written than the rest of the volume, and has '(Ode est finis.)' written beneath it.

Clarke's optimistic self-dedication to poetry on his twenty-fifth birthday, 15 December 1812 (item 38), was not copied into the commonplace book until after he had met Leigh Hunt in the summer of 1813. The meeting seems to have stimulated Clarke to a review of his own earlier poetry, which he transcribed into his manuscript, along with new work (items 38, 43–4, 46, and 48–50). Ironically, Clarke's flurry of poetic activity in the summer of 1813 and early 1814 nearly coincided with (and may even have stimulated) Keats's first known poems, which date from 1814. Keats quickly left Clarke behind. Yet Keats's precociousness was even more deeply indebted to Clarke than has been recognised. Clarke's commonplace book gives the pattern of beliefs and allegiances, poetic and political, which governed Keats throughout his writing career.

NOTES

1 See 'Recollections of John Keats' in Charles and Mary Cowden Clarke, *Recollections of Writers* (London, 1878), 120–57. For the biographical notes prepared by Clarke for Monckton Milnes, Mar. 1846, see *KC*, ii. 146–53.

2 'Charles Cowden Clarke's Commonplace Book and its Relationship to Keats', *K–SJ* 29 (1980), 83–95. The commonplace book is part of the Novello-Clarke Collection, Brotherton Collection, University of Leeds. I am grateful to the Librarian for permission to quote from the manuscript, and to Mr Chris Sheppard for advice and help.

3 That these are the dates of transcription rather than composition is clear from the dates given to those poems which Clarke chose to reprint in *Carmina Minima* (priv. ptd., 1859). For details see items 43, 44, and 51–4.

4 There were 19 blank pages between **p. 276** and the end of the volume. There was a further blank at **p. 39**. Today the following pages are empty, **pp. 39, 279, 287, 314–15**. When Hunt saw the commonplace book in 1816 (see pp. 67–8) those pages and **pp. 280–3** (see item 51) were empty.

5 Keats is normally believed to have left Enfield School in summer 1810. Robert Gittings argues that Keats must have left in 1810 in order to complete his five years' apprenticeship in time to be admitted to Guy's. This involves arguing that the copy of Bonnycastle awarded to Keats in 1811 was not a regular prize; see *John Keats* (London, 1968; Harmondsworth, 1979), 56–7 and n..

6 Unpublished letter, Novello-Clarke Collection. This, and other unpublished letters by both Clarke and Hunt, give an interesting account of their relationship between 1813 and 1818 which I hope to publish shortly.

7 Rollins gives two possible identifications of the sonnet, an unidentified poem by Clarke or Horace Smith's sonnet 'To the Setting Sun' published in 1821 (*Letters*, i. 113 n.). Robert Gittings in his *Letters of John Keats: A New Selection* (Oxford, 1970), 1 n., rejects Smith's sonnet as 'not yet . . . written'. Coldwell (89–90) adds Ollier's name to those of Clarke and Smith, but fails to conclude that Keats must be referring to Ollier's sonnet, which has exactly the title used in Keats's letter. Clarke is not known to have written a sonnet on the sun, but Keats knew (and later echoed) his 'irregular effusion' on the sunset which was copied into the commonplace book on 26 June 1813 (see item 43): Keats would not confuse a sonnet with an 'effusion'.

8 Whichever was the case, his praise of Ollier – 'it is no mean gratification to become acquainted with Men [Hunt and Ollier] who in their admiration of Poetry do not jumble together Shakespeare and [Erasmus] Darwin' – is disingenuous if based on the evidence of this weak poem. As Coldwell (90) implies, Keats's interest in Ollier was more likely (already) to have been in meeting a possible publisher rather than an 'Author'. In his next letter to Clarke on 31 October he asks for Ollier's address (*Letters*, i.114–15).

9 Coldwell (95) speculates that the Brotherton commonplace book may be the 'Portfolio' to which Keats refers in his letter to Clarke of 9 October 1816, the same letter in which he mentions Ollier's sonnet (*Letters*, i.113–14). She believes that when Keats wrote that Clarke had something in his portfolio which he should 'by right see', Keats was arguing that 'because he had shown his own work to Clarke, Clarke should now "by rights" reciprocate'. A portfolio and a commonplace book are very different things, and Keats shortly after recorded his pleasure in Leigh Hunt's conversation about art on 'opening a portfolio' (*Sleep and Poetry*, 11. 337–8). Playful metaphors abound in Keats's letter, of course, but as Hunt's letter shows Clarke had more than one commonplace book, and Keats refers to only a single 'Portfolio'. If Coldwell is right, Keats had not been allowed to read Clarke's collections.

10 These are normally but not always marked with an asterisk in the text of the commonplace book, and listed in the index under 'C'.

11 Unpublished letter, Novello-Clarke Collection.

12 See Burke's observation that 'the King of Great Britain ... most certainly does not owe his high office to any form of popular election . . .' (*Reflections*, 17).

13 Nor does it occur in Cambridge University Library Ddd. 25.205[1], a bound volume with ten satires, including *Politics for the People* (1794), from this period. I am very grateful to Dr Frank Felsenstein and Dr John Whale for their help in trying to locate the original.

14 See above, pp. 67–8.

15 *Shelley: His Life and Work* (2 vols., London, 1927) ii. 394–401.

16 See Donald S. Taylor and Benjamin B. Hoover (eds.), *The Complete Works of Thomas Chatterton* (2 vols., Oxford, 1971) i. 304–5 (ll. 196–end).

17 Ibid. i. 388–91.

18 For the full text see ibid. ii. 709–12.

19 Thomas Percy (ed.), *Reliques of Ancient English Poetry* (3 vols., London, 1765) iii. 202 ff.

20 (7 vols., Oxford, 1980–93) iii. 86, 424–5. See also Molly Tatchell, 'Byron's *Windsor Poetics*', *Keats–Shelley Memorial Bulletin* 25 (1975), 1–5. For the fullest list of manuscript copies, see Barbara Rosenbaum and Pamela White, *Index of English Literary Manuscripts, Volume IV 1800–1900: Part I Arnold–Gissing* (London and New York, 1982), 364–6 and Addenda. There are two further copies of Version C in the commonplace books of Mary and Sarah Leigh dating from 1814 or 1815 (Keats House, Leigh Browne–Lockyer Collection, pp. 45 and 25 respectively). The Leighs, who lived near Sidmouth, were friends of James Rice and John Hamilton Reynolds, and, a little later, Benjamin Bailey. One of these probably supplied the text.

21 There are no italics in McGann's text. Clarke's text is closer to the Galignani version than to Northcote's ms copy in the Bodleian (MS. Eng. Misc. e. 143). The substantive variants from Galignani are as

follows: l. 8 Vampires join to breathe] Vampyre wakes to life *Galignani*; l. 9 What now shall] Ah! what can *Galignani*; they] these *Galignani*.

22 See Hunt's letter of 25 May 1813, Thornton Hunt (ed.), *The Correspondence of Leigh Hunt* (2 vols., London, 1862) i. 87–8.

23 According to *DNB*, Webbe went to Liverpool in 1798 and only settled in London about 1817; I have found no trace of a printed setting. The variants are as follows: l. 6 crown] prove *Examiner*; l. 9 bereft of all] abandoned to *Examiner*; l. 10 wondring . . . fall] grieving their strength should go *Examiner*.

CHAPTER 5

History, self, and gender in Ode to Psyche

Daniel P. Watkins

> An interpretation . . . is generally effective only when it visibly or even violently rewrites the surface appearance of the text, that is, when the restoration of the deep structure alters our initial reception of the sentences themselves.[1]

What does 'Keats and History' mean? Political events, and their representation in the poems – or literary history, the relation of Keats's poetry to classical and English literature? Does 'history' relate to extraliterary concerns – social history and the place of Keats's poetry within the frames of economic and ideological life? Is Keats's poetry a social–historical object?[2] More problematically, can 'history' be said to designate only matters from the past? Must it not also define the historical positions from which current criticism attempts to understand Keats?

Equally troubling for historical investigation is the meaning of *Keats*. When we speak of 'Keats', do we mean a person about whom certain biographical facts may be ascertained? Or, more abstractly, a cultural idea whose authority assigns meanings and values to poetic texts? To what extent does Keats – as person or cultural idea – control the critical investigation of poems associated with his name, and to what extent ought (can) that investigation to resist the constraints that the name might impose?

In what follows, I examine *Ode to Psyche* in an attempt to specify some of the larger issues associated with such questions about Keats and history, particularly those having to do with ideology, social relations, and sexual power. My investigation begins with the historical materialist assumption that criticism necessarily finds its richest territory at the level of the poem's deep structure. Here one not only finds major sources of poetic inspiration, but also certain socially charged currents that often contradict – even while they shape – poetic expression. For at this level of the poetic text, the dialectics of

88

history are acknowledged prior to their reconciliation and resolution in theme and imagination.

The primary deep historical pressure operating on *Psyche* – and, more generally, on English Romanticism – involves the demise of aristocratic feudalism and the triumph of industrial capitalism and bourgeois ideology in the late eighteenth and early nineteenth centuries.[3] One motivating desire in Keats's poetry, including *Psyche*, is to shape meaning out of, and express hope in the face of, certain powerful political, economic, and cultural conditions associated with this historical transformation. These conditions included: the quantifying pressures of an emergent and powerful commercialism that would transform all things (including poetry) into commodities to be exchanged on the open market; an increasingly militarised state apparatus established to secure and extend the operations of capital; the demise of religion as a master discourse, and its replacement by an individualist ethic grounded in a cash nexus; new forms of government repression; rampant urbanisation and its accompanying problems of unemployment and poverty.[4] Under historical conditions such as these, a poem like *Ode to Psyche*, which describes its titular goddess as a member of a 'faded hierarchy' (25), and as a beautiful, noble victim of a declining world, is more than a poetic celebration of a classical goddess. It is more, even, than a nostalgic expression of pure love. It is also, necessarily, a symbolic register of the deep structural realities constituent of the world in which Keats produced the poem, the decline of Psyche's world registering the decline of another world before the poet's eyes – the world of aristocratic feudalism. The descriptions of Psyche, and the ambitious and noble vision of human warmth and love, reach beyond the poem's classical subject matter to form a series of anxious responses to the social instability of Keats's own day, responses which range from disenchantment to hope that a new world order might provide unprecedented opportunities and possibilities.[5] The poem finds in the story of Psyche reasons to insist that love and integrity are humanly attainable, but at the same time it expresses a strong apprehension that 'in these days so far retir'd/ From happy pieties' (40–1) the imagination may be unable to achieve the beautiful idealisms that the poet would associate with Psyche.

Some of the anxieties that characterise the poem are indicated in the opening lines, though their social and historical dimensions are not immediately visible. The poet asks that his 'tuneless numbers' be

heard by Psyche, states that the poem itself has been 'wrung' from
him, albeit by 'sweet enforcement', and asks pardon for it (1–3).
Besides displaying the trepidation that a poet might be expected to
experience when addressing a figure from classical mythology, these
opening comments suggest a historical nervousness arising in part
from the poet's sense of his own existence in a world lacking the faith
and intense imagination that allegedly existed in the past. It is as
though the poet hopes that recollection and exaltation of a mythological
character such as Psyche might revivify a modern world that, he
believes, has lost its enchanting qualities, and yet, as early as the
opening lines, he betrays his doubt that this is possible.

To read the poem's anxieties as an expression of the incongruity
between the modern and classical worlds helps to elucidate a more
particular (though barely visible) determining pressure on Keats's
imagination. Even as the poem struggles to overcome anxiety by
describing a world of imaginative possibilities – by nobly attempting
to create a world of freedom from a world of necessity – it remains
transfixed by the claims of the present, and especially so by the
cultural authority of commodity exchange. Under that authority the
poem circulates within specific social networks – economic and
ideological – and its *value* is determined by its circulatory path. Its
meanings, moreover, are conditioned, in significant ways, by the kinds
of value that are attached to it by commodity culture. Of course, the
poem is not a commodity in the crudest sense, produced for sale on the
open market, but its value and meanings arise from *within*, and are
shaped by, frames of cultural reference governed by commodity
exchange. Keats's poem competes for ideological space within these
frames of reference, and in so doing it necessarily registers their
values, assumptions, and logic.

Before approaching the specific significance of this argument for
Psyche, it may be recast in slightly different terms in an attempt to
situate the poem more clearly among its determining social relations.
Marx defines the commodity, generally, as 'an object outside us, a
thing that by its properties satisfies human wants of some sort or
another'. 'The nature of such wants', Marx continues, 'whether, for
instance, they spring from the stomach or from fancy, makes no
difference.' The commodity, moreover, possesses two forms – 'a
physical or natural form, and a value-form' – the latter of which is
characterised by 'a purely social reality'. That is, the value of the
commodity is not inherent to itself, but always depends upon its social

situation. To insist upon the social definition of the commodity's value is, among other things, to secularise it, to deny that there is a 'universal equivalent' of value in some trans-social or transhistorical sphere. If there is to be a universal equivalent of value, according to Marx, then society itself must create it.[6]

Under capitalism, the commodity takes on an even more specific meaning than I have described above, one determined by the paths of bourgeois social relations along which it circulates. No longer an objective product meant only to satisfy some human need, the commodity comes to be defined, rather, in terms of its relation to other commodities as an exchange value. As Marx puts it, the 'circulation of commodities is the starting point of capital'.[7] The commodity is now bought and sold in the open market, valued not for its use but for its perceived ability to contribute to an escalating process of exchange and accumulation. Use value is given over entirely in favour of exchange value, and human labour itself is thus transformed from a qualitative into a quantitative value, as it becomes inextricably attached to the demands of commodity exchange: human labour becomes reified, alienated, broken into units capable of being managed by the culture and economics of exchange value.

To view *Psyche* within the strict terms of commodity exchange is to see that it is a product of human labour that performs a human function; that its value is social value alone; and that its social value is determined by its circulatory path. Its circulatory path, moreover, as defined by exchange value, sets limits to both its formal and expressive character according to the social and cultural demands of exchange. Expressive intention, textual detail, and poetic beauty arise from within these parameters, and to the extent that they do so they are quantities, abstracted from human practice to satisfy the demands of commodity culture. This is not to say that *Psyche* is a poem about buying and selling, but that its vision must be understood within the historical and cultural reality of buying and selling, within the social reality of reification and alienation.

This is admittedly a sterile and grim view of poetry that does not explain all that poetry is, or might become. Poetry is also an expression of human need and desire, and as such it possesses a utopian dimension that (one might hope) may be socially transform-ative. But not to situate Keats's poem among the specific social relations that enable and control its value and meaning may reduce its social function to the mystification of social relations – absorbing the contradictions of social life and resolving them into a nostalgic vision of what once was, but never more shall be.

While in *Psyche* there are no overt references to the market-place that might clearly demonstrate its position within a culture of commodity exchange, the poem nonetheless reveals quite forcefully at least one of the major ideological features of commodity culture. The poem's vision of transcendental possibility is grounded in a specifically bourgeois sensibility that is of a piece with the capitalist economic order of commodity exchange. It is a sensibility characterised most impressively by 'that rich, monadic, properly psychological autonomy' of the individual subject.[8] That autonomy assumes, among other things, that the individual is an isolated being circulating along various social paths freely chosen by itself. (As I shall argue, however, one path that is not – and cannot – be chosen within such a system is the path of communal hope: the individual can enter society, but only as one subject among an aggregate of other subjects.) The price of this individual autonomy, ultimately, is the privatisation of human life, insofar as the subjective vision of transcendental possibility requires the exchange of the social world for isolation, and the conversion of human value into a small, discrete territory of pleasure meant for consumption only by the individual subject. In *Psyche*, this point is driven home by the poet's acceptance of diminished territory for imaginative play; the world, which the poet asserts has lost its enchanting quality, is given over in favour of 'some untrodden region of [his] mind' (51), which, he believes, will be furnished with his own self-generated emblems of value. Standing hauntingly behind this vision is the sure loss of community, the isolation of the individual from the social world, and the conversion of human desire into a medium of exchange and consumption, wherein collective hope is sold in return for a private world.

This argument about the isolation and commodification of human value in *Psyche* echoes Christopher Caudwell's reading of Keats. Describing Romanticism as that phase of the 'bourgeois illusion' ushered in by the industrial revolution, Caudwell says that 'Keats is the first great poet to feel the strain of the poet's position . . . as producer for the free market'. That strain

led him to a position which was to set the keynote for future bourgeois poetry: 'revolution' as a flight *from* reality. Keats is the bannerbearer of the Romantic Revival. The poet now escapes upon the 'rapid wings of poesy' to a world of romance, beauty and sensuous life separate from the poor, harsh, real world of everyday life, which it sweetens and by its own loveliness silently condemns.[9]

Caudwell emphasises here that Keats's poetry is mediated in important ways by the social and historical energies of an emergent industrial capitalism (particularly those energies that isolate the imagination, reducing it to a private form effectively managed by the demands of commodity exchange) and that these energies are manifest in the very *aesthetic* qualities of Keats's imagination. The value, desire, and hope expressed in Keats's poetry (no less than its expressions of despair, disenchantment, and hardship) are *real* enough, but their shape and content are never independent of the historical situation within which they emerge.

Caudwell's point can be sharpened by casting it more specifically in terms of *Psyche*: the demise of Psyche's world, Keats emphasises, has left her without temple, shrine, grove, oracle (28–35) – an alienation that tells also of the spiritual desiccation of Keats's own times. Born into the modern world that Caudwell describes, the poet has lost the faith that, he imagines, must have belonged to an earlier age; Keats also is 'too late for antique vows' and 'Too, too late for the fond believing lyre' (36–7). The only region remaining for his faith and hope, as for Wordsworth before him, is the 'untrodden region of [his] mind'. This being the case, it is not surprising that the poem energetically (and hopefully) explores this uncharted region, while betraying an uncomfortable realisation that the modern world has been lost to an unseen and unspoken – yet definitive – authority that has left *only* the mind in the control of individuals.

If in *Psyche* Keats celebrates his imaginative ability to revive and invest with new meaning a character from the mythic past, providing a momentary resistance to the quantifying pressures of his own world, subsequent readers of Keats (from T. S. Eliot to Earl Wasserman to Helen Vendler) have coincided with him. By accepting the poet's definition of what counts as meaningful and elaborating it in a vocabulary consistent with the demands of modern critical sensibility, scholars and critics have done much to preserve and disseminate the beautiful imaginings in Keats's poetry. But, as Jerome McGann has shown, they have often done so at the cost of excluding the historical conditions (as described by Caudwell, for instance) with which Keats's imagination contended.[10] This exclusion means not only that our understanding of Keats today remains incomplete, but also that the loss of the world, registered in a poem like *Psyche*, is also the loss of our own world: criticism remains as much a private enterprise as Keats's poem, seeking its purpose away from a world that no longer cares to hear its voice.

One obvious feature of *Psyche*'s imaginative struggle with (and within) history is its tendency to appropriate the past as nostalgia. However true it may be that Psyche and Cupid's world is forever lost – and the poem does not deny this fact – the *recollection* of that world is rich with a sense of past greatness far surpassing anything found in the present. This curious, paradoxical imaginative manoeuvre is seen in Keats's readiness to acquit the past of responsibility for Psyche's alienated divinity, transferring this burden to the present day as a commentary on its imaginative and spiritual poverty:

> O brightest! though too late for antique vows,
>   Too, too late for the fond believing lyre,
> When holy were the haunted forest boughs,
>   Holy the air, the water, and the fire;
> Yet even in these days so far retir'd
>   From happy pieties, thy lucent fans,
>   Fluttering among the faint Olympians,
> I see, and sing, by my own eyes inspired.   (36–43)

This manoeuvre completed, he turns once again to the past, imaginatively recreating it as stable, inviting, and rich in possibility.

But of course the imaginative recreation of Psyche's world is not so much a retreat into the past as a labour to make an idealised vision of the past available as a redemptive power for the present. Like all nostalgia, this poetic move attempts to create a space where loneliness is at least temporarily laid to rest and alienation defeated. With his own world much too threatening to negotiate imaginatively, the poet remakes the long-dead world of the mythic past to express what he would like to find, but cannot, in his own world. And he shapes that material as he would like to shape his own world, a world which he stresses is 'far retir'd' from spiritual and imaginative well-being.

Everywhere in this poem about classical fictions and the inner recesses of the individual mind are traces of a troubling reality characterised by the conflict between myth and history, present and past, the individual and the world – by the conflict between the *form* of Keats's imagination and certain unspoken historical currents that make that particular form possible. The poem admittedly *desires* freedom and happiness, but can give shape to that desire only in accordance with a material situation that insistently obstructs freedom and happiness. Therefore, until that situation is known, the nature of the desire arising from it cannot be fully understood.

Within the frame of the foregoing discussion, is authorial intention no longer significant? Certainly, intention remains crucially important, though not in the ways that critical practice once assumed. It matters that Keats *chose* Psyche as his subject matter; that he believed he was writing a poem that, in its vision, surpassed the work of writers such as Mrs Tighe whom he once greatly admired; that he relied for information on the writings of Apuleius and Lemprière; that he knew he was celebrating a 'hethen Goddess'. Such details and others, long known to Keats scholars, are important not only because they provide information about Keats's intellectual interests and psychological quirks, but more importantly because they help to focus one level of historical interest in the poem. That Keats was drawn to things Hellenic and pagan as subjects for expressing his understanding of beauty and truth says much about the shape of the Romantic world: its paucity of attractive topics for poetry, and its challenge to poets to shape vision from their belated circumstances. Keats's intentions and motives are important, in short, because they are one set of details that might provide information about the *genesis* of the poem.[11]

Authorial intention is ultimately, however, contingent rather than constitutive, though this fact does not make it any less important or illuminating in historical terms. It is one condition of meaning within a larger set of historical conditions, and its precise significance for literary study is that it focuses and enlivens – even as it may threaten to mystify – the historical situation of poet and poetic text. In the case of *Psyche*, Keats's intentions, recorded in his journal letter to George and Georgiana Keats, March–April 1819, help readers to understand the choices available to him as a poet in post-Waterloo England.

The issue of intention, or at least of authorial presence, may be elucidated by reference to Keats's discussion of the world as a 'vale of Soul-making' (*Letters*, ii. 101–2), which immediately precedes the transcription of *Psyche* for his brother and sister-in-law. This letter is one of Keats's most eloquent statements describing his impatience with orthodox Christian explanations of human life, and his sense of the extent to which material circumstance shapes and empowers, in fundamental ways, human value, hope, and activity. As such, it provides a helpful gloss on certain ideas uppermost in his mind at the time he composed *Psyche*.

At the centre of Keats's letter are two major concerns that suggest the intellectual position at which, following Hazlitt, he had begun to arrive in 1819: *identity* and *circumstance*. In his three-part formulation – '*Intelligence* – the *human heart*... and the *World*' – he not only asserts the determining role that material circumstance plays in human life ('man was formed by circumstances') but, more importantly, seeks to explain why the authority of circumstance is proper and valuable in human life: 'Do you not see how necessary a World of Pains and troubles is to school an Intelligence and make it a soul?' He knowingly distances himself from a Christian explanation that would see human life as irretrievably fallen, and capable of salvation only by professions of faith and prayers calling for the aid of God. Unlike Christianity, he says, the 'system of Salvation' that he imagines 'does not affront our reason and humanity' because it finds a way to exist meaningfully within circumstances that, in Keats's view, provide the necessary bases of human knowledge and capacity (see *Letters*, ii. 102–3).

In this explanation of human salvation, Keats focuses on the question of identity, to show that identity is not pre-given but rather emerges from situations of conflict and difficulty. His account approaches what would now be called a materialist explanation of identity, and goes a long way toward rewriting certain assumptions about identity that had governed the vision of some poets only a generation earlier, especially Wordsworth. But the explanation that he offers is itself implicated in the very circumstances that it is meant to address, so that its materialist intention is only partly realised. That is, the explanation, while rejecting Wordsworth's view of the defining authority of the individual imagination, points toward a view of identity as the happy influence of painful circumstantial pressures in forming a spiritually meaningful essence: identity becomes synonymous with salvation, and thus it is, finally, but a modified version of the Christian idealism to which Keats objects.

Keats's position articulates a desire to believe that turbulent circumstance can, and does, produce intelligence, identity, and soul. Such desire is, on some level, itself a response to and product of circumstance, which, on its own terms, cannot guarantee the fulfilment of which Keats speaks. In fact, his effort to cut through the idealism governing many of the intellectual forms of his age actually duplicates that thought, insofar as it assumes that individual identity is an essence corresponding to a transhistorical essence (God). Keats affirms the formative pressures of circumstances on individual life (and this was felt with particular force in the critical post-Waterloo years) yet, at the same time, he seeks to preserve something of the nostalgic notion of identity as a focus of transcendent meaning, possibility, and reward. The letter, in other words, is an act of individual subject construction, motivated by a conviction that '*Intelligence* [is] *destined to possess the sense of Identity*' (Keats's emphasis). According to this logic, whatever Keats might say about the determining authority of circumstance, it is in fact secondary to an individual identity capable of shaping circumstance to its own ends. While it is asserted that circumstance is pivotal to Keats's argument, it is cast as that which serves the individual subject (Keats's real concern) and in this respect the materialist edge of his argument is dulled.

The 'vale of Soul-making' letter is important to *Psyche* because it helps to elucidate Keats's strong drive to situate himself as a stable identity in a turbulent world. This is precisely what he attempts in *Psyche*, which might be regarded as a poetic representation of the idea of soul described in the letter. The relation between these two documents is seen not only in the obvious attention that Keats gives, in the poem, to Psyche as soul, or in his exploration of the soul's home in 'some untrodden region of [his] mind'. It is seen, more compellingly, in the laborious process of soul-making that he describes in the poem's final stanza. Here the poet describes himself as dedicated to 'build[ing] a fane/ In some untrodden region of my mind' (50–1); his efforts will be enabled by 'a working brain' (60), whose 'shadowy thought' will 'win' what it can for the soul (65). Such dedication, carried out entirely within the frame of the individual mind, will, it is hoped, produce a mental territory – an intelligence and a soul – where love can dwell in luxurious warmth.

This final stanza of *Psyche* allows us to see clearly what goes largely unremarked in the letter, namely the active *construction* of identity. The poem traces, in imaginative form, the world of circumstance – with its 'enforcement' (2), 'surprise' (8), spiritual void (36–41), and 'pleasant pain' (52) – and, at the same time, it describes the process of producing identity out of circumstance. Moreover, that identity is emphatically shown to be individual, rather than communal, with its desires, integrity, love, and hope housed entirely within the mind. It is as though circumstance is a necessary starting point for the poet, but only that; circumstance is eventually abandoned in favour of the mind's imaginings that resolve circumstantial tensions within the authority of self-identity.

This obsessive concern with individual identity and possibility is, perhaps, the key ideological feature of the emergent bourgeois self in the eighteenth and early nineteenth centuries. A visibly changeful world generates tremendous liberating energies, which, though they transform society, leave people without full control of, or access to, that world. What people are left with, instead, is their own privatised self-identity, which they mistake for freedom. Within the frame of such transformation, human desire and hope are real, but mistaken, claiming freedom under the very conditions of its denial.[12] In *Psyche*, the ideological movement of the poem is very much in this direction: the poem's *expression* is full of goodness, while its political unconscious carries within it the very contradictions, inconsistencies, and injustices that the poet believes have been overcome.

The problems and dynamics surrounding the issue of identity – particularly the relation between identity and reification – are nowhere more evident than in the poem's handling of gender relations. The social and historical matters traced above are at every turn mediated by the presence of Psyche, so that the poet's comments on himself and on the world are also, necessarily, comments on relations of gender in the poem. The formulation of those relations energises, in quite specific ways, the poet's struggle against the debilitating pressures of his world, and enables him to begin constructing an autonomous identity for himself and a transcendental vision of human possibility. Gender is central, therefore, to the hopeful cast of the poem, and has to be considered if the grounds of that hope are to be understood.[13]

The first social fact that must be observed with respect to gender in *Psyche* is now a commonplace in feminist criticism of Romanticism, succinctly described by Janet Todd:

The Romantic poet's world is infinite, eternal and one, and the one, like the one of matrimony, is male. In the poetry of Wordsworth, Coleridge, Keats and even of Blake and Shelley, the female enters not usually as creating subject but as the symbol of otherness and immanence by the side of male transcendence, as a component in metaphors of reconciliation and integration, as emanation, shadow, mirror and epipsyche.[14]

This is precisely the way that Psyche enters Keats's poem – as the symbolic projection of the masculine poet's dreaming ego – and it is one sign of the fragmentation and reification of human life that arise with commodity culture. While the poem purports to be about Psyche, offering a laudatory description of her, it actually focuses on the male poet's imagination. Throughout, Psyche is passive, silent, ideal, while the poet is active, vocal, and imaginatively industrious. The apparent idealisation of Psyche becomes in fact the idealisation of the poet himself.

This strategy discloses the process of masculine subject construction under the pressure of an emergent bourgeois world; it is a process that energises the autonomous self through the paradoxical denial of self – and it is a process that can exist *only* within particular (bourgeois) hierarchical frames of reference.[15] The poem gives the impression throughout that the poet is subordinate to the female figure he would worship: he is apologetic (1–4), proceeds almost as if against his will (1–4), and seems committed, in the face of all obstacles (36–7, 40–1), to praising Psyche as 'loveliest' of the Olympians. Each gesture and manoeuvre, however, calls attention to the poet himself, often in quite explicit ways. In the initial diffident expressions, for instance, it is clear that the poet, for all his timidity, is sufficiently bold to address the goddess – 'And pardon that thy secrets should be sung/ Even into thine own soft-conched ear' (3–4) – even as he apologises for doing so. Read literally, these lines state the poet's relation to his subject, establishing him as a benevolent, though nonetheless controlling, presence, who alone gives voice to (and shapes the value of) her 'secrets' – which of course, insofar as he controls them, are not her secrets at all, but signs of his determining authority.

Possession of Psyche's secrets alone, however, is insufficient to the poetic task of accomplishing the transcendence of the imagining mind. The poet ultimately claims to control and shape every dimension of his subject, and in establishing this claim he erases Psyche's character entirely. While she is the figure he most wishes to celebrate, she is poorer, in every respect, than her better-known counterparts, and in fact the poet identifies her enthusiastically and entirely in terms of what she lacks:

> . . . temple thou hast none,
> Nor altar heap'd with flowers;
> Nor virgin-choir to make delicious moan
> Upon the midnight hours;

> No voice, no lute, no pipe, no incense sweet
> From chain-swung censer teeming;
> No shrine, no grove, no oracle, no heat
> Of pale-mouth'd prophet dreaming. (28–35)

This is certainly a curious poetic expression of esteem and desire, insofar as it implies that Psyche wants the elaborate paraphernalia of devotion and worship. According to these lines, all will in fact be given to her, or provided for her, by the poet himself. Just as previously he had informed her of her own secrets, he now lays the foundation for creating the character who possesses those secrets.

The remainder of the poem describes the ideological process whereby the poet invests Psyche with all that he desires to worship in her. Here again the poetic strategy is one of apparent self-effacement that is in fact self-construction, necessarily involving the conversion of Psyche into an object. After lamenting the decline of the modern age, the poet sets about describing the energy and labour that he will generate out of his own being in the cause of deifying Psyche. Specifically, the poet imagines himself as a 'priest' (50) with a 'working brain' (60); he is a spiritually devout intellectual labourer capable of creating, in his own mind, a 'fane' that will invest Psyche with spiritual significance. All of the devices of spiritual and intellectual accomplishment – 'voice', 'lute', 'pipe', 'incense sweet', 'shrine', 'grove', 'oracle' (46–8), 'branched thoughts' (52) – are compressed into his own mind as a hard crystal of individual identity. In gathering imaginative energy for the purpose of claiming – of insisting upon – his unique ability to elevate Psyche as a goddess equal to 'Olympus' hierarchy', the poet brings Psyche under his own control as a way of asserting his transcendence of the world before him. The act of exalting Psyche is an act of the poet's authority, the description of her an affirmation of his own transcendental wish. On such a view, her beauty and truth appear most significantly in her consumability as an object that will quench the poet's desire to be aligned with godhead.

The fairly conventional feminist explanation that I am offering here is extended by consideration of class issues that distinguish Keats's poetic voice and help clarify the specifically bourgeois character of gender relations in the poem. For even as the poem is a masculine play of authority against a constructed feminine other, that authority is cast in terms of a spiritualised labour which anticipates, perhaps, Carlyle's admonitions on the redemptive value of work. In aspiring to be a labouring priest in the service of Psyche, the poet imagines himself as unalienated and whole, fully a master of the surplus value of his labour. His 'working brain' and 'the gardener Fancy' (62) cultivate a rich world of intellectual and spiritual plenitude, a world in which labouring activity produces 'Love' (67), human warmth, and meaningful life. Such desires, of course, are grounded in the historical reality of alienated labour and class division.

The poem's stress on labour may be seen as a sign of Keats's own class position. At that moment when the poet is most triumphant in his imaginings, he is still lower class, his identity firmly set outside the domain of wealthy leisure. And even as the poem valorises productive labour, imagining the possibility of fulfilment in work, it duplicates the deep structure within which alienated labour under industrial capitalism is always set. In this duplication can be glimpsed the operations of bourgeois patriarchy, for even while the poet envisions himself happily labouring his way to self-fulfilment, his accomplishment is predicated upon a silent Psyche. Although he views himself in terms of his work, in fact he manages, or oversees, the instalment of Psyche as an object worthy of his devotion. On this account, the surplus value that the poet enjoys comes not entirely from his own productive capacities, but also from what has been denied to Psyche as an autonomous identity equal in value to the poet. Fragmentation, alienation, and reification have not been transcended, but rather pushed further down into the inner recesses of social life, until they are almost hidden away in one of the most basic relations of human existence – sexuality.

Gender in the poem has another, more disturbing aspect as well. The masculine identity articulated on the surface structure arises from a much deeper pornographic, and Sadeian, logic, which itself emerged with capitalism and carries within it a need for violence against feminine existence. Admittedly, this is a strong expression of one kind of operation in the poem, but it nevertheless describes an important dimension of the relation between the poet and Psyche, and gender and society. For at the heart of Sadeian logic is not physical violence, but rather the absolute domination of femininity by masculinity, and the definition of pleasure *as domination*. At the heart of pornographic logic is a universalised masculine ego capable of inserting itself, at will, into any sexually desirable situation. Indeed, one dimension of Romanticism might be seen as an ideal displacement of these operations.

To begin with pornography. The manoeuvre whereby the poet inserts his own identity into a sexual situation initiated and conducted by individuals other than himself is remarkably simple. The poet describes a scene in which he wanders (whether dreaming or awake is unclear) 'thoughtlessly' (7) across a landscape of natural beauty; during his wandering he comes unexpectedly upon Cupid and Psyche, who

> . . . lay calm-breathing on the bedded grass;
>   Their arms embraced, and their pinions too;
>   Their lips touch'd not, but had not bade adieu,
> As if disjoined by soft-handed slumber,
> And ready still past kisses to outnumber
>   At tender eye-dawn of aurorean love . . .   (15–20)

This erotic scene constitutes the only description in the poem of Cupid, even though the Cupid–Psyche embrace is the determining event for all subsequent musings. Immediately following this scene the poet erases Cupid entirely from his imagination, in one stroke substituting himself for the god in whose arms Psyche lies enfolded, emphatically claiming the ability to serve Psyche in ways superior to her erstwhile lover. Such a move drains the sexual energy from Cupid onto the identity of the poet, and at the same time establishes the poet's authority over a god. The act of worshipping and serving Psyche is also an act of self-transcendence, achieved through the strange logic of imaginatively possessing the sexual prowess of Cupid.

The logic of pornography, as many recent studies have persuasively demonstrated, is not simply a matter of private masculine desire, but also a matter of power relations, as private desire is necessarily acted out in terms of other people.[16] Recognition and disclosure of these power relations were the great contributions of Sade, who surrounded his pornography with long commentaries on the philosophy of sexual relations. At the centre of Sade's thought is the assumption that the active pleasure of one individual derives from the denial of pleasure to another. Among other things, Sade discloses the tremendous anxiety permeating individual life in the late eighteenth and early nineteenth centuries, an anxiety that arises with the new age of exchange value and economic scarcity and, in line with that age, takes for granted that there is not enough pleasure to go around: what little there is must be fought over by competing individuals. While Sade states this position in all its ugliness and mean-spiritedness, it is an attitude made manifest in many less disturbing – and often quite palatable –

ways, occasionally even in the form of romantic desire and romantic identity construction.[17]

In *Psyche*, a sanitised and idealised form of Sadeian logic emerges precisely at that moment when the poet displaces Cupid and begins to imagine himself as the 'priest' most suitable for worshipping Psyche. In his initial gesture toward her, as we have seen, the poet denies Psyche an autonomous subject position (28–35), despite the fact that when he first discovers her she is happily (see line 22) wrapped in a love-embrace with Cupid. This denial is quite emphatic – no fewer than ten negative expressions appear over fewer than ten lines – and it is complemented by the poet's subsequent assertion of his own identity and pleasure. The celebratory tone of the poem (proceeding toward a moving pronouncement of 'warm Love' [67]) may seem to qualify any description of this relation in terms of oppression. Yet the poet's desire, the poet's pleasure, the poet's need, the poet's identity, the poet's imagination – all of these appear and are shaped within the context of what the poet actively denies to Psyche, although, in her early relation with Cupid, she is an autonomous being, an agent of her own pleasure. The poet's vision is not a liberating myth, an alternative to the poet's original recognition of Psyche as lovely though 'faded', for her situation does not change significantly from the classical past to the Keatsian present. Rather, she has in effect been shifted from one sort of helplessness to another; in the modern world she is made to serve the poet's desire for transcendence, even as the poet claims to be liberating her from a past that never properly acknowledged her beauty.

It is important to call the logic of this masculinist poetic strategy *Sadeian*, because the word suggests the severity of the poem's portrayal of gender and helps to link various social and cultural energies of the age within a single historical and cultural framework. The logic of the poem is not entirely under the control of Keats the poet; it is, rather, the logic of an age, and Keats's Romantic vision is constrained by that logic even as he invests it with his own particular shaping desire. While he attempts to break free of a modern age that no longer knows 'happy pieties', 'antique vows', and 'the fond believing lyre', and to offer a vision of hope and possibility, he remains situated within the historical moment of an emergent industrial capitalism, his imagination implicated in the broad and deep controls that it would transcend. Those controls are both bourgeois and patriarchal.

In *Ode to Psyche*, the past is devoured and recast as nostalgia in the poet's effort to establish himself as an autonomous identity. So the past is made to appear as a domain of infinite possibilities for the noble and loving imagination. And yet nostalgia remains tinged with present difficulties, difficulties that take the form both of bourgeois alienation and patriarchal oppression. One question that readers may therefore ask is whether the historical realities that the poem is unable to overcome compromise its noble expression of hope and love. The answer must be that the poem's importance is not diminished but enhanced by recognition of its historical situation, because the poem's desire to transcend history provides an avenue into history, and into the conditions of the desire for escape. Thus while the poem may not offer what Keats wished it to offer, and while its meanings may not be entirely containable within frames of reference that some modern readers might prefer, it nonetheless provides something of what historical understanding needs: an example of the controlling authority of material circumstance and of the imaginative effort to shape and direct that circumstance.

To begin reading Keats's poetry from the perspective of its energising social and historical relations is to recognise that expressive intention, textual detail and discontinuity, and reader response all carry specific, or individual, significances, but are ultimately important as pressures and effects within a much larger context that is ideologically burdened and politically charged. To insist, moreover, on moving Keats's poetry away from more traditional liberal humanist approaches is not to deny the beauty of the poetry, or to deny the grand contributions of liberal humanism. It is, rather, to reinvigorate the poetry, not as nostalgia, but as history – as a beautiful idealism capable of teaching valuable lessons about the past and, thereby, helping to inspire hope in the present for a transformed world, where beauty, compassion, and love are at last realised.

NOTES

1 Fredric Jameson, *The Ideologies of Theory: Essays 1971–1986* (Minneapolis, 1988) i. 19–20.
2 For Keats's poems in the historical and political contexts of his age, see *KHM* and Thomas A. Reed, 'Keats and the Gregarious Advance of Intellect in *Hyperion*', *ELH* 55 (1988), 195–232; Kenneth Muir, 'The

Meaning of *Hyperion*', in K. Muir (ed.), *John Keats. A Reassessment* (Liverpool, 1969), 103–23; June Q. Koch, 'Politics in Keats's Poetry', *JEGP* 71 (1972), 491–501. For Keats's relation to literary history see John Middleton Murry, *Studies in Keats* (London, 1930); Morris Dickstein, *Keats and His Poetry: A Study in Development* (Chicago and London, 1971); M. R. Ridley, *Keats's Craftsmanship: A Study in Poetic Development* (Oxford, 1933); and Robin Mayhead, *John Keats* (Cambridge, 1967). For the economic and ideological dimensions of Keats's poetry, see Kurt Heinzelman, 'Self-Interest and the Politics of Composition in Keats's *Isabella*', *ELH* 55 (1988), 159–93.

3 While I differ in textual interpretation and in my conclusions from Christopher Caudwell, my assumptions about the relations of Romanticism to the decline of aristocracy and emergence of the bourgeoisie are heavily indebted to his study *Illusion and Reality: A Study of the Sources of Poetry* (1937; rpt. New York, 1977), especially 101–13.

4 For further discussion see my *KPP* and *KL*. For a more general and theoretical study of the relations of Romanticism and capitalism, see Robert Sayre and Michael Lowy's essay, 'Figures of Romantic Anticapitalism', in G. A. Rosso and Daniel P. Watkins (eds.), *Spirits of Fire: English Romantic Writers and Contemporary Historical Methods* (London and Toronto, 1990), 23–68.

5 Keats scholars have long recognised that transformation is an important theme in the poem, but have tended to speak of transformation in terms of a 'fall' from myth into history. See for instance Kenneth Allott, 'The *Ode to Psyche*', in Jack Stillinger (ed.), *Twentieth Century Interpretations of Keats's Odes* (Englewood Cliffs, N.J., 1968), 17–31, and Stuart M. Sperry, *Keats the Poet* (Princeton, 1973), 249–61.

6 Karl Marx, *Capital: A Critique of Political Economy* (1954, rpt. Moscow, 1977), 43, 54, 90. According to Marx, money stands as the universal equivalent of value, enabling all other commodities to 'represent their value' (90).

7 Ibid., 145.

8 Jameson, 'The Ideology of the Text', *The Ideologies of Theory*, 52–3.

9 *Illusion and Reality*, 107, 108.

10 *The Romantic Ideology. A Critical Investigation* (Chicago and London, 1983).

11 For Keats's reference to Psyche as 'hethen' see his letter to George and Georgiana Keats, March–April 1819, *Letters*, ii. 106. For relevant discussions of intention, see Robert Weimann, *Structure and Society in Literary History* (Baltimore, 1984); Jerome J. McGann, *A Critique of Modern Textual Criticism* (Chicago and London, 1983), 65–80; and Annabel Patterson, 'Intention', in Frank Lentricchia and Thomas McLaughlin (eds.), *Critical Terms for Literary Study* (Chicago and London, 1990), 135–46.

12 See Russell Jacoby, *Social Amnesia: A Critique of Conformist Psychology from Adler to Laing* (Boston, 1975), 113.

13 For Keats's portrayal of women, goddesses, and 'the feminine' see Sperry, *Keats the Poet*, 101–3; David Perkins, *The Quest for Permanence* (Cambridge, Mass., 1959), 222–3; Beth Lau, 'Keats's Mature Goddesses', *PQ*, 63 (1984), 323–41; Geoffrey Hartman, 'Reading Aright: Keats's "Ode to Psyche"', in Eleanor Cook et al. (eds.), *Centre and Labyrinth: Essays in Honour of Northrop Frye* (Toronto, 1983), 210–26; Mario d'Avanzo, *Keats's Metaphors for the Poetic Imagination* (Durham, 1967), 25–31; and especially Marlon Ross, *The Contours of Masculine Desire: Romanticism and the Rise of Women's Poetry* (New York and Oxford, 1989), 167–86.

14 *Feminist Literary History* (New York, 1988), 114.

15 For specific features of bourgeois patriarchy, see for instance Zillah R. Eisenstein, 'Developing a Theory of Capitalist Patriarchy and Socialist Feminism', in Z. R. Eisenstein (ed.), *Capitalist Patriarchy and the Case for Socialist Feminism* (New York, 1979), 5–40.

16 For recent debates surrounding pornography, see Donald Alexander Downs, *The New Politics of Pornography* (Chicago and London, 1989).

17 The best materialist analysis of the historical significance of Sade's thought is Angela Carter's *The Sadeian Woman and the Ideology of Pornography* (New York, 1978).

CHAPTER 6

Isabella in the market-place: Keats and feminism

Kelvin Everest

In some English writers of the Romantic period we find an extraordinary sophistication and subtlety in the representation of modes of oppression suffered by women. This kind of highly conscious and developed concern with central problems of feminism may be found in, for example, the poetry of Shelley, where there is a very acute analysis of the role of individual consciousness in assenting to social orders which in fact limit and damage the potentialities of the assenting individual. A direct and fully conscious representation of similar issues is found even more strikingly, and centrally, in Blake, and especially in some of the astoundingly original earlier illuminated 'Prophecies' such as *The Book of Thel*, *Visions of the Daughters of Albion*, and *Europe*.

There is, secondly, a quite different kind of engagement with feminist issues in Romantic writing. Here the thematic concerns are still direct and overt, but the level at which the problems of female social role and identity are conceived is markedly less sophisticated and, so to speak, disablingly imprisoned within the deep ideological structures of English culture. Mary Wollstonecraft's work, for example, may be understood in such terms. Her *Vindication of the Rights of Woman* (1792) is limited in its power and scope by a constraining awareness of the realities of the male status quo, which vitiates the drive of the argument towards a truly radical perspective. In Wollstonecraft's novels the problem emerges in a series of lamely sentimental images of the ideal sexual and marital relation, which is all that the novels can offer to set against the savage human abuses of prevailing social practices. When an entirely different and implicitly oppositional social model does threaten to emerge into coherence – as it does for instance in the sketching of a saving and supportive idea of female friendship in *The Wrongs of Woman* (1798) – the possibilities are left undeveloped and unaccommodated at the level of plot.

There is however a third kind of engagement with problems of gender and sexuality in texts of the Romantic period, where the thematic interests appear not conscious and direct at all, but displaced and skewed in a way which can produce writing of a compelling and enigmatic power. Mary Shelley's *Frankenstein* (1818) is a text of this sort, opening up questions of a depth and implication of which the novel's controlling intelligence seems only incompletely aware. This is not to patronise the achievement of the novel; it is manifestly fully conscious of many of its own operations and contexts, literary and cultural and indeed autobiographical, and there is an important sense in which we may read *Frankenstein* as a careful meditation upon the destructive domestic effects of what the young Mary may well have considered the dangerously unbridled radical idealism of her husband and her father. Nevertheless, the novel activates inquiry and reflection on themes of sexuality and gender roles, in the family and in society at large, which do not easily fit any scheme of reading offered by the terms of the novel itself.

Keats is another such example. In some of his poetry we are conscious of thematic issues which are not present to the overt controlling intelligence. I realise that it is not very fashionable to talk in such terms. But to speak of the liberating or oppositional capacities of a criticism which disregards such controlling intelligence is, of course, and rightly, simultaneously to credit texts with possessing such things. It is often important and valuable to 'read against' the voice of a text, in the manner so frequently recommended and sometimes practised by various varieties of post-structuralist, deconstructionist, Marxist, and feminist criticisms. But the power of the technique depends upon and presupposes a resistant textual presence which is being subverted in the critical act. Keats's *Isabella* provides an interesting test case for these propositions; that issues of importance to a feminist criticism are raised by the poem, and that these issues are not germane to the conscious purposes of the poem.

Isabella is an early poem. Keats was twenty-two when he was working on it between late February and late April of 1818. It is a work which bears obvious marks of immaturity. The passages directly addressed from the narrator to the reader seem to lack self-assurance, in a nervous way which produces an almost apologetic tone. This quality in the poem has often been taken as an early and uncertain form of what was to become a characteristic concern of Keats with his own status and role as a poet. The diction and versification of *Isabella* constitute a marked improvement on *Endymion*, Keats's first genuinely ambitious and sustained poetic venture which had been completed towards the end of 1817, and revised at the beginning of 1818. But traces do still remain in the style of *Isabella* of the so-called 'cockneyfying' influence of Leigh Hunt, whose stylistic mannerisms – a kind of prettifying ornateness and fussiness – affect Keats's early development quite markedly. These traces give the writing in *Isabella* an uneven quality, and this effect is compounded by the manner of Keats's rendering of his source story in Boccaccio's *Decameron*, which is oddly proportioned, and (for instance) allows too much time to the opening introductory account of the young lovers.

Indeed, the treatment of the lovers in the poem has consistently presented the poem's biggest difficulty for twentieth-century readers. It is a bad sign that they presented no such difficulty for nine-teenth-century readers, such as the Pre-Raphaelites, who generally cultivated an image of Keats which served cultural needs and circumstances which no longer exist (we must return later to this question of Keats's cultural image). To present-day readers the presentation of Lorenzo and Isabella can often appear mawkishly sentimental, by turns morbid, grotesque, and lushly ornamental in its treatment of such insistently serious concerns as love, death, and, presumably, insanity.

Keats himself seems to have had reservations about the poem. Some eighteen months after completing it he wrote to his friend Richard Woodhouse explaining why he did not at that time propose to publish the poem:

I will give you a few reasons why I shall persist in not publishing The Pot of Basil – It is too smokeable – I can get it smoak'd at the Carpenters shaving chimney much more cheaply – There is too much inexperience of live [*sic*], and simplicity of knowledge in it – which might do very well after one's death – but not while one is alive. There are very few would look to the reality. I intend to use more finesse with the Public. It is possible to write fine things which cannot be laugh'd at in any way. Isabella is what I should call were I a reviewer 'A weak-sided Poem' with an amusing sober-sadness about it. Not that I do not think Reynolds and you are quite right about it – it is enough for me. But this will not do to be public – If I may say so, in my dramatic capacity I enter fully into the feeling: but in Propria Persona I should be apt to quiz it myself – (21, 22 September 1819; *Letters*, ii. 174)

This account has been taken to indicate that Keats came to consider the poem limited and implausible, in a way which corroborates the reactions of modern readers. But in fact the judgements in the letter need to be understood more circumspectly. Keats's expression 'smokeable' does not mean 'easily exposed in its faults' (as has been suggested), but rather 'too easily made fun of'. The wariness of Keats's letter probably owes much to the savage mauling that *Endymion* had received from certain reviewers, and there is nothing actually to suggest that Keats felt *Isabella* to be a failure. Rather the feeling is that the poem's style and concerns laid themselves open too readily to the mockery of an unsympathetic critical perspective. The central point here is that there is no good reason in Keats's own judgement to write off *Isabella* as a mannered and immature oddity. It earns the right to a more serious and attentive reading; Keats's nervousness was understandable but misleading.

There are two kinds of critical assumption which are commonly brought to bear in readings of *Isabella*. The first kind, taking its cue from a hasty reading of the letter quoted above, simply dismisses the poem as manifestly early in Keats's development, and emphatically limited in various ways because of that. As we have already noted, there is some truth in this. The second common kind of critical assumption actually builds on the first kind, but in a very particular way. The assumption here is that the poem gives, in an uncomfortably exaggerated way, a representation of human experience which is nonetheless typical and central in Keats.

We may characterise this assumedly central and typical representation as follows. The arrangement and feel of the poem are founded upon an opposition between – in one formulation – 'Romantic enchantment' and 'colder actuality'. This opposition is very familiar in Keats criticism, and takes various related forms. 'Romantic enchantment' will be understood to include love, and especially young love which embraces a physical dimension; a luxuriant richness of sensory experience; the imagination and its projected forms; poetry itself. Set against these are the predicates of 'colder actuality': the pragmatic, workaday imperatives of real experience, limited in space and time, and subject to disciplines and necessities which are variously contrary to desire and its fulfilment. The historian E. P. Thompson has cogently formulated this widely operative conception of a fundamental opposition at the heart of Keats's poetic intelligence:

This conflict [in Keats's poetry] sometimes appears as one between the sensuous and the philosophic life ('O for a life of Sensations rather than of

Thoughts!'), sometimes as between science and imagination ('Do not all charms fly/ At the mere touch of cold philosophy?'): more often it is deeply embedded in the very structure of the poems themselves, in the acute tension between the richness of the life of the senses and imagination and the poverty of everyday experience, and in Keats's struggle to reconcile the two. It is his intense awareness of this conflict (which was of central importance to English culture), which gives greatness to his achievement.[1]

These are persuasive formulations, but if we accept them then the nature of Keats's achievement is made to conform to a cultural model of the 'Romantic' which considers it a rejection of all forms of social engagement. And it then follows that, for all of the idealism, the capacity for pleasure, and the intense power of human sympathy which prompt the wish to escape 'the poverty of everyday experience', Keats's poetry cannot usefully be read as an imaginative mode of positive engagement with the realities of his social life.

I wish to avoid this way of reading Keats, and to show that even in an underrated poem such as *Isabella* we may find, on the one hand, a far more subtle and meditated set of purposes at work in the poem, and also, on the other hand, a rich diversity of significations which may be read across or against the real subtlety of the poem's intentions. This is not to deny that certain features of *Isabella* do appear to lend themselves to the terms of Thompson's account. It is rather too easy to find in the poem an impulse to escape reality that is merely naive, insubstantially posed, and sentimental. The lovers in particular are something of an embarrassment, if we decide that we must take them 'straight' – on their own terms, as it were – and consider the whole poem as an exercise in sentiment, if a weirdly grotesque one. Keats very considerably enlarges the role of the lovers relative to their treatment in the source story, so their prominence in the poem is definitely calculated. If the poem is to be judged a failure in this respect, it is a failure of a markedly willed and deliberated kind.

The other main term of the central thematic opposition which has often been discerned in the poem is provided by Isabella's merchant-capitalist brothers. They set against young love and mutually absorbing sexual passion a coolly and grimly calculating spirit of mercantile enterprise. They embody the heartless world of work and gain. It is through their agency that the sentimental idyll of the lovers is destroyed. To interpret the thematic pattern of the poem in this way also justifies an interpretation of the later main episodes, the visit of Lorenzo's ghost, Isabella's excavation of the grave and bizarre cultivation of her dead lover's head, as successive forms of lament for the loss of innocence, pleasure, and imaginative fulfilment, under the inexorable pressure of social and economic exigencies. Viewed in this way the latter part of the poem might be considered as sometimes carried off quite affectingly, and sometimes frankly laughable; in other words, just as Keats himself in his letter thought that readers might take the poem.

The broad terms of these thematic oppositions may be widened to incorporate other very important levels which are frequently found to be at work within Keats's poetry. One crucial level at which Keats's poetry is seen to be founded on recurring oppositions is that of philosophical orientation. An imaginative idealism is found in contrast and conflict with rationalist empiricism. The conflict is perhaps most sharply dramatised in *Lamia*, but it is not difficult to produce a reading of *Isabella* which also conforms to a similarly contrastive thematic opposition. The lovers in the poem embody an idealism, founded on an imaginary conception of the good life in a close union of spiritual and physical modes of fulfilment, which is opposite to, and thwarted by, the cold, hard-headed pragmatic realism and financial acumen of the brothers. And yet, in spite of the easy assent that such readings have for a long time now commanded, it is in the practice of reading really very difficult to sustain such an opposition in the poem with any persuasive coherence. It is interesting, for example, to compare the different ranges of knowledge and understanding displayed by the groups of characters on either side of this opposition. The lovers consistently demonstrate an inward, excluding mutuality in their reciprocal absorption in love:

> Parting they seem'd to tread upon the air,
>   Twin roses by the zephyr blown apart
> Only to meet again more close, and share
>   The inward fragrance of each other's heart.
> She, to her chamber gone, a ditty fair
>   Sang, of delicious love and honey'd dart;
> He with light steps went up a western hill,
> And bade the sun farewell, and joy'd his fill.
>
> All close they met again, before the dusk
>   Had taken from the stars its pleasant veil,
> All close they met, all eves, before the dusk
>   Had taken from the stars its pleasant veil,
> Close in a bower of hyacinth and musk,

> Unknown of any, free from whispering tale,
> Ah! better had it been for ever so,
> Than idle ears should pleasure in their woe. (73–88)

The intimacy of the lovers is sustained even while they are apart by a kind of entranced oblivion to other human society. Their mutually sustained apartness is insisted upon by the mannered repetition of the second quoted stanza, but it is also more subtly and more tellingly caught in the cameo representations of her solitary singing and his happily self-sufficient solitary walking. The verse makes us feel that even the poem's readers constitute the kind of unwelcome intrusion of a larger human society for which their love never wished to find a place.

This almost wilfully self-blinding marginality to the wider range of human activity is in obvious contrast with the outlook of the brothers, who manifest a much more pervasive, cold scrutiny:

> How was it these same ledger-men could spy
> Fair Isabella in her downy nest?
> How could they find out in Lorenzo's eye
> A straying from his toil? Hot Egypt's pest
> Into their vision covetous and sly!
> How could these money-bags see east and west? –
> Yet so they did – and every dealer fair
> Must see behind, as doth the hunted hare. (137–44)

It is plain from the manner of these lines that the capitalist mentality of the brothers is offered as unattractive and humanly limited. But it is not in fact any more limited than the inwardness of the lovers. Indeed the far greater range and manipulative capacity of the brothers' perspective is one of the various ways by which a certain *vulnerable* quality is suggested in the mode of experience which is yet represented as the preferred mode of the poem's moral outlook. This vulnerability in the way that the lovers behave implicitly questions the viability of their idealism, and renders them almost culpable in their own fate. They invite the pragmatic manipulation which destroys them. The thematic opposition embodied in these contrasted outlooks is thus significantly modified. The power of an imaginative as against a rational mode of understanding is implicitly questioned by the poem's refusal to endorse without irony the experience of the lovers in the early stanzas of the poem.

Something similar also happens at the level of stylistic contrasts within the writing of *Isabella*. Part of the poem is emphatically coloured by the stylistic qualities which marked Keats out so distinctively from all of his contemporaries, and which made him such a ready target for hostile reviewers. The medievalism of *Isabella*, for example, is elaborated with a largely unironised relish; the action takes place amongst Italianate settings which imbue the obvious Englishness of the countryside with a dreamy stage-Gothic. Added to this is Keats's deliberately 'primitive' refusal of a Pope-like polish and finish in his versification. This is noticeable in the handling of the *ottava rima* stanzas. In sharp contrast to other English practitioners, Fairfax, or Byron, Keats's *ottava rima* is far from sophisticated, and reaches instead for a quirky, idiosyncratic use of outlandish epithets, often in prominent rhyme-positions. Critics throughout the nineteenth century often pointed to an apparent clumsiness, especially in the handling of rhyme, which they assumed to indicate an uncultured and homemade quality in Keats's poetic English. The effect, which they castigated as at once pretentious and ludicrous, is of a literal sense in the verse which is constantly being pulled about by the exigencies of awkward or eccentric rhyme-words:

> 'To-day we purpose, ay, this hour we mount
>   To spur three leagues towards the Apennine;
> Come down, we pray thee, ere the hot sun count
>   His dewy rosary on the eglantine.'
> Lorenzo, courteously as he was wont,
>   Bow'd a fair greeting to these serpents' whine;
> And went in haste, to get in readiness,
> With belt, and spur, and bracing huntsman's dress. (185–92)

The striking and rather laboured rhymes here on 'Apennine' and 'eglantine' clearly work to import into the stanza an Italian and medieval atmosphere, but they also establish a demand in the rhyme-scheme which is met in the phrase 'these serpents' whine', which seems at once grammatically forced, and unluckily inapt (serpents don't whine). But such stylistic features are in fact anything but crude. Keats's rejection of a tradition of smooth facility in English versification was meditated and purposeful, even if his early work does show the influence of mannered models which could obscure his achievement. *Isabella* wears its 'primitive' artifice on its sleeve. It is a poem which suits its rhetoric to the pre-industrial freshness of its setting and materials. This is what Keats is driving at in his letter about the poem: 'If I may say so, in my dramatic capacity I enter fully into the feeling'. Keats's style struck contemporaries not so much as mannered, but as almost embarrassingly weak and amateurish. But its true originality lies in the way in which it offers brilliant commentary upon, and modification of the lines of development in English verse which precede it (quite a close parallel to the nature of Keats's originality is offered in the jazz piano style of Thelonius Monk). The primitive roughness of versification effects a transformation in the possibilities of poetic language quite as profound and far-reaching, for example, as the stylistic innovations of Wordsworth and Coleridge, which are indeed in many ways the crucial precursors of Keats's style.

A characteristically Keatsian outlandishness of style is, however, balanced in *Isabella* by a quite different and contrasting manner. This element in the style of the poem reaches after the kind of effects found in Romantic mock-Spenserianism. The manner was a legacy of the satiric mock-Spenserianism of James Thomson's very influential poem *The Castle of Indolence*, which was first published in 1748. Wordsworth used it in his 'Stanzas Written in my Pocket-Copy of Thomson's "Castle of Indolence"' (1802; 1815) although the satiric tone is subdued to elegiac feeling in the self-portrait:

> Great wonder to our gentle Tribe it was
> Whenever from our Valley he withdrew;
> For happier soul no living creature has
> Than he had, being here the long day through.
> Some thought he was a lover, and did woo:
> Some thought far worse of him, and judged him wrong:
> But Verse was what he had been wedded to;
> And his own mind did like a tempest strong
> Come to him thus, and drove the weary Wight along. (28–36)[2]

These same elements of style – a mock-archaic diction combined with details from eighteenth-century 'stock diction' ('tribe', 'Wight'), and a deliberated narrative pace marked in the pattern of the Spenserian rhyme-scheme – are used in a more definitely satirical context by Byron in the early stanzas of *Childe Harold's Pilgrimage* (1812):

> Whilome in Albion's isle there dwelt a youth,
> Who ne in virtue's ways did take delight;
> But spent his days in riot most uncouth,
> And vex'd with mirth the drowsy ear of Night.
> Ah, me! in sooth he was a shameless wight,
> Sore given to revel and ungodly glee;
> Few earthly things found favour in his sight
> Save concubines and carnal companie,
> And flaunting wassailers of high and low degree.

> (Canto I, 10–18)[3]

Used in this Byronic way the style offers a cynical and worldly-wise tone, slickly alert to the realities of human ways, and unillusioned about them. In *Isabella* the commercial world of the brothers is introduced by a striking variation of style which falls into exactly this idiom; the preceding stanza needs to be quoted here too, to demonstrate the abrupt and unmistakable nature of Keats's shift in register:

> But, for the general award of love,
> The little sweet doth kill much bitterness;
> Though Dido silent is in under-grove,
> And Isabella's was a great distress,
> Though young Lorenzo in warm Indian clove
> Was not embalm'd, this truth is not the less –
> Even bees, the little almsmen of spring-bowers,
> Know there is richest juice in poison-flowers.
>
> With her two brothers this fair lady dwelt,
> Enriched from ancestral merchandize,
> And for them many a weary hand did swelt
> In torched mines and noisy factories,
> And many once proud-quiver'd loins did melt
> In blood from stinging whip; – with hollow eyes
> Many all day in dazzling river stood,
> To take the rich-ored driftings of the flood.   (97–112)

The Spenserian manner is introduced emphatically in the prominently rhymed archaism 'swelt', and there is too a new industrial and productive reference in the diction – 'factories' – and an eighteenth-century manner of abbreviated grammatical forms suggesting a tendency to abstraction and personification ('from stinging whip', 'in dazzling river'). The style recurs with reference to the brothers, suggesting an entirely different mode of experiencing the world, which is much more far-seeing, workaday, and businesslike than the perspective of the lovers:

> Yet were these Florentines as self-retired
> In hungry pride and gainful cowardice,
> As two close Hebrews in that land inspired,
> Paled in and vineyarded from beggar-spies;
> The hawks of ship-mast forests – the untired
> And pannier'd mules for ducats and old lies –
> Quick cat's-paws on the generous stray-away, –
> Great wits in Spanish, Tuscan, and Malay.   (129–36)

This odd stanza, with its determination to catch the character of a crafty and canny but still blinkered and viciously exploitative commercial mentality, was followed in Keats's manuscript fair copy of the poem by a further stanza, later dropped. In these cancelled lines Keats all but spells out the terms by which the brothers are set in thematic opposition to the lovers; a juxtaposition that is also strongly emphasised by stylistic contrasts:

> Two young Orlandos far away they seem'd,
>   But on a near inspect their vapid Miens –
> Very alike, – at once themselves redeem'd
>   From all suspicion of Romantic spleens –
> No fault of theirs, for their good Mother dream'd
>   In the longing time of Units in their teens
> Of proudly-bas'd addition and of net –
> And both their backs were mark'd with tare and tret.

It is however again misleading to conceive of these stylistic qualities as participating in a direct and schematic set of oppositions in the rhetoric of the poem. The satirical, socially alert Byronic manner is indeed associated with the brothers, and steadily contrasted with the medievalism and natural-descriptive language which characterise the verse Keats uses in relation to the lovers. But these stylistic contrasts are not in reality clear-cut or mutually excluding. Keats's poetic language is always striving to register a direct sensory engagement with the real – with what he would have described as the 'feel' of reality – in ways which are manifest on both sides of the supposed opposition. The brothers' exploitative merchant-capitalist mentality is given at times with a sensuous relish which properly belongs on the other side of the contrastive scheme, in for example the graphic detailed rendering of colour, and of physical movement and sensation:

>   . . . with hollow eyes
> Many all day in dazzling river stood,
> To take the rich-ored driftings of the flood.
>
> For them the Ceylon diver held his breath,
>   And went all naked to the hungry shark;
> For them his ears gushed blood . . .   (110–15)

The styles are in fact mixed here. We have already noted the elements of eighteenth-century 'stock' diction associated, in Keats as in other Romantic practitioners, with worldly mock-Spenserian satire. But the sensuous 'feel', usually inseparable from a recognisably Romantic handling of phrasing and rhythm, is also emphatically present – 'rich-ored driftings', 'ears gushed blood' – and makes for a much more complex overall effect than the apparently schematic organisation of the poem would suggest.

Just as the philosophical or epistemological oppositions turn out to be more subtle and mutually ironising than the critical tradition has allowed for in *Isabella*, so the stylistic oppositions too reward more careful attention. And, where the poetic discourse of the brothers is modified by a language which holds it in relation to its apparently opposite conditions, so Keats enters an implicit reserve about the lovers by his handling of natural-descriptive language in relation to their experience:

> . . . soon into her heart a throng
>   Of higher occupants, a richer zest
> Came tragic; passion not to be subdued,
> And sorrow for her love in travels rude.
>
> In the mid days of autumn, on their eves
>   The breath of Winter comes from far away,
> And the sick west continually bereaves
>   Of some gold tinge, and plays a roundelay
> Of death among the bushes and the leaves,
>   To make all bare before he dares to stray
> From his north cavern. So sweet Isabel
> By gradual decay from beauty fell,
>
> Because Lorenzo came not.   (245–57)

This elegiac passage brings in a suggestion of the lovers' thwarted participation in the natural cycle. Imagery of warmth, seasonal fluctuation, and flowers, here as throughout the poem, does not serve straightforwardly to guarantee the rightness and naturalness of their relationship, but rather to dramatise its tragic dislocation from the recurring natural cycles which are the background to their experience. In both thematic and stylistic contexts, then, it is difficult to sustain the paradigms which have long been considered typical in Keats. At the heart of these paradigms is the opposition of reality – empirical knowledge, the limits to experience set by space, and time, the need to work, and the practical exigencies of life – to a fulfilling imaginative idealism. This central opposition in particular is not in fact sustainable in relation to Keats, with its odd suggestion, for example, that certain frankly physical experience is somehow less 'real' than knowing about the workings of trade, or the spectrum, or being able to do arithmetic, or blackmail people.

Considered in such terms the opposition itself is real and damaging enough, but its terms are not offered as mutually excluding in Keats's poetry. The opposition as it appears in *Isabella* is more productively understood as a *dramatic* function of the characters in the narrative. The poem is generally conscious of dimensions in the experience of the characters, of which they themselves display no awareness. The brothers, as we have seen, cannot share in the lovers' order of experience. They can, however, discern it; and the language associated with them in the poem also bears traces of the stylistic qualities associated with its opposite condition. The lovers, on the other hand, labour under an equally or even more limiting perspective, in that their experience blinds them to its antithetical forms. Their mutually absorbed assurance in love is indeed assailable *per se*, in its willed and culpably vulnerable exclusion of the real. Its self-conscious, conventionally posed quality averts attention from the activities and intentions of the brothers, but also from the true nature of their *own* experience, the physicality of sexual love. In discovering this kind of ironising distance in Keats's treatment of the lovers we can also then establish justification for the elaborate and sustained introductory account, in *Isabella*, of the courtship of Lorenzo and Isabella. The tone in these passages is not at all sentimental or coyly posed; these qualities are being fixed as limitations in the characters, in a narrative manner of firm but gentle parody:

> Fair Isabel, poor simple Isabel!
>   Lorenzo, a young palmer in Love's eye!
> They could not in the self-same mansion dwell
>   Without some stir of heart, some malady;
> They could not sit at meals but feel how well
>   It soothed each to be the other by;
> They could not, sure, beneath the same roof sleep
> But to each other dream, and nightly weep.
>
> . . .
>
> He knew whose gentle hand was at the latch,
>   Before the door had given her to his eyes;
> And from her chamber-window he would catch

> Her beauty farther than the falcon spies;
> And constant as her vespers would he watch,
>   Because her face was turn'd to the same skies;
> And with sick longing all the night outwear,
> To hear her morning-step upon the stair.
>
> A whole long month of May in this sad plight
>   Made their cheeks paler by the break of June:
> 'To-morrow will I bow to my delight,
>   To-morrow will I ask my lady's boon.' –
> 'O may I never see another night,
>   Lorenzo, if thy lips breathe not love's tune.' –
> So spake they to their pillows; but, alas,
> Honeyless days and days did he let pass . . .   (1–8, 17–32)

The delicate mockery here, of the young lovers' willing subjection of themselves to sentimental conventions of courtship, is a gentle and sympathetic mode of critical awareness; but it is mockery nonetheless. The lovers' wan and pining attitude is in ironic contrast with the onset of high summer, as the days drift through 'A whole long month of May' up to 'the break of June'. Their coy, embarrassed self-denials in the face of their own feelings are deftly marked in the imagery of illness – 'malady', 'sick longing' – and in the odd negative 'Honeyless', which invokes the condition it denies.

The poem demonstrates how self-destructive such apparently innocent self-delusion can become. In the harshly pragmatic, unloving, and profit-seeking world of the brothers, such an absorption in conventions of sentiment makes for easy prey. As we have seen, the oppositions of *Isabella* establish a subtle perspective on the strange action; the dream world, aching for a realisation of the perfect and the ideal, is destroyed by an uncongenial reality, but this destruction is in fact represented as a working-out of limitations inherent in the character of the dream world. To put it another way, the destructive agency of the brothers in the action of the poem provides an extended dramatic form for the working out of flaws in the relationship of the lovers.

The visit of Lorenzo's ghost to Isabella is particularly interesting in the context of such a reading. In sadly eloquent speech, the ghost evokes his marginalised social being:

> 'I am a shadow now, alas! alas!
>   Upon the skirts of human-nature dwelling
> Alone: I chant alone the holy mass,
>   While little sounds of life are round me knelling,

And glossy bees at noon do fieldward pass,
  And many a chapel bell the hour is telling,
Paining me through: those sounds grow strange to me,
  And thou art distant in Humanity . . .'   (305–12)

The sense is of a radical dislocation from the purposeful business of the working world. Chapel bells tell off the hours ('Paining me through' beautifully gives the swinging rhythm and metallic resonant thrill of the chimes), as bees pass 'fieldward' and the air is filled with 'little sounds of life'. But Lorenzo is at the margins of this activity, a passive and remote observer, like one who lies bed-bound in illness as the day passes outside the window. He dwells on 'the skirts of human-nature', and his increasing distance from humanity is insisted upon in the repetition of 'alone'. This isolation is not a negation of his living experience, but a logical extension of it; it dramatises the inward-looking and unsocial character of his relationship with Isabella.

But other features of the description of Lorenzo's ghost point in another direction. The ghost's incipient physical decay is rendered with a disconcerting directness; this ghost is also a body who has been lying buried in the ground:

It was a vision. – In the drowsy gloom,
  The dull of midnight, at her couch's foot
Lorenzo stood, and wept: the forest tomb
  Had marr'd his glossy hair which once could shoot
Lustre into the sun, and put cold doom
  Upon his lips, and taken the soft lute
From his lorn voice, and past his loamed ears
Had made a miry channel for his tears.   (273–80)

This is in fact a more physically present Lorenzo than Isabella had been used to receive 'at her couch's foot'. The reality of his body is now eerily inescapable, with its 'glossy hair', 'loamed ears', and face streaked through the mud with channels cut by tears. The full force of Keats's opening account of the conventionally sentimental courtship can now emerge. For it involved a denial of the body, of the physical and sensual basis of their attraction. Now that the real physical body is dead, the reality of love's sensory basis is cruelly brought home to Isabella. A strong erotic charge enters the poem only in Isabella's half-deranged and obsessive efforts to recover the corpse:

She gaz'd into the fresh-thrown mould, as though
  One glance did fully all its secrets tell;

Clearly she saw, as other eyes would know
    Pale limbs at bottom of a crystal well;
Upon the murderous spot she seem'd to grow,
    Like to a native lily of the dell:
Then with her knife, all sudden, she began
To dig more fervently than misers can.

Soon she turn'd up a soiled glove, whereon
    Her silk had play'd in purple phantasies,
She kiss'd it with a lip more chill than stone,
    And put it in her bosom, where it dries
And freezes utterly unto the bone
    Those dainties made to still an infant's cries:
Then 'gan she work again; nor stay'd her care,
But to throw back at times her veiling hair.

That old nurse stood beside her wondering,
    Until her heart felt pity to the core
At sight of such a dismal labouring,
    And so she kneeled, with her locks all hoar,
And put her lean hands to the horrid thing:
    Three hours they labour'd at this travail sore;
At last they felt the kernel of the grave,
And Isabella did not stamp and rave.   (361–84)

There is a frank eroticism, in for example the line 'Her silk had play'd in purple phantasies' (where the embroidered glove Isabella recognises is endowed with the suggestive power of a sexual dream), which marks a decisive shift in the atmosphere of the poem. The reality of love and death is not now simply inescapable; Isabella's belated recognition of her sexual feeling for Lorenzo grotesquely exaggerates her own former illusions. Her 'infancy' has been 'school'd' (334); she has learned to understand something of herself, and her world, but much too late. And, coming so much too late, her understanding serves horribly to mock her, in a manner reminiscent of the ironies of Shakespeare's *Romeo and Juliet* (a play which haunts *Isabella* as much as it does *The Eve of St. Agnes*).

This dimension in the poem's thematic interests raises an interesting general question. The carefully ironised oppositions between the worlds of the lovers and the brothers can be shown to operate at a level of conscious and deliberated intention in the poem. But the representation of the relationship between Isabella and Lorenzo, on the other hand, opens up possibilities of interpretation which are less easily reconciled with notions of intentionality. A similar problem is raised, for instance, in the *Ode on a Grecian Urn*. In that poem a set of thematic polarities are established early in relation to the subjects represented on an imaginary Greek vase. The thematic polarities in question set a perfected, timeless, and unageing artistic representation of human experience against the fevered and ceaseless flux of real human experience in time and space. But the human experience upon which these polarities are made to pivot is an orgiastic scene of sexual struggle and pursuit (5–10) which raises questions that are at a tangent to the intentional programme of the poem. Keats's primary overt concern in the poem is with the differing claims and limitations of this experience in its reality, and in its representation; the poem is about the relationship between art and life. But the example chosen by Keats also emphatically posits ravishment of women by men as an intensely desirable and pleasurable experience, and in so doing the poem is obviously male in its orientation, and may legitimately strike non-sexist and especially women readers as in this respect offensive and blinkered.

Isabella offers a similar problem for readers. The palpable design of the poem is to offer a subtle, carefully qualified, and ironic juxtaposition of opposed modes of understanding. But the oppositions of the poem are further complicated for present-day readers by the possibilities of a feminist perspective, and these possibilities activate new and different possibilities of meaning within the designed possibilities of Keats's conception. The crucial element in this transforming new perspective is the ability to understand that there is a deep connectedness between the flaws within the relationship of the lovers – flaws which are recognised and dramatised by Keats – and the assumptions of the capitalist brothers. Lorenzo and Isabella both subordinate their mutual sexual feeling to a code of sexual behaviour and courtship. This code sentimentalises and disguises the motivating desire of the relationship and subdues it to forms which express the commodified status of the woman in sexual relations. Lorenzo plays the coy courtly lover, and Isabella too willingly goes along with the role of demure and passive object. But these roles in sexual conduct are in fact in the service of larger economic interests, where the making and sealing of marital alliances is closely bound up with financial and property deals. The brothers' motive in their murder is indeed specifically economic; they are alarmed by the possibility of a liaison which will interfere with their plans for Isabella in the market-place:

These brethren having found by many signs
    What love Lorenzo for their sister had,
And how she lov'd him too, each unconfines
    His bitter thoughts to other, well nigh mad
That he, the servant of their trade designs,
    Should in their sister's love be blithe and glad,
When 'twas their plan to coax her by degrees
To some high noble and his olive-trees.   (161–8)

This is not to suggest that there is anything false or specious in the
mutual attraction and love of Isabella and Lorenzo; but their feeling
is falsified, disguised from themselves, by codes of social behaviour
which have been shaped to the purposes of those social interests to
which they appear to be opposed. The strange, even bizarre tone of
the poem's closing stanzas then stands as a cruel exposure of the real
sexual experience which had been masked in the early courtship of
the lovers. Isabella loses her reason when she confronts the realities of
sex and death, but the conventions which had earlier blinded her to
those realities are actually operating to the advantage of her brothers
and their kind, who shape and control feeling to serve economic power.

Such a reading runs across the grain of the poem's thematic
orientation, but it is not precluded by it, nor does it involve us in any
falsification of the poem's rhetoric and organisation. This is a
crucially important feature of any reading which seeks to tease out or
expose possibilities of interpretation which are not present to the
conscious purposes of a poem. *Isabella*, like most of Keats's poetry,
seeks very successfully for carefully wrought effects and meanings;
meanings and effects beyond these meditated ones are certainly
possible, and indeed inevitably given the changing contexts and
histories of subsequent generations of readers.

But the fact that a poem's meanings will necessarily always change,
and grow, and be modified in the guts of the living, does not offer *carte
blanche* for readers. New meanings remain circumscribed by the
possibilities to which the verbal facts and formal organisation of a
poem limit interpretation. These determining limits of interpretation
may be helpfully characterised by reference to the work of Roland
Barthes. In a brilliant essay 'The Struggle with the Angel', first
published in 1971, Barthes sketches a distinction between 'structural'
and 'textual' analysis which can yield very useful perspectives in the
consideration of critical practice. By 'structural' analysis Barthes
means analysis of those units of a text, and the relations between

them, which remain constant in otherwise widely diverse interpretations. We might think, for example, of the structural features of Keats's *Isabella* as including in Barthes's sense the opposition, on both stylistic and thematic levels, between the lovers and the brothers. This would include questions of local aesthetic quality such as diction and rhythm. But these structural features, once recognised and established in their proper presence for analysis, then themselves become interpretative counters in what Barthes terms 'textual' analysis. Barthes describes his conception of 'textual' analysis as follows:

Such an analysis endeavours to 'see' each particular text in its difference – which does not mean in its ineffable individuality, for this difference is 'woven' in familiar codes; it conceives the text as taken up in an *open* network which is the very infinity of language, itself structured without closure; it tries to say no longer *from where* the text comes (historical criticism), nor even *how* it is made (structural analysis), but how it is unmade, how it explodes, disseminates – by what coded paths it *goes off*.[4]

This sense of 'textual' analysis enables us to think of interpretation as virtually limitless in practice through time, and yet also always necessarily responsible to those 'structural' features – '*how* [the poem] is made' – upon which widely divergent modes of reading can still agree. We can then also recognise and honestly acknowledge that the reading of Keats, as of any seriously demanding poet, must answer to the conscious artistry, the presence of the poet to his or her own creation, which makes reading a discipline as well as a focus for interpretation.

Such honest acknowledgements must then make a difference to the status of our interpretations. The reading of *Isabella* which has here been proposed seeks to find an implicit representation in the poem of conventions for expressing love and sexual feeling which are unwittingly complicit with the economic and social realities to which they appear to be opposed. But it can be argued that the controlling intelligence of the poem's rhetorical organisation does not itself countenance this meaning. Indeed, it is by virtue of its silence effectively at odds with it. Keats does not represent the relationship that we can yet discern in his materials, given the different emphases and history of our experience as readers of his poetry. We are, in short, *in dialogue* with Keats's poetry. We should therefore allow always for the possibility that, while new theoretical frameworks may point to possibilities and contradictions in the poetry, the poetry also has the power to realise possibilities, and to expose contradictions and limits, within our theoretical framework.

NOTES

1 *William Morris: Romantic to Revolutionary* (London, 1977), 11.
2 Nicholas Roe (ed.), *William Wordsworth. Selected Poetry* (London, 1992), 189–92.
3 Jerome McGann (ed.), *Lord Byron: The Complete Poetical Works* (7 vols., Oxford, 1980–93) ii. 9.
4 *Image–Music–Text*, trans. S. Heath (London, 1977), 126–7.

CHAPTER 7

Keats, fictionality, and finance: The Fall of Hyperion

Terence Allan Hoagwood

'. . . I, Moneta, left supreme
Sole priestess of his desolation'
The Fall of Hyperion, I. 226–7

The substitutive symbolism of monetary form was a theme widespread in the economic literature of Keats's times. Adam Smith's *Wealth of Nations* (1776) had contended that 'labour was the first price . . . that was paid for all things', and the point was reaffirmed in 1817 by David Ricardo's observation that the value of a commodity rests not upon the money paid for it, but rather the material labour exacted by its production. Also in 1817, William Cobbett argued that paper money was a mere inscription that no longer purported to represent the substantial values of gold or silver; indeed, Cobbett made an explicit comparison with religious symbol-systems, and suggested that a demystification of paper finance was crucially necessary.[1]

These formulations were familiar to Keats from frequent discussions in the columns of the *Examiner*. In the paper-money economy of the depressed post-Waterloo years, speculative capital increased and, as it did so, the relation between the derivative fiction (money) and the foundational praxis (labour) became antagonistic and contradictory. A financial theory of illusion emerged as forms of monetary value were shown to be fictitious – encoding, as it were, a symbolic interval: the fictitious term of the dyad (money) was treated pejoratively as an illusion; the materiality of productive action lamented as absent and lost.

Keats writes frequently in his letters and poems about money worries but the larger importance of this financial semiotic extends beyond the poet's biography. Keats's works reproduce the signifying form of the illusionistic dyad: a fictive term purports to designate an absent substance. Keats's poems question this relationship, however, and the use of signifiers detached (like paper money) from absent realities. At the level of topic and theme, K. K. Ruthven, Daniel P.

Watkins, and Marjorie Levinson have argued for the importance of money in the symbolism of Keats's poems.[2] This essay's reading of the *Fall of Hyperion* suggests that patterns of surrogation within the poem repeat, paradigmatically, the symbolic action of cash as a token, a sign whose meaning presents the absence of the real. Intentionally or otherwise, Keats writes poems situated in a symbolic economy.

To appreciate the special use Keats makes of everyday figures of language, it is useful to recognise those figures which were current in the language of the day. To read *After dark vapours have oppressed our plains*, for example, in context with the *Ode on a Grecian Urn* will reveal different meanings from those which emerge when one reads the poem in the context of Hunt's political journalism, the poem's immediate frame on its original appearance.

The *Examiner* for 19 January 1817 included an unsigned article, 'Mr Pitt – Finance – Sinking Fund', which was in large part a review of *An Inquiry Concerning . . . the National Debt., by Dr Hamilton*. The article, like the book, argued that when the 'Sinking Fund' borrowed what it paid, compound interest was 'a mere hypothesis'. This contention about financial fictions was linked to the topic of political crisis; an angry population had been 'transformed into paupers', and the people were 'indignant at the change' (36–7). A month later the *Examiner* for 23 February 1817 printed an article entitled 'Friends of Revolution. – Taxation' in which an important figure appeared: government administrators were said to 'have torn the nation from its base, rooted up the sturdy peasant from his native soil, and left him to wither on its surface' (113). The *Examiner*'s economic point was reinforced by the fact that the harvests of 1815 and 1816 had been poor. The article continued by defining a popular, nostalgic response to this crisis: 'when goaded into the perception of a necessity for alteration, [the people] almost always sanctify some *past* period in their imagination' (113). So compensatory phantasies were said to arise from present oppressions. The machinery of that oppression included financial fictions: the administrators who uproot the peasant have 'dealt in phantoms and fictions, – imaginary capital' (113). Paper money and national debt were parts of a scheme that was understood at the time to generate nostalgic yearnings for an imaginary past.

A recurrent theme in the *Examiner*'s columns was the critique of empty language: on 9 March 1817, for instance, Hunt ridiculed Castlereagh's use of metaphor ('the people will not turn their backs on themselves'; 145). Furthermore, the *Examiner* was frequently explicit in drawing analogies between verbal art and the wiles of political and economic deception: 'It is really too much for such tremendous tragedians [i.e., the authors of the current economic crisis], such enactors of war, famine, and desolation, to turn round upon their victims for insinuation that the Dramatis Personae might be amended' (23 February 1817, 114). Metaphor and mythic allusions were assimilated with the machinery of 'imaginary capital' and real afflictions, while the 'mistiness' of state rhetoric was identified by the *Examiner* as appropriate to 'an experienced Pythoness' (a mystic or soothsayer).

As well as treating politics as art, the *Examiner* also politicised poems: 'Demanders of Constitutional Reform . . . You are descendants of CHAUCER . . . who was a Reformer in his day, and set his face both against priestly and kingly usurpation'; 'you are descendants of MILTON, who vindicated your ancestors the "People of England" against the pedantic hirelings of despotism'. 'Statesman who were worthy to guide an intellectual people' were, according to the *Examiner*, 'masters of the language' (9 March 1817, 145). Enemies of the people, by contrast, misused language and, like Castlereagh, framed bad metaphors.

The same issue of the *Examiner* addressed political and economic affairs and mingled these with various poetical concerns. It contained articles which discussed the Habeas Corpus Suspension Bill and the Seditious Meetings Bill, petitions for reform, the demise of the crown, 'Irish Lunatic Poor', 'rioting among the Colliers', 'disturbances . . . expected to take place at Manchester', 'the Unfunded Debt in Exchequered Bills', and also published two poems by Keats – *To Haydon with a Sonnet Written on Seeing the Elgin Marbles* and *On Seeing the Elgin Marbles*. The *Examiner* for 16 February 1817 sustained this mixture of politics and poetry, accompanying 'A Warning to Men of Rank and Fortune' with Keats's sonnet *To Kosciusko* which compares the leader of the armed rebellion in Poland with King Alfred (who was shortly afterwards noticed by Hunt as an ancestor in the cause of English liberty; 2 March 1817, 129). The *Examiner* for 23 February 1817 reproduced the text of an 'infamous placard' which proclaimed that 'The Regent must be put aside for the advancement of the general good' and called for the death of 'Caesar' (124). The same page included an article entitled 'Military Torture' and Keats's sonnet, *After dark vapours have oppressed our plains*. The *Examiner* for 25

May 1817 included an article about the trial of Thomas Jonathan Wooler for alleged libel in his periodical, *The Black Dwarf* (366); an article contending that the current system of parliamentary representation was founded on 'noon-day bribery and corruption, in maintaining large expenditures and standing armies' (322); and a review of *Poems by John Keats* (345).

To facilitate funding of the war, the government adopted a monetary policy founded in the illusionistic dyad of fictive paper and absent referent. By the Restriction Act of 1797, the government had abolished the gold standard; currency remained without the gold standard (like a signifier without a signified) until 1821. Reformers who opposed the war also opposed the machinery of debt, but larger meanings were involved in their opposition as well. Following a similar line of argument to the *Examiner*, in *A Philosophical View of Reform* Shelley said that 'the rich . . . have invented this scheme [i.e., public credit and the national debt] that they may rule by fraud'. And in 1817 Ricardo wrote that 'in all rich countries, there is a number of men forming what is called the monied class; these men are engaged in no trade, but live on the interest of their money, which is employed in discounting bills, or in loans to the more industrious part of the community'.[3] Money, which arose as a signifier, eventually counted as value itself – its meaning severed from its referent.

Such a form of value is literally fabricated, which is to say fictitious (*fictus* = 'fabricated' or 'shaped'). To fund the war, Shelley wrote, the government has 'fabricated pieces of paper'; 'at the bottom it is all trick'. Here Shelley followed Cobbett, who pointed out that 'the Bank Company . . . at no time could have in hand gold and silver enough to pay off *all* their notes at once'; no substance was necessary, however, 'as long as the people regarded those notes as being equally good with gold and silver'. '"Public credit," as it is called . . . may more properly be called *The credit of bank notes*' or 'SUSPICION ASLEEP.' Existing merely 'in name', paper money is like a word without a referent.[4] In Keats's time, as we have seen, paper money generated a debate about the nature of credit, which extended to all imaginary systems including religion and poetry.

Marx wrote that 'value . . . presents itself as an independent substance, endowed with a motion of its own . . . [I]nstead of simply representing the relations of commodities, it enters now, so to say, into relations with itself.' As Gilles Deleuze and Felix Guattari explain, money paid to a worker is valued by the worker in relation to goods and services; but the money in the profit column of a commercial or investment firm is valued there only in relation to the money-form itself.[5] In the arguments of Cobbett, Shelley, and Marx, the social and political consequences of this development are important, but at a higher level of thought the realisation emerges that the paper-money system is a self-perpetuating illusion.

The arguments of Ricardo, Cobbett, and others during the Regency suggested that money was involved with a regression in semiotic substitutions: all money is funny money, false coin. The money-flow was a flux of surrogates without foundation in reality. Paper money and credit economy amounted to windmill-giants; Will-o'-the-wisps. To use John Locke's estimate of figurative applications of words, these are 'perfect cheats'.[6] I will argue below that, apart from Keats's references *to* money in the *Fall of Hyperion*, symbolic substitution is inherent to the process of that poem. It is a sequence of surrogates; a chain of figures; metaphors of metaphors; ultimately, a dream within a dream. The narrator's attendant anxiety about delusion and vacancy is a related and important theme. Before illustrating my case from the poem, it may be helpful to reconsider, from Keats's own statements, how these forms of thought and language, from the discourse of money, appear in his ordinary, informal writing – in his letters.

The discourse of money often enters Keats's letters in rhetorical figures. For example, he writes to John Hamilton Reynolds (3 February 1818): 'Every man has his speculations, but every man does not brood and peacock over them till he makes a false coinage and deceives himself' (*Letters*, i. 223). Keats is referring to the philosophical poetry of 'Wordsworth &c', but one should not overlook the wider implications of the term 'false coinage'. The tenor of 'false coinage' is self-deception, and a comparable thought about poetry appears with the metaphor of money in Keats's letter to Benjamin Bailey of 13 March 1818: 'I am sometimes so very sceptical as to think Poetry itself a mere Jack a lanthern to amuse whoever may chance to be struck with its brilliance – As Tradesmen say every thing is worth what it will fetch, so probably every mental pursuit takes its reality and worth from the ardour of the pursuer – being in itself a nothing' (*Letters*, i. 242). This passage assimilates to the fictional symbolism of money not only poetry but likewise the structure of 'every mental pursuit'; and money is said to be 'in itself a nothing', though, as Ricardo pointed out, in its fictitious autonomy it is the *only* valued measure among 'Tradesmen'.

Keats's letters use both money and religion as representative examples of deceptive structure and exploitative fictions. To Reynolds he writes (3 May 1818) of Milton:

In his time englishmen were just emancipated from a great superstition – and Men had got hold of certain points and resting places in reasoning which were too newly born to be doubted . . . Protestantism was considered under the immediate eye of heaven, and its own remaining Dogmas and superstitions, then, as it were, regenerated, constituted those resting places and seeming sure points of Reasoning . . .   (*Letters*, i. 281–2)

In a treatise which Keats seems to have known, Holbach had also written of Christianity as 'superstition', using the word 'fanatic' to describe the mental operation of Christians 'deluding themselves by force of allegories, subtilities, commentaries, and forced interpretations'.[7] Apart from the specific content of Keats's and Holbach's remarks, I would point out their shared metaphors of the false front, the delusive image, mere fictions. For each of them, dogma amounted to a false coinage.

In the letter in which Keats first mentions writing the *Fall of Hyperion* (to George and Georgiana Keats, 16 December 1818–4 January 1819), he returns to these topics again summarising his view of the world as 'people think of nothing but money-getting' (*Letters*, ii. 14). Later in the same letter, Keats copies out two quotations from the 1818 *Examiner*, firstly Hazlitt's review of Godwin's *St Leon* and, specifically, Hazlitt's observations on the 'tormenting' effects of riches and 'the desert of society' (*Letters*, ii. 24–5). He then transcribes his own poem, *Bards of passion and of mirth*, which intimates a kind of socialised and naturalised immortality belonging to writers:

> Thus ye live on Earth and then
> On the Earth ye live again . . .
> Here your earth born souls still speak
> To mortals of the little week
> They must sojourn with their cares . . .

Unwelcome 'cares' were constraining his own productivity, as his letter makes clear. '[W]ith respect to my livelihood I will not write for it', he says to Haydon on 8 March 1819 (*Letters*, ii. 43). Later that year, however, he mentions (in a letter to John Taylor, 23 August) that he and Brown 'have together been engaged (this I should wish to remain secret) in a Tragedy [*Otho the Great*] which I have just finish'd; and from which we hope to share moderate Profits' (*Letters*, ii. 143).

When Keats writes of money specifically, he does so in ways that (like the 'false coinage' metaphor) entail illusion and deception. One episode that runs across a sequence of letters to Benjamin Robert Haydon, for example, is both sad and instructive. On 22 December 1818 he writes of his own willingness to provide money for Haydon, as a loan; 'but let me be the last stay – ask the rich lovers of art first . . . I have a little money which may enable me to study and to travel three or four years – I never expect to get any thing by my Books . . . Try the long purses' (*Letters*, i. 415). In the event, he did not have even the 'little money' he had thought he possessed. In January 1819 he writes to Haydon again: 'I shall have a little trouble in procuring the Money and a great ordeal to go through'; he adds, 'I do not think I shall ever come to the rope or the Pistol' (*Letters*, ii. 32) – but he is, as that sentence shows, *thinking* of suicide, and that rhetorical fact alone may indicate something about the seriousness of the expected 'ordeal'.

Keats's explanation appears in his letter to Haydon, 18 February 1819: 'What I should have lent you ere this if I could have got it, was belonging to poor Tom [his brother, who had recently died] – and the difficulty is whether I am to inherit it before my Sister is of age' (*Letters*, ii. 40). Further comments appear in the letter of 13 April 1819: 'When I offered you assistance I thought I had it in my hand . . . [there are now] difficulties . . . affairs being still in a Law[y]er's hand . . . I cannot do two things at once, and thus this affair has stopped my pursuits in every way'. '[M]y accounts are entirely in my Guardians Power', he goes on, 'I find myself possessed of much less than I thought', and adds that he is 'hurt at the slight[l]y rep[r]oachful tone of your note' (*Letters*, ii. 54–5). His mistaken belief that he had money when in fact he had none, and the merely conventional means by which it was kept from him (having to do with nominal guardians and legal fictions) were painfully joined for Keats in his deceptive offer of aid to Haydon. He had not *meant* to deceive Haydon, nor had he meant his inscribed promise to be false coin; but so it was.

Sometimes Keats's treatments of figurality and fictitiousness involve the common topic of social codes and the necessary suppressions conducive to 'good manners': 'The notions of Society will not permit a Parson to give way to his temper in any shape . . . He is continually acting' (*Letters*, ii. 63). His letters also treat both military enterprise and religion as instances of deception: 'The soldier who is cheated into an esprit du corps – by a red coat, a Band and Colours for the purpose of nothing – is not half so pitiable as the Parson who is led by the nose by the Bench of Bishops . . . a poor necessary subaltern of the Church' (*Letters*, ii. 63). Keats's treatments of politics characteristically elaborate a theme of subterfuge and its power over mental formations; for example, 'These Reviews too are getting more and more powerful and especially the Quarterly – They are like a superstition . . . I was in hopes that when people saw, as they must do now, all the trickery and iniquity of these Plagues they would scout them, but no they are like the spectators at the Westminster cock-pit' (*Letters*, ii. 65).

Like money, therefore, religion and politics are thus exposed and demystified in Keats's letters; as Cobbett had written in 1817, some 'seem to regard the Bank of England as being as old as the Church of England, at least, and some of them appear to have full as much veneration for it'.[8] It is the form of this suspicion, however, rather than its topical reference, which seems to me most important for a critical understanding of Keats's poems: 'they are very shallow people who take every thing literal [.] A Man's life of any worth is a continual allegory – and very few eyes can see the Mystery of his life – a life like the scriptures, figurative' (*Letters*, ii. 67). The mix of 'figurative' semantics with theory of value ('worth') recurs in Keats's poetry, which I now approach via some contemporary histories of writing and figurality.

The opening phrase of the *Fall of Hyperion* – 'Fanatics have their dreams' – refers to the discourse of political philosophy, as what is said of 'dreams' would indicate: with them, fanatics 'weave . . . a sect'. Psychological as well as cultural phenomena are mentioned, when 'the savage too' guesses about heaven according to 'the loftiest fashion of his sleep' (I. 3–4). The topic of writing is raised: the fanatic and the savage 'have not/ Trac'd upon vellum or wild Indian leaf/ The shadows of melodious utterance' (I. 4–6). Written fictions may be absent in primitive cultures, but other fictive formations are apparent nonetheless: 'every man whose soul is not a clod/ Hath visions' (I. 13–14). In the dream-form, the writing-form, and the consciousness-form, fictiveness may be said to occur because in each case images are fabricated.

In his *Outlines of an Historical View of the Progress of the Human Mind*, Condorcet, in sketching the historical progress of the human mind in ten epochs, had defined the third epoch as 'the Progress of Mankind from the Agricultural State to the invention of Alphabetical Writing'. At that stage of societal development, Condorcet said, a need is felt for a mode of communicating ideas to those absent and 'of stating, in a way less liable to change, those respected customs to which the members of any society agree to submit their conduct.' The art of writing was invented as an image-forming activity: first, 'absolute painting, to which succeeded a conventional painting . . . Afterwards, by a kind of metaphor . . . the image of a physical object became expressive of moral ideas. The origin of those signs, like the origin of words, were liable in time to be forgotten; and writing became the art of affixing signs of convention to every idea.'[9] Representation, or image-substitution, is the buried act, contrived to preserve customs but rendered invisible when it becomes customary.

Among the Encyclopedists, Holbach explained that the writing of customs involved codifying institutions: 'History points out to us the most famous legislators as men, who . . . first gave to nations their Gods – their worship', with forms of 'theology, of jurisprudence, of mysteries, etc.' As with Keats's fanatical sect-former, 'the entire of nature, as well as all of its parts, was personified' by primitive leaders who were sovereigns and priests: 'Here then is the great macrocosm, the mighty whole, the assemblage of things, adored and deified by the philosophers of antiquity, whilst the uninformed stopped at the emblem under which this nature was depicted, at the symbols under which its various parts, its numerous functions were personified'.[10]

Figurality is not only a personal or mental phenomenon; it is also a social and political act, and it is in these respects that figurality is itself thematised in the *Fall of Hyperion*. The practice of inscription is historical in its consequences as well as its origins. Blake (on plate 11 of *The Marriage of Heaven and Hell*) and Shelley (in *A Defence of Poetry*) also suggest that this activity of forming symbolic images is historically connected with the establishment of religions and law. Holbach writes, for example, about an important mythic parallel for the *Fall of Hyperion*: the 'fable of the . . . *rebellious angels*', a story whose punitive theme is imposed on 'the ignorant multitude' who credit its authoritarian morality.[11]

The *Fall of Hyperion* encloses its fiction within two frames: the narrator's dream of Moneta, and her narrative of the fallen gods. The poem's narrator is uncertain whether the dream whose content will constitute the narrative 'Be poet's or fanatic's' (I. 16–17). In this case, the generic apparatus of the dream-vision has added significance: it helps to extend the trope of symbol-formation, and suggests that the related problems of fictionality and delusion pertain to (extra-poetic) history. Like the works of Holbach (and other Encyclopedists) and Condorcet (and other ideologists), the poem treats the problem of delusion in terms of cultural and even institutional history.

Inside the frame of the dream, all of the narrative content is the poet's vision of Moneta. As Ruthven has pointed out, 'Moneta' means 'money', according to accounts of mythology that Keats knew. In *The Pantheon* (1698), Andrew Tooke showed that Moneta is another name for Juno, treasurer for the Olympians, while Robert Burton's *The Anatomy of Melancholy* defined 'Moneta' as 'Queen Money, to whom we daily offer sacrifice, which steers our hearts, hands, affections, all: that most powerful goddess, by whom we are reared, depressed, elevated'.[12] The modern word 'money' derives from the Latin *moneta*, 'mint', 'coin', 'money', the origin of which appears from the fact that the ancient Romans minted their coins in the temple of Juno Moneta. These lexical details are important for interpreting the *Fall of Hyperion*, though I do not think that *any* symbol in the poem is susceptible to flat allegorical equivalence. The poem is preoccupied with the *action* of fabricating imagery and with paradigms of delusion. Money furnishes a central cluster of images in the poem; money constituted an important case of figural trickery in the social world in which Keats lived and worked, and it works within the poem to represent the structures of deception, and not *only* particular economic facts.

The first paragraph of the narrative (after the opening reflections about poetry and fanaticism) begins with the uncertainty of 'Methought I stood' (I. 19). The exotic description which follows is tentative and conditional, as for example in the brief allusions to myth: the figment of fruit 'seem'd refuse of a meal/ By angel tasted, or our mother Eve' (I. 29–31). Likewise, the 'fabled horn' and 'Proserpine' are mentioned only as hypothetical analogies (I. 35, 37). When the narrator confesses that the 'transparent juice' which he drank 'is parent of my theme' (I. 42, 46), he emphasises the artificial generation of the entire poem, as it is said to be drug-induced (the narrator compares 'Asian poppy' (I. 47), 'poison' (I. 49), and 'elixir fine/ Of the soon fading jealous caliphat' (I. 47–8)). The 'full draught' induces a 'cloudy swoon', when the speaker falls into a profound trance within his own dream, 'sunk/ Like a Silenus on an antique vase' (I. 46, 55–6). The narrator does not awaken in a different scene, but dreams that he does. The fair illusory 'trees were gone' (I. 59), but of course they were never actually present. He finds a 'domed monument', the temple of Moneta, whose associations with material treasure are emphasised by biblical allusion: 'in that place the moth could not corrupt' (I. 71, 75), alluding to Matthew 6.19, where Matthew quotes Jesus Christ's metaphor of the corrupting moth in his warning about earthly treasure. The surrounding imagery is opulent: 'Robes, golden tongs, censer, and chafing dish,/ Girdles, and chains, and holy jewelries' (I. 79–80). A little further on, the narrator hears a voice: 'If thou canst not ascend/ These steps, die on that marble where thou art' (I. 107–8). The steps which the narrator ascends lead to the 'horned shrine' of Money. And at this point another mythic parallel is mentioned in the allusion to Jacob's vision of a ladder that reached to heaven': 'I mounted up,/ As once fair angels on a ladder flew/ From the green turf to heaven' (I. 137, 134–6).

The ironic juxtaposition of money's shrine and heaven in this passage also had an important function in contemporary political iconography: to mention one striking example, James Gillray's engraving, *Confederated Coalition: – or, The Giants storming Heaven, with the Gods alarmed for their everlasting abodes* (1804), shows Charles James Fox leading the rebel angels in an attack, with cannon, on the besieged treasury; Gillray used a line from *Paradise Lost* as an epigraph: 'Not to destroy! but root them out of Heaven' (VI. 855).[13] Conventionally 'heaven' may function iconographically as 'royalty', and 'earth' as the ruled multitudes. As Henry More, a contemporary of Milton's at Cambridge, explained, '*Ascending into Heaven* signifies the Acquisition or Increase of Political Dignities and Honours.'[14]

In the shrine of Money, the dreaming narrator is told that those who 'find a haven' in the world, where they enjoy a 'thoughtless sleep', rot when they come to the shrine of Moneta (I. 151–3). Ironically, Moneta, Goddess of Money (who remembers the fall of the Titans) advises the dreamer to beware of illusory surfaces and to 'think of the earth' (I. 169). Indeed, historical change is one of the poem's subjects – not a specific example of change (e.g., the French Revolution; the rise and fall of Napoleon), and not merely the *concept* of change (as in Spenser's *Two Cantos of Mutabilitie* (1609)), but rather the process of historical change itself.

Moneta emphasises the violence of historical change when she refers to 'the thunder of a war' fought by 'giant hierarchy/ Against rebellion' (I. 222–4). Her role in this violent overthrow – the role of Queen Money – is stated explicitly: she shows the narrator an image of the fallen king, and says, 'I, Moneta, [am] left supreme/ Sole priestess of his desolation' (I. 226–7). Whether Queen Money's account of revolutionary change is adequate or not, it enjoyed considerable currency in Keats's lifetime. The replacement of a hierarchy of inherited nobility by a new regime of acquired wealth was an acknowledged historical change of great magnitude and with markedly violent effects.

As I have emphasised, the poem does not settle into topical reference. It thematises its own fictionality in ways that complicate a quest for a positive reference, as for example when the narrator 'aches' to see 'what high tragedy/ In the dark secret chambers of her skull/ Was acting' (I. 276–9). The tale of the gods is seen in her head, and not in the world. Further, even on the screen of consciousness, it is a fictitious *enactment* of an event, and not the event itself. Moneta reminds the dreamed image of a narrator that what he sees are simulacra: 'the scenes/ Still swooning vivid through my globed brain . . . Thou shalt with those dull mortal eyes behold' (I. 244–7). For the narrator the prospect of gazing on the inner scenes of Moneta's brain is described in terms of earthly wealth and exploitation that identify the dreamer as a devotee of Milton's Mammon (*Paradise Lost* I. 678–90):

> . . . As I had found
> A grain of gold upon a mountain's side,
> And twing'd with avarice strain'd out my eyes
> To search its sullen entrails rich with ore.   (I. 271–4)

After their visionary transportation to 'the shady sadness of a vale' (I. 294), Moneta says of the spectacle that she displays for the narrator: 'So Saturn sat/ When he had lost his realms' (I. 301). Symbolic recapitulation is doubled here, because, having seen an 'old image' of Saturn (I. 224), the narrator is with Moneta transported in vision to a vale where he sees

> . . . an image huge,
> Like to the image pedestal'd so high
> In Saturn's temple.   (I. 298–300)

The language denotes similitude, not proper existence. The scene displayed by Moneta is consequently a figment which *represents* what is not there: Saturn is absent from the spectacle of Saturn, which was –

paradoxically – exactly how the realmless Titan had described his own fallen state in *Hyperion*:

> ' – I am gone
> Away from my own bosom: I have left
> My strong identity, my real self,
> Somewhere between the throne, and where I sit
> Here on this spot of earth.' (I. 112–16)

In *The Fall of Hyperion*, the 'Unsceptred' monarch (I. 324) is addressed by Thea in words we never hear,

> . . . words, which in our feeble tongue
> Would come in this-like accenting; how frail
> To that large utterance of the early Gods! (I. 351–3)

Instead, we are offered a translation the inadequacy of which is emphasised even before it is uttered (I. 354–63). The translation of Thea's speech articulates a pattern that is common to several recent usurpations, including the troubled governments of revolutionary France, the career of Napoleon, or the restored monarchs of Europe. But it is this common pattern, and not a single example, which is the passage's larger reference: 'thy sharp lightning in unpracticed hands/ Scorches and burns our once serene domain' (I. 364–5).

Language shifts from ostensive reference into similitude: referring to Thea's speech, the narrator says:

> As when, upon a tranced summer night,
> Forests, branch-charmed by the earnest stars,
> Dream, and so dream all night, without a noise,
> Save from one gradual solitary gust,
> Swelling upon the silence; dying off;
> As if the ebbing air had but one wave;
> So came these words, and went . . . (I. 372–8)

This breathtaking passage is evidently offered as a complex figure of speech; but, further, within the sentence the propositional content is fantasy (forests cannot literally be said to dream). The tenor is fantastic, as well as the vehicle. Elsewhere, characters are likened to artefacts and simulacra: Saturn is 'motionless,/ Like sculpture' (I. 382–3). When Saturn speaks, he articulates a Lucretian naturalism (I. 418–24), after which the narrator again emphasises his earthly (rather than ideal) reference: 'Methought I heard some old man of the earth/ Bewailing earthly loss' (I. 440–1). This instance of narrated supposition is followed by a return to the topic of writing, which closes the first canto of the poem:

> . . . she spake on,
> As ye may read who can unwearied pass
> Onward from the antichamber of this dream,
> Where even at the open doors awhile
> I must delay, and glean my memory
> Of her high phrase . . .   (I. 463–8)

Canto II of *The Fall of Hyperion* opens with a direct reference to metaphoric construction:

> 'Mortal, that thou may'st understand aright,
> I humanize my sayings to thine ear,
> Making comparisons of earthly things;
> Or thou might'st better listen to the wind,
> Whose language is to thee a barren noise,
> Though it blows legend-laden through the trees.'   (II. 1–6)

The phrase, 'Making comparisons of earthly things', need not translate upward into the ideal forms of Platonic or Spenserian symbolism. It can translate downward, naming the figural act itself, the practice of using poetry to represent 'earthly loss'.

The interpretative point is not wholly a question of whether mythological symbols have terrestrial referents. The process of the poem is functional as a meaning, no less than its narrative content. Just before the second canto breaks off, a recollection of the earlier *Hyperion* appears, when at line 50 'Mnemosyne' is mentioned in place of 'Moneta' (a similar instance appears at I. 331). From this point onward, the narrative content of the poem overlaps with that of the earlier *Hyperion*. Among the changes in the development of the *Fall of Hyperion* from the earlier fragment, *Hyperion*, I would suggest that the most important are these: the frame enclosing the narrative of the fallen hierarchy within a specified and limited point of view, and the enclosure of the dream to remove the narrative to yet another level of figurality. The hermeneutics of earthly reference (the specification that the mythographic action is like 'earthly loss') is also new to the later version.

The critical preoccupation with figurality is not unique to the *Fall of Hyperion*, nor is the location of the money-symbol as a crucial case, even a governing case, of figural substitution. Despite the individualising and aestheticising tendencies that have been ascendant in Keats studies since Arnold's and Pater's appreciations of his poetry, the great poems of Keats's last years all tend to enact in their figural substitutions the crises of conflict, displacement, illusion, and violent change which sometimes furnish even the manifest content of their narrative surface. In those cases in which Keats evidently portrays historical substitutions (as in *Otho the Great*), and in those cases where historical substitution is evidently occurring *without* such intentional control (as in the confusion of earlier Mnemosyne with later Moneta), surrogation, and consequently interpretive substitution, appear in the foreground of the poetic works themselves.

The fictionality of the money-form is centrally important in the poems' contextual field, I would suggest, not only as a salient figure within the poems' narrative action and reference, but likewise as a paradigm of symbolic substitution, which is at once the poetry's mode of operation and also the meaning of *The Fall of Hyperion*. Through the money-form, that figurative operation removes the poetry from the magic circle of reductive specialisation (poetry *per se*); precisely because it treats critically the illusionistic dyad of presence and absence, Keats's work is in and of the world.

NOTES

1 See Smith, *An Inquiry into the Nature and Causes of the Wealth of Nations* (1776), ed. E. Cannan (2 vols., London, 1904) i. 32. Ricardo, *On the Principles of Political Economy and Taxation* (1817), in *The Works and Correspondence of David Ricardo*, ed. Piero Sraffa (9 vols., Cambridge, 1951) i. 11. Cobbett, *Paper Against Gold* (London, 1817), 8–9.

2 See Ruthven, 'Keats and *Dea Moneta*', *SIR* 15 (1975), 445–59; *KPP*, 156–76 (on *The Fall of Hyperion*); *KL*, 255–61 (on *Lamia*). Paul Hamilton, 'Keats and Critique', in Marjorie Levinson et al., *Rethinking Historicism: Critical Readings in Romantic History* (Oxford and New York, 1989), 127–32, suggests as part of a discussion of Keats an analogy between poetry and capital.

3 R. Ingpen and W. E. Peck (eds.), *The Complete Works of Percy Bysshe Shelley* (10 vols., London and New York, 1926–30) vii. 25. Ricardo, *Works*, i. 89.

4 Shelley, *Works*, vii. 27–8. Cobbett, *Paper*, 11, 14, 21.

5 Karl Marx, *Capital*, trans. Ernest Untermann (3 vols., New York, 1967) i. 154. Deleuze and Guattari, *Anti-Oedipus: Capitalism and Schizophrenia* (1972), trans. Robert Hurley, Mark Seem, and Helen R. Lane (Minneapolis, 1986), 226–31.

6 *An Essay Concerning Human Understanding*, ed. Alexander Campbell Fraser (2 vols., New York, 1959) ii. 146.

7 In 1819, Richard Carlile published (as the second volume in a series of pamphlets called *The Deist*) Paul-Henri Thiry, Baron d'Holbach's *Christianity Unveiled* (under an erroneous attribution to Boulanger). Carlile also published an edition of Paine's *Age of Reason*, for which he was imprisoned. On 14 February 1819, Keats mentions *The Deist* in a letter to George and Georgiana Keats; see *Letters*, ii. 62. The passage quoted is drawn from Carlile's text of *Christianity Unveiled; Being an Examination of the Principles and Effects of the Christian Religion, Translated from the French of Boulanger* (London, 1819). On 'the political effects of the Christian religion', see pp. 99 ff.; Holbach uses the word 'fanatics' p. 19 and *passim*.

8 Cobbett, *Paper*, 8.

9 *Outlines of an Historical View of the Progress of the Human Mind: Being a Posthumous Work of the Late M. de Condorcet. Translated from the French* (London, 1795), 8–9, 40.

10 *The System of Nature, or Laws of the Moral and Physical World* (1770), trans. H. D. Robinson (Boston, 1853), 175, 177, 179. This work first appeared in English translation (anonymous) in London in 1795.

11 Ibid., 184.

12 Tooke, *The Pantheon* (London, 1713; rpt. New York, 1976), 107–8; Burton, *The Anatomy of Melancholy* (Oxford, 1621; rpt. London, 1964) i. 65. Both Tooke and Burton are cited in connection with Moneta in the *Fall of Hyperion* by Ruthven, 'Keats and *Dea Moneta*', and *KPP*, 161–2.

13 The engraving is reproduced in *The Works of James Gillray* (1851; rpt. New York, 1968).

14 'A compendious Alphabet of certain Prophetick Schemes', *Synopsis Prophetica* (1664), in *The Theological Works of the Most Pious and Learned Henry More* (London, 1708), 536.

CHAPTER 8

'When this warm scribe my hand': writing and history in Hyperion and The Fall of Hyperion

Michael O'Neill

Too often invocations of 'history' in recent criticism of Romantic poetry accompany a banal demystification of poetic achievement. History, as ventriloquised by certain critics, does not seem able to help or pardon Romantic poems; rather, it is encouraged to weep crocodile tears over the poetry's alleged blindnesses, elitism, and negation of social realities. Pity Keats, pilloried by snobbish reviewers in his own life, now patronised by politically correct critics who think that systems of social relations hold a poet's pen, inscribing sombre, predictable secrets into texts.

The fact, for instance, that *Ode on a Grecian Urn* was originally printed in *Annals of the Fine Arts* (4 January 1820) does not indicate any simplistic belief, on Keats's part, in art for art's sake. Instead, *Ode on a Grecian Urn* poses its reader a central question: can the claim that art has significance outlasting a particular historical moment be justified? With a cunning peculiar to poetry, the poem does not so much make as include this claim; the urn, symbol of art and art's ambitions, is seen as just that – a symbol – at the start of the final stanza: 'O Attic shape! Fair attitude!' (41) cries the poet, pulling back from the previous stanza's involvement in irretrievable historical realities that art seems to come out of and gesture towards. The 'little town' whose 'streets for evermore/ Will silent be' is the 'desolate' twin of the urn's 'silent form' teasing 'us out of thought/ As doth eternity' (38–40, 44–5). The famous phrase – 'dost tease us out of thought' (44) – plays with a pair of meanings: the urn baffles thought, it takes us beyond mere reason.[1] It offers a likeness of 'eternity', its suppression of temporality both perplexing and intriguing.

One thing that teases out of thought in each of the senses just sketched is the fact that the 'historical realities' to which the urn might allude can only be imagined; it is the poet's questioning imagination which pursues the figures on the urn to the 'little town' where their 'real-life' counterparts are surmised as having lived. Art, on this reading, exists when history has been 'emptied' (37), a word which starts to resonate as soon as it is spoken. 'The last stanza enters stumbling on a pun', remarked Robert Bridges,[2] but the wry pseudo-punning conveys 'stumbling' semi-exasperation on Keats's part that something which is a question of 'shape' and 'attitude' has power, through the fact of its 'form', to 'tease us out of thought'.

Yet semi-exasperation passes into sobered recognition that though art cannot alter the facts of mortality and suffering it can remain 'a friend to man' (48). It does so by repeating its prevailing, unavailing message that '"Beauty is truth, truth beauty"' (49); here at least the urn's silence is violated, and an assertion offered which the poem cannot be reduced to nor divorced from. Set apart at the start of the line for maximum emphasis, the famous equation is also caught in the net of a syntax that links the utterance of an artefact to the fact of ongoing 'woe' (47). The poem debates in its own terms the relationship between art and history: the 'Cold pastoral' of art and the world of 'silence and slow time' which art incorporates within itself (45, 2). As a linguistic structure the poem mediates between the urn as 'Sylvan historian' (3) and 'history'. In doing so the poem half-frees itself from the limitations located in the sculptured urn. As it wonders about the urn's meanings and message, the poem enacts the struggles of consciousness and creates an illusion of presence and immediacy; the urn, by contrast, is opaquely other, teasing out of thought because apparently transcending the culture out of which it comes. *Ode on a Grecian Urn* is affecting because its protest against the artifice of art coexists with awareness that the poem, too, is an artefact, a product of 'breathing human passion' (28) perhaps, but destined to take on a life that fights free of a particular time and culture. Historical critics, like other critics, are fated to behave to the poem as the poem behaves to the urn; and as the urn resists the poem so the poem resists the critic, historical or otherwise. That the poem knows as much about itself is part of its achievement; the danger this essay seeks to avoid is of ignoring the insight into its procedures and nature of which a poem is capable.

Consequently, the purpose of this essay is not to deny the importance of 'history', but to explore the nature of Keats's imaginative involvement with writing and history, especially in *Hyperion* and *The Fall of Hyperion*, and to reassert the value of the terms Keats himself chose to express this involvement. The essay takes issue with two common and loaded uses of 'history'. The first has just been adumbrated: the view that history writes poetry – or, more precisely, that poetry's terms are misrepresentations of history, and need to be corrected by reference to some master code. 'We cannot take idealism at its own estimation of itself' writes Paul Hamilton with reference to Keats's poetry.[3] Hamilton's 'We' hoists a polemical flag, but the way 'idealism' is used as a synonym for 'poetry' causes disquiet. Hamilton treats conflicts in poetry as attention-seeking or attention-diverting devices: attention is sought for the poem's aesthetic status; attention is diverted from the poem's complicity in extra-poetic forces. He works his way towards the tendentious conclusion that the *Hyperions* engage in 'euphemistic betrayal of the historical fact that, within their aesthetic, criticism and creation, disownment and renewal, abandonment and progress have to take place in the same words, through the same effects, powered by the same talents, clenched in the same narratives'.[4] This critical narrative has its own clenched eloquence, as it seeks to implicate and vindicate, entrapping Keats's poetry even as it allows the poetry the capacity for self-critique. However, the sorrowful drama outlined by Hamilton is based on a disputable privileging of something he calls 'historical fact' over the poems' 'aesthetic': this privileging is disputable because it underplays the degree to which Hamilton's supposed historical fact is a critical fiction. I would urge the counter-truth (critical fiction) that poems often know fascinating things (a knowledge not simply reducible to 'critique' of their own procedures) about the relationship between history and poetry. Keats's thinking about 'history' is increasingly prepared to concede, and able to accommodate, perplexity. In *Endymion*, Book II, the opening passage shows a Keats for whom 'pageant history' is dismissed in favour of the poetic attempt to place 'Love's standard on the battlements of song' (II. 14, 41); there, the metaphor wrests its associations from 'the universe of deeds' (II. 15), thus implicitly acknowledging the force of history which Keats is explicitly denying. By the time of the *Hyperions* and the odes, Keats does not remain content with such naive, easily deconstructed oppositions; instead he works more meditatively, more aware, in the case of the odes, of the scope for 'lyric debate'.[5]

The second use of 'history' which this essay contests is amusingly described by Paul H. Fry as the practice of 'arranging a few beads like Peterloo, Pentridge, the Holy Alliance, and the arrest of Major Cartwright along the string of class conflict, and calling it history'.[6]

Such a method risks opportunism, as does the allied procedure of taking the lack of overt historical allusion as in itself historically significant. According to this latter approach, the truest political poetry often turns out to be that which feigns its lack of interest in politics. Absence is presence; the natural imagery of *To Autumn* is read as political code. Keats is either aestheticising social reality or using language that 'cannot finally exclude a negative historical actuality'.[7]

But such readings, however stimulating, refuse to see a poem as itself an occurrence of a particular kind, one which has an existence which may be resistant to causal explanation. The debate about the disturbances of 1819 and *To Autumn* frequently supposes that the poem must be in a dialectical, reflex, subordinate, or marginal relation to historical forces. Undoubtedly such forces prompted Keats's wish, expressed a few days after writing the poem, 'to put a Mite of help to the Liberal side of the Question before I die' (*Letters*, ii. 180). Set that statement beside the last stanza of the ode, though, and the limitations of contextualist readings declare themselves. True, the stanza turns its back on 'the songs of spring' (23), which could be interpreted as poems of political hope (such as Shelley's 'Ode to the West Wind', written a month later). Yet it would falsify the poem to see it as glorifying 'Englishness' in any chauvinist sense or as avoiding political involvement out of timidity. Keats would have read in the *Examiner* the previous month a leader entitled 'Lamented Irreligion of the Reformers', which pointed out that 'The French revolution is always used as a bugbear or Gorgon's head to petrify resistance of every sort' (8 August 1819, 498). In September he was 'much pleas'd with the present public proceedings' (*Letters*, ii. 180), referring to the reformers' responses to Peterloo. He was certainly in touch with current unrest and sympathetic to reform. But unless one takes the view that all human discourse is political in a partisan sense, what is most striking about the third stanza of *To Autumn* is its refusal to take sides, except the side of its own art, its own music, a music which is, miraculously, also on the side of the life it represents. Striking, too, as in all achieved poems is the way it obeys its own formal laws, laws which are not imposed on the language but emerge from it. Such a law is at work dictating the unexpected stress on 'bloom', which at once offsets and coalesces with 'soft-dying'; another such law shapes the bracing rhyme of 'mourn' and 'bourn', and endstops the line in which 'bourn' occurs (25, 27, 30), discouraging movement of the eye and mind beyond the scene and, in doing so, contrasting with the 'solitary thinkings; such as dodge/ Conception to the very bourne of heaven,/ Then leave the naked brain' in *Endymion* (I. 294–6). Keats's gaze takes on that 'steadfast' quality he yearns for in his *Bright star* sonnet; however, to watch 'with eternal lids apart,/ Like nature's patient, sleepless eremite' (*Bright star, would I were stedfast as thou art*, 3–4) requires, as the simile concedes, the resources of art and rhetoric. In *To Autumn* Keats looks at nature through the medium of art and discovers, by virtue of the intensity with which he handles his medium, a way of articulating a greeting of the spirit that is remarkable for its selflessness. Caught between the disagreeables of political agitation and personal crisis, the poet reaffirms the 'music' he is able to win from self-transcendence and contemplation. And he does so in a way that is locked into time ('and now', 31) yet transhistorical. Moreover, the stanza's celebration of 'music' (24) is alert to the cadences of mourning, attaining a composed acceptance of loss, presence, and change. And to this extent the poem – for all its resolute exclusion of opinion – connects with the letter-writer who a few months previously in his 'vale of Soul-making' letter had attacked naive doctrines of 'perfectibility' (*Letters*, ii. 102, 101).

Keats wrote *To Autumn* around 19 September 1819, mentioning the poem in a letter to John Hamilton Reynolds. The relevant section of the letter moves by associative leaps. After describing the autumn Keats goes on to let slip that he 'composed upon' the fact that 'Somehow a stubble plain looks warm – in the same way that some pictures look warm'; a quick eddy of self-deprecation ('I hope you are better employed than in gaping after weather') passes into a restrained hint of the poet's present mood ('I have been at different times so happy as not to know what weather it was'). He will not 'copy a parcel of verses', but switches to talk of Chatterton, whom he associates with autumn and whose 'genuine English Idiom in English words' serves as the springboard for an account of his reasons for giving up the *Hyperion* project (of which more below) (*Letters*, ii. 167). Keats's restlessness, his mixture of forthcomingness and reticence in the letter, bear witness to the fact that though a poem emerges from a life it takes on a life of its own; often the two lives will not be straightforwardly related. And I use 'straightforwardly' to encompass McGann's 'dialectically' when he writes of the poem's autumn as 'an historically specified fiction dialectically called into being by John Keats as an active response to, and alteration of, the events which marked the late summer and early fall of a particular year in a

particular place' (*KHM*, 61). McGann's adverb lends his discourse
an air of 'scientific' authority, but it should be noted that he allows for
authorial agency; there is no reason why Keats should not have
created a 'fiction' whose 'dialectical' relation with particular 'events'
is more unfathomable than McGann allows.

Keats's transcription of *To Autumn* in a letter to Richard Woodhouse
contains the following line: 'Then in a wailful quire the small gnats
mourn' (*Letters*, ii. 171). The variant spelling of 'choir' is intriguing.
'Quire' meaning 'folded sheets of paper' is a quirkily reflexive,
suppressed under-meaning. On the same day Keats began a letter
with the words: 'letter writing is the go now; I have consumed a Quire
at least' (*Letters*, ii. 178). The 'music' of Autumn is written out in a
'wailful quire', though the epistolary quire, like the poem, is 'wailful'
only obliquely. The pun, seemingly haphazard and almost certainly
unconscious, supports the opinion that Keats does not pass his poem
off as 'natural', even as he wishes it to assume the self-sufficiency of
pictorial art. Absence *is* presence; the poem knows about its status as
writing, about its deliberate refusal to refer to recent historical events,
yet it knows these things in a spirit that demands respect for its status
as art. *La Belle Dame sans Merci*, written some months before *To Autumn*
was composed, is more equivocal in its fathomings of imaginative life.
Anticipating *The Fall of Hyperion*, the poem laments yet proclaims the
power of dream; it turns from enchantment to nightmare while
developing a sense of the way men of action – 'pale kings, and princes
too,/ Pale warriors' and the knight-at-arms himself – are 'in thrall' to
La Belle Dame (37–8, 40): the ballad's 'language strange' (27) can be
read as indicating history's subservience to whatever drives lead to
the writing of poetry, the fashioning of dreams.

The letter to Woodhouse mentioned above also contains transcriptions
from *The Fall of Hyperion*, and it is fugitively haunting that two
passages deal indirectly and a third directly with writing. For the
letter has at its core the secrecy of a poet who knows that talk about
poetry can never replace the thing itself. 'I will give you', Keats says,
'a few lines from Hyperion on account of a word in the last line of a
fine sound' (*Letters*, ii. 171); he goes on to quote the start of Canto II of
The Fall (missing out the fifth line). The start of Canto II reads:

> 'Mortal, that thou may'st understand aright,
> I humanize my sayings to thine ear,

Making comparisons of earthly things;
Or thou might'st better listen to the wind,
Whose language is to thee a barren noise,
Though it blows legend-laden through the trees . . .'

(II. 1–6)

Keats emphasised 'legend-laden'; the word does indeed have a 'fine
sound', but it is a sound whose fineness derives from its semantic
freight. 'Legend-laden': the very word says much about Keats's
impulse to create imagined worlds, values, possibilities, and about the
potentially burdensome nature of this impulse. Experience is 'laden'
with 'legends', with 'what is to be read', to draw on the etymology of
'legend'; the interrogating poet is confronted by residual or vanishing
pointers, signs, hieroglyphics. 'What leaf-fring'd legend haunts about
thy shape . . .?' (5) he asks the urn. In *Endymion*, II. 827–53, Keats
describes a tale repeated by nature to a poet who 'sang the story up
into the air,/ Giving it universal freedom' (II. 838–9), where
'universal freedom' has its eye on a 'freedom' that is glimpsed as a
condition made possible by imaginative writing. 'The legend cheers/
Yon centinel stars' (II. 841–2): Keats's hyperbole here is later crossed
by compassionate ironies when he dwells on 'Madeline asleep in lap of
legends old' (*The Eve of St. Agnes*, 135). But in *The Eve of St. Agnes*
'legend' is written about so as to seem 'real'; imaginative enchantment
usurps reality. In the above passage from *The Fall* Moneta conjures
up a ghostly choir of unheard melodies, just out of range of the poet's
hearing; 'barren noise' is all he would hear did she not make
'comparisons of earthly things'. The poem wants to tackle issues that
bear profoundly on 'earthly things' – the verb 'humanize' illuminates
a central ambition of *The Fall* – yet the 'barren noise' of self-concern
has its part to play in the poem's chastened music.

This self-concern appears in the opening passage, the first eleven
lines of which Keats copied out for Woodhouse. Nothing ensures a
more immediate pitch of consciousness in a poem than awareness of
its own becomings, of the burdens and exhilaration of writing; at the
same time no subject is more calculated to damage a poem's health.
Moneta rebukes the poet-dreamer in *The Fall of Hyperion* as 'a
dreaming thing;/ A fever of thyself' and enjoins him to 'think of the
earth' (I. 168–9). Yet *The Fall* matters because of the grave, alert way
it treats its essentially undignified, even shaming theme: the 'fever' of
self-consciousness, subjectivity, reflexiveness. What is the use of
poetry? Am I a poet? Is it the case, as Hazlitt asserted controversially,

that 'The principle of poetry is a very anti-levelling principle'?[8] The
questions reverberate throughout the poem's opening:

> Fanatics have their dreams, wherewith they weave
> A paradise for a sect; the savage too
> From forth the loftiest fashion of his sleep
> Guesses at heaven: pity these have not
> Trac'd upon vellum or wild Indian leaf
> The shadows of melodious utterance.
> But bare of laurel they live, dream, and die;
> For Poesy alone can tell her dreams,
> With the fine spell of words alone can save
> Imagination from the sable charm
> And dumb enchantment. Who alive can say
> 'Thou art no poet; may'st not tell thy dreams'?
> Since every man whose soul is not a clod
> Hath visions, and would speak, if he had lov'd
> And been well nurtured in his mother tongue.
> Whether the dream now purposed to rehearse
> Be poet's or fanatic's will be known
> When this warm scribe my hand is in the grave.   (I. 1–18)

Post-Romantic reflexiveness is ushered in by these lines, even as they
can be viewed as speaking out of that 'felt helplessness' which
Raymond Williams sees as afflicting Romantic poets.[9] Wallace
Stevens lurks in the wings of the induction, and yet Keats's passage
affects because it lacks the fictive poise one associates with Stevens.
Stevens plays with argument; Keats gets stuck in an argumentative
mire of his own making. Hence the 'spawning of empty distinctions'
which John Jones complains about; but the passage calls for a more
inward, sympathetic reading than Jones offers.[10] Certainly the lines
begin a journey into a labyrinth where rays from history shine
obscurely. The passage sways rather eerily between quiet-voiced
sureness and puzzlement; it marks a cultural moment at which the
poetic self recognises that strength lies in weakness; that the recording
of uncertainty by 'this warm scribe my hand' is a necessary mode. The
enlightened and democratic sense that poetic ability is potentially
present in everyone 'whose soul is not a clod' rubs shoulders with a
dispirited yet heroic note of social alienation. Keats's 'fine spell of
words' sees words as agents of illusory enchantment yet asserts their
power. Later the poet-dreamer will ask Moneta to take note of those
'Who love their fellows even to the death;/ Who feel the giant agony of
the world;/ And more, like slaves to poor humanity,/ Labour for

mortal good' (I. 156–9); but the recommendation hardly helps his case, sharpening his anxiety about poetry's usefulness; and yet part of the poem nurses a doubtful hope that it is the poet as much as the practical philanthropist, Robert Owen, who should receive the praise in the *Examiner*:

such a man is the very identical man to be listened to at a time, when human beings have at once acquired heaps of knowledges and means, and are suffering under such inequalities of privation, as is agreed on all hands cannot long be endured. That 'something,' as the phrase is, 'must be done' before long, every body seems to allow. That nobody well knows what to do, especially the existing authorities, is also pretty well known to be the fact by *all* descriptions of people.   (4 July 1819, 417)

This passage defines a certain liberal disaffection, however ironically 'nobody well knows what to do' is meant, and helps to contextualise the mood of introspective searching characteristic of *The Fall of Hyperion*.

   The poem (subtitled 'A Dream') seeks to 'rehearse' a dream both like and unlike that of a 'fanatic'. It is the affinity between fanatic and poet which is most troubling – precisely because the writing is so deliberately untroubled, Keats expressing 'pity' that the dreams of 'fanatic' and 'savage' have not achieved articulation. 'Fanatic' carefully avoids specificity; whether the word alludes to followers of Christ, Godwin, or Johanna Southcott is impossible to say. The poem is never able to clarify its sense of the difference between the dreams of poet and fanatic (any more than it is able fully to accept Moneta's assertion that 'The poet and the dreamer are distinct', I. 199). It would appear at first that whereas 'Fanatics have their dreams', 'Poesy alone can tell her dreams' (I. 1, 8); but the final opposition between poet or fanatic implies that a fanatic's dreams can be told; however, only in so far as they are told without being told can they be known to be the dreams of a fanatic. On this reading the poet is one who commands language, who saves imaginative promptings from 'dumb enchantment'. Yet if this sounds like a claim (which it is) it is bound up with uncertainty about poetry's status; poetry, Keats suggests, works at a remove, is involved in tracing 'The shadows of melodious utterance' (I. 6). Perhaps fanatic and savage are closer to 'dreams' than the poet; the tangle of feelings involved here looks forward to the topsyturvy judgements that take place in the dreamer's later encounter with Moneta. The poem's 'I' is both privileged and cursed, self-convicted of 'utterance sacrilegious' (I. 140) but attaining a height which his moral betters are not accorded since it would not occur to them to desire the painful ordeal that poetic self-recognition involves. As Moneta says, in her tauntingly illogical, severely consoling way, 'They come not here, they have no thought to come –/ And thou art here, for thou art less than they' (I. 165–6).

Yet what overrides uncertainty about the poet's fitness and cultural role is the fact that such uncertainty achieves melodious utterance, and in the final lines of the induction Keats faces down self-doubt in the act of giving it fuller and freer expression. 'If the poem will only be recognizable as poetry by a later age, it is not poetry now': thus Paul Hamilton, trapping the passage within his argument's 'Hegelian conundrum'.[11] One retort is that the passage overcomes doubt by voicing it. The 'warm scribe' is only the agent of the poet and concedes that poetry involves 'writing', a cultural practice; but the lines do not so much put at risk as reassert the authority of the writing's source. Long after the 'warm scribe' is in the grave the lines will continue to be read, challenging readers to work out whether the lines are the product of poet or fanatic, and thus obliging readers to sense and accept the high value placed on poetry by the passage and the poem. The poet's 'living hand, now warm and capable/ Of earnest grasping' (*This living hand, now warm and capable*, 1–2) is engaged in the drama of creating a poetry of experience, at the centre of which is the experience of creating poetry; and the hand in both passages throws down a gauntlet to the reader, challenging him or her to propose a mode of knowledge superior to that of the poet, or a mode that feels so powerfully what it means to be 'living'.

The *Hyperions* bear witness to a paradox with which Keats's poetry confronts his readers: it shapes a verbal world which the senses can authenticate, yet it is often concerned with itself, with the desire to be a poet, or with inquiries into poetry. 'The Naiad 'mid her reeds/ Press'd her cold finger closer to her lips' (*Hyperion*, I. 13–14); this picture that is more than merely pictorial illustrates the first part of the proposition; the last three lines (I. 16–18) of the opening of *The Fall* illustrate the second part. What both aspects reveal is a concern with possibly unattainable 'presence': either the object is verbally transubstantiated, the limping hare and the words rendering it sharing in one another's life; or the subject who sees and sings by his own eyes inspired comes before the reader as the sole authority for his imaginings.[12] Keats at his most negatively capable or egotistically sublime is always prepared to allow that reality may be elsewhere. Yet out of such an allowance comes a poetic force that 'cheats' the reader, to use the *Nightingale* ode's verb, into accepting the poem as a place where the world, reworked through words, seems available. And when 'history' is his subject Keats tends to posit an engaged if isolated poetic self confronting what may seem 'alien' or 'forlorn' but is quickly sympathised with and humanised. Niobe, Ruth, Saturn, Moneta: all these figures exercise the poet's capacity for sympathy and do so in a way that elides distances of time and culture.[13] In this sense the poet 'pours out a balm upon the world', as Keats has Moneta say in *The Fall of Hyperion*, unlike the dreamer who merely 'vexes it' (I. 201, 202).

However, that is a touchingly buoyant view of poetry spoken in a poem which comes close to bidding such a view adieu. Even the 'naive' Keats is never less than 'sentimental'. *Hyperion*'s relationship with 'history' shares in the 'knowledge of contrast, feeling for light and shade' (*Letters*, ii. 360) informing the poem. It is a poem about the loss of authority (that of the Titans) which seeks to assert the authority of a poet (Keats); a poem of great stylistic control whose most powerful moments concern loss of control (especially as experienced by Saturn and Hyperion); a poem that rehearses one myth (that of evolutionary progress) only to find its imaginative sympathies engaged by an elegiac mood (that induced by the spectacle of fallen greatness); a poem that withdraws from the contemporary but is responsive to Napoleon's dubious bequest, his legacy of paralysed aftermath. Unlike Hazlitt, Keats was no admirer of Napoleon, insisting that even Wellington should receive his due (*Letters*, i. 144); yet Keats, too, may have felt, with Hazlitt, that Napoleon 'put his foot upon the neck of kings, who would have put their yoke upon the necks of the people' (*Examiner*, 15 August 1819, 524). Arguably, *Hyperion* represents an oblique, even cryptic, response to the failed hope embodied for many by Napoleon's career. Above all, *Hyperion* is a poem which uses its story to explore Keats's view of the role of the poet in relation to history, but fails to complete itself as a story. It is a Romantic fragment poem whose fragmentariness articulates its inability to believe full-bloodedly in a liberal, optimistic version of history. And for all the voices set free in Book II's debate it is a poem that does not try to vocalise the aspirations of 'the people' – unless Keats's own aspiration to don Miltonic robes can be seen as, in part, a class-motivated denial of his 'Cockney' origins and poetic affiliations.

The two *Hyperion*s read each other. The first version elects for earliness; even if it picks up its primal story at a point of aftermath, following the defeat of the Titans, it strives to be in at the beginning as if Keats were willing himself into a state where his own career as a poet (embodied in the figure of Apollo) and history (at the outset of change for the better) could be tied together. The second version chooses and is chosen by belatedness; in this version everything except the capacity to imagine happened a long time ago. The poem's 'I' drinks a 'draught' that takes him out of a post-lapsarian 'arbour' into a place where 'The mossy mound and arbour were no more' (I. 46, 25, 60), a line whose rhythm is an iambic study in loss. The poet-dreamer (it is a part of the poem's sure confusions that one wavers between applying either word to the poem's 'I') enters and conjures up a landscape of Dantesque sublimity that dwarfs 'The superannuations of sunk realms' (I. 68). The Keatsian surrogate who was on the verge of poetic incarnation in *Hyperion*, Book III, is now invoked as 'faded, far flown Apollo' (I. 204); Moneta is named potently by the poet as 'The pale Omega of a wither'd race', a 'conjuration' which wins him the power to 'see as a God sees' (I. 288, 291, 304). In *The Fall* the poet's burden is not to know so as to be in a position to prophesy or control, but rather to know so as to suffer, 'Without stay or prop/ But [his] own weak mortality' (I. 388–9). Both poems concern themselves with problems of representation, whether in relation to history or the self. If the first version seems the would-be objective myth and the second version the painfully subjective critique, it is also the case that the second constructs its own myth (of the solitary artist undergoing purgatorial ordeal) and the first drops hints of self-concern in the act of seeming to repress concern with self.

At the start of *Hyperion*, where the reader might expect a plea for the breath of inspiration, Keats offers a statuesque evocation of windlessness and voicelessness.[14] This evocation indicates Keats's studied determination to breathe new life into epic tradition by conceding its potential deathliness; the labour of recreation is spent on the imagining of a once heroic figure whose identity has gone and whose stillness parodies the calm repose used to describe 'poesy' in *Sleep and Poetry*: ''tis the supreme of power;/ 'Tis might half slumb'ring on its own right arm' (236–7). However, the loss of identity Keats himself undergoes in *Hyperion* – his abandonment of the role conferred on him by Hunt and hostile reviewers alike – signals his interest in writing a poem which does not have a clear case to make. For Keats to dwell on Saturn is to open his poem to an influx of feeling at odds with any progressivist message of a simply didactic kind. The poem is ideologically complex, elusive, and, for all its austerity, hospitable to different approaches. Among the poet's contemporaries, Shelley, one might speculate, liked it because he read it as using myth as the vehicle of a gravely mature optimism; Byron because it forswore the uppity, bourgeois callowness of *Endymion*. This elusiveness is made possible by the pursuit of sublimity; the poem longs for and mimes a majestic certainty of utterance, as in the far from decorative epic simile beginning 'As when, upon a tranced summer-night . . .' (I. 72): far from decorative because the fascination with the way in which Thea's words came and went links with the desire for some breath of inspiration to sweep through the poem: 'one gradual solitary gust/ Which comes upon the silence, and dies off,/ As if the ebbing air had but one wave' (I. 76–8). This 'solitary gust' might stand for the poet's desire to exercise aloof control over the complexities his mythic imaginings have set in motion. Significantly, the initial paragraph of blank verse is fourteen lines long.[15] Keats, who experimented restlessly with the form, recasts the sonnet most originally in his would-be epic; *Hyperion*'s aimed-for objectivity is immediately complicated by suggestions of the inwardness and structural self-awareness virtually inseparable from the sonnet form.

By comparison with Keats's earlier poems the diction of *Hyperion* may be 'more native in origin, and more strongly consonantal in texture'.[16] But it knows it is these things, is consciously them, and takes a deliberated pleasure in being so, a pleasure that is also a summoning of artistic nerve: the medium occupies centre-stage. One sees this at work in the first line's lingering over 'vale'; as used by Milton (in *Paradise Lost*, I. 321), the word provoked Keats to a rhapsodic gloss: 'There is a cool pleasure in the very sound of vale . . . It is a sort of delphic Abstraction, a beautiful thing made more beautiful by being reflected and put in a Mist.'[17] 'Reflected and put in a Mist' might describe the artful treatment of Saturn's misery.

When Keats rehouses the opening of *Hyperion* in the changed world of *The Fall of Hyperion*, he brings it into connection with his subjectivity and poetic ambitions. Seeing 'what first I thought an image huge,/ Like to the image pedestal'd so high/ In Saturn's temple' (*The Fall*, I. 298–300), the poet defamiliarises the earlier version, seen within the new poem as itself an 'image', an artefact.

This tactic flushes out into the open the earlier version's secret wish to sculpt a permanent image, 'quiet as a stone' (*Hyperion*, I. 4). But the moment in *The Fall* also takes the reader into the theatre of the mind, achieving, for all its artfulness, an effect of truth-telling. Moneta's 'So Saturn sat/ When he had lost his realms' (*The Fall*, I. 301–2) is equally startling; reader and narrator are about to witness a replay of what has already happened. The major set piece of the first version has become an event that signifies only in so far as the self-conscious poet can be made to feel it on his imaginative pulses. History is what has happened; the poet in search of forgiveness for being a poet seeks to come to terms with the 'high tragedy' (*The Fall*, I. 277) to which, he surmises, past events have been converted within Moneta's brain.

To this end Keats sacrifices some of the finest lines in the first version. Attention in *The Fall* is focused less on the sorrowing Saturn than on the poet's attempt to grapple with his 'lofty theme' (I. 306), to ravel out the rest of the web. Stasis is the subject which lends Keats creative energy in the first version; in the second version it is an internalised condition which at crucial moments – the climbing of the steps, say, or the vision of Moneta's face – is partly overcome. A concern with suffering, and more especially the artist's need to suffer his poem's subject, is present, in different ways, in both poems. The poet's duty is less to warn than to bear witness to his concern to bear witness; such a conviction manifests itself in the lines which conclude *Hyperion*, Book I. Coelus, himself 'but a voice', has urged Hyperion to be 'in the van/ Of circumstance', to 'seize the arrow's barb/ Before the tense string murmur', and sends him off 'To the earth' (I. 340, 343–5). Hyperion's response to this quietist's call for deeds is less to act than to look:

> Ere half this region-whisper had come down,
> Hyperion arose, and on the stars
> Lifted his curved lids, and kept them wide
> Until it ceas'd; and still he kept them wide:
> And still they were the same bright, patient stars.
> Then with a slow incline of his broad breast,
> Like to a diver in the pearly seas,
> Forward he stoop'd over the airy shore,
> And plung'd all noiseless into the deep night.   (I. 349–57)

One is reminded by these lines that Hyperion serves as a poetic alter ego as much as Apollo, his apparent rival but covert confrère. Satan on the verge of Chaos and Mulciber falling from the crystal battlements ghost these lines; but transgression and punishment give way to a moment of tranced contemplation. Here the Sun-God prepares for his 'plunge' into 'the deep night' of loss and futile struggle; though the consequence is likely to be failure, what haunts Keats is the thought of a gaze that is open-lidded, steady, aware of the need for a patience equal to that of the 'bright, patient stars'. To the degree that he assumes such a gaze Hyperion is allowed a glimmer of godlike understanding, which marks an advance on his previous condition when he 'Unus'd to bend, by hard compulsion bent/ His spirit to the sorrow of the time' (I. 300–1). The 'pearl' his dive into history will turn up is, the passage suggests, the gift of acceptance, as Oceanus's speech (II. 173–243) will later make explicit. But Hyperion's role differs from and is more sombre than that of Oceanus. Through Hyperion Keats tries to come to terms with 'the sorrow of the time' by seeing it as a sorrow which has to be endured; a small hope persists that open-lidded endurance will allow a glimpse of escape from sorrow, even if Hyperion's appearance in Book II serves to betray misery 'To the most hateful seeing of itself' (II. 370). Oceanus puts forward a stoically optimistic reading of history, though his account is not complacently endorsed by the poem. But in his squaring-up to 'the pain of truth', his desire 'to bear all naked truths,/ And to envisage circumstance, all calm' (II. 202–4) and his readiness to accept change, Oceanus articulates a vision of history which part of Keats wishes to recommend.

Though Keats speaks of having 'relapsed into those abstractions which are my only life' (*Letters*, i. 370), the poem's escape into the abstractions proposed by Oceanus is partial. A month after Peterloo, Keats reformulates the view of progress which Oceanus expounds: 'All civiled countries', Keats writes, 'become gradually more enlighten'd and there should be a continual change for the better' (*Letters*, ii. 193). In that shift from 'become' to 'should', however, the quickness to glide over the problem of pain, which undoes Oceanus's speech for some readers, betrays itself. In *Hyperion* there are other 'naked truths': the unignorable, hard to accommodate facts of misery and distress. Enceladus's put-down, 'Dost thou forget, sham Monarch of the Waves,/ Thy scalding in the seas?' (II. 319–20), momentarily invites the reader to see Oceanus's speech as unctuous rhetoric. At the same time the poem is half in love with easeful sorrow, persuading itself into a state where 'Sorrow more beautiful than Beauty's self' (I. 36) admires its cadenced, dignified representation. The historical impli-

cations of such a self-persuasion are equivocal: Keats's epic becomes a
way of responding to suffering yet it abandons specificity, even as the
poem's 'transcendental cosmopolitics' are a means of interrogating
political vantage-points.[18]

Historical attitudes current in Keats's time are at once recycled
and challenged in the poem. For instance, Saturn can be viewed as a
mythic version of Napoleon or of George III, Shelley's old, mad,
blind, despised, and dying king; but he can be also seen as a reworking
of Lear ('Look up, and tell me if this feeble shape/ Is Saturn's' (I.
98–9)), a figure more sinned against than sinning. Historical allusion
is complicated by self-sustaining literary effects and surprising
switches of perspective. *Hyperion* may wish to represent a painful but
necessary revolution, a wish with obvious political implications when
one remembers the social unrest of post-Waterloo Britain and the
ongoing debate about the implications of the French Revolution. Yet
the task of sustaining such a vision within the poem alights finally on
Apollo, a character whose weakness is stressed and whose appearance
coincides with the weakest writing in *Hyperion*. Contrasting the
already written *Endymion* with the still-to-be-composed *Hyperion*,
Keats writes in January 1818 that 'the Hero of the written tale being
mortal is led on, like Buonaparte, by circumstance; whereas the
Apollo in Hyperion being a fore-seeing God will shape his actions like
one' (*Letters*, i. 207). But, despite Keats's avowed desire to imagine a
poet-hero untarnished by historical limitations, Apollo, the poet of a
new order, lives in 'fearless yet in aching ignorance' (*Hyperion*, III.
107). Such 'aching ignorance' seems flimsy beside the 'horrors,
portion'd to a giant nerve' which 'Oft made Hyperion ache' (I.
175–6). The contrast is between a tragically compelling, doomed old
order and an only half-believed-in new order, between a poet
(Hyperion) trapped but humanised by suffering and a poet (Apollo)
who unconvincingly strives 'to search wherefore I am so sad' (III.
88). *Hyperion*'s myth may be a form of representing history, but that
representation is always on the verge of creating a secondary myth:
the myth of the artist preoccupied and vexed into utterance by the
lack of a clearcut role.

Keats, as is well known, was the severest critic of his attempt in the
two versions of *Hyperion* to recapture a Miltonic epic grandeur. In his
letter to Reynolds of 21 September 1819 announcing that he has
'given up Hyperion', he presumably refers to *The Fall of Hyperion*, on
which he had been working over the summer:

there were too many Miltonic inversions in it – Miltonic verse cannot be written but in an artful or rather artist's humour. I wish to give myself up to other sensations. English ought to be kept up. It may be interesting to you to pick out some lines from Hyperion and put a mark X to the false beauty proceeding from art, and one || to the true voice of feeling. (*Letters*, ii. 167)

As is the case elsewhere in Keats's letters, this shows him thinking on the hoof, generating categories which it would be wrong to reify. Behind his remarks lurks the following question: can a difference be established between an 'artist's humour' and 'the true voice of feeling'? In his recoil upon himself, Keats senses the difficulty of enforcing this opposition. 'Upon my soul', he writes, "twas imagination I cannot make the distinction – Every now & then there is a Miltonic intonation – But I cannot make the division properly' (*Letters*, ii. 167). This rider may be the most interesting, if least commented on, aspect of an almost too famous letter.

The Fall of Hyperion is embroiled in the struggle to make its art the means of voicing truly its feelings about art. At the centre of this struggle, with its implications for Keats's exploration of the modern poet's function, is the encounter with Moneta. Here Keats recasts a weak scene in the first *Hyperion*, the confrontation between Apollo and Mnemosyne. This takes place in Book III, the 'vulgarity' of which is read by Marjorie Levinson as signifying Keats's 'attempt to vex the strong utterance of the first two books'.[19] Certainly the effect of the writing is such a vexation, whatever the poet's intention. Epic grandeur sustained at a severe cost in the first two books gives way to something more openly bewildered. The invocation to the Muse which the reader was denied at the start of *Hyperion* now materialises, though the strongest note is sounded by the poet's self-thwarting confession of inadequacy: 'O leave them, Muse! O leave them to their woes;/ For thou art weak to sing such tumults dire' (III. 3–4). Apollo's moment of poetic incarnation is announced in a quasi-orgasmic shriek just before the poem breaks off, while his sense of imminent deification is rendered with disregard for what its abstractions might entail: 'Knowledge enormous makes a God of me./ Names, deeds, gray legends, dire events, rebellions,/ Majesties, sovran voices, agonies,/ Creations and destroyings, all at once/ Pour into the wide hollows of my brain' (III. 113–17). The writing here is distinctly smokeable; that 'all at once' is ludicrously opportunist, though one notices Keats's wish that his poetic tyro should be in possession of 'Knowledge enormous', a moment which comes as close as any to defining his poem's stance in relation to history. *Hyperion* is less a poem written in order to take sides than to instruct Keats in the 'Knowledge' necessary for any imaginative purchase on history.

Indifferent as it may appear in places, the third, unfinished book of *Hyperion* was the point from which some of the finest poetry in *The Fall of Hyperion* was able to depart. As if in reaction to that 'all at once' Keats approaches the altar at the foot of Saturn's image deliberately, 'Repressing haste, as too unholy there' (*The Fall*, I. 94), 'too unholy' implying the poet-dreamer's subliminal knowledge that the very act of wanting to be a poet will involve some element of violation. Apollo 'in the morning twilight wandered forth' (*Hyperion*, III. 33); but the poet-dreamer in *The Fall* is shut off from origins, earliness, all the primacy Keats had tried to body forth in the myth adumbrated by *Hyperion*. Instead, the poet-dreamer exists in a world of leavings, 'refuse', 'imageries', traces; north and south are columns, 'ending in mist/ Of nothing', where the omission of an article, definite or indefinite, before 'mist' speaks volumes about a state of epistemological doubt; to the east 'black gates/ Were shut against the sunrise evermore' (*The Fall*, I. 30, 77, 84–6). Whereas *Hyperion* breaks off banally with 'Apollo shriek'd; – and lo! from all his limbs/ Celestial' (III. 135–6), the nightmarish ascent of the steps in *The Fall of Hyperion* redeems 'shriek'd' from banality or melodrama: 'I shriek'd; and the sharp anguish of my shriek/ Stung my own ears' (I. 126–7).

'[T]he wide hollows of my brain', perhaps the most impressive moment in the passage quoted from *Hyperion*, become the implicit setting of *The Fall*. Such hollows are further internalised in *The Fall of Hyperion* as an inwardness the poem longs for and fears: the dreamer is simultaneously fated and privileged to behold 'the scenes/ Still swooning vivid through my globed brain' (I. 244–5), as Moneta puts it. The words stay in touch with a physical swooning even as they conceptualise the physical. Does this physicality also accommodate a materialist critique, an awareness that, in Daniel Watkins's words, 'poetry in the modern world necessarily passes through the market-place'? Watkins, following K. K. Ruthven, asserts that Moneta represents the goddess of money. Provocative as Watkins's argument is, it involves a great deal of reading-in. It is one thing to claim that a poem has a 'political unconscious', quite another to catalogue the contents of that political unconscious in a poem which Watkins himself admits is resistant to his approach. Watkins's reading consequently tends to reduce enigma. Moneta is viewed as seeking to 'hegemonize the world' and as encouraging poets to treat their art as opium for the masses (Watkins's interpretation of the line 'The one pours out a balm upon the world'); in addition, she is associated with 'a past of political conservativism'.[20]

In responding to Watkins's case, I would argue that he grants the wrong kind of thematic centrality to a figure of speech. After viewing Moneta's face, the poet 'ached to see what things the hollow brain/ Behind enwombed' (I. 276–7); this ache is compared to one who 'twing'd with avarice' (I. 273) looks for gold ore in the earth. Does this mean Moneta equals money? I think not, though the comparison does indeed alert the reader to the presence within the poem's 'political unconscious' of concern with money. Yet in context, a context which only a few lines earlier has associated Moneta with Christ-like suffering, the twinge of avarice serves to highlight the poet's longing for knowledge. It hints, too, at the element of trespass felt by the poet as he concedes this longing. Moreover, Moneta's associations with memory, poetry, and admonishment are pervasive; her illogicalities do not undermine her authority; rather, they correspond to uncertainties within the poet who is ventriloquising her remarks. But to underplay her role as muse, so evident in the text, because the *Examiner* ran a number of articles about the bullion controversy, is to skew the poem's response to history.[21] *The Fall of Hyperion* is worried by the role of poetry in the modern world, but it does not subscribe to a Marxist view of the relations between modes of production and cultural activity. Myth and Dante allow Keats to reassert, albeit in often anguished tones, the theme of poetry as the vehicle for spiritual quest. That Saturn is a product of an old order does not mean that sympathy for his sufferings is felt by the poem to be dubious.

For once again Keats is seeking to know through sympathy. This very sympathy can act as a brake upon the desire to know. Moneta's brain as womb contains secrets which the poetry recoils from exploring even as it is compelled to do so; this ambivalence is at work throughout *The Fall*, and can be seen as the consequence of the poet's desire for reverence (towards his muse, poetic tradition, conscience, social ideals), a desire which compensates for the poem's drive, almost despite itself, to rearticulate what it is to be a poet. For all its wish to believe in the usefulness of poetry, the poem also believes – and herein lies its modernity – that the utilitarian and the imaginative are likely to be in tension with one another. Certainly, though, the desire for reverence just referred to inheres in the poem's nurturing and mothering associations: every man would speak, the induction asserts, 'if he had lov'd/ And been well nurtured in his mother tongue'; the poet-dreamer initially detects what 'seem'd refuse of a meal/ By angel tasted, or our Mother Eve' (I. 30–1), and invokes the myth of Proserpine and Ceres (giving it a briefly happy ending that relates ambiguously to the poet-dreamer's search for the lost mother); the draught which takes him out of the pleasant arbour into the dream-enclosed-within-a-dream world of the sanctuary is 'parent of my theme' (I. 46); Moneta tells the poet-dreamer that unless he ascends the steps, 'Thy flesh, near cousin to the common dust,/ Will parch for lack of nutriment' (I. 109–10); Moneta's admonitory words 'As near as an immortal's sphered words/ Could to a mother's soften' (I. 249–50); Keats invokes her 'By great Apollo, thy dear foster child' (I. 286). What the reader witnesses in and through these references is Keats's wish to believe in a beneficent, caring, parenting, and most of all mothering poetic tradition, a tradition serving as an emblem of what he hopes history has to offer the self-discovering poet. This longing never grows sentimental and is the more touching for never being assuaged; what Keats will discover is that nurturing by his muse involves terror, acceptance of the burden of the mystery, and isolation. He may claim for himself the deification experienced so abruptly by Apollo, asserting that 'there grew/ A power within me of enormous ken,/ To see as a God sees' (I. 302–4). Yet Keats is forced to experience the pain which Moneta told him he would not feel, rather than the wonder she promised him (I. 248). Some of the most searing lines he ever wrote express the intolerable burden of beholding the suffering he projects onto his own imaginative creations:

> . . . Oftentimes I pray'd
> Intense, that death would take me from the vale
> And all its burthens. Gasping with despair
> Of change, hour after hour I curs'd myself;
> Until old Saturn rais'd his faded eyes,
> And look'd around, and saw his kingdom gone . . .
>
> (I. 396–401)

Here the word 'vale' sheds the literary, pastoral air it has in the first line of *Hyperion*. And the poem strikes its most authentic note of suffering, attaining knowledge less of 'the miseries of the world' (I. 148) than of the pain endured in writing a poem that seeks such knowledge.

However, *The Fall of Hyperion*, like *Hyperion*, seeks throughout to establish relationship with otherness, with what lies beyond the self. If the pathos of the unfinished *Hyperion* lies in the way Keats keeps imagining, only to be denied, the possibility of saving contact with tradition and history, *The Fall* is at its finest in the passage where Keats comes closest to gaining access to another: where he views Moneta's face (I. 256–71). Moneta shares in the doubleness of a muse: external goddess and inner voice, remote from the poet and an externalising of the poet's conception of the task he should be setting himself. Gazing, he sees the features of 'high tragedy'; 'deathwards progressing/ To no death was that visage' (I. 260–1), an embodiment of the terrible, cold immortality of art that Keats explores in the *Ode on a Grecian Urn*. Like the urn, unable to protect human beings from 'waste' but a 'friend to man' (46, 48), Moneta's eyes offer unconsoling consolation, as the syntax of the closing lines of the description of her face brings out: 'they saw me not,/ But in blank splendor beam'd like the mild moon,/ Who comforts those she sees not, who knows not/ What eyes are upward cast' (I. 268–71). The longing for relationship, a longing that is answered and thwarted here, defines the special plight and courage of this poem, a poem that affects the reader by virtue of its attempt not to be 'visionless entire . . ./ Of all external things' (I. 267–8). Most affecting is the fact that shortly before his fragment breaks off Keats has internalised Moneta's suffering; he too is 'deathwards progressing/ To no death'. However, by exploring the 'burthens' of the poetic calling (as the High Romantics were forced to confront it), Keats produced in *The Fall of Hyperion*, unpublished until 1857, a poem which still speaks eloquently if enigmatically about the relation between writing and history.

NOTES

1 See John Barnard (ed.), *John Keats. The Complete Poems* (Harmondsworth, 1973), 651.
2 Bridges is quoted in *AP*, 537.
3 'Keats and Critique', in Marjorie Levinson et al., *Rethinking Historicism: Critical Readings in Romantic History* (Oxford and New York, 1989), 137.
4 Ibid.
5 Walter Jackson Bate, *John Keats* (Cambridge, Mass., 1963), 510.
6 'History, Existence, and "To Autumn"', *KP*, 217.
7 See *KHM passim* and William Keach, 'Cockney Couplets: Keats and the Politics of Style', *KP*, 196.
8 'Coriolanus', *Characters of Shakespear's Plays* (London, 1817), quoted from

The Round Table: Characters of Shakespear's Plays (London and New York, 1969), 214.

9 *Culture and Society: 1780–1950* (Harmondsworth, 1977), 63.

10 *John Keats's Dream of Truth* (London, 1969), 99.

11 'Keats and Critique', 136.

12 Examples taken from *The Eve of St. Agnes*, 3, and *Ode to Psyche*, 43, respectively.

13 Niobe appears in *Endymion*, I. 337–43; Ruth in *Ode to a Nightingale*, 65–7.

14 See Geoffrey H. Hartman, 'Spectral Symbolism and the Authorial Self: An Approach to Keats's *Hyperion*', *EinC* 34 (1974), 15.

15 Ibid.

16 Walter Jackson Bate, *The Stylistic Development of Keats* (London, 1958), 66.

17 Quoted from 'Keats's Marginalia to *Paradise Lost*', in E. Cook (ed.), *John Keats*, Oxford Authors Series (Oxford and New York, 1990), 338.

18 Leigh Hunt's phrase in *The Autobiography of Leigh Hunt* (3 vols., London, 1850) ii. 202.

19 *KL*, 194.

20 *KPP*, 175, 164, 163, 168, 169, 171.

21 Ibid., 162.

CHAPTER 9

Keats, history, and the poets

Vincent Newey

Keats's relation to 'the poets' is as much a factor in his thought and writing as are the fall of Napoleon or civil unrest in England, Waterloo or Peterloo, the public events which recent scholarship has rediscovered as not only the backdrop to his work but vital constituents of its meaning.[1] To observe this relation is not, it should be said, to walk a blind alley of 'reflexiveness', where the subject of literature becomes nothing but literature itself; nor does it simply confirm theories of maturation or 'influence', where creativity develops through the strong poet's encounters with prior authority.[2] The story of Keats and the poets is sometimes linear, as such theories tend to be, and sometimes contrapuntal – figuring change yet involving a mass of ongoing issues, partisan interactions, and contemporary affairs. It also reveals a Keats rather more conservative in outlook than is commonly assumed.

There is, especially in the early poems, a surprising vein that leads back to William Cowper, an advocate of sobriety with whom Keats might be expected to have had little or nothing in common. Cowper has been identified as the source of Keats's complaint of tardy and unfocused inspiration in the lines *To Charles Cowden Clarke*, where the imagery – 'With shatter'd boat, oar snapt, and canvass rent/ I slowly sail' (17–18) – foreshadows, as we shall see, a more famous moment of concern with personal identity and progress.[3] Also in 1816, however, Keats may well have been recalling the libertarian and patriotic sentiment of Cowper's *The Task* (1785) – lines of which, on the horrors of the Bastille, had been declaimed by Charles James Fox from the pro-Revolutionary side in parliamentary debate – when he outlined his positive hopes for 'Posterity's award' in a verse letter to George Keats:[4]

> The patriot shall feel
> My stern alarum, and unsheath his steel;
> Or, in the senate thunder out my numbers
> To startle princes from their easy slumbers.
>
> (*To My Brother George*, 73–6)

We shall find close resemblances between parts of *The Task* and Keats's extended comments, two years later, on the weakness of the government, which he contrasts with the 'Spimpicity' ['Simplicity'] and 'Strength' of the commonwealth of Oliver Cromwell (*Letters*, i. 396). Keats's radicalism in politics always maintained a conservative thread, and this is one with a larger strain of virile humanism which Marjorie Levinson and others have made efforts to deny in favour of his more subversive 'anti-nature' or 'vulgarity'.[5] But for the moment I wish only to underline the fact of his commitment to a well-tried English liberalism that zealously upheld the popular rights won during the Civil War and under William III but was firmly nationalistic and far from undisciplined. One prominent expression of this allegiance is his indignant riposte to the ringing of bells on the anniversary of the restoration of Charles II:

> Infatuate Britons, will you still proclaim
> His memory, your direst, foulest shame?
>   Nor patriots revere?
> Ah! when I hear each traitorous lying bell,
> 'Tis gallant Sydney's, Russell's, Vane's sad knell,
>   That pains my wounded ear.
>
> (*Lines Written on 29 May, the Anniversary of Charles's Restoration* . . ., 1–6)

The clear, sonorous rhetoric, which reminds us of Cowper's preference for a 'manly' line that 'plows its stately course',[6] is the stylistic counterpart of Keats's high-minded interest in a cause that laid rigorous stress, as Cowper again puts it, on the 'blessing' for which 'our Hampdens and our Sidneys bled', the refusal of 'chains and bondage, for a tyrant's sake' which had inspired the opponents of Charles I and Charles II alike to throw off 'the shackles of usurped control'.[7]

This hard-driving Whig perspective also has a place in the writings of Leigh Hunt, alias 'Libertas', who, for example, lauded the victory of the Allies over Napoleon in 1815 in a 'National Song' that places England with 'On the left of thee Freedom, and Truth on the right'.[8] Though Keats and Hunt adhere to the same basic tradition as Cowper, however, they are of a different generation and cast.

Cowper's deprecation of 'authority grow[n] wanton' is the moderate's defence of constitutional monarchy against George III's insistent use of patronage and royal prerogative during the American War.[9] Hunt and Keats belong to the headier and more intensely combative era that saw the restoration of the Bourbons under the standard of Divine Right and, in England, the reactionary government of the Regency. Both declare an aggressive belief in setting limits to princely power, as when Keats's advice to the peoples of Europe at the end of the war with France in 1814 – 'Give thy kings law – leave not uncurbed the great' (*On Peace*, 13) – echoes Hunt's assertion that 'he [Louis XVIII] will not have power to play the tyrant like some of his predecessors, his subjects will take care, if they remain true to their new charter'.[10] Then, later on, Keats follows victory in one of Hunt's poetry contests with bolder, seemingly republican visions of 'A trampling down of what the world most prizes,/ Turbans and crowns, and blank regality' (*On Receiving a Laurel Crown from Leigh Hunt*, 11–12). But the best known of the several sonnets directly linking the two poets is that in which Keats, in February 1815, commemorates Hunt's release from prison, where he had spent two years for telling *The Morning Post* that its 'Adonis in loveliness', the Prince Regent, was really a corpulent man of middle age who had done his country no good.[11]

The lines *Written on the Day That Mr. Leigh Hunt left Prison* were published in Keats's first collection of poems in 1817, and were quoted in full in John Lockhart's subsequent attack on Keats in *Blackwood's*.[12] The wrath of the Tory press was no doubt stoked by the particular references to the Prince as 'Minion of grandeur' and his followers as a 'wretched crew', as well as by the designation of Hunt himself, the public enemy, as 'immortal spirit' (5, 14, 3). The gibe 'wretched crew' would have been especially cutting at a time when the supporters of contemporary monarchy were being satirised widely, in cartoons and other publications, as a rabble of Circean monsters. Yet there is something else in Keats's defiance, which is the contrast between the 'true', productive life of imagination and deluded, sterile temporal authority. The 'daring Milton' with whom the incarcerated Hunt is said to take inward creative flight 'through the fields of air' (11) is another hero of the English revolution, but his importance on this occasion is much more as the type of the imaginative artist, or what Keats called elsewhere one of the 'Men of Genius' as opposed to the 'Men of Power' (*Letters*, i. 184). It has been argued that the point of this elevation of imagination is 'escape' – a 'political gesture' certainly, but also an 'evasion of politics'.[13] There is a marked element of this in Keats of course: the cultivation of aesthetic and sensuous values as a 'negation' of the established order – Herbert Marcuse's 'Great Refusal'.[14] But to understand the situation fully we must look beyond this idea of recalcitrance to the proactive workings of Keats's creativity, which include sustained engagement *with* politics. For Keats the 'Men of Genius' are 'great as certain ethereal Chemicals operating on the Mass of neutral intellect'. How then does the major project of his own early career, *Endymion*, so operate?

It has gone unrecognised, I think, that *Endymion* grew in certain respects out of Hunt's long narrative poem, *The Story of Rimini*, and the controversy surrounding it. Published in 1816, *Rimini* treats the story from Dante's *Inferno* of the adulterous and incestuous love of Paulo, Prince of Rimini, for Francesca, his brother's wife. Whereas Dante consigns the lovers to eternal punishment, however, Hunt shifts the emphasis over from sin to sympathy, and to the conditions that engendered the fatal act. The city of Ravenna, Francesca's home and site of her impending marriage to Giovanni, lord of Rimini, which seems at first a world of perfect order and happiness, is gradually exposed as a scene of 'intrigue and art' (II. 33), oppressive power-structures, and venality. The crowd that greets the bride stands in 'sullen silence' till the herald scatters a 'bag of money' (II. 84–94), but by far the greater shadow of self-interest is cast by the conspiracy between Giovanni and Francesca's father, Guido, to 'secure' the princess by having the more attractive brother, Paulo, woo and marry her as a proxy (II. 18–83). The 'secret snare' (III. 217) works all too well, and Francesca, legally married to Giovanni, finally unites with Paulo in the garden that has become the ambivalent symbol of her psychological imprisonment and her burgeoning desires:

> And Paulo, by degrees, gently embraced
> With one permitted arm her lovely waist;
> And both their cheeks, like peaches on a tree,
> Leaned with a touch together, thrillingly; . . .
> Sacred be love from sight, whate'er it is.
> The world was all forgot, the struggle o'er,
> Desperate the joy. – That day they read no more.
>
> (III. 591–4, 606–8)

Nothing is more certain than the holiness of the heart's affections; beauty is truth, truth beauty, even in cases of sexual transgression.[15]

To use the formulations of Hunt's own justifications of the poem, he keeps tolerant faith with 'natural impulses', and throws the blame for misfortune (Paulo falls on his brother's sword during a duel, Francesca dies of a remorseful and broken heart) squarely on the 'first cause' of the tragedy, which was 'the habit of falsehood' that encouraged this action and remains 'the great social mistake, still the commonest amongst us'.[16]

The poem, then, was intended to inculcate a sense not only of true justice but also of possible improvement in human affairs, since suffering is shown to arise out of 'want of knowledge rather than defect of goodness'.[17] The Tory reviewers did not see it like that at all: they issued diatribes against its 'extreme moral depravity', and against an analogous impurity of style. Lockhart, in the first of his *Blackwood's* articles on 'The Cockney School', fulminates against Hunt's 'glittering and rancid obscenities'. Others drew attention to 'low and vulgar' expressions and 'ungrammatical, unauthorized, chaotic jargon', quoting, for instance, the phrases 'a scattery light' and 'a clipsome waist' as unacceptable neologisms.[18] Hunt's experiments in diction and prosody, his search (as he says in his original preface to *Rimini*) for 'a freer spirit of versification' than the closed Augustan couplet, were, for his opponents, all one with the corruptness of his mind and politics.

Endymion is, like *Rimini*, a critique of society and a valorisation of 'love of truth'[19] and of love itself. For the Marxist critic Daniel P. Watkins this means an account of the emergence of 'individual subjectivity' out of 'social disintegration',[20] as evidenced by Endymion's tribute to the power of passion to win men from the arena of public interest and ambition:

> Aye, so delicious is the unsating food,
> That men, who might have tower'd in the van
> Of all the congregated world, to fan
> And winnow from the coming step of time
> All chaff of custom, wipe away all slime
> Left by men-slugs and human serpentry,
> Have been content to let occasion die,
> Whilst they did sleep in love's elysium. (I. 816–23)

Yet Keats's own attachment to love, and to friendship, the 'steady splendour' only just below in humanity's 'crown' (I. 800–7) does not in fact preclude him from political action. Even in the quoted passage he has it two ways – on the one hand evoking the pleasures of sensuous detachment but on the other, in language Shelley was to take up with devastating force in *Adonais*, attacking the inhuman, or rather subhuman, molluscan, and reptilian, machinations of the Regency government and their literary allies.

The political animus of Book I, however, goes much deeper than this overt counter-abuse, and relates to a broader set of events. The 'gloomy days' referred to in the induction (I. 9) are those of the excesses of the restored Bourbon regime and the support given to it by the British government, both of which were attacked by Hunt in *Examiner* articles throughout 1817: kings 'by the modern revived theory of Legitimacy, have a right like God, to do what they will ... to waste provinces, to persecute individuals, to nourish superstition, to gorge their favourites with the fat of the soil'; the Government taxes 'our eatables, our drinkables, wearables' only to 'enable the King of FRANCE to keep a good table'.[21] Against a background of high prices and bad harvests, the years 1815 and 1816 had seen petitioning movements and riots against distress in manufacturing towns and in East Anglia; while early in 1817, when *Endymion* was begun, an assault on the Prince Regent's coach led to the so-called 'Gag Acts'. The trial of the radical William Hone, for satirising government policy in his parodies of the Catechism, Litany, and Creed, was a *cause célèbre* of 1817. His acquittal in December 1817 is possibly the subject of Keats's enigmatic poem, 'Nebuchadnezzar's Dream' (*Before he went to live with owls and bats*),[22] and is certainly celebrated in a journal letter to George and Tom Keats as 'encouraging – his *Not Guilty* is a thing, which not to have been, would have dulled still more Liberty's Emblazoning' (*Letters*, i. 191).

Book I of *Endymion* has its own hidden agenda. What Watkins sees only as a picture of a society caught up in decadent nostalgia is in truth Keats's positive vehicle for meeting Hunt's rallying call for the young and intelligent to 'assist by every means in your power, the new growth of taste, liberality, popular feeling, and a love of nature and justice'.[23] The community to which Endymion, shepherd–ruler, belongs is, unlike that of Hunt's Ravenna, one where degree means cohesion rather than oppression, as a 'goodly company' (I. 129) of young and old, men and women, labourers and leaders, 'children garlanded', 'damsels', 'crowd of shepherds', 'venerable priest', 'chieftain king' and 'common lookers on', '[m]others and wives' (I. 110, 135, 139, 149, 172, 176, 207), all gather for the festival of Pan; where humankind exists in productive harmony with 'nature's lives and

wonders', as baskets overflow with 'April's tender younglings', and
'teeming sweets' are piled in thanksgiving on the altar of the god of the
year's 'completions' (I. 105, 138, 224, 260); where resources are fairly
distributed, whether in times of 'plenteous stores' or when, in
straitened circumstance, men 'shar'd their famish'd scrips' (I. 389–92);
where the life of mind is honoured, in the quest for 'universal
knowledge' and in 'solitary thinkings' alike (I. 289, 294); and where
the spirit of Nature is invoked to feed the processes of a constant renewal:

> . . . be still the leaven,
> That spreading in this dull and clodded earth
> Gives it a touch ethereal – a new birth:
> Be still a symbol of immensity;
> A firmament reflected in a sea;
> An element filling the space between;
> An unknown – but no more . . .   (I. 296–302)

All of this constitutes a vision that is at once retrospective and
prospective, evoking a classical and mythic realm of 'simple times' (I.
171), not for its own sake or merely as an escape from a sordid present,
but as a model of how 'better times' might be.

It is also a forcibly partisan vision. The repetition of 'our' seven
times in ten lines (213–22) of the priest's opening address to the
assembled people of Latmos – 'Our vows . . . our lowing heifers . . . our
wide plains . . . our lord' – suggests a covert call for solidarity among
the people of England, and a proclamation of democratic values in
the areas of property and the franchise. The whole spontaneous ritual
of dance and 'circle' (I. 185) suggests those that had broken out in the
first dawn of the French Revolution, such as Wordsworth depicts in
Book VI of *The Prelude* (1805, VI. 391–413), where Englishmen,
'forerunners in a glorious course', had joined the newly emancipated
French and 'form'd a ring/ And, hand in hand, danced round and
round the Board'. Though by 1817 concern for France had given way
in England to debate over the legitimacy of government, social
justice, and institutionalised corruption, the language of revolutionary
zeal continued. In the Latmian's call for 'a touch ethereal – a new
birth' (I. 298) we see a version of the apocalyptic imagery of Blake,
and the semi-mystical faith in the power of Nature expressed at the
beginning of Paine's *Rights of Man* in a quotation from a speech of La
Fayette – 'Call to mind the sentiments which Nature has engraved in
the heart of every citizen, and which take a new form once they are

solemnly recognized by all: For a nation to love liberty, it is sufficient
that she knows it.'[24] The word 'ethereal' is twice used by Keats in a
poem *To Hope* in 1815 to describe the hope he opposes to his fears of
liberty being stifled by 'the base purple' (39) of regality after the
abdication of Napoleon.

The historical dimension of *Endymion* Book I can be further brought
out by reference to another of Hunt's poems – *The Descent of Liberty*,
the masque written in 1815 in response to the allied victory over
Napoleon. Keats adopted from this work both his pastoral setting and
the ideal of an organic community where, to quote from the *Descent*,
'all live well together,/ The high in rank, the low in liberty' (I. 52–3)
under the leadership of Eunomus, and where in gatherings 'on every
lightsome green' the people are taught by Liberty to know that
henceforth 'masters' may be chosen as best befits '[their] free selves'
(III. 677–716). Yet whereas Hunt, in the flush of post-Waterloo
enthusiasm, is concerned with identifying and consolidating gains,
Keats, in the much darker and beleaguered atmosphere of 1817, is
polemical and unsure. Certainly, he puts no faith in the nations but
builds instead upon two subsidiary emphases in Hunt's masque – the
force of love and the force of poetry. Both of these are situated by Hunt
on the margins of a topography of good government and societal
organisation. Love is a token of universal fellowship, where 'heart is
full, but love for all/ Swims at the top', in a world that has learned to
resist 'tyrannic juggler[s]' (III. 138–9, II. 8). Poetry appears as one of
the agents of 'Truth and Right' – in a procession which, culminating
in the enthroned shapes of Chaucer, Shakespeare, and Milton, aligns
truth and right with English cultural tradition. In Keats, in a
movement from Book II through the rest of the poem, Love and
Poetry are placed at the centre of a much less conventional vision of
redemptive possibilities.

It has been claimed that at the beginning of Book II Keats rejects
history in favour of 'a private world of desire'.[25] In fact, the history he
renounces is specifically that of martial conflict and prowess – 'The
woes of Troy', the exploits of Alexander and his 'Macedonian
numbers', 'the death-day of empires' (II. 8, 24–5, 34). When he calls
'pageant history' a 'gilded cheat' and a 'Wide sea' on which rotten
boats are transformed to 'goodly vessels' (II. 14–20) he may well be
pointing to the 'naumachia', or mock naval battle, centre-piece of the
'national jubilee' organised on 1 August 1814 by 'the councils of the
Prince Regent' to celebrate peace – and the accession of the House of

Brunswick, for whose centenary this date was chosen.[26] History, he implies, is constructed in the service of political interests. But history is a 'cheat' for Keats also because it fails to inscribe what is most valuable in human experience – above all, love itself. His own cause will be to serve *this* 'sovereign power', 'striving to uprear/ Love's standard on the battlements of song' (II. 1, 40–1). The military terms signal the co-option of the language of conventional warfare into Keats's own cultural offensive – his writing, not of an alternative history, but an altogether different set of values for humankind, a new way of governing and measuring being-in-the-world.

The project reaches its climax in Book III, in the account of the 'great enfranchisement' (299) wrought by Endymion in the story of Endymion and Glaucus. There is a topical sub-text in this episode too. Glaucus has been imprisoned in a spell of inaction by the sorceress Circe, and, as June Q. Koch long ago made clear, in both satirical cartoons and the *Examiner* itself, legitimacy, in the person of Louis XVIII, had been identified with Circe. On 4 February 1816, Hunt writes of how the 'French wags have converted the title of the new order of loyalty, *Compagnons du Lys*, into *Compagnons d'Ulysse*, whom Circe changed into swine'; while a widely circulated print by Cruikshank shows Louis and a host of pigs wearing fleur-de-lis ribbons being put to flight by bees and bursting shells.[27] The legend to this caricature, 'Wake! drowsy Sluggard wake & see/ The Lily yielding the active *Bee*/ Hear Europe cry with one indignant voice/ The People's sovereign is the *people's choice*!!', casts light back upon the people's gathering in Book I and the priest's bearing of 'valley-lilies, whiter still' (I. 157), and suggests an appropriation in Keats of the reactionary colour, white, to the popular side.[28] That Keats has the evils of tyranny more generally in mind, moreover, is evident from his recall of the speeches of the American patriot, Patrick Henry – 'give me liberty or give me death'[29] – in one victim's challenge to Circe's thraldom – 'Or give me to the air, or let me die!' (III. 542). While the 'grovelling, serpenting . . . deformities' of the Circean multitude represent the effects of authorised oppression and self-abasement, Endymion's release of Glaucus from the 'scummy slime' of 'long captivity' (III. 330–7) expresses hopes that the chains might be broken. That Keats intends this message is all the more certain from the fact that he altered Ovid's original narrative (*Metamorphoses*, XIV. 37–74), where Glaucus resists Circe in the first place.

Koch, then, is right to say that Keats's poem declares 'the need for political action',[30] and Endymion plays a central role in this theme. Glaucus himself is, whatever else, a type of the Poet, bearing the insignia of 'book', 'wand', and priestly 'stole' (III. 196–230); Endymion, 'the youth elect', is at once his counterpart – they are 'twin brothers in this destiny' (III. 713) – and his successor. Endymion's first encounter with the old man – 'Upon a weeded rock this old man sat,/ And his white hair was awful, and a mat/ Of weeds were cold beneath his cold thin feet' (III. 193–5) – is a recollection of Wordsworth's meeting with the Leech-gatherer, the 'oldest Man . . . that ever wore grey hairs';[31] but Keats rolls over the plot of 'Resolution and Independence' so as to bring to the fore the Poet's status as redeemer, agent of both individual (that is, Glaucus's) and collective renewal. Whereas in Wordsworth's psychodrama the narrator is rescued from solipsism and fear by the example of the Leech-gatherer's firmness and persistence, in Keats the youthful wanderer restores the aged Glaucus, who is caught in the stasis of self-preoccupation, reading the book in which is inscribed his *loath'd existence* (III. 691). When Glaucus tears up his scroll he abdicates in favour of one who transforms the dead letter into the potent means of a present awakening:

> . . . [he] onward went upon his high employ,
> Showering those powerful fragments on the dead.
> And, as he pass'd, each lifted up its head,
> As doth a flower at Apollo's touch.   (III. 783–6)

In this is proclaimed a new Romantic order, where words not swords hold magnificent sway. The affirmation of the true sublimity and superior lordship of the Poets is carried into the very heart of the poem.

But what are we to make of the terms in which Endymion finally *consummate[s] all* (III. 710) – resurrecting the host of shipwrecked lovers that Glaucus has laid out beneath the sea? Even here political points are being made. Pushing to the limit Hunt's valorisation of Love and Beauty, Keats opposes to the orthodox ways of the world a vision of reconciliation and joy, with 'gladness in the air – while many, who/ Had died in mutual arms devout and true,/ Sprang to each other madly' (III. 792–4). His main reservation about Napoleon was that his example had taught the nations of Europe, especially 'the divine right Gentlemen', 'how to organize their monstrous armies' (*Letters*, i. 397): in *Endymion* there is positively no 'army' of 'haughty Mars' (III. 728), whether under the flag of Revolution or of Reaction, but its antitype, a 'Paphian army' of sexual passion, marching to pay homage to

> . . . Neptune on his throne
> Of emerald deep: yet not exalt alone;
> At his right hand stood winged Love, and on
> His left sat smiling Beauty's paragon.　　　(III. 862–5)

The message is clear: make love, not war. This is the Marcusean 'Great Refusal' in extreme form – a denial not only of earthly regalities but, in the just-quoted allusion to the Trinity, the dogma on which their authority is (fraudulently) predicated.

Endymion thus sustains its blend of idealism and sharp political animus. Yet something is amiss. In the final analysis the erotic specificity of Keats's imagined realm compromises the poem's affirmative and ideological thrust, pressing to near-parody the cult of the sensuous and the aesthetic:

> 　　　　　　Cupid, *empire-sure*,
> Flutter'd and laugh'd . . .
> 　　　　　Then dance, and song,
> And garlanding grew wild; and pleasure *reign'd*.
> In harmless tendril they each other *chain'd*,
> And strove who should be *smother'd* deepest in
> Fresh crush of leaves.　　　(III. 931–7: italics mine)

This is hedonistic fantasy. The italicised words make us aware of, and so expose to question, the imperial hauteur, trammels, and oppressiveness of the established order, and in particular perhaps of the Regency Court; but the overall impression is of a mental topography in which the contours of that other world have been both inverted and introverted. A self-sufficient scene of 'ardent listlessness' (I. 825), the lines constitute no practical model for adjusting or transforming society, or for effectively shaping present circumstance.

This is important, for it contradicts Keats's wish to be of constructive use to his generation. He insisted on one occasion that he would 'jump down Ætna for any great Public good' (*Letters*, i. 267), but saw that 'good' as arising not so much from being in perpetual opposition as from formulating a corporate framework of belief. This outward-looking concern becomes oddly explicit at the start of Book IV, where, in addressing the 'Muse of my native land' (IV. 1), he honours the idea of being a national poet, and sadly admits, in humble 'lowliness of heart' (IV. 29), that in *Endymion* he has failed to be so – 'Great Muse, thou know'st what prison,/ Of flesh and bone, curbs, and confines, and frets/ Our spirit's wings' (IV. 20–2). The imagery of confinement and flight suggests that the collective wisdom Keats now has in mind might be a transhistorical ontology, imagination as a means of grace, rather than plans for the just ordering and advancement of society.[32] Overall, however, *Endymion* accomplishes neither of these articles of faith. There are traces still in Book IV of a preoccupation with social well-being, as when, near the end, it is predicted that 'the shepherd realm shall prosper well' (IV. 863); but these are faint vestiges of a political purpose which has, after all, been overwhelmed by the pull of the psychic realm – for example, the Cave of Quietude, that 'Dark paradise' which is a 'space/ Made for the soul to wander in and trace/ Its own existence' (IV. 512 ff.). When in this Book it is announced that 'Pan will bid/ Us live in peace, in love and peace' (IV. 634–5) it is precisely in connection with a retreat from 'the abodes of mortals' (IV. 628) into an enclave of private desire, Watkins's 'compensatory [but troubled] subjectivity'.[33]

There is one section of Book IV, however, which does project an aspect of national life and identity, though without Keats knowing it, and paradoxically within an apparent international perspective. The stanzas in question, the Indian maiden's 'roundelay', range outwards on a global scale that embraces details of 'Osirian Egypt kneel[ing] adown' and of how 'kings of Inde their jewel-sceptres vail,/ And from their treasures scatter pearled hail' (IV. 145, 263–4). The story is of Bacchus's mythic journey through the East, but there is a hard contemporary significance that has wider implications for an understanding of Keats's involvement in history. It is ironical that the verses are sung by the Indian maid whom Endymion discovers lost and in need of protection, for the subcontinent was by the second decade of the nineteenth century very firmly subjected to British political and economic control, after progressive underpinning of the victories over French, and indeed native, interests (the third and decisive defeat of the Pindaris and Marathas took place in 1817). An Indian voice becomes the unquestioning vehicle of Keats's unwitting but definite imaginative consumption, and entrepreneurial representation, of the Orient.

Sometimes, it is true, Keats does think about the fact of empire, and takes a critical stance towards it. Ceylon, captured from the Dutch in 1795 and formally ceded to Britain by treaties of 1802 and 1815, is the focus of the inhuman and dehumanising outreach of Isabella's brothers (*Isabella*, 113–15). Later, Keats talks of how the government fears to prosecute the radical bookseller Richard Carlile because 'they are afraid of his defence: it would be published in all the papers all

over the Empire' (*Letters*, ii. 194); the lines of communication that
enable imperial expansion also make it vulnerable to the spread of
ideas. Yet, for all his libertarianism and exposure of abuses, Keats
(unlike Byron in his treatment of the East in the 'Turkish Tales') gives
no evidence of valuing cultures in contradistinction to his own, or
even of respecting their otherness, though he may recognise their
strangeness. He is highly conscious of problems of national identity
but none the less assumes the centrality, and indeed superiority, of
England and Englishness.

This is especially apparent in his response to America, which was
never for him the *exemplum* of successful revolution or bastion of
freedom, but a stage for acquisitive self-interest against which the
high-minded culture of England, or at least of one English tradition,
could be highlighted:

Dilke . . . pleases himself with the idea that America will be the country to
take up the human intellect where england leaves off – I differ there with him
greatly – A country like the united states whose greatest Men are Franklins
and Washingtons will never do that – They are great Men doubtless but how
are they to be compared to those of our countrey men Milton and the two
Sidneys – The one is a philosophical Quaker full of mean and thrifty maxims
the other sold the very Charger who had taken him through all his Battles –
Those American's are great but they are not sublime Man – the humanity of
the United States can never reach the sublime – Birkbeck's mind is too much
in the American Stryle [*sic*] – you must endeavour to infuse a little Spirit of
another sort into the Settlement . . .   (*Letters*, i. 397–8)

The closing sentences declare a private set of references that tends
often to operate in or behind Keats's judgements on the United
States. It was to Morris Birkbeck's Settlement of 16,000 acres in
Illinois, purchased from the Government for resale, that the George
Keatses, addressees of this journal letter, were heading. Keats had
originally consented to his brother's plans to go abroad as a farmer
because he felt him to be 'of too independant and liberal a Mind to get
on in trade in this Country' (*Letters*, i. 287). But the fact is that, after a
long and tortuous journey that eventually took him elsewhere than
Illinois, George fell victim to a business swindle which left Keats more
convinced than ever that the Americans were 'fleece[rs]', and
embroiled him in troublesome and futile efforts to raise funds in
London to put George back on his feet. It is odd to think of Keats in
Hampstead or Winchester having such certain and complicated links
with a vast new world in the making. Yet, peculiarly personal though

they were in origin, these links served to raise larger issues, and above all to intensify his interest in his native civilisation. In the above letter to the George Keatses he also complains of the present government's departure from 'Simplicity' and the standards of 'national Honesty' associated with Milton, Algernon Sidney, and the Whig tradition latterly represented by Cowper, whose long lament in *The Task* for a situation where 'th'age of virtuous politics is past,/ And we are deep in that of cold pretence' (V. 493–4) is firmly called to mind by Keats's reference to the absence of anything 'manly' or 'sterling' in the government and to the reign of 'interest', 'Vanity', and a dishonourable 'Officinal Atmosphere' (*Letters*, i. 396). This is the letter, too, in which Keats, associating himself with the Whig 'sublime', disassociates himself from political extremes, both the revolutionary 'Madmen . . . who would like to be beheaded on [T]ower Hill merely for the sake of eclat' and intellectuals like Leigh Hunt 'who from a principle of taste would like to see things go on better'. The sceptical, even dismissive tone towards his erstwhile mentor is unmistakable. Here, in October 1818, Keats wants neither to pull things down nor simply to espouse fashionable causes for improvement. He wants to bind the nation together in uncertain times and to help it to understand itself in positive terms.

Hyperion, commenced in mid-August 1818, reflects these aims. The decision to write in *blank verse* was itself significant, signalling a move away from Hunt and alignment with the more conservative poetics of Milton and, especially, Wordsworth. Keats had predictable reservations about Wordsworth's canvassing for the Tory Lowthers in the election campaign of summer 1818 – 'Wordsworth versus Brougham!! Sad – sad – sad – and yet the family has been his friend always' (*Letters*, i. 299) – but his abandoning of what Lockhart had called 'the loose, nerveless versification, and Cockney rhymes of the poet of *Rimini*' (*KCH*, 104) in favour of the measure of *The Excursion* represents a definite and public shift of position in the politics of style – a sign of his wanting to come in from the margins, where the reviewers had placed him, to the centre.

Keats always respected Wordsworth, but there was at this point in his career a discernible increase in the seriousness with which he took him as a model. On 3 February 1818 he acknowledges Wordsworth's 'grandeur' yet says he 'will have no more of it', taking it as the type of modern authoritarian poetry, which 'has a palpable design upon us', as opposed to a poetry that is 'great & unobtrusive' (*Letters*, i. 224).

Significantly, the imagery used to qualify this 'grandeur' is of regality and strict government: each of the moderns 'governs his petty state' like an Elector of Hanover, knowing how many straws are swept up daily in all his dominions and continually itching to ensure that all domestic coppers are well scoured. In art, as in politics, Keats, at this stage, favoured evident democratic ideals, and indeed in a letter of 19 February he actually develops the idea of 'a grand democracy' in his discourse on the spider and the bee, which asserts that almost everyone is potentially creative 'like the Spider spin[ning] from his own inwards', everyone a prospective member of a 'fellowship' in the giving and receiving of intellectual and spiritual nourishment (*Letters*, i. 231–2). The same anti-authoritarian emphasis is still present, perhaps, in the later opposition between the 'Wordsworthian or egotistical sublime' and the species of 'poetical Character' which Keats claims for himself, which is to have 'no Identity', but to be constantly – selflessly and without discrimination – conceiving, or being subsumed in, the identities of others (*Letters*, i. 386–7). By now, however, Keats had also discovered another Wordsworth, 'deeper than Milton' the supreme 'Philosopher', which is the Wordsworth who sees into 'the human heart', bears the burden of a 'World . . . full of Misery and Heartbreak, Pain, Sickness and oppression' (*Letters*, i. 281–2). This is the Wordsworth he follows in *Hyperion* – though there is a prominent place, too, for the Philosopher. In this later letter the imagery has changed from webs and topographies of organic interaction to the 'grand march of intellect', suggesting Keats's interest both in progress and in a process whereby 'a mighty providence subdues the mightiest Minds [like Milton and Wordsworth] to the service of the time being'. In *Hyperion* he seeks to insert himself alongside Wordsworth in the van of that 'march', interpreting the present to the present, in both humanistic and theoretical terms.

Hyperion's treatment of the events and concerns of 'the time being' has been given thorough attention elsewhere.[34] What I wish to emphasise here are the main strategies Keats offers for coping with, and looking constructively at, contemporary upheaval. If the original objective of *Endymion* is to unsettle, that of *Hyperion* is to enlighten and console. Central to this thrust, of course, is Oceanus's great speech (II. 173–243) which brings both 'comfort' and 'truth'. Just as the Titans arose to rule 'new and beauteous realms' (II. 201), so have they been succeeded:

'for 'tis the eternal law
That first in beauty should be first in might:
Yea, by that law, another race may drive
Our conquerers to mourn as we do now . . .' (II. 228–31)

This is the manifest philosophic side of the poem, and its most direct
recipe for satisfying the rage for order in the face of chaos. Part of a
debate in dramatic form, it avoids didacticism, a 'palpable design'
upon the reader, but it does project a clear message – a benign
necessitarianism, an account of historical process that subsumes
problems of Power and Revolution under the concept of Evolution.
Everything is in essence determined by 'Nature's law', and this leads
onwards and upwards from 'purer life' to 'fresh perfection' (II. 181,
211–12). Change is inevitable, continuous, and decidedly for the
better. For Keats, struggle, and death, are (at least for the moment)
part and parcel of a universal pattern of decline and renewal that is
fundamentally progressive.

This broadly optimistic teleology – pragmatic and serviceable
where *Endymion* had been improbably idealistic in its elevation of
organicist social formations and of Love – remained useful to Keats as
a way of explaining history. He applied it, for example, in the
aftermath of Peterloo, in probably his most considered attempt to
place present happenings within a larger context. Keats argued that
'All civiled countries become gradually more enlighten'd and there
should be a continual change for the better', and identified three
'great changes': the 'annihilation of the tyranny of the nobles' and (in
England) concomitant emplacement of constitutional monarchy; the
rise of despotism in Europe and the ensuing French Revolution,
which, however, had the 'unlucky' result of prompting the Court to
reactionary policies and of 'put[ting] a stop to the rapid progress of
free sentiments in England'; and the 'present struggle in England of
the people . . . to destroy [the] superstition' against 'in[n]ovation and
improvement'. 'Perpaps on this account', he goes on,

the pres'ent distresses of this nation are a fortunate thing – tho so horrid in
the[i]r experience. You will see I mean that the french Revolution put a
tempor[a]ry stop to this third change, the change for the better – Now it is in
progress again and I thing in an effectual one. This is no contest beetween
whig and tory – but between right and wrong.   (*Letters*, ii. 193–4)

This is Keats standing firmly, sensitively, intelligently, as he wished to
be, on 'the Liberal side of the Question' (*Letters*, ii. 180).

At the same time, however, we can hardly miss the recurrent note of tentativeness in this statement (*'should* be', *'Per[h]aps'*, 'I *thin[k]'*) and Keats's sudden qualification of his abstract view of suffering in 'distresses . . . are a fortunate thing – *tho so horrid in the[i]r experience'* (italics mine). This is important, for it links with the pointing within *Hyperion* itself to the limitations of the rationalising stance represented by Oceanus, valuable though his theory is as a means of making sense of things. We cannot altogether dismiss either Enceladus's description of his fellow Titan as 'over-wise' or the emotional force of his outcry, 'Much pain have I for more than loss of realms' (II. 309, 334). The wisdom of *Hyperion* as a whole includes the cerebral detachment of the Oceanus passage but also outreaches it by looking into 'the human heart', the 'dark passages' of life, as Wordsworth, in Keats's view, had so pre-eminently done (*Letters*, i. 281–2). The dying splendour of Hyperion and the Titans 'chain'd in torture' are relevant here, but most obvious is the experience of Saturn himself, his 'realmless eyes . . . closed' (I. 19):

> 'I am gone
> Away from my own bosom: I have left
> My strong identity, my real self,
> Somewhere between the throne, and where I sit
> Here on this spot of earth . . .
> Search, Thea, search! and tell me, if thou seest
> A certain shape or shadow, making way
> With wings or chariot fierce to repossess
> A heaven he lost erewhile: it must – it must
> Be of ripe progress – Saturn must be King.
> Yes, there must be a golden victory . . .'
>
> (I. 112–16, 121–6)

This is the unseeing Man of Power, 'blind from sheer supremacy' (II. 185); unable to imagine regeneration, or indeed existence itself, except in the ironic shape of a former self which has been irretrievably lost. Behind the portrayal of Saturn undoubtedly lies recall of Napoleon's escape from Elba, the Hundred Days of his bid to re-establish his reign, and his defeat at Waterloo; and the above-quoted passage appears to owe something to Hunt's statuary dethroned Emperor in the prologue to *The Descent of Liberty*, who 'Sits wrapped in double gloom, listening at times,/ With half a fear, to catch the expected sound/ Of numbers coming in their fresh revenge' (24–6). But where Hunt is allegorical Keats unveils the human meanings present in history. The precise cue for the figure of Saturn comes of course from Shakespeare's study in purblind regality, Lear, who similarly must be King – or nothing.

Thus is Keats alert to the sufferings of those caught up in the drama of history, and this plainly connects with his ever-increasing sense of life as a precarious state of nature. Reflecting upon America and upon the epoch of Louis XIV, he concluded that 'the people' of all societies, primitive and civilised, are burdened alike by 'mortal pains'; 'Man' is ineluctably 'a poor forked creature' (another recollection of *Lear*), and although capable of advancing his physical and material welfare he remains subject to 'hardships and disquietude of some kind': 'If he improves by degrees his bodily accomodations and comforts – at each stage, at each accent there are waiting for him a fresh set of annoyances' (*Letters*, ii. 100–1). This was written just as *Hyperion* was abandoned, and it can be argued that the collapse of the poem, its refusal of closure, is due, not to Keats's professed dissatisfaction with the extent of its 'Miltonic inversions' (*Letters*, ii. 167), but to a clash between the secular optimism of evolutionary theory and a stubborn religious insistence on unavoidable human ordeals (not exactly Judaeo-Christian, since Keats rejects 'superstitious' notions of 'a vale of tears' from which we are 'redeemed' (*Letters*, ii. 101–2), yet haunted none the less by the shadow of the Fall). The young Apollo, who should be the end point and guarantee of the eternal law of progress, turns out in the event to be 'Apollo anguish'd' not only from a knowledge of history ('Names, deeds, gray legends, dire events . . .') but from being in the world itself, as he passes through a liminal state to 'Die into life' (III. 130, 114, 130). As well as this structural, and ideological, impasse, of course, the advent of Apollo signals Keats's turning-in, and becomes in *The Fall of Hyperion* the site of his grappling, often bewildered, with the question of his own function as poet: is he a mere 'dreaming thing' or is he 'a sage;/ A humanist, physician to all men' (I. 168ff., 189ff.)? In Book I of *Endymion* he had been a 'dreamer' of sorts, figuring an ideal social formation, 'weav[ing]/ A paradise for a sect' (*The Fall*, I. 1–2); but there had always been that other aspiration, to bear and heal amidst 'the agonies, the strife/ Of human hearts' (*Sleep and Poetry*, 124–5), and the treatment of suffering in *Hyperion* exemplifies the most obvious of all consoling strategies in Romanticism, or any other discourse. Keats's Titans – in effect strangely like Milton's Adam and Eve making their solitary exit from Eden – are life in a symbolic attitude, configurations of a grand pathos, art hallowing tribulation and lack. This is transcendence through aestheticisation. *To Autumn*, as we shall see, spreads the same balm more potently, because in more concentrated form and without the encounter with subjectivity which in *Hyperion* finally exposes the limits, the relativism and artifice, of imaginative affirmation – though the very success of the poem has rendered it especially controversial and vulnerable to ideological attack in recent times. First, however, there are good reasons to consider the opposite pole of the theme of Keats and history – self-chronicling, the I-realm.

On First Looking into Chapman's Homer (1816) is as much a cultural narrative as *Hyperion*, but one centring, at least initially, in questions of individual rather than collective need and potentiality. Complicating the poem's evident status as the young Keats's bid for entry into English poetic tradition, Marjorie Levinson's brilliant (if overextended) analysis argues for a reading of the text as a profoundly radical projection of 'the authority of an *anti*-nature'.[35] Lockhart's vitriolic early review cues such an angle, when, sneering at Keats's origins and lack of education, he comments that he 'knows Homer only from Chapman' (*KCH*, 103). The remark has a double implication: not only does Keats have no Greek, he enjoys Homer through Chapman's eccentric Elizabethan translation rather than the received version by Pope, one of Lockhart's favourite disciplined writers. Moreover, as Levinson stresses, Keats doesn't actually *read* Homer at all, even second-hand, but *looks into* it, absorbing bits and pieces, as he likes, opportunistically. Lockhart's reaction highlights both the oddity and the challenge of this *parvenu* poet's relation to literature, learning and the institutions they represent – at once askew *and* appropriative, in search of space and possession. It is this latter, acquisitive, strain that Levinson underestimates. She takes the fulsome claims to literary ease at the beginning of the sonnet as histrionic hyperbole that undermines 'the premise of natural authority'. But the effect is also of aggressive amplification, an ambiguous mixture of cocksure difference and dedicated conformity to conventional goals that is present throughout the opening section. 'Much have I travell'd in the realms of gold' (1): 'travell'd' suggests 'travailed', Keats working his passage – and still working it – where others, more privileged, have made a leisurely grand tour. 'Round many western islands have I been' (3): the preposition, foregrounded by its location at the head of the inverted syntax, carries particular weight, emphasising how this intending poet circumnavigates the place which established 'bards' actually 'hold', occupy, if only as vassals of ('in fealty to') Apollo. He exists on the periphery, the circumference; yet he has reconnoitred the territory, marked a circle around it, staked a definite claim. Keats is an oppositional outsider, but his urge is to be on the inside, to make it his own. He seeks to empower himself, by right, *within* a culture which, though available, is his neither by birth nor even upbringing.

This is paradigmatic both of Keats's usual brand of 'radicalism' and of the conservative wing of Whig, Protestant, middle-class tradition to which it broadly belongs. *On Chapman's Homer* inscribes, not revolutionary dissidence, but a progressive ideology of upward mobility, inward penetration and procurement. Its imagery is drawn immediately from the voyages of discovery, Cortez and Balboa, but, given Keats's background and objectives, it evokes, too, the profitable 'bourgeois' adventures of Robinson Crusoe and *The Pilgrim's Progress*; no longer adrift in uncertainty, as when he had been mentally at sea with 'oar snapt, and canvass rent' in the epistle to Cowden Clarke, Keats has his course confidently set for gain and recognition. Levinson contends that in the sonnet's last four lines, Keats's sympathy is all with the 'men' who are rendered 'free and vital', in contrast to the 'master', who is 'stuck [and] frozen'. This is narrow assertion, predicated on a forced reading of 'wild' as meaning simply 'free' (which is in fact one definition Johnson's *Dictionary* does *not* list): we should take the text more at face value, and see Keats as indeed feeling 'like stout Cortez', whom we should see in turn, not as (in Levinson's dismissive phrasing) a mere 'solid citizen', but as intrepid, and manifestly virile, explorer, whose stoutness suggests the virtues of resolution and control as well as, perhaps, a capacity for loyal service. 'Travell'd', 'loud and bold', 'eagle eyes', also imply stalwart effort and resources; and these are qualities the poem finally valorises, together with freedom of spirit and sublime exaltation. Critics often cite Keats's confusion here of William Robertson's accounts of Balboa's first sight of the Pacific and Cortez's of Mexico City, but equally important is the recall of William Gilbert's commentary on his poem, *The Hurricane*, as quoted in one of Wordsworth's notes to *The Excursion*: 'when he ... contemplates, from a sudden promontory, the distant, vast Pacific – and feels himself a freeman in this vast theatre, and commanding each ready produced fruit of this wilderness, and each progeny of this stream – his exaltation is not less than imperial'.[36] The fall upon 'imperial' is especially forceful in drawing out the latent concern in Keats's sonnet with conquest and command

– both of course called to mind by the very name of Cortez, and by his *over-seeing* of the productive landscape before and beneath him. Keats's text is a private dream of self-elevation, but it nevertheless reproduces and endorses the values of the status quo, even as it challenges the hegemony of an entrenched Establishment. His desire for advancement and the possession of space enacts at the individual level the core impulses of a competitive and expansionist – incipiently imperialist – society.

The same impression of art being bound up – inescapably but unconfessedly – with the disposition and exigencies of a materialist culture is raised at the very outset of the poem in the phrases 'realms of gold' and 'many goodly states and kingdoms', which, though on a figurative level proclaiming a pure world of imaginative riches, make that world easily translatable back into a sphere of ownership and economic quest – art itself, or more precisely writing, as dominion and a rate of exchange. In the discourse of the letters the connection between poetry and prosperity, or the lack of it, in Keats's thought and experience is often less guarded. In his usual money trouble, he once considered taking a job as ship's surgeon on an Indiaman, or of emigrating to South America (*Letters*, ii. 114–15): but mental voyaging offered the readier chance of making good, in actuality as well as fantasy. He was idealistic enough to say that he would not 'Mortgage [his] Brain' by producing essays for the rebarbative *Blackwood's*, yet, with that exception, he would 'spin . . . any thing for sale' (*Letters*, ii. 178–9); and when he writes to George Keats in September 1819 he dignifies authorship with the title of 'literary Pilgrimage' but reveals its ends as in practice anything but selfless and spiritual, speaking as he does of being 'in the way of acquiring property', of wishing to 'employ [him]self', or, with regard to a possible contract, of the probability that the publisher Murray would '[since] my reputation is very low . . . not have negociated my bill of intellect or given me a very small sum' (*Letters*, ii. 210–11). Commissions – he goes on – are in any case a bad thing since they are a sacrifice of the 'great benefits which one's own untramell'd and free industry may bring one in the end'; yet industry is 'free' of course only in this specialised sense, and Keats's texts, poetic or otherwise, inevitably operate under – though they may also reformulate, react against, even provisionally transcend – the impress, socio-structural, historical, discursive, of the world he inhabits.

Even *To Autumn* is by no means unmarked by such contingencies.

Ever since Jerome J. McGann's essay 'Keats and the Historical Method' it has been difficult to read the poem without thinking of the event which Keats had just witnessed and refers to in a letter the day before composition began – 'Orator' Henry Hunt's 'triumphal entry' into the metropolis after being released on bail pending his trial as leader of the reform meeting at St Peter's Fields, Manchester (*Letters*, ii. 194). For McGann, as I understand his rather testing conclusion, it is hard to feel 'anything but shame' in the presence of a lyricism, like that of *To Autumn*, which sets aside harsh political realities – Peterloo, the Six Acts restricting freedom of speech and assembly, distress caused by economic crisis and a run of bad harvests, the riots in manufacturing towns – in a celebration of 'the sufficiency of the imagination' (*KHM*, 61–5).

It can be argued that the background which McGann apparently considers to be wilfully excluded from the text is in fact curiously there in traces: the process of 'Conspiring' (3) that evokes the very nature of political action; the 'bees' that, as we saw from political cartoons, may emblematise the populace, or even workers; the 'clammy cells' that suggest the government lock-up and/or sweatshops (and it is obvious which side Keats is on from the imagery of self-help in 'load[ing] and bless[ing]' and of happy unexpected profusion in 'o'er-brimm'd', 3, 11). But to unpick this thread is to enforce rather than challenge McGann's argument. The only real answer to McGann perhaps – and it is a necessary one if we are not to collude in making of Romanticism a bankrupt ideology of evasion – is to reverse his emphasis and unashamedly embrace *To Autumn* as a poem of positive transhistorical value, a model process of sustained forgetting out of which comes a spiritual calm and refreshment. Conflict and oppressive power are forgotten in the image of nature's beneficent conspiracy to 'load and bless'; deprivation is forgotten in plenitude; revolution among men is forgotten in the cycle of the seasons; labour, the getting of the earth's fruits, is forgotten in the figure of 'careless' Autumn sitting, sleeping, gliding steadily over obstacles, watching the press – which we hardly, if at all, register as a machine – endlessly extracting sustenance; violence is forgotten, as the 'hook/ Spares the next swath' (17–18); even illusion is forgotten, for it is the bees, not the poet or humankind, that are captivated by a utopian present, 'think[ing] warm days will never cease' (10). And there are in the poem, too, vestiges of other, more intimate experiences, transformed into aspects of a benign and beautiful topography of 'natural good': do we not see in the 'bloom' and 'rosy hue' of the 'soft-dying day' (25–6) a projection and dissolution of the features of the tubercular Tom Keats, who had died the previous December, and even, speculatively, of Keats himself, who was suffering from sore throats? Do we not find in the curiously genderless, though deeply sensuous, figure of Autumn, 'hair soft-lifted' (15), a sublimation of Keats's disturbed desire for Fanny Brawne, from whom he was trying to 'wean' himself (*Letters*, ii. 160)? In *Endymion* Keats had spoken of heavenly 'Powers' who commune with earth, 'every sense/ Filling with spiritual sweets to plenitude,/ As bees gorge full their cells' (III. 30–4). *To Autumn* ties the production of 'spiritual sweets' firmly to a tellurian dimension, a reciprocity between recreative (in both senses) imagination and the materials of this world: it exists, a thing of beauty in midst of woe, as a comprehensive consolation, where self, history, nature as it is, have become constituents of a new and surpassing 'reality'.

Clearly, McGann's foregrounding of Peterloo is itself an ideological and tendentious manoeuvre (Marxist-led, in fact), rather than the open, generous recovery of history that he would have us believe his 'method' to be.[37] Keats's long journal letter of 17 to 27 September 1819 contains not only the references to 'Orator' Hunt, and reflections on the 'distresses of the people', but a concern with the petty materialism of the Americans, amply attested by the fraud apparently perpetrated upon his brother (*Letters*, ii. 185, 210–12, 217). It is here that we are made aware with particular force of Keats being strangely touched by the rhythms of a changing world – a world that was in one sense rapidly expanding, not least through the development of north America, and in another was contracting through business connections and improved communications. The intenser feeling for questions of national identity and cultural heritage which was one clear result of these circumstances then comes out in Keats's decision to give up tinkering with the idea of joining George: 'it is quite out of my interest to come to America – What could I do there? How could I employ myself? Out of the reach of Libraries' (*Letters*, ii. 210); 'interest' and 'employ' signal again the meritocratic and pecuniary motives that so haunt Keats's texts, yet 'Libraries', the repositories of accumulated wisdom, which the fledgling States do not have, are the *sine qua non* of all effective performance. Plainer chords, however, are struck on the same theme, for much of this letter is taken up with a retrospective account of Keats's tour of Scotland in the summer of 1818, packed with information and observations on that nation's history, customs, and scenery (*Letters*, ii. 195–9); and, nearer home, he is equally fascinated by the Englishness of Winchester and its vicinity, not only in the often-quoted passage on 'chaste weather . . .' (*Letters*, ii. 167), but in a kaleidoscope of responses to landscape and architecture, ranging from 'door steps always fresh from the flannel', through the various churches of this 'ancient aristocratical place', to the 'Cathedral yard', 'gardens', and 'clear river' of the mental perambulation against the background of which Keats asserts his intention to develop 'a more thoughtful and quiet power' in his poetic writing (*Letters*, ii. 166, 189, 209).

The impulses behind the 'quiet power' of *To Autumn* – and McGann takes no note of this – include nationalistic ones. Most revealing of all is his interest in an Englishness of idiom. His turning from Miltonic style because it was too 'artful', 'a beautiful and grand Curiosity', is common knowledge, but it is less often realised that on two occasions this renunciation was accompanied by a celebration of pure English, the chief exponent of which was, in Keats's view, Thomas Chatterton: 'I always somehow associate Chatterton with autumn. He is the purest writer in the English Language. He has no French idiom, or particles like Chaucer's . . . English ought to be kept up' (*Letters*, ii. 167):

The Paradise lost though so fine in itself is a curruption of our Language . . . The purest english I think – or what ought to be the purest – is Chatterton's – The Language had existed long enough to be entirely uncorrupted of Chaucer's gallicisms and still the old words are used . . . I prefer the native music of it to Milton's cut by feet . . .   (*Letters*, ii. 212)

And Chatterton is duly echoed in *To Autumn* – especially the passage in *Aella* (1777), 'When the fayre apple, rudde as even skye,/ Do bend the tree unto the fructyle ground' (184–5) – along with prominent evocations of Thomson and of Coleridge.[38] Even when there is neologism or rare usage, as with 'oozings' or 'plump' (22, 7), the roots are germanic. The word 'plump', adjective made verb, is one of the expressions in *To Autumn* taken forwards from *Endymion* (see IV. 377), and very much the type of linguistic smartness condemned by hostile reviewers of the Cockney School.[39] This raises the question of how far *Endymion* itself reflects a desire to create for the present an English idiom, by getting back beyond French and classical influences – and 'create', of course, is the word – for the 'purity' of Keats's language, as of Chatterton's, is notional, and is predicated essentially on the basis of difference (in the case of *To Autumn*, non-Miltonic, non-Wordsworthian) and exclusion. Certainly, when, in the early manifesto *Sleep and Poetry* (1816), Keats lauds Hunt as the saviour of English poetry it is alongside a recuperation of the 'manhood' and 'high Imagination' of the Elizabethans representing the central poetic line, in opposition to the 'foppery and barbarism' of the French-influenced 'schism' of eighteenth-century neo-classicism (162–229):[40] the Cockneys, cast by their opponents in the role of fanciful and unprincipled rebels, were really hard-core traditionalists. *To Autumn* is the unorthodox route, via Chatterton's made-up early Englishness, to the orthodox goal of an uncorrupted language. In style as well as content it is a national poem.

But this designation should not be understood too narrowly. *To Autumn* is at once local *and* universal, geographically specified *and* unspecific, of its time *and* timeless. It is tempting to see it as realising the authority sought in *On Chapman's Homer*: affirming the creative subject – the individual and his imagination – as the locus of world-disclosure. That, however, would not be quite satisfactory, for subjectivity and making are as much under the head of erasure, or, to use my own previous phrase, of 'forgetting', as any other factors in the poem: the vision of *To Autumn* is postulated as something given, as absolute rather than relative, as revelation (in a strong sense) of nature's own autonomous 'life' and 'truth'. The self-assertiveness, 'loud and bold', of *On Chapman's Homer* and its valuing of power and possession have been replaced by self-reticence: the activity of stanza one belongs all to Autumn itself; it is not the poet who discovers Autumn, but '*whoever* seeks abroad' (13: italics mine); and even when a question is asked (suggesting an operative interrogator) it is to attest an anterior, extra-linguistic notation – 'thou hast thy music too' (24). One of Keats's early admirers sounded immediately the coming response: these are lines 'which bring the *reality of nature* more before our eyes than almost any description that we remember'.[41] Not only the appeal of *To Autumn* but its force as a cultural icon depends crucially upon its 'naturalness': the myth of nature's abundance and unfailing beauty, a version of paradise, is made actual and available to all, and is grounded, so literally that we do not register or think about the fact, in a small corner of England – which is everywhere.

The last word, however, must be that there is never one way of taking a text. As the passages quoted will tell, including those which (on inspection) so pointedly abnegate self in favour of nature, Keats's 'forgetting' stores in its occlusions and silences that which is being overlooked – political turmoil, labour, disease, and death, the constructive 'I'. Thus is *To Autumn*, in the fullest analysis, trying rather than triumphant, a projection of desire and of a freedom eternally beset by limits, existentialist in its strategic – magnificent but incomplete – transcending of those limits. Ultimately, we do not have to choose between a traditional, positivist reading of the poem's 'quiet power' as imaginative insight or poetic artifice (represented in our own time by, say, Geoffrey Hartman's work on its place as redemptive 'fiction') and McGann's lament for its escapism (which is conceived in substantial part as a corrective to Hartman's essay).[42] No poem puts greater value on poetic process, whether for individual or collective ends, but it declares at the same time the *in*sufficiency of that process as an agency of liberation from the ontological tensions of which experience of historical and social circumstance is a major – though not the only – source.

NOTES

1 Significant earlier work in the field by Thorpe, Muir, and Koch is cited in note 1 of the Introduction, to which subsequent references here are keyed. See also *KHM, KP*, and *KPP*. Parts of the present essay are based on my earlier piece, '"Alternate uproar and sad peace": Keats, Politics, and the Idea of Revolution', in J. R. Watson (ed.), 'The French Revolution in English Literature and Art', MHRA *Yearbook of English Studies* 19 (1989), 265–89, which I am conscious, variously, of confirming, modifying, and correcting.

2 See especially Harold Bloom, *The Anxiety of Influence: A Theory of Poetry* (London, 1973).

3 Cf. Cowper, *On the Receipt of My Mother's Picture* (1790), 102–3: 'Me howling winds drive devious, tempest toss'd,/ Sails ript, seams op'ning wide, and compass lost'; H. S. Milford (ed.), *Cowper: Poetical Works*, 4th edn, rev. Norma Russell (London, 1971), 396.

4 For Cowper's peculiarly prophetic attack upon the Bastille, see *The Task*, V. 379–445. Fox's use of the passage in the Commons was reported by William Hayley in his 1812 edition of the poet's works; see H. T. Griffith (ed.), *Cowper: The Task* (Oxford, 1875), 262.

5 *KL*, 1–38 and *passim*.

6 See *Table Talk*, 522 (Milford, *Cowper: Poetical Works*, 12), and letter to Joseph Johnson, Jan. 1781, J. King and C. Ryskamp (eds.), *The Letters and Prose Writings of William Cowper* (5 vols., Oxford, 1979–86) i. 433.

7 See, *inter alia*, *The Task*, V. 331–537.

8 H. S. Milford (ed.), *The Poetical Works of Leigh Hunt* (London, 1923), 144. For Keats's references to 'Libertas', see *To My Brother George*, 24, and *To Charles Cowden Clarke*, 44.

9 Cowper, *Table Talk*, 226. For detailed consideration of this subject, see my 'William Cowper and the Condition of England', in V. Newey and A. Thompson (eds.), *Literature and Nationalism* (Liverpool, 1991), 120–37.

10 *Examiner*, 1 May 1814, 273.

11 See Anne Blainey, *Immortal Boy: A Portrait of Leigh Hunt* (London, 1985), 54.

12 'Cockney School of Poetry. No. IV', *Blackwood's Edinburgh Magazine*, Aug. 1818, 519–24; in *KCH*, 97–110, esp. 109.

13 Morris Dickstein, 'Keats and Politics', *KP*, 176.

14 Marcuse advances this concept in *Eros and Civilization* (New York, 1962): see Dickstein, 'Keats and Politics' in *KP*, 176.

15 Hunt argues at length for these Keatsian ideas in his theoretical essay 'What is Poetry?', as when he proclaims that 'beauty and truth become identical in poetry, and . . . pleasure, or at its very worst, a balm for our tears, is drawn out of pain'; E. D. Jones (ed.), *English Critical Essays: Nineteenth Century* (London, 1916), 305. Published in 1844, 'What is Poetry?' was influenced by Keats's writings; but the same emphases are already implicit in *The Story of Rimini*, as, also, is the view (expressed by Hunt in defence of his sympathetic treatment of Paulo and Francesca) that 'the world . . . [is] capable of receiving its best profit through the medium of pleasurable, instead of painful, appeals to its reflection' ('Author's Preface to the Edition of 1832', Milford, *Poetical Works*, xxiv). Cf. Keats's belief in a poetry that is 'unobtrusive' rather than overtly didactic (*Letters*, i. 224) and his insistence on the relish of the 'poetical Character' for 'light and shade' alike and on the way it leads to 'speculation' from its delight in 'the dark side of things': 'What shocks the virtuous philosop[h]er, delights the camelion Poet' (*Letters*, i. 386–7).

16 'Preface [to *Foliage*], including Cursory Observations on Poetry and Cheerfulness' (1818), L. H. Houtchens and C. W. Houtchens (eds.), *Leigh Hunt's Literary Criticism* (New York, 1956), 132; 'Author's Preface', Milford, *Poetical Works*, xxiv.

17 'Author's Preface', Milford, *Poetical Works*, xxiv.

18 See Lockhart, 'The Cockney School of Poetry', *Blackwood's*, Oct. 1817, quoted in Edmund Blunden, *Leigh Hunt: A Biography* (London, 1930), 129, and the following reviews of *The Story of Rimini*: Francis Jeffrey, *Edinburgh Review* 26 (June 1816), 491; John Wilson Croker, *Quarterly Review* 14 (Jan. 1816), 477. For other similar examples, see John O. Hayden, *The Romantic Reviewers, 1802–1824* (London, 1969), 179–82.

19 Hunt, 'Author's Preface', Milford, *Poetical Works*, xxv.

20 *KPP*, 43.

21 *Examiner*, 6 Apr., 31 Aug. 1817; quoted in Koch, 493.

22 *AP*, 289 approves Aileen Ward's argument to this effect in 'Keats's Sonnet, "Nebuchadnezzar's Dream"', *PQ* 34 (1955), 177–88.

23 *Examiner*, 1 Mar. 1818; quoted in Koch, 501.

24 Quoted in Stephen Prickett, *England and the French Revolution* (London, 1989), 6. Prickett explores both trains of imagery, the 'apocalyptic' and that of 'nature', in detail.

25 *KPP*, 44.

26 *Annual Register*, 1 Aug. 1814, 67; quoted and discussed (in another context) by *AP*, 207.

27 See Koch, 498–500.

28 White had been the colour of Jacobite 'reaction', as well as of monarchist parties in the post-Revolutionary period (sometimes called in England the years of the 'White Terror'). David Pirie, however, in a lecture at the first conference of the British Association for Romantic Studies, King Alfred's College, Winchester, 1989, indicated that it was also the emblem of the Peterloo petitioners and their radical leader 'Orator' Hunt. The recurrence of the epithet 'white' in Book I of *Endymion* may thus, apart from the obvious connotations of purity and innocence, signify either the chosen badge of dissent or an ironical take-over of the standard of established authority, or both.

   There was a flourishing tradition of reference to the labouring classes as 'active' bees, in contrast to the idle drones who battened upon their forced produce. Shelley uses this metaphor of the social hive in 'Song to the Men of England', where he addresses the 'Bees of England' (9); see P. M. S. Dawson, *The Unacknowledged Legislator: Shelley and Politics* (Oxford, 1980), 50–1, where several other examples are presented from radical literature, including one from Tom Paine himself. The community depicted in Keats's poem is not politically aggressive in spirit, but it is, as we have seen, a sharing and justly ordered one, a model formation.

29 Address to the Virginia House of Delegates, 23 Mar. 1775. William Wirt's popular *Sketches of the Life and Character of Patrick Henry* (Philadelphia, 1817) gave wide circulation to his speeches: see *AP*, 228.

30 Koch, 500.

31 Wordsworth, 'Resolution and Independence', in Nicholas Roe (ed.), *William Wordsworth. Selected Poetry* (London, 1992), 186. For closer treatment of Keats's dialogue with this text, see my '"Alternate uproar and sad peace"', 275.

32 Keats might here have contemplated a new direction, leading from social to experiential values, under the influence of the introspection of the third canto of Byron's *Childe Harold*, published in 1816, a few months before book IV of *Endymion* got under way. Byron's sense of possible transcendence is closely shadowed by doubt: as, for example, in stanza xiv, on the 'clay', the mortal bondage, which holds back the 'spirit' in its projected happy 'flight'. It may also be that Keats is recalling, and inverting, Cowper's celebration of the inner liberty – freedom of spirit as distinguished from political freedom – that no oppression or affliction 'can cripple or confine' (*Task*, V. 763–78).

33 *KPP*, 44.
34 See '"Alternate uproar and sad peace"', 277–84. Apart from Muir seminal statements include Marilyn Butler, *Romantics, Rebels, and Reactionaries. English Literature and its Background 1760–1830* (Oxford and New York, 1981), 151–4 and Alan J. Bewell, 'The Political Implication of Keats's Classicist Aesthetics', *KP*, 220–9.
35 Here and in the following discussion I refer to *KL*, 11–15.
36 (1814), III. 931 n.; E. de Selincourt and H. Darbishire (eds.), *The Poetical Works of William Wordsworth* (5 vols., Oxford, 1940–9) V. 422–3.
37 'A comprehensive theory will show that we need not doubt the relevance of "extrinsic" methods and materials; rather, what the critic must weigh are the problems of how best and most fully to elucidate the poem's (presumed) networks of social relations' (*KHM*, 18).
38 For Chatterton, Thomson and Coleridge echoed in *To Autumn*, see *AP*, 651–5.
39 See, for example, Croker on 'the new words with which, in imitation of Mr Leigh Hunt, he [Keats] adorns our language' (*KCH*, 114).
40 Keats's attack upon the school of Pope, with its 'musty laws lined out with wretched rule' (195), continues that of Cowper, for whom Pope 'Made poetry a mere mechanic art' (*Table Talk*, 654). The accusations of 'foppery', moreover, are directly in line with Cowper's condemnation of the modern vogue for 'push-pin play' and 'whipt-cream' poetry (*Table Talk*, 542–55); see Milford, *Cowper: Poetical Works*, 14, 12.
41 Review (unsigned) of Keats's 1820 volume, *Monthly Review* 92 (July 1820), 305–10; rpt. *KCH*, 159–63. See esp. 162; italics mine.
42 See Hartman, 'Poem and Ideology: A Study of Keats's "To Autumn"', in *The Fate of Reading and Other Essays* (Chicago and London, 1975), 124–46; *KHM*, 49–50, 56, 59–62.

CHAPTER 10

Keats's commonwealth

Nicholas Roe

Sad sixteenth of August! accursed be the day;
When thy field, oh, St. Peter! was crimson'd with gore . . .
'Manchester Y——Y Valour', *Manchester Observer*, 18 September 1819

When Keats's readers opened *Lamia, Isabella, The Eve of St. Agnes, and Other Poems* they discovered that the book began with an apology. The publisher's Advertisement (which famously angered Keats) drew attention to 'the unfinished poem of HYPERION', explaining that the unfavourable reception of *Endymion* had 'discouraged the author from proceeding'. By noticing Keats's discouragement, Taylor and Hessey hoped to forestall hostile criticism of his third collection of poetry, and it has recently been suggested that a quality of passive reconciliation is characteristic of the volume as a whole. 'Keats's 1820 poems . . . were issued not to provoke, but to allay conflict', Jerome McGann has said:

The *Lamia* volume represented Keats's effort to show his readers how they might, by entering his poetic space, step aside from the conflicts and tensions which were so marked an aspect of that period. The whole point of Keats's great and (politically) reactionary book was not to enlist poetry in the service of social and political causes – which is what Byron and Shelley were doing – but to dissolve social and political conflicts in the mediations of art and beauty.[1]

In McGann's account the poems in Keats's 1820 volume define a 'reflexive world' that the same critic has elsewhere identified with Romantic Ideology, an ideal space far, far removed from contemporary history. Ironically, in seeking to historicise Keats's poems, McGann has emphasised their distance from the turbulent world in which they were written, first published, and reached their earliest readers. But that distance, or 'displacement', becomes in turn an index of historical pressures at work on and in the poetry. So McGann argues in *The Romantic Ideology* that 'Shelley's idealism, Byron's sensationalism, and Keats's aesthetic poetry are all displaced yet fundamental vehicles of cultural analysis and critique: a poetry of extremity and escapism which is the reflex of the circumstances in which their work, their lives, and their culture were all forced to develop'. And, yet more emphatically: 'Byron and Shelley are most deeply *engaged* (in a socialist–activist sense) when they have moved furthest along their paths of displacement and escape.'[2]

In differentiating Keats's 'reactionary' poems from the socially and politically 'enlisted' writings of Byron and Shelley, however, McGann apparently concedes the inadequacy of Romantic ideology to discriminate the full spectrum of the poets' various relations to historical conflicts and tensions. Furthermore, printing *'engaged'* in italics does not effectively demonstrate how social–political enlistment, in Byron's and Shelley's poems, coincides with the extremities of ideal displacement. The difficulty appears in the strong polarisation of this view of Romantic poetry and history, which obscures a wide range of possible attitudes and responses that intervene between social–political 'engagement' and 'paths of escape'. As a result, the unique texture of the individual poem is flattened, erasing the complex and subtle negotiations with history that may be traced through various aspects of the poem's vocabulary, form, style, and generic identity.[3] A more accommodating view of the 'mediations of art and beauty' (at the levels of word, image, emblem) is necessary in order to comprehend the involvement of history and Romantic idealism – and this will be one of my concerns in the present essay.

As Susan Wolfson demonstrates elsewhere in this volume, Shelley had done much to initiate the myth of Keatsian 'escapism' when, in his Preface to *Adonais*, he described Keats's genius as 'delicate', 'fragile', 'beautiful', a 'young flower . . . blighted in the bud'.[4] Nineteenth-century commentators elaborated this vulnerable figure into an unworldly genius, but they did so by way of assimilating a poet otherwise perceived as unsettling to contemporary literary, political, social, and sexual orthodoxies.[5] Thomas De Quincey, recalling Keats in 1846, demonstrated this clearly. 'As a man, and viewed in relation to social objects', De Quincey said, 'Keats was nothing':

It was as mere an affectation when he talked with apparent zeal of liberty, or human rights, or human prospects, as is the hollow enthusiasm which many people profess for music, or most poets for external nature. For these things

Keats fancied that he cared; but in reality he cared not at all. Upon them, or any of their aspects, he had thought too little, and too indeterminately, to feel for them as personal concerns.

De Quincey ridiculed Keats's liberal, humane imagination by insisting (like other hostile critics since the poet's lifetime) on Keats's 'thoughtless' youth; 'childish years and childish inexperience'. The source of his irritation appears elsewhere in the essay, where De Quincey recognised Keats's poems as a powerfully articulate challenge to received ideas about linguistic and stylistic decorum: 'the most shocking revolt against good sense and just feeling'; 'the most shocking abuse of his mother tongue'; 'the deep treason of these unparalleled offences'.[6]

The subversive force of Keats's writing, acknowledged here by De Quincey, had been widely remarked in early reviews of the 1817 volume, and of *Endymion* in particular. Critical responses to the 1820 collection were generally welcoming, with *Lamia* and *Isabella* attracting favourable comment, although the volume did not allay conflict altogether. Indeed a number of reviewers continued to distrust Keats's politics, indicating that some contemporaries did not perceive the reactionary, escapist tendencies dwelt upon by later critics.

John Scott, writing in Baldwin's *London Magazine* (September 1820), protested at Keats's treatment by the *Quarterly* and *Blackwood's*, observing that 'the miserable selfishness of political party has erected itself into a literary authority'. Yet his review actually conceded the political ground on which the Tory critics had attacked Keats: 'his spirit is impregnated with a flippant impatience, (irritated and justified by a false philosophy) of the great phenomena of society, and the varieties of human nature'. According to Scott, the caricature of Isabella's brothers ('these same ledger-men . . . these money-bags', 137, 142) betrayed 'all sorts of dissenting, and altercating principles and opinions', and he concluded 'it will easily be seen that [Keats] has very much, and very incautiously exposed himself to attack'. Josiah Conder, in the *Eclectic Review* (September 1820), agreed with Scott in asserting that 'there does not occur, if our recollection serves us, throughout [Keats's] present volume, a single reference to any one object of *real* interest, a single burst of virtuous affection or enlightened sentiment, a single reference, even of the most general kind, to the Supreme Being, or the slenderest indication that the Author is allied by any one tie to his family, his country, or his kind'. Both of these critics were in fact well-disposed to Keats's ambitions as a poet; nevertheless, each recognised Keats as a 'malcontent'. An alternative view of Keats's politics appeared in the *Indicator* (2 August 1820), where Leigh Hunt argued that the 1820 poems were 'coloured by the modern philosophy of sympathy and natural justice' and 'a high feeling of humanity'; the expression of 'an age of poetry [that] has grown up with the progress of experiment'.[7]

As with Keats's earlier publications, therefore, the response to his 1820 collection divided according to 'political party'. The liberal disposition welcomed by Hunt was condemned by reviewers such as Conder, for whom Keats's poetry expressed a treacherous sensibility recalling the Jacobins of the 1790s: 'At present, there is a sickliness about his productions, which shews there is a mischief at the core.'[8] Furthermore, by echoing *To Autumn*, Conder associates 'mischief' with a poem that has been widely understood as an expression of Keats's quietism. In Geoffrey Hartman's celebrated essay 'Poem and Ideology', for instance, it is presented as 'a poem without explicit social context', the voice of a 'true impersonality'.[9] Taken together, these contrasting responses to the poetry suggest that the liberalism of the 1820 volume may have been expressed in *To Autumn* as a covert mischief, the more potent for working under the sign of disinterested imagination, or 'negative capability'.

To Autumn offers an ideal, 'impersonal' image of the season. History, in this poem, has been assimilated to the natural revolutions of seasonal change, processes that are arrested, almost, and redeemed by autumnal beauty and plenitude. For Hartman *To Autumn* was best understood as a *Convito*, a banquet of English sounds and foods that nourished Keats's imagination after he had abandoned the sublime, Miltonic voice of the *Hyperion* poems.[10] A collateral interpretation has been offered by McGann, who reads *To Autumn* as 'the finished expression' of Keats's tranquil mood at Winchester during September 1819; 'Winchester, and his time there, are repeatedly seen [in Keats's letters] as a respite from the tensions not only of his own personal affairs, but of the contemporary social scene at large.' As McGann puts it, Keats 'found Winchester a wonderful refuge'; 'The city and its environs [were] magical in their ability to carry him away to a charmed world far removed from the quotidian press of his money affairs and the dangerous political tensions of his society' (*KHM*, 58). In this contextual reading of *To Autumn* McGann coincides with Hartman's (manifestly anti-historical) understanding of the poem as 'enchanted ground', a spellbound refuge from history. But maybe a less mysterious interpretation of history in *To Autumn* is possible. In the following pages I shall seek to locate the poem in relation to contemporary discourses of political and social conflict, inflecting the poem so that 'the mediations of art and beauty' may be understood as historical intervention rather than 'an attempt to "escape" the period which provides the poem with its context'.[11]

To be sure, Keats was impressed by the 'ancient aristocratical' city of Winchester, although his letters at this time dwelt at greater length on his vexing financial problems, his fragile health, and his need to 'wean' himself from Fanny Brawne: 'I am all in a mist; I scarcely know what's what'; 'I am all in a Mess here – embowell'd in Winchester'; 'I should *do* something for my immediate welfare'; 'were it not for the assistance of Brown & Taylor, I must be as badly off as a Man can be . . . I have pass'd my time in reading, writing and fretting'.[12] For a time he believed his letters were being opened in the post, a paranoia driven by his personal distress and the extremity of the times. Indeed, between 10 and 15 September Keats's private affairs overlapped with contemporary public events, when he returned to London to secure funds for his brother George. It is this brief visit which provides a focus for the composition of *To Autumn* during a period of acute unsettlement – personal, public, political, and social.

A SERIOUS CONSPIRACY IN MANCHESTER

Just published. THE GAME BOOK FOR 1819 . . . by means of which an account may be kept with ease and accuracy of the different kinds of Game, when, where, and by whom killed, how disposed of, and other particulars.

Advertisement in the Champion (29 August 1819)

On the afternoon of Monday 13 September 1819 Keats joined the large crowd gathered in The Strand to welcome 'Orator' Henry Hunt on his arrival in London. 'I[t] would take me a whole day and a quire of paper to give you any thing like detail', Keats wrote to his brother and sister-in-law: 'I will merely mention that it is calculated that 30.000 people were in the streets waiting for him – The whole distance from the Angel Islington to the Crown and anchor was lined with Multitudes' (*Letters*, ii. 194). Henry Hunt had been the principal speaker at the mass-meeting of reformists in St Peter's Fields, Manchester, a little under a month before on 16 August 1819. When the Manchester and Salford Yeomanry, on horseback, moved into the crowd to apprehend Hunt and the others, the peaceful meeting was swiftly transformed to violent confusion in which (perhaps) eleven were killed and as many as five hundred people wounded: the Peterloo Massacre. 'Confusion' and 'perhaps', because what exactly happened in Manchester that day remains controversial. Certainly, the emotive and often contradictory accounts of the tragedy in newspapers of the day encouraged rumour and dismay throughout the country. 'Within two days of Peterloo, all England knew of the event', according to E. P. Thompson: 'Within a week every detail of the massacre was being canvassed in ale-houses, chapels, workshops, private houses.'[13] Hunt and the others on the tribune were arrested and imprisoned, although the immediate charge of 'conspiracy and sedition' was soon dropped. His triumphal reception in London on 13 September reflected widespread jubilation among the reformists, but this was mingled with resentment at the behaviour of the militia, the judiciary, and – especially – the government which had endorsed without delay the actions of the soldiers and magistrates at Manchester.

In this highly-charged political environment, conspiracy theories flourished. When one reads *To Autumn* with this context in mind, the opening lines start to resonate in unusual and, I think, intriguing ways:

> Season of mists and mellow fruitfulness,
>   Close bosom-friend of the maturing sun;
> Conspiring with him how to load and bless
>   With fruit the vines that round the thatch-eves run . . .

The verb 'to conspire', from the Latin *conspirare*, literally means 'to breath together' and thus 'to accord, harmonize, agree, combine or unite in a purpose' (*OED*). So in 'conspiring' together the powers of the season and sun combine to make earth fruitful. Yet this genial conspiracy is shadowed by the contrasting sense of the word, glossed by *OED* as to 'plot mischief together secretly', and this mischievous sense of conspiracy was the primary definition of the word in Samuel Johnson's *Dictionary* (1755). In one reading, 'conspiracy' in *To Autumn* is a plot of nature to 'fill all fruit with ripeness to the core' (6) – an impersonal process of natural abundance. But that expression of nature's fruitfulness is modified by the alternative, treasonable discourses of conspiracy that were circulating widely in September 1819.

On behalf of the government, the Home Secretary Lord Sidmouth advised that the leading reformists were to be charged 'for a treasonable conspiracy to alter by force the constitution of the realm as by law established'. To Lord Eldon, the Chancellor, the meeting had been 'an overt act of conspirators, to instigate . . . specific acts of treason'.[14] *The Times* pronounced on the 'dreadful fact' of the violence at Manchester *before* the detailed account from the paper's reporter, John Tyas, had arrived in London. This leading article established the popular belief 'that nearly a hundred of the King's unarmed subjects have been sabred by a body of cavalry in the streets of a town of which most of them were inhabitants' – although Tyas's eyewitness version, published in the same edition of *The Times*, 19 August 1819, contradicted the leading article in some details. Both the leader and Tyas's report were widely reprinted and appeared in two opposition newspapers that published Keats's writings and which he is known to have read. These were the *Examiner*, edited by Leigh Hunt, and the *Champion*, edited in 1819 by John Thelwall – a leading reformist since the 1790s. Both journals followed *The Times* in agreeing on the 'dreadful fact' of what had happened in Manchester, but of course interpretations of the event differed (and still do so today). The *Examiner* reported 'disturbance' and 'atrocities' at Manchester; the *Champion* warned about 'ANARCHISTS in MILITARY UNIFORM', the breakdown of justice, and the possibility that military action against the people might provoke a violent revolution. When Henry Hunt and other leading reformists were arrested and imprisoned, the *Champion* noted that the magistrates 'brought against them a charge of *conspiracy* to alter the laws by force and threats'.[15] During the weeks after Peterloo, the *Champion* elaborated an alternative theory of conspiracy in which the powers of the state were aligned against the liberties and democratic aspirations of the people.

   For Thelwall, the reformists at Peterloo were to be identified with 'the cause of the people at large – of the Laws and the Constitution'. At St Peter's Fields the crowd had called for annual parliaments and universal suffrage; in one section of a banner held aloft in the crowd, 'Justice' was represented 'holding the scales in one hand, and a sword in the other'. From Thelwall's point of view, the military intervention was an act of 'lawless, and ruthless murder', an 'abhorrent massacre'.[16] Then, on Sunday 19 September 1819 – the day on which Keats first drafted *To Autumn* – the *Champion* published an analysis of contemporary events:

There is indeed, we believe, A SERIOUS CONSPIRACY IN

MANCHESTER – a Conspiracy of those whom fortune has favoured, to depress and keep down the less fortunate multitude whose labour has been the instrument of that favour: – a Conspiracy of the Rich against the Poor – a species of conspiracy certainly not less frequent (as it is certainly much more practicable) than a conspiracy of the poor against the rich: – nay a conspiracy which we might almost venture to say, always precedes, and not unfrequently produces, that of the latter description. These Opulent Conspirators wish to prevent the labouring classes from aspiring to any political rights – because political rights have a tendency to secure personal liberty and personal consideration. The confederacies and combinations they practice among themselves, they would interdict entirely their poorer brethren, that they may keep them in abject and entire dependence: and what the law cannot, or will not insure for them, in this respect, they would accomplish by the terrors of the sword. If nothing else will keep down the half-famishing labouring poor and stifle the cry of their complaints, it has been thought that massacre would.[17]

Keats could not have read this column on 19 September (it would have taken a day for copies to reach Winchester from London). On the other hand, political debate in August and September 1819 focused on the word 'conspire', and Thelwall was evidently responding to – and amplifying – theories of state conspiracy that were current in the broad range of reformist discourse in the months after Peterloo. The various theories of conspiracy were available to Keats in the national journals, and in material from those papers reprinted locally in the *Salisbury and Winchester Journal*.[18] But Keats's poem is not radical polemic like Thelwall's articles in the *Champion* or, for that matter, Shelley's incandescent response to Peterloo in *The Masque of Anarchy*. How can one make a credible link between the ongoing discussion of political crisis in the newspapers and conspiracy in *To Autumn*, so as to elucidate the politics of autumnal beauty in Keats's poem? A possible answer, I think, is via the literary and political columns of Leigh Hunt's *Examiner*.

THE CALENDAR OF NATURE

And Libra weighs in equal scales the year . . .
'Autumn', James Thomson, *The Seasons*

The *Examiner* for 5 September 1819 (just before Keats's visit to London) contained much on Peterloo, and also Leigh Hunt's regular monthly column entitled 'The Calendar of Nature'. The latter item has been noticed before in criticism of *To Autumn*, most recently in

William Keach's essay on the political and cultural significances of Keats's poetic styles.[19] Hunt's 'Calendar' has not been reproduced fully in this context, however, so that its relation to Keats's poem may reward some further consideration. The 'Calendar' begins with the 'September' stanza from Spenser's *Mutabilitie Cantos*, long recognised as the source for some images in *To Autumn*:

> September.
> Next him September marched eke on foot;
> Yet was he heavy laden with the spoyle
> Of harvest's riches, which he made his boot,
> And him enriched with bounty of the soyle:
> In his one hand, as fit for harvest's toyle,
> He held a knife-hook; and in th'other hand
> A paire of weights, with which he did assoyle
> Both more and lesse, where it in doubt did stand,
> And equal gave to each as justice duly scanned.   Spenser.

The poet still takes advantage of the exuberance of harvest and the sign of the Zodiac in this month, to read us a lesson on justice.

Autumn has now arrived. This is the month of the migration of birds, of the finished harvest, of nut-gathering, of cyder and perry-making, and, towards the conclusion, of the change of colour in trees. The swallows, and many other soft-billed birds that feed on insects, disappear for the warmer climates, leaving only a few stragglers behind, probably from weakness or sickness, who hide themselves in caverns and other sheltered places, and occasionally appear on warm days. The remainder of harvest is got in; and no sooner is this done, than the husbandman ploughs up his land again, and prepares it for the winter grain. The oaks and beeches shed their nuts, which in the forests that still remain, particularly the New Forest in Hampshire, furnish a luxurious repast for the swine, who feast of an evening in as pompous a manner as any alderman, to the sound of the herdsman's horn.

But the acorn must not be undervalued, because it is food for swine, nor thought only robustly of, because it furnishes our ships with timber. It is also one of the most beautiful objects of its species, protruding its glossy green nut from its rough and sober-coloured cup, and dropping it in a most elegant manner beside the sunny and jagged leaf. We have seen a few of them, with their stems in water, make a handsome ornament to a mantle-piece, in this season of departing flowers.

The few additional flowers this month are corn-flower, Guernsey-lilies, starwort, and saffron, a species of crocus, which is cultivated in separate grounds. The stamens of this flower are pulled, and dried into flat square cakes for medicinal purposes. It was formerly much esteemed in cookery. The clown in the Winter's Tale, reckoning up what he is to buy for the sheepshearing feast, mentions 'saffron to colour the warden-pies'. The fresh trees and shrubs in flower are bramble, chaste-tree, laurustinus, ivy, wild honeysuckle, spires, and arbutus or strawberry-tree, a favourite of Virgil, which, like the garden of Alcinous, in Homer, produces flower and fruit at once. – Hardy annuals, intended to flower in the spring, should now be sown; annuals of curious sorts, from which seed is to be raised, should be sheltered till ripened; and auriculas in pots, which were shifted last month, moderately watered.

The stone-curlew clamours at the beginning of this month, wood-owls hoot, the ring-ouzel reappears, the saffron butterfly is seen, hares congregate; and, at the end of it, the woodlark, thrush and blackbird, are heard.

September, though its mornings and evenings are apt to be chill and foggy, and therefore not wholesome to those who either do not or cannot guard against them, is generally a serene and pleasant month, partaking of the warmth of summer and the vigour of autumn. But its noblest feature is a certain festive abundance for the supply of all creation. There is grain for men, birds, and horses, hay for the cattle, loads of fruit on the trees, and swarms of fish in the ocean. If the soft-billed birds which feed on insects miss their usual supply, they find it in the southern countries, and leave one's sympathy to be pleased with an idea, that repasts apparently more harmless are alone offered to the creation upon our temperate soil. The feast, as the philosophic poet says on a higher occasion,

> The feast is such as earth, the general mother,
>   Pours from her fairest bosom, when she smiles
> In the embrace of Autumn. To each other
>   As some fond parent fondly reconciles
> Her warring children, she their wrath beguiles
>   With their own sustenance; they, relenting, weep.
> Such is this festival, which from their isles,
>   And continents, and winds, and oceans deep,
> All shapes may throng to share, that fly, or walk, or creep.
>   Shelley.

Just below the stanza from the 'philosophical poet' Shelley's *Revolt of Islam* is the heading 'LAW. Surrey Sessions. *Tuesday, Aug. 31.* Seditious Placards', returning the reader to an article about the controversial politics of the day.

The similarities between Hunt's 'Calendar of Nature' and *To Autumn* extend beyond 'harvest's riches' and the harvester's 'knife-hook' in Spenser. Details such as the migrating birds, cider-making, swallows and insects, warm days, and even the chill and fog all reappear in Keats's poem.[20] Most interesting in the present context, however, is the schooling that Hunt draws from Spenser and elaborates in his commentary and with the quotation from Shelley: 'The poet still takes advantage of the exuberance of harvest and the

Figure 10.1   *Manchester Heroes*, attributed to George Cruikshank

sign of the Zodiac in this month, to read us a lesson on justice.'

Spenser's harvester uses a 'paire of weights' to divide the produce of autumn justly and equably. The image of the balance is especially appropriate to September (as Hunt notices) because the latter part of this temperate month lies under the constellation Libra, which depicts a pair of scales. Keats had been familiar with the image and seasonal significance of Libra since his schoolboy reading in John Bonnycastle's *Introduction to Astronomy*: 'LIBRA, the Balance, one of the twelve signs of the zodiac, into which the sun comes about the 20th of September, or the beginning of autumn'.[21] In addition to these seasonal and astronomical associations, during autumn 1819 the scales had immediate emblematic force in political debate. The reformists' banners at Peterloo had been emblazoned with the figure of Justice holding her scales, as an expression of their call for democratic rights and universal suffrage. And contemporary satirical prints such as 'Manchester Heroes' represented the *injustice* of Peterloo and its aftermath in a cartoon image of the Prince Regent as the fulcrum of a set of unbalanced scales. In this wider emblematic context, the point of Leigh Hunt's 'lesson on justice' in his September 'Calendar of Nature' becomes apparent in mediating between political turmoil and seasonal fruitfulness. The 'exuberance of harvest' (literally *ex-uber*, from the breast of nature) is appropriately the season of justice, depicted by Hunt as a commonwealth – 'a certain festive abundance for the supply of all creation'. And Shelley's autumnal *Convito*, the 'banquet of the free' in Canto Five of *The Revolt of Islam*, points the revolutionary meaning of Hunt's observations. The exuberance of 'earth, the general mother' feeds and reconciles the 'warring children', who share with all creation in the plenty of the season.

Turning from Spenser, Shelley, and 'The Calendar of Nature' to Keats's *To Autumn*, the conspiracy of sun and season may now appear less of an escape from historical tensions, than as a harvest-home fulfilling the call for justice from 'the less fortunate multitude'. There are of course no scales of justice overtly represented in *To Autumn* (as they had been in Spenser's verse, and as depicted on the protestors' banners at Peterloo). Nevertheless in formal terms and in some verbal details the three stanzas of Keats's poem exhibit a fine equity, resuming the current discourse of (in)justice as a politics of style; as Hartman has already pointed out, 'Each stanza . . . is so equal in its poetical weight, so loaded with its own harvest'.[22] Hartman's perception of the poem's global equipoise as lyric can be substantiated further in specific images and emblems of balance, disclosed in the central stanza amid the store of autumn's plenty. The tress of hair, for example, is 'soft-lifted', floating upon the breath of the 'winnowing wind'; indeed, the version of the poem transcribed in Keats's letter to Richard Woodhouse, 21 September 1819, has 'winmowing wind', a misspelling that seems to concentrate in a single word the whole process of harvest in mowing, winnowing, and – perhaps – windmilling. The furrow of corn is 'half reap'd', the next swath 'and all its twined flowers' yet to be harvested. And then there is the marvellous balancing movement of

> . . . sometimes like a gleaner thou dost keep
> Steady thy laden head across a brook . . .

– 'Stready', as Keats wrote in his copy of the poem for Woodhouse (*Letters*, ii. 170), intimating, as Christopher Ricks notes, both 'straight and steady': a justified progress.[23] In all of these verbal and emblematic details the poem identifies balance and equity as particularly appropriate to autumn, 'a medium between summer and winter', articulating the beauty of the season in language and imagery that were also circulating in discourses of political and social justice after the outrage at Peterloo.

The third stanza of *To Autumn* returns the poem to the westering world of change, loss, and mortality – already sensed, perhaps, in the 'clammy cells' of the bees – but with the acceptance of those processes of time that has been remarked by many readers of the poem. Crucially, however, that acceptance has been achieved through contemplation of natural abundance that was laden with intense social and ideological significance at the season of the poem's composition. There is, moreover, a biblical resonance to the language and imagery of *To Autumn* that deserves to be mentioned, for it enables us to hear the distant commotion of Peterloo even in the final *sotto voce* cadences of Keats's poem. Behind Keats's benign and generous harvest was the terrifying, apocalyptic reaping of the earth in Revelation 14:

19. And the angel thrust in his sickle into the earth, and gathered the vine of the earth, and cast it into the great winepress of the wrath of God.
20. And the winepress was trodden without the city, and blood came out of the winepress, even unto the horse bridles, by the space of a thousand and six hundred furlongs.

Some contemporary responses to Peterloo echoed these dreadful 'last oozings' from the winepress,

> – May the ghosts of the murdered your slumbers infest,
> And drops of their blood be found in your wine . . .[24]

– and Shelley in his *Masque of Anarchy* draws from the same source to orchestrate the 'ghastly masquerade' of the murderers,

> Drunk as with intoxication
> Of the wine of desolation.   (48–9)

Elsewhere, 'the conspirators against the privileges of the People' were denounced in the prophetic voice of Revelation:

They shall not smell sweet and blossom in the dust; the wrongs which they have heaped upon society will adhere to them like the leprosy . . . time will disclose the secret; and then they may call on the heavens to hide, and the hills to cover them, but the outstretched arm of Offended Justice will seize these children of blood, even at the uttermost bounds of the earth.[25]

In the temperate lyrical clime of *To Autumn*, these sanguinary tones are chastened, residual, but discerned nonetheless, I think, in the reaping 'hook', the 'last oozings' of the 'cyder-press', the 'soft-dying day', and the 'rosy hue' of the 'stubble-plains'. Through such verbal details the apocalyptic harvest of the fields of St Peter is quietly acknowledged, even as it is subdued in the slow gathering of the season and the poem itself towards a close. The figure of 'Offended Justice' remains, and it is to this focus of restitution in Keats's poem that I now wish to turn.

'WHO HATH NOT SEEN THEE?'

pray tell me what that tall majestic lady is, that stands there, beautified with yellow hair, and crowned with a turbant composed of ears of corn; her bosom swells with breasts as white as snow. Her right-hand is filled with poppies and ears of corn, and in her left is a lighted torch.

Andrew Tooke, *The Pantheon*[26]

Scarcity and want shall shun you;
Ceres' blessing so is on you.

The Tempest (4. 1. 116–17)

'Who hath not seen thee oft amid thy store?' As has frequently been pointed out (by Ian Jack, Helen Vendler, John Creaser, and others), Keats's personification of autumn has numerous mythical referents, the most notable of these being the goddess Ceres.[27] A well-informed classicist, Keats had known about Ceres from his schoolboy reading in Ovid's *Metamorphoses* and (more especially) a number of classical dictionaries and anthologies of classical literature.

Three texts, which Charles Cowden Clarke recalled Keats reading at school, identify the various mythical associations of Ceres. Lemprière's *Bibliotheca Classica; or, A Classical Dictionary*, which Clarke says Keats 'appeared to *learn*', provides the typical image of Ceres, 'goddess of corn and harvests . . . represented with a garland of ears of corn on her head, holding in one hand a lighted torch, and in the other a poppy, which was sacred to her'. Ceres' resemblance to the figure on the Peterloo banner, with the torch and scales of justice, was not a coincidence – as will shortly appear. Joseph Spence's *Polymetis*, also read at school by Keats, offers an identical image of Ceres 'regarding the laborious husbandman from heaven; and blessing the work of his hands with success'.[28]

There are notable parallels between Lemprière, Spence, and *To Autumn* apparent in these short extracts. It is Andrew Tooke's *Pantheon*, however, which elaborates the symbolic roles of Ceres in greatest detail, glossing a passage from the *Metamorphoses* which associates her with fruitfulness, labour on the land, and the origins of justice:

> Ovid . . . tells us that *Ceres* was the first that made laws, provided wholesome food, and taught the art of husbandry, of plowing and sowing: for before her time the earth lay rough and uncultivated, covered with briars and unprofitable plants. Where there were no proprietors of land, they neglected to cultivate it; when nobody had any ground of his own, they did not care to fix land-marks; but all things were common to all men, till Ceres, who had invented the art of husbandry, taught men how to exercise it: and then they began to contend and dispute about the limits of those fields from whose culture they reaped so much profit; and from thence it was necessary that laws should be enacted to determine the rights and properties of those who contended. For this reason Ceres was named the *Foundress of laws*.[29]

Here, Ceres presides over land originally 'common to all men'; over food, farming, cultivation, and prosperity; and over the laws determining 'rights and properties' among contentious humankind. She represents nature's abundance, and also the rights and laws that determine a just distribution of that plenty.

If one glances back at Thelwall's account of the reformists at St Peter's Fields, one might contend that Ceres was the appropriate emblem of those 'labouring classes . . . aspiring to . . . political rights . . . personal liberty and personal consideration'. Certainly, the mythical associations of the goddess, uniting fruitfulness and justice, would have gained an extra resonance at a season when killings, trumped-up prosecutions, and rumoured conspiracies seemed likely to provoke a revolution. Perhaps, as Josiah Conder had said, there was mischief indeed at the core of Keats's 1820 collection. Yet in *To Autumn*, the goddess is a shadowy figure, not explicitly invoked although her presence may be assumed in the question 'Who hath not seen thee oft amid thy store?' The interrogation is knowing and very finely balanced, however, addressing the community 'who hath seen' but with a glancing acknowledgement of those who have not done so, in that they are unjustly excluded from their due share in autumn's plenty. This latter sense was in fact emphasised in Keats's draft of *To Autumn*, where the question was abbreviated as 'Who hath not seen thee?' And the succeeding lines of the draft momentarily admit the deprived in search of restitution, 'Sometimes whoever seeks for thee may find thee', subsequently revised to 'Sometimes whoever seeks abroad may find thee'.[30]

When in 1821 Leigh Hunt republished his 'Calendar of Nature' as a volume entitled *The Months*, he prefaced the book with an advertisement mentioning that 'The good-nature with which this Calendar was received on its appearance in 1819 . . . has induced its republication in a separate form, with considerable additions'. Hunt made no revisions to the text of 'September', but he did make one notable addition: the second and third stanzas of *To Autumn*.[31] 'A living poet has happily personified autumn in some of the pleasantest shapes under which her servants appear', Hunt wrote, and incorporated Keats's poem within his own celebration of autumnal exuberance. In so doing, however, he explicitly associated *To Autumn* with the seasonal 'lesson on justice' that he had drawn from Spenser. If Hunt's 'Calendar of Nature' had offered Keats some ideas and images for *To Autumn*, in *The Months* the poem was republished by Hunt in a context that acknowledged the poem's fruitful conspiracy as an expression of Keats's commonwealth: 'a certain festive abundance for the supply of all creation'.

The generous equanimity of *To Autumn* was discovered amid the mists of personal anxieties and public unsettlement in September 1819. But to describe Keats's poem as 'escapist' is to assume the utter dissolution of those histories, and the ready access of ideal beauty as a reflexive alternative to the conflicts of the world. Indeed a current orthodoxy in Romantic criticism has understood the imagination as reactive and evasive, displacing history in the quest for a transcendent refuge. Scant attention has been accorded in such criticism to the intricate verbal processes by which history is acknowledged and addressed through the varied mediations of art and beauty. Conspiracy in *To Autumn* suggests that it may be helpful to reexamine the strategies by which such poems negotiate with history through lyrical intervention: to understand the thing of beauty as 'a joy forever', certainly, but also, and more immediately, as 'sylvan historian'.

NOTES

Research for this essay was supported by a grant from the British Academy, for which I am grateful. I have gained from suggestions made on occasions when the essay was delivered as a paper at the Universities of Dundee, Durham, and Glasgow, and at the Wordsworth Summer Conference, Grasmere, 1993. David Fairer of Leeds University helpfully pointed out the apocalyptic harvest in Revelation 14.

1 *KHM*, 53.
2 See *The Romantic Ideology. A Critical Investigation* (Chicago and London, 1983), 117, 124, and *KHM*, 61–2 where, in discussing *To Autumn*, McGann defines the 'reflexive world of Romantic art' as 'the very negation of negation itself, wherein all events are far removed from the Terror, King Ludd, Peterloo, the Six Acts, and the recurrent financial crises of the Regency, and where humanity escapes the inconsequence of George III, the absurd Prince Regent, the contemptible Wellington'. For a questioning response to McGann's assertion, see the conclusion of Vincent Newey, '"Alternate uproar and sad peace": Keats, Politics, and the Idea of Revolution', in J. R. Watson (ed.), 'The French Revolution in English Literature and Art', MHRA *Yearbook of English Studies* 19 (1989), 265–89.
3 See Terry Eagleton, *Marxism and Literary Criticism* (London, 1976), 14, for 'a whole series of "levels" which "mediate" between text and social economic conditions'.
4 See D. Reiman and S. Powers (eds.), *Shelley's Poetry and Prose* (New York and London, 1977), 390–2. Shelley quotations will be from this edition.
5 See Susan Wolfson, 'Feminizing Keats', in H. de Almeida (ed.), *Critical Essays on John Keats* (Boston, 1990), 317–57, and my 'Keats's Lisping Sedition', *EinC* 42 (1992), 36–55.
6 'Notes on Gilfillan's "Gallery of Literary Portraits". John Keats' in *Tait's Edinburgh Magazine* (April 1846); rpt. *KCH*, 308–10.
7 For Scott, Conder, and Hunt, see *KCH*, 219–27; 232–9; 165–77.
8 *KCH*, 238. For the 'dangerous voices' of childish sensibility in the 1790s, see David Fairer, 'Baby Language and Revolution: The Early Poetry of Charles Lloyd and Charles Lamb', *Charles Lamb Bulletin* 74 (April 1991), 33–52.
9 'Poem and Ideology: A Study of Keats's "To Autumn"', in *The Fate of Reading and Other Essays* (Chicago and London, 1975), 126, 146.
10 'Spectral Symbolism and the Authorial Self in Keats's *Hyperion*', in *The Fate of Reading*, 57–73.
11 *KHM*, 61. See also Paul Fry's dissenting response to McGann, 'History, Existence, and "To Autumn"', *KP*, 211–19.
12 See Keats to Fanny Brawne, 13 Sept. 1819; J. H. Reynolds, 21 Sept.; Richard Woodhouse 21–2 Sept.; C. W. Dilke, 22 Sept.; the George Keatses, 17–27 Sept.; *Letters*, ii. 160, 167, 169–75, 178, 185.

13 See *The Making of the English Working Class* (Harmondsworth, 1968), 753–6. For a full-length reassessment of Peterloo, see Robert Walmsley, *Peterloo: The Case Reopened* (Manchester, 1969).

14 Walmsley, *Peterloo*, 247, 339–40.

15 See *The Times* (19 Aug. 1819); *Examiner* (23 Aug.); *Champion and Sunday Review* (22 Aug.), 525; *Champion and Sunday Review* (19 Sept.), 595.

16 *Champion* (22 Aug. 1819), 526, 532; (12 Sept.), 574.

17 Ibid. (19 Sept. 1819), 591.

18 I am grateful to John Barnard for information about the political columns of the *Salisbury and Winchester Journal*, in 1819.

19 'Cockney Couplets: Keats and the Politics of Style', *KP*,182–96.

20 Ian Jack noted two further literary sources for Keats's autumnal imagery: illustrated editions of Thomson's *Seasons*, and John Aitkin's *Natural History of the Year*. See *Keats and the Mirror of Art* (Oxford, 1967), 238–40.

21 (London, 1786), 420.

22 'Poem and Ideology', 129.

23 *Letters*, ii. 170–1, and Ricks, *Keats and Embarrassment* (Oxford, 1974), 72–3.

24 'Manchester Y——Y Valour', in Walmsley, *Peterloo*, 263–4.

25 'Manchester Politics', *Manchester Observer* (11 Sept. 1819), in Walmsley, *Peterloo*, 273.

26 (London, 1698; London and Edinburgh, 1783), 177–8.

27 See *Keats and the Mirror of Art*, 232–43; Vendler, *The Odes of John Keats* (Cambridge, Mass., and London, 1983), 233–88; Creaser, 'From "Autumn" to Autumn in Keats's Ode', *EinC* (1988), 190–214.

28 Charles and Mary Cowden Clarke, *Recollections of Writers* (London, 1878), 124; J. Lemprière, *Bibliotheca Classica; or, A Classical Dictionary* (3rd edn, London, 1797), unpaginated; Spence, *Polymetis; or, An Inquiry Concerning the Agreement between the Works of the Roman Poets, and the Remains of the Ancient Artists* (2nd edn, London, 1755), 103.

29 *Pantheon*, 179.

30 See the draft of *To Autumn* reproduced in Jack Stillinger (ed.), *John Keats. Poetry Manuscripts at Harvard. A Facsimile Edition* (Cambridge, Mass., and London, 1990), 222. For a reading of *To Autumn* as 'an apotheosis of contemporary Spencean articles of faith about English natural abundance and fertility' see David Worrall, *Radical Culture. Discourse, Resistance and Surveillance, 1790–1820* (Hemel Hempstead, 1992), 201–2.

31 *The Months Descriptive of the Successive Beauties of the Year*, 5, 102–9.

CHAPTER II

Keats, ekphrasis, and history

Theresa M. Kelley

INTRODUCTION

In 'Keats and the Historical Method', Jerome McGann argued the need for an historical method in literary criticism that would engage the circumstances of poetic composition and publication together with relevant contextual matters such as Keats's poetic embodiment of the aesthetic values of Romantic Hellenism. Whereas Byron and Shelley respond directly to their times, Keats chooses instead to celebrate the ideal, timeless world of Greek art and literature. The critical irony of this assessment is worth noting: by applying the historical method to Keats, we discover just how much his poems seek to occupy a universal space *outside* history and culture. So construed, Keats is one instance of what McGann later identified as the Romantic ideology – a transcendent poetic vision that works assiduously to exclude historical reality as injurious to the autonomy of Romantic selfhood.[1] If Wordsworth is the designated driver of this ideology, Keats is its prototype and Byron its antitype. From this critical vantage point, the *Ode on a Grecian Urn* celebrates works of art as, in McGann's words, 'perfect and complete embodiments of a perfect and complete idea of The Beautiful' that derives from the Romantic Hellenism of Keats's early mentor and friend, the historical painter Benjamin Robert Haydon, and other contemporaries (*KHM*, 51–3, 44).

This reading critiques more than Keats's ode. Its ultimate target is the New Critical principle (whether silently or explicitly at work in post-structuralist formalist criticism) that poems, like urns, ought to be read as well-wrought wholes.[2] So positioned, the *Ode on a Grecian Urn* becomes a test or limit case for the interpretive gains of an historical, as opposed to a strictly formalist, critical method. At issue in the historicist challenge to a purely formalist approach is the power of Keats's lyricism. Because the ode is an ekphrasis – a poetic description of a work of art – it is highly self-conscious about its lyric capacity to match the beauty of the urn with beauties of its own. And because this lyric impulse foregrounds the expressivity of figures, it subtly discourages critical notice of the historicising impulse embedded in the ode's narrative difficulties.

McGann's essay, like the formalist criticism it interrogates, reifies a way of reading Keats's poetry that warrants scrutiny. To the formalist extreme implied by reading poems as verbal objects sealed off from history and culture, he replies with its mirror opposite: a quasi-determinist contextual apparatus that fixes poems as surely as they were fixed by the New Critical disposition to praise Keats for fashioning well-wrought poetic urns. To illustrate this method, McGann argues that the ode reflects the circumstances of its two publications in 1820. It was first published in the January issue of the *Annals of the Fine Arts*, a periodical dedicated to the cultivation of the arts according to Romantic Hellenic principles and published by Haydon's friend and champion James Elmes. In June the ode was reprinted in the *Lamia* volume of Keats's poems, with added quotation marks around '"Beauty is truth, truth beauty,"' a compelling textual example of the critical consequences of a nonverbal or 'silent' variant. With the earlier critical reception of *Endymion* and the current political climate very much in mind, Keats's publishers Taylor and Hessey argued against including politically radical or indecent (that is, explicitly erotic) material in the volume. On both occasions, McGann surmises, Keats acquiesced to others' wishes: first to the idealist aesthetic of Romantic Hellenism and then to the demands of his cautious publishers. McGann observes that the *Lamia* volume thereby avoids the 'explicit ideological attack' on establishment culture found in roughly contemporary volumes, the cantos of Byron's *Don Juan* published in 1819 and 1823, and Shelley's *Prometheus Unbound*, published in 1823. Unlike these volumes, Keats's *Lamia* volume is preoccupied with 'art, myth, and imagination' (*KHM*, 51–3).

In this essay I want to redirect the historicist programme of McGann's influential essay.[3] Like most discussions of Keats's interest in art, it assumes that Keats was throughout guided by Haydon's and others' defences of Romantic Hellenism, much as other critics have assumed that the version of *La Belle Dame sans Merci* published in the *Indicator* was dictated or supervised by its editor Leigh Hunt. I have claimed elsewhere that this poem shows Keats at play among the circumstances of its composition and publication, not subservient to

editor and periodical.[4] Here I want to extend that argument to
suggest how we might read Keats's poems within and against their
historical and cultural moment. To locate this poet in his times, critics
have too often assumed with Pierre Bourdieu that one's situation or
moment, which Bourdieu calls one's 'habitus', determines or constrains
invention on all sides. If we apply this view of agency and culture to
Keats, we are likely to claim that Haydon's mentorship is a
determining factor in Keats's preference for Greek art and culture
and his interest in the sister arts of painting and poetry.[5]

In successive modulations of Bourdieu's theory of innovation,
Anthony Giddens has argued that individuals modify and redirect
the habitus they find on all sides by a process he calls 'structuration' –
an ongoing refabrication of the habitus that subtly contorts what it
finds. I adapt Mary Robertson's analysis of contortion in feminist
literary theory and practice to argue that Giddens's theory of
structuration models an inventional strategy that is not bound to the
programmatic constraints of 'originality', but manifestly capable of
using and contorting what lies at hand.[6] As I understand this strategy,
it works itself out by way of figures that resist or redevise the material
it finds, whether that material comes from a poetic or literary
tradition or from cultural and social artefacts. Either way, this
strategy does not appear to be governed by a discursive, intentionalist
logic. Thus I do not believe Keats explicitly decided that he would
challenge Haydon's aesthetic principles by writing the *Ode on a Grecian
Urn*. The figural pathways of Keats's resistance to Haydon are more
subtly embedded in his poems about works of art, especially Greek
art. In this essay, therefore, I am interested in how matters of history
and narrative are raised in Keats's ekphrastic poems, but particularly
the *Ode on a Grecian Urn*, the sonnet on Chapman's translation of
Homer, the Elgin Marbles sonnet, and *Hyperion*. My reading of these
poems emphasises their ambivalent commitment to the goal or desire
of *ekphrasis* – the effort to describe an object completely; to make, in
William Carlos Williams's words, 'the ear and the eye lie/ down
together'.[7]

I argue further, and on a contextualist hook, that the English
acquisition of the Elgin Marbles at the beginning of Keats's career
works against the lyric and ekphrastic impulse so evident in his
poetics. Indeed, the debate over the acquisition of marble statues and
other sculptural pieces removed from the Parthenon is the moment in
English Romantic culture when the preference for Greek art (according

to criteria J. J. Winckelmann developed a half century earlier) encounters the liberal critique of spoliation disguised as the cultural recovery of precious artefacts. The arrival of the marbles in England in 1803 and the acrimonious public debate fifteen years later about what to do with them, frame an instructive cultural moment in English Romanticism. As Haydon put it in 1816 (with uncharacteristic understatement): 'This year the Elgin Marbles were bought, and produced an Aera in public feeling.'[8] I argue that this 'Aera' became a commonplace – a rhetorical turning-point – in the English celebration of Greek Hellenism. As I use the term 'commonplace', it designates a rhetorical figure or idea that speakers, as actors within culture, consult not simply to imitate or echo what others have said, but to invent arguments from within the range of rhetorically available topics.[9]

As Keats revisits this commonplace, he reimagines its key arguments about cultural hierarchies, Greek art, and a progressive or evolutionary view of history. By observing how he does this, we may recognise how his poems contort a cultural habitus by putting its figures to work for ends not envisaged by Haydon, or William Hazlitt, the other contemporary whose views on art Keats's poems, including the *Ode*, echo. Whereas the materialist approach of McGann's essays wards off the seductive verbal shape of poems as artefacts by exposing their historical blindnesses, I contend that the aesthetic form of the *Ode on a Grecian Urn* belongs to a diffused, but nonetheless compelling, argument about history and art that permeates Keats's poetic career. By examining this argument through the lens of the Romantic debate about the Elgin Marbles, we are better situated to see how Keats's poems rework this cultural material toward their own poetic ends.

THE ELGIN MARBLES

The first shipment of the marbles was stored at Lord Elgin's house and not exhibited to a private audience until 1807. During 1811 the marbles were moved to a windowless outbuilding in the grounds of Burlington House, and were joined there in 1812 by a second shipment. Space was short, and some of the marbles had to be left outside, exposed to the elements. In 1816 (after protracted wrangling and a report published by a Select Committee of the House of Commons) Parliament agreed to buy the marbles for considerably less than Elgin believed was justified by his efforts in transporting them from Greece. The marbles were then moved to the British Museum, where Keats first saw them in Haydon's company in March 1817 and again, perhaps more than once, with the painter Joseph Severn. After seeing the marbles for the first time, Keats composed and sent Haydon two sonnets, one about the marbles and another praising Haydon for defending their authenticity.[10]

The debate about what to do with the marbles was also carried on, with ample vituperation, in the periodical press. Indeed, for years afterward various pseudonymous contributors to the *Annals of the Fine Arts* chastised R. P. Knight, George Beaumont, and anyone else who had even briefly dared to question Haydon's assessment of their authenticity and value.[11] On the liberal side of the question, Byron's *The Curse of Minerva* excoriated Elgin for an act of spoliation that was in fact greater in degree but not in kind than what earlier explorer/travellers like Edward Clarke, J. B. S. Morritt, and even Byron himself had attempted or managed to do. In several articles on the marbles published during Keats's lifetime, and some later pieces that Keats never saw or heard, Hazlitt praised the marbles repeatedly and used them to illustrate his theory of ideal or natural art.[12] The debate over the marbles addressed two principal concerns, whether they embodied the ideal image of Greek beauty which Romantic Hellenism derived from Winckelmann, and whether they should have been taken from Greece.

According to Winckelmann's luminous description of the Apollo Belvedere, ideal Greek beauty is immortal and universal: 'an eternal spring, like that of *Elysium*, blends the grandeur of man with the charms of youth . . . Here sick decay, and human flaws dwell not, blood palpitates not here . . . Peace dwells in blest tranquillity.'[13] Despite his occasional impatience with the idealist rhetoric of Winckelmann's lectures on ancient art, Haydon's energetic defence of the Elgin Marbles as the work of the Greek sculptor Phidias extended Winckelmann's influence to include the marbles taken from the Parthenon. Indeed, for Haydon, Sir Thomas Lawrence, and Hazlitt, among others, the marbles expressed the highest form of Greek art because they were naturalistic, so lifelike that Hazlitt called them 'living men turned to stone'. The editor of the *Champion*, John Scott, indicates the view of the marbles that eventually prevailed, in large measure because Haydon successfully championed that view against all comers: 'the ruins and scanty remnants of ancient Greece, are more perfect in beauty, more fresh in the fragrance of elegance, more living and life-giving, than all the preserved and prized stock of what genius has since effected'.[14]

Haydon's protracted defence of the marbles thus overlooked their fragmentary, ruined state: no small achievement given the extensive public discussion of their ruined condition. In 1803, before the marbles were exhibited privately, the *Monthly Magazine* published a letter 'relative to Lord Elgin's collection of Grecian antiques, and of Lord Hamilton's late travels in Greece', praising Elgin's efforts to 'enrich his country with the spoils of ancient Greece . . . the precious *remains* of antiquity' (my emphasis).[15] At the first private exhibition, Grant Scott notes, viewers were more taken by the marbles' dismaying condition than their grandeur. Joseph Farington reports that the painter Ozias Humphrey found the marbles 'of a high stile of Sculpture, but the whole was "a Mass of ruins"'. Beaumont recommended, 'the mutilated fragments brought from Athens by Lord Elgin should be *restored* as at present, they excite rather disgust than pleasure in the minds of people in general, to see parts of limbs, & bodys, stumps of arms, etc.' Byron espoused much the same view in *English Bards and Scotch Reviewers* (1809), calling the marbles 'Phidian freaks,/ Mis-shapen monuments, and maimed antiques'. In 1817, Hazlitt's *Encyclopaedia Britannica* article on 'Fine Arts' acknowledges the marbles' fragmentary, ruined condition as does Felicia Hemans in *Modern Greece*.[16]

KEATS AND EKPHRASIS

In his sonnet *On Seeing the Elgin Marbles*, Keats presents the sculptures a good deal more equivocally than Haydon or even Hazlitt. As Scott astutely observes, Keats's sonnet exhibits a Winckelmannesque (and Haydonesque) enthusiasm for them as 'wonders', yet calls them 'a shadow of a magnitude' (11, 14). This second perspective prevails in the poem's ekphrastic imitation of the marbles as diction and metre articulate the mortality and ruin he identifies with the marbles. A profusion of dactyls ('magnitude', 'heavily', 'pinnacle', 'luxury', 'opening', etc.), Scott explains, 'contribute to the weak or falling rhythm of the sonnet', while enjambements unhinge expectations about what ought to follow. By such means, Keats's sonnet becomes what it describes – a ragged, if splendid, collection of broken, ruined monuments that prompt the speaker's anguish about his own mortality.[17] The last line of the sonnet also reverses the terms of

Hazlitt's 1816 *Examiner* recommendation that the marbles be acquired for the improvement of the fine arts in England. Echoing contemporary criticism that English art needed improvement (much of it directed by Haydon against painters he thought inferior), Hazlitt declared:

It is to be hoped, however, that these Marbles with the name of Phidias thrown into the scale of common sense, may lift the Fine Arts out of the Limbo of vanity and affectation into which they were conjured in this country about fifty years ago, and in which they have lain sprawling and fluttering, gasping for breath, wasting away, vapid and abortive ever since, – the shadow of a shade.[18]

By reassigning a version of Hazlitt's last phrase to the marbles themselves, Keats suggests that they, not the English art they are supposed to revive, may be 'gasping for breath, wasting away'. It is the marbles, after all, which cause the speaker of the sonnet to feel a 'pain,/ That mingles Grecian grandeur with the rude/ Wasting of old time' (11–13). By refiguring Hazlitt's diction, Keats creates a different argument about what English painters and poets might learn from the marbles.

   Haydon's effusive reply to Keats's sonnet, '*I* know not a finer image than the comparison of a Poet unable to express his high feelings to a sick eagle looking at the Sky', cheerfully misses the irony of Keats's ekphrasis.[19] For the sonnet foregrounds the decay of the marbles, not Haydon's or Hazlitt's praise for their perfect realisation of natural human beauty. The irony belongs to an array of concerns in poems Keats wrote before and after he first saw the Marbles. These include: the spoliation of the New World as well as the ancient classical one, the status of Greek vs. Egyptian art, the progressive view of history and culture, Keats's youthful desire to imitate Apollo as the ideal Greek embodiment of a divine poet, and the gradual deterioration in his regard for Haydon.

   On First Looking into Chapman's Homer was written in October 1816, after the Select Committee of the House of Commons ended its deliberations and published its report on the Elgin Marbles, and after Hazlitt's *Examiner* essay.[20] In the sonnet, the speaker shuttles metonymically between two 'realms of gold' – the New World and the ancient classical world of Homer's poetry. Marjorie Levinson has argued that by such means Keats pillages Homer and Greek culture by way of Chapman's English translation.[21] By 1816, as even Hazlitt's *Examiner* essay recognises, the figure of pillage cut in both directions and included the three explorers commonly identified with the Spanish conquest of the New World – Cortez, Balboa, and Pizzaro. William Robertson's semi-apologetic account in his *History of America* and Helen Maria Williams's more polemical epic poem *Peru* suggest that what all three did best was pillage.[22] From this perspective, whether it was Balboa or Cortez who discovered the Pacific hardly matters: the common denominator is spoliation. If Keats's sonnet figures exploration and colonisation as the work of the poet, it also figures both as the wealth (or pelf) of nations – whether acquired from ancient Greece or the New World. For Keats, who later asserted his wish to write 'on the liberal side of the question' (*Letters*, ii. 176), this view of discovery as theft rather than reclamation probably inflects the sonnet's praise for Homer and the 'realms of gold'.[23] In 1816, these poetic figures look principally like the 'bold' gesture of a Cockney poet determined to locate himself among those poets whose legitimating feudal lord is Apollo. Framed by contemporary notice of spoliation in the ancient and new worlds, the same figures stand ready to complicate Keats's poetic idealisation of Apollo and Hellenic Greek art.

Keats's poetic interest in the fallen Titans in both Hyperion poems is a strong indication that the complication which had been available to him in 1816 had taken hold by 1818, when he began work on *Hyperion* during Tom Keats's last illness. In that poem, Keats ascribes to the Titans a measure of the pathos so evident in letters to friends about his brother. As other readers of the Hyperion poems have remarked, the poet who had early taken Apollo as his model and declared his belief in a 'grand march of intellect' ought to have been more eager to proceed with Apollo's succession and the rise of Hellenic Greece than either Hyperion poem suggests he was.[24] Instead, Keats lingers with the Titans – figuring and refiguring their gigantic, fallen, sculptured forms. Hazlitt's haunting observation that the Elgin Marbles are like 'living men turned to stone' succinctly indicates their similarity to Keats's Titans as monumental, fallen gods 'Like natural sculpture in cathedral cavern' (*Hyperion*, I. 86). But the Titans are evidently not Greek. The earlier *Hyperion* makes ancient Egyptian art the prototype for Thea:

> She was a Goddess of the infant world;
> By her in stature the tall Amazon
> Had stood a pigmy's height: she would have ta'en
> Achilles by the hair and bent his neck;

Or with a finger stay'd Ixion's wheel.
Her face was large as that of Memphian sphinx,
Pedestal'd haply in a palace court,
When sages look'd to Egypt for their lore.
But oh! how unlike marble was that face:
How beautiful, if sorrow had not made
Sorrow more beautiful than Beauty's self.   (I. 26–36)

As a colossal goddess who might easily crush Homer's Greek heroes, Thea's alliance with Egyptian sculpture destabilises the evolutionary model of history and culture that dominates Enlightenment and Romantic aesthetics. According to that model, Hellenic Greece is the cultural successor to ancient Egypt. There despotic power and priestly mysteries had enslaved a culture, whereas Apollonian reason assisted the emergence in Greece of a free and enlightened culture and polity. As Alan Bewell observes, this argument is freely invoked in the Romantic periodical press and by Keats in a letter to Reynolds (3 May 1818; *Letters*, i. 281) that describes the epic argument of *Hyperion*.[25]

In part, Keats's description grants all this. The 'Memphian Sphinx' stood in a court 'when sages *look'd* to Egypt' (my emphasis). But the figural interest of Thea's Egyptian likeness also participates in a cultural fascination with Egypt inaugurated by Napoleon's scientific and military expedition there in 1798.[26] Like the simile later used to describe Hyperion ('a vast shade/ In midst of his own brightness, like the bulk/ Of Memnon's image at the set of sun' II. 372–5), Keats's 'Memphian sphinx' probably responds to the arrival of several Egyptian pieces of statuary and sculpture at the British Museum during 1818. The next year, Keats and Severn saw the sculptures, including one Keats called a 'Sphinx' (*Letters*, ii. 68). As reported by the *Annals of the Fine Arts*, that Sphinx was initially identified as a 'Colossal Head, said to be of Memnon', an 'enormous fragment' transported with difficulty down the Nile from Thebes to Alexandria. Despite its apparent interest in Egyptian antiquities, a year later the same magazine declares that Egyptian sculptures 'bear the character of the infancy of art, rude in their design, yet imposing in their massiveness and extraordinary size'.[27]

Keats's interest in Thea and Hyperion as versions of the head or bust said to be the Egyptian Memnon is differently poised. As figures, they are accorded something of the sense of mortality Keats invokes to describe the Elgin marbles in that earlier sonnet: like the marbles,

Keats's Titanic doubles of the Egyptian Memnon are colossal, but ruined forms and deities. Much as the sun (Hyperion, Apollo) in ancient times drew melodious sounds from the ancient statue of Memnon (silent except when struck by the sun's first rays), so does the poet (a devotee of Apollo) stir these massive, sculptured figures to utterance.[28] Viewed this way, in a retrospective that momentarily collapses Egyptian and Greek antiquity into a single frame, both cultures exist only as massive, broken fragments, and both offer equally moving evidence of the ravages of time and decay. What interests me is the critical role of figures in this argumentative strategy: because they contort or reconfigure the hierarchy Romantic Hellenists and later Hegel superimpose on the history of art (primitive Egypt succeeded by more advanced Hellenic Greece), they make it possible for Keats to put aside Haydon's anything-but-silent claim that the Elgin Marbles are the highest expression of antiquity.

Of the five odes Keats wrote during the spring of 1819 after giving up *Hyperion* and before revising it as the *Fall of Hyperion*, three take some measure of the aesthetic and historical location of Greek divinities and art. In *Ode to Psyche*, the goddess's status as the 'latest born and loveliest vision far/ Of all Olympus' faded hierarchy' (24–5) situates Apollo and the entire Greek pantheon in a faded past; in the *Ode on Indolence* the speaker says that the female figures who pass 'like figures on a marble urn' are 'strange to me, as may betide/ With vases, to one deep in Phidian lore' (5, 9–10). What is peculiar and, as Martin Aske notes, evocative of the speaker's bewilderment in *Ode on a Grecian Urn*, is the assertion that someone who is immersed in 'Phidian lore' might well not be able to comprehend who those passing figures are.[29] The logic of this surprising ineptitude may owe something to a conflict in the expert testimony reported to the Select Committee that dealt with the Elgin Marbles. Against all objections, Haydon consistently argued that the marbles were the work of the Greek sculptor Phidias. Among those who disagreed, some who claimed that the statues were Greek nonetheless insisted that the sculptor was someone other than the great Phidias.[30] The speaker of Keats's ode may thus exact a small ironic return on the earlier debate and, in particular, on Haydon's obsession with the 'Phidian lore' of the marbles.

During the same period Keats's letters chronicle a series of disagreements with Haydon about money and, less overtly, aesthetic values. In January 1820, the same month the *Ode on a Grecian Urn* was

published in the *Annals*, Keats peevishly wrote to his sister-in-law
Georgiana Keats, 'standing at Charing cross and looking east west
north and south I can see nothing but dullness'. His catalogue of
'dull' particulars includes 'Haydon's worn out discourses of poetry
and painting' (*Letters*, ii. 244). He had been angry with Haydon
before, mostly because he had asked to borrow money that Keats did
not have or because Haydon was unwilling or unable to repay the
loan Keats finally agreed to make. To Haydon's first appeal for
money, Keats replied in December 1818, 'ask the rich lovers of art
first' (*Letters*, i. 415). Haydon's chief patron in that category was the
painter and connoisseur Sir George Beaumont, with whom he had
once disagreed about the marbles but whose aesthetic principles
basically accorded with Haydon's. Both were frequent contributors
to the *Annals* and both advocated the revival of history painting as
'poetic painting', the representation of scenes from great narrative
poems in classical or English literature, a project that made extensive
use of the 'sister arts' tradition. The slight edginess of Keats's refusal
seems, in brief, to target Haydon's aesthetics along with his chronic
impecuniousness.

After this incident, Keats's irritation with Haydon increased in the
midst of other, seemingly unrelated concerns, among them Keats's
extensive poetic composition during late spring and summer 1819.
Sorted roughly by date, these are the pertinent exchanges and events:
Haydon's requests for money in January and March and Keats's
solicitations of funds from Richard Abbey during the same period;
Keats's April letter refusing Haydon's second request for a loan,
which was however soon followed by a loan; loans to Keats from
Abbey and from Keats's publishers Taylor and Hessey; Keats's
apologetic letter to his publishers, sent with some of the books he had
borrowed from them; assorted letters during July in which Keats asks
Haydon and other friends to repay loans he had made them; and the
September journal letter in which Keats tells his brother and
sister-in-law that his friendship with Haydon is 'at an end' (*Letters*, i.
415; ii. 31, 44, 53, 54, 111, 125, 206). Taken altogether, these
comments and activities suggest that Keats was settling accounts,
acquitting himself of debts wherever possible, and assuming new ones
out of the sheer mental necessity of needing to employ himself by
writing poems. Unable to repay Taylor and Hessey with income from
publishing poems, Keats returns most of their books. He cannot lend
Haydon money because Keats himself has to borrow money, but then

he lends Haydon money anyway. Keats later tries to recoup all loans and, a few months after that, declares his friendship with Haydon is over. With that account closed, Keats tells his sister-in-law the following January that he is fed up with Haydon's discourses on poetry and painting.

This chronicle ends just as the *Annals of the Fine Arts* publishes the *Ode on a Grecian Urn*: the ekphrastic poem whose formal beauties McGann and others have read as evidence that Keats assented to the Romantic Hellenic principles Haydon and his contemporaries celebrated in the pages of the *Annals* and in the Select Committee's report on the Elgin Marbles. As I read the ode, however, it works (less vindictively than his letters) to settle Keats's debt to his early mentor Haydon by interrogating the strengths and liabilities of poetic ekphrasis; that is, the art of describing a work of art with such fidelity that the outcome is either perfect sisterhood (the avowed ideal of the sister arts tradition) or a poem whose verbal beauties surpass the object of its mimesis. To achieve this, Keats returns by a different route from that of *Hyperion* to the relative demands and effects of history and ruin on art.

The fourth stanza of the ode grants that history is loss but it is precisely because the speaker is mortal and self-conscious about time's ravages that he can and does imagine in this stanza what the urn must logically omit: the town emptied of inhabitants once they join the procession depicted on the urn. Imagination is here the sign of a restless historical consciousness that is critical of the urn's willingness to suspend time in order to make pictures. By such means, the speaker learns to contend with the power of the urn as a work of art whose shape compels, even invites, his ekphrastic rivalry.

Keats's aesthetic desire for a perfect ekphrasis is inscribed on the verbal surfaces of the ode, which at once replicates and challenges the shape of the object it describes. That challenge is at first submerged in the questions the speaker asks about the figures on the urn and the story or stories it depicts; it becomes overt in the fourth stanza as the speaker imagines a town 'emptied' of its inhabitants. This imaginative turn from the urn's representations intimates that its images are isolated, forever sealed off from worldly existence, temporality, and above all history.

Yet the effort to describe the urn cannot be dismissed as duplicitous or misguided because the ode is marked at every turn by the ekphrastic tradition it at once evokes and resists. Keats's exploration of the limits of ekphrasis and the strength of ekphrastic desire suggests how even well-wrought poems break open to admit the claims of history and temporality as the 'other' which well-wrought urns do not or cannot disclose. If Keats's ode is about art, myth, and imagination, as McGann asserts, it takes exception to the ideological and critical premises that would make these topics safe poetic terrain.

Although the term ekphrasis can refer to any verbal description of any object, its rhetorical power emerges more fully if the text in question gives, in Jean H. Hagstrum's resonant phrase, 'a voice or language to an otherwise mute object'.[31] When Keats's ode speaks of and finally for the urn, he invokes this more strongly marked version of ekphrasis. In equally precise fashion, the ode indicates its indebtedness to a famous pastoral ekphrasis, the description of a wooden cup in Theocritus's first *Idyll*. Keats's speaker alludes to classical pastoral when he asks whether the landscape depicted on the urn is in Tempe or Arcady and again when he calls the urn a 'Cold Pastoral' (45). As Leo Spitzer and others have observed, the ekphrastic occasion Keats shares with Theocritus, a cup or urn decorated with figures carved or set in relief, gives the poet a rare opportunity to match a circular object and visual narrative with its verbal equivalent – a perfectly crafted, closed poetic form whose symmetry rivals or exceeds that of the work of art it describes.[32] For Spitzer, the New Critics, and McGann, Keats's ode does just this.

The differences between the way each poet and speaker conducts his ekphrasis tell another story. Pope had complained that Theocritus's description of the cup (which takes up most of the *Idyll*) is 'much too long'.[33] But here length is an index of poetic assurance. Theocritus willingly delays the pastoral song of the shepherd Thyrsis so that the goatherd might describe the wooden cup and the goat he will give to Thyrsis if only he will sing. Much like this goat, which gives bountiful milk, Theocritus is generous, even prodigious in the length and quantity of ekphrastic detail. Theocritus's goatherd says (in a much reprinted eighteenth-century translation), 'My large two-handled Cup, rich wrought and deep;/ Around whose Brim, pale Ivy seems to creep,/ With Helichryse entwin'd: Small Tendrils hold/ Its Saffron Fruit, in many a clasping Fold'.[34] He describes the landscapes as well as the human figures carved inside the cup, explaining what they are wearing, doing, and thinking. He also supplies verbal transitions from one scene to its neighbour.

Although Keats later (and ironically) reworks the 'rich wrought' cup into the urn's 'overwrought' 'brede/ Of marble men and maidens' (41–2), his speaker is otherwise taciturn where Theocritus's goatherd is voluble: end-stopped lines and questions resist the pleasures of ekphrasis. Indeed, at first Keats's speaker half-yields his narrative power to the urn as the 'Sylvan historian' that might respond to the question: 'What leaf-fring'd legend haunts about thy shape?' As Ian Jack and McGann note, this line may pun on the appearance of classical urns in engravings, where the images are framed by printed 'leafy' borders. Furthermore, the question – like those that follow – may echo Henry Moses's early nineteenth-century observation that scholars had often found it difficult to identify the figures depicted on ancient urns.[35] Thus, instead of amplifying the detail of a curling vegetative border as Theocritus's goatherd does, Keats puns on the appearance of antique urns as engraved illustrations in the leaves of books, then withdraws into a shorthand narration whose laconism is for Walter Benjamin the sign of a good story-teller, someone who 'commends a story to memory' by telling it with 'chaste compactness'.[36] In Keats's ode, too, too much compactness and too many questions make it hard to know precisely which story or stories to remember.

The different functions of Theocritus's cup and Keats's urn also signal the ode's resistance to its genre. As the goatherd makes clear, Theocritus's cup is for drinking goat's milk. The (unacknowledged) funerary purpose of Keats's urn seems an uneasy substitute. Theocritus's goatherd gently reminds Thyrsis that he will gain nothing by saving his song for Hades, where songs will be forgotten; in Keats's ode the stasis and perhaps the forgetfulness of death are already there. Except in its title, the ode does not acknowledge the urn's identity and function. Even so, Keats's ode obliquely learns from Theocritus the hard lesson of pastoral: that escape from the world into such an idyll is necessarily temporary. Otherwise, the pastoral world and those who inhabit it, as Bruce Thornton observes, 'indulge an inauthentic desire to escape the contingencies of time, death, and the world in which we must live'.[37]

The speaker's competing desires to say what the urn depicts and to acknowledge what it does not and cannot depict are implied in the first stanza. Calling it a 'still unravish'd bride of quietness' and 'foster-child of . . . slow time' suggests, as Spitzer argued, that the urn has survived intact although separated from its origin by centuries. Yet the strangeness of these figures cannot be explained by this

more-or-less accurate paraphrase. Spitzer suggests further that they
refer to a newly discovered urn 'which has not as yet been violated by
archaeological or historical scholarship'.[38] But urns had been the subject of
extensive investigation since the eighteenth century, when Winckelmann and others first proposed that they were not Etruscan but
Greek. By the early nineteenth century, most agreed that the
collections included many Greek vases and that if some were
Etruscan-made, even these were decorated with legends or myths
extracted from Greek sources. By calling them 'neo-Attic urns', Ian
Jack neatly bridges the dispute about their origin.[39]

As a 'still unravish'd bride', the urn is threatened by the sexual
violence this figure keeps just at bay: it too can be violated, broken.
Seen against the larger record of antiquity and ruin that was
available to Keats as he looked at urns and fragments of the
Parthenon frieze in the British Museum, the hint of alienation and
potential violence embedded in these figures may designate what the
speaker's idolatry of the urn as a superior 'historian' has so far
suppressed.[40] If he does not want to break this idol, he may well want
to break its hold on him, its potential silencing of his 'rhyme' as less
sweet, less pure than those 'ditties of no tone' (14) he identifies with
the pipes depicted on the urn.

The speaker's resistance to ekphrasis thus obliquely indicates his
resistance to the urn. For by restricting his verbal description to a
series of questions, he can direct attention away from the beauty of the
urn as a self-contained form toward the history it does not represent.
By most critical reckonings, the urn depicts three scenes: a collective
'pursuit' of 'maidens loth' in the first stanza; a 'Bold lover' who never
quite kisses the 'she' of the second stanza; and in the fourth a sacrificial
procession that includes a lowing 'heifer'. The intervening third
stanza proclaims the happiness of the lovers in the preceding one.
Although the 'mad pursuit' and 'maidens loth' could be an earlier
moment in a narrative that proceeds toward the 'Bold lover' and 'she'
in the second stanza, the shift from singular to plural encourages
readers to imagine these two scenes as isolated vignettes from different
stories.

Whether the source of this narrative discontinuity is the urn or the
speaker, it echoes a scholarly debate about Etruscan funerary urns
which began in the early eighteenth century. Until the late nineteenth
century, classicists were puzzled by the Etruscan use of isolated
vignettes in box-like enclosures. Unlike Etruscan urns, Greek and

Roman vases and friezes used various devices to indicate the larger narrative to which individual scenes belonged. Successive scenes might present the same figure in different actions or in different sacred and historical registers. Called 'stacking' or 'stratification', this redundancy made thematic or narrative continuity possible in a visual medium. Even without such codes, the classical observer could be expected to know the narrative to which depicted scenes belonged, either as key episodes or as popular digressions. Eighteenth- and nineteenth-century classicists explained the lack of narrative continuity they found on Etruscan urns by suggesting that the Etruscans had borrowed piecemeal from Greek sources, which had in turn borrowed from Greek literary cycles that were subsequently lost. As literary works were transmitted by different media and cultures, crucial narrative threads disappeared, leaving only fragmented images which the Etruscans used as best they could.[41]

By inventing a 'Grecian' urn whose isolated vignettes mimic Etruscan urns, Keats makes short work of this scholarly debate. He also denies the claim that Greek urns exhibit the narrative coherence Etruscan urns lack. By way of these adjustments, Keats's ode generalises its ekphrastic dilemma to suggest that no urn can represent history or time in motion. Arguing against the doctrine of *ut pictura poesis* – the claim that painting and poetry are 'sister arts' – Lessing insisted that whereas painting can represent only one moment, poetry can chronicle an entire narrative. However, the painter who depicts what Lessing calls the 'most pregnant moment' in a story – the moment that suggests what comes before and after – may accomplish by visual means what the poet does much more easily with words. Lessing's praise for the Laocoön statuary suggests that its achievement is in part to have surmounted its generic limitations, to have done at least as well what a poem, by virtue of its linear and thus narrative dimension, does more easily.[42] By this turn of argument and example, Lessing exposes the formalist bias half-hidden in his basic disagreement with the *ut pictura poesis* doctrine.

The third stanza of Keats's ode transforms Lessing's pictorial moment from an asset into a liability as the repetition of 'happy' makes readers uneasy about the advantage of being forever young, not kissing or unkissed. Similarly, the repetition of 'still' works against assigning unequivocal value to the still moment of happiness offered by the urn. Finally, the inverted syntax of the line 'All breathing human passion far above' (28) has a surprising and disconcerting effect: the depicted lovers do not exemplify 'All breathing human passion'; rather they are 'far above' it. This diction, which echoes Hazlitt's 1816 declaration that the beauty of Greek statues raises them 'above the frailties of pain or passion', manages to reformulate Hazlitt's praise as something less.[43] Whereas Hazlitt, Haydon, and other admirers of the Elgin Marbles insist that they seem like living human bodies, Keats says that the arrested lovers depicted on the urn are 'above' living passion. Placed beside contemporary praise for the marbles, this assertion begins to look equivocal. For if it is the case that the urn's lovers do not know love's satiety, they also do not know 'breathing human passion'.

Keats's ode makes another adjustment of Hazlitt's aesthetic principles. In his 1815 essay 'On the Ideal', Hazlitt began to develop a Romantic definition of the ideal which insists that what is truly ideal will also be historical. For this to occur, the human face and figure must be particularised – this beard, that expression, those shapes of muscle and bone. To this inventory Hazlitt adds 'passion', arguing that a face 'becomes historical by the mere force of passion', which 'moulds figures into the same emphatic expression.'[44] The lovers on Keats's urn are, in short, not historical or particular. And in the fourth stanza of the ode, the speaker makes this liability more explicit.

In that stanza, the speaker locates the procession depicted on the urn in a narrative sequence that begins with the 'little town' emptied of inhabitants and ends at a 'green altar'. For the doomed heifer 'lowing at the skies . . . her silken flanks with garlands drest' (33–4), the procession qualifies as an apt instance of Lessing's 'pregnant' moment. We may not know precisely how the heifer got there, but we may surmise what is about to happen to her. The historicality of that attention recalls both Hazlitt's definition (the historical is particular, animate, and passionate) and Keats's verse letter to Reynolds a year earlier, in which another scene of a heifer being led to sacrifice is 'touch'd into real life' by the 'Titian colours' of the poet's reverie (25 March 1818, *Letters*, i. 260). Jack's suggestion that the source for this image is the Elgin Marbles returns the ode's historicality to the pieces of Parthenon sculpture that had earlier prompted Keats's interest in the pathos of antiquity.[45]

In the *Ode on a Grecian Urn*, Keats's speaker is only briefly attentive to heifer and sacrificial moment before turning elsewhere, to the imagined 'little town'. His uncertainty about 'town' and 'green altar' emphasises that this narrative begins and ends off the urn. A. W.

Phinney argues that the best Keats's speaker can do is imagine or speculate about the provenance of the people in that procession. What we get is not verifiable history but 'phantasy', the work of a belated speaker who does what he can with what the urn and antiquity have left for him to do. But such a reading misses the point of the anti-ekphrastic gesture of Keats's poem. As Susan Wolfson has noted, the term *historia* means a 'method of learning by inquiry' – precisely what the speaker attempts in addressing the urn, whose very nature resists such inquiry (it is what it is and has no time for inquiry).[46] *Contra* Lessing, Keats suggests that the singularity of the urn's representations cannot convey an extended history.

The historicising impulse of Keats's ode is not an isolated phenomenon even in the annals of Romantic Hellenism. Like Winckelmann, Romantic Hellenists urged the recovery of cultural and historical contexts. In their long disagreement about the Elgin Marbles, Richard Payne Knight sought to persuade Haydon that his defence of the statues was mistaken on historical grounds. The tension between the desire for an accurate historical record and the establishment of the British Museum, where antiquities could be displayed with relatively little discussion of the cultures or sites from which they had been taken, is, as Phinney observes, inscribed throughout Keats's ode.[47]

Yet for all its resistance to ekphrasis as a device that seals descriptions, like the objects they mimic, from historical and cultural embeddedness, the ode is enmeshed in ekphrastic desire. Were it not, it could not have served formalist analysis as well as it has done and will continue to do.[48] As technical terms that refer to classical shape and line, the speaker's last figures of address ('O Attic shape! Fair attitude!', 41) explicitly recognise the urn's classical form. Although succeeding lines betray an edge of irritation with the power of the urn's 'overwrought' and 'silent form' to 'tease us out of thought', the ode concludes by delivering the urn's message.

Part of what some earlier critics claimed for that message has been abbreviated in Jack Stillinger's edition, which gives the urn the first half of the penultimate line ('"Beauty is truth, truth beauty"') and the speaker the rest ('– that is all/ Ye know on earth, and all ye need to know'). As readers have often observed, if the speaker distances himself from the urn's message, he also rejects Keats's famous comments on beauty and truth in his letter to Benjamin Bailey (22 November 1817; *Letters*, i. 184), and Haydon's use of a similar formula in an 1818 essay on Raphael in the *Annals of the Fine Arts*.[49] I would surmise further that Keats worked out his reservations about Romantic Hellenic principles as occasions warranted, trying out Haydonesque principles because they still attracted him even after he wrote the Elgin Marbles sonnet, but then putting them aside in the poem whose questions point toward historical and material realities that exceed the terms of the equation between beauty and truth. This surmise is directed by the remark that precedes Keats's passionate version of the traditional equation between beauty and truth in his letter: 'dont because you have suddenly discover'd a Coldness in Haydon suffer yourself to be teased'.

To whom the speaker of the ode addresses the last line and a half, whether to the urn or to us, remains at issue. The archaic 'Ye' usually refers to a plural addressee, but until the late nineteenth century it could also be singular. To argue with Stillinger and Phinney that we are the 'Ye' for whom the urn's message is 'all [we] need to know' would be to assent to formalist claims about well-wrought (if double) messages and poems.[50] We might argue instead that the speaker replies to the urn's aphorism 'Beauty is truth, truth beauty' by indicating this is the urn's truth, not his and, presumably, not ours. Whereas the text of the 1820 *Lamia* volume separates the urn's aphorism from what follows, earlier versions do not: deciding whether the urn's view of truth and beauty is all we need to know was not any easier for Keats than it has been for his modern readers.

As I read these lines, the speaker tells the urn that its aphorism is all *it* needs, but the referential wobble of 'Ye' tells readers the rest of the story. Keats's speaker remains divided between his desire to have the urn's history suffice and his recognition that it cannot suffice. This self-division expresses more than simply nostalgia for a world defined by the urn's representations. It argues that those representations leave out the sense of history that the speaker replaces by imagining life going on off the urn or, more precisely, by imagining that the urn will forever hold the inhabitants of an entire town captive and leave that town empty and, as it were, suspended in the urn's eternal, lyric time. The fact that the ode, as lyric and as ekphrasis, conveys this point obliquely also tells us something about the shape of history in poetic texts. Working against the seductions of its aesthetic form, the historical consciousness of Keats's ode asserts that history is particular ('What men or gods are these? What maidens loth?' Keats's speaker asks, 8) and animated by passion. It is not, in other words, 'Cold

Pastoral' or the 'Coldness in Haydon'. Finally, the ode figures present history as what is always going on elsewhere as events occur and slip past the moment of any single representation. For this reason, history can be indicated, but not encased, by poems and works of art: they work instead like indexical signs that point (obscurely or explicitly) to events, other material objects, beliefs, feelings, and suppositions about how all these do or do not impinge on each other – the whole array of phenomena that constitute what we know or call history. Shaped by Benjamin's theory of history, this observation returns modern historical consciousness to its Romantic antecedents.[51]

By such figural means Keats's *Ode on a Grecian Urn* contorts expectations implied by the circumstances of its 1820 publication. In January, when he complained about Haydon's tired 'discourses on poetry and painting', Keats let the ode appear in the *Annals of the Fine Arts*, precisely where he might have chosen not to make a public point of his resistance to the aesthetic principles championed by Haydon and the *Annals*. After preliminary skirmishes with Taylor and Hessey over the sexual explicitness of a substituted stanza in *The Eve of St. Agnes* in the spring of 1819, Keats was well aware that his publishers would be chary of any poem that might stir up controversy.[52] Yet he allowed them to publish the ode with the added quotation marks that invite notice of reservations about ekphrasis and the Elgin Marbles he had harboured for at least two years. Thus if Keats's ode does not openly attack the establishment, it does challenge aesthetic and more broadly cultural principles that Haydon, Hazlitt, and other contemporaries advocated in the name of Greek art.

COMMONPLACES AND CRITICAL METHODS

As a commonplace in Romantic English culture, the debate about the Elgin Marbles does not determine Keats's mediations between historical consciousness and ekphrasis in the *Ode on a Grecian Urn* and earlier poems. That debate is rather an occasion whose positions and figures Keats takes up, then reinvents. Understood via Giddens's theory of agency, this process allows Keats to refashion the habitus within which he becomes a poet, figure by figure and poem by poem. By calling this process 'structuration', Giddens suggests that it is roughly akin to the way surveyors triangulate points to map the contours of a field. To Giddens's figure of definitive, even mathematical agency within a fixed material field, I would add two codas. First,

individual agents do not simply map what is there: they find their
own rhetorical paths and arguments (this may only be another way of
saying that in charting a terrain a surveyor also invents a model of
that terrain). Second, Keats's sustained and ambivalent engagement
with ekphrasis invites us to imagine agency and invention as
something more than precipitates of will. I think it is clear that the
aesthetic pleasures of ekphrasis made significant demands on Keats as
a poet. He artfully resists those demands at the beginning of the *Ode*,
but that resistance is tuned to an ekphrastic bow and, as the poem
proceeds, Keats makes poetic space for this contradictory (or dialectical)
recognition. This inventional shuttle manages a Keatsian version of
what Richard Poirier finds in Emerson: a sense that human agents are
made as much by casualties that arrive casually (the pun is Emerson's),
with no sense of their occasion in our lives. In return, says Poirier, 'any
one of us assists, accelerates, tropes within this flow of things, and out
of the profusion one invention easily becomes the casualty of
another'.[53] It is no accident that Keats's reconsideration of ekphrasis
in the light and shadow of the Elgin Marbles debate is tropological:
the play of figures allows him to mark poetic moments in the 'flow of
things' – what we might also call history.

This view of agency and invention rejects a critical method that
fixes poems, like so many dead butterflies, in a preserving solution
called 'history' or 'culture'.[54] It also rejects a method that isolates
poems as brilliant artefacts suspended far above human history. The
outcome of either method is, oddly, much the same. Perceived as art
objects or materialist data, poems become fixed, served-up portions
for critical delectation. Keats's poetic practice suggests a different
way to configure the work of writing poems and the task of reading
them. The inventional path of his figural arguments about ekphrasis
and the Elgin Marbles seems both active and reactive, as though the
poet and the poems were forged in the shuttling of figures back and
forth across the array of topics I have described, and others I have not.

The critical model that informs this description is evidently
contextualist, whatever my disagreements with the specifics of
McGann's critical practice. But my argument is also, to borrow
David Perkins's distinction, immanent to the extent that I read Keats
via formalist and structuralist concerns generated by the ekphrastic
ambitions of the poems. Arguing that absolute knowledge is an
unattainable ideal, Perkins is sceptical about the possibility of literary
history – whether contextualist or immanent (although he clearly

favours the second of these). In one sense, he is right: no essay or reader will discover all there is to learn about a given work, cultural moment, or genre. And because no single critical focus will survey all evidence, it is logically impossible to say with certainty that one's argument is adequate or representative.[55] But the vectors of this scepticism need to be redirected to acknowledge that if all this is true, it is also true to life. As agents, we do the best we can by triangulating between and among the propositions, texts, and events that collectively register the acts (and self-contradictions) of being and knowing. As critics, we are faced with an allied, but different enterprise. To read Romantic poems, even those that appear to be brilliant verbal shapes far above the fray of Romantic cultural history, we need to grant that such poems are both capacious and permeable. As such, they reconfigure what is at hand, whether it is a genre, traditional figures, or the verbal shape any culture and moment gives to its material life. To read poems in this way, we need to risk flexible surmises about poems, poetic agency, and their mutual histories. Nothing more and nothing less than this will suffice.

NOTES

1 See in particular McGann's discussion of *Ode on a Grecian Urn*, *KHM*, 43–6; *La Belle Dame*, *KHM*, 31–7; the *Lamia* volume, *KHM*, 51–3. See too *The Romantic Ideology. A Critical Investigation* (Chicago, 1983), 81–92.

2 See Cleanth Brooks's essay, 'The Well-Wrought Urn', in *The Well-Wrought Urn* (New York, 1947), 151–6. For a recent restatement with reference to the ode, see Philip Fisher, 'A Museum with One Work Inside: Keats and the Finality of Art', *K–SJ* 33 (1985), 102.

3 For its impact on recent historicist critics see, for example, *KL*, 41 n., and Grant F. Scott, 'Beautiful Ruins: The Elgin Marbles Sonnet in its Historical and Generic Contexts', *K–SJ* 39 (1990), 124 n. Scott's argument undermines McGann's contention that the ode acquiesces to aesthetic principles identified with *Annals of the Fine Arts*.

4 See my 'Poetics and the Politics of Reception: Keats's "La Belle Dame sans Merci"', *ELH* 54 (1987), 333–62.

5 Bourdieu, *Outline of a Theory of Practice*, trans. R. Nice (Cambridge, 1977), 78. See also Ian Jack, *Keats and the Mirror of Art* (Oxford, 1967), for Haydon 23–45; the *Annals*, 46–57; and Keats's ode, 214–24. Jack, 223, suggests that Keats assents to the urn's idea of beauty. I thank Frederick Hoerner for conversations about limitations imposed by Bourdieu's 'habitus' and Giddens's idea of structuration (see note 6).

6 See Giddens, 'Structuration Theory: Past, Present and Future', in C.

Bryant and D. Jary (eds.), *Giddens' Theory of Structuration* (New York, 1991), 207–21. See Robertson, 'Deconstructive "Contortion" and Women's Historical Practice', *Poetics Today* 7 (1986), 712–17.

7 For Romantic and post-Romantic ekphrasis, see J. Hollander, 'The Gazer's Spirit: Romantic and Later Poetry on Painting and Sculpture', in G. W. Ruoff (ed.), *The Romantics and Us* (New Brunswick, 1990), 130–67. Williams, *Song* ('beauty is a shell'), *Collected Poems*, ed. A. W. Litz and C. MacGowan (2 vols., Manchester, 1987–8) ii. 395.

8 W. B. Pope (ed.), *The Diary of Benjamin Robert Haydon* (5 vols., Cambridge, Mass., 1960–3) ii. 76, quoted by Martin Aske, *Keats and Hellenism* (Cambridge, 1985), 15.

9 For further discussion of 'commonplace', see my essay 'The Case for William Wordsworth: Romantic Invention vs. Romantic Genius', in D. Bialostosky and L. Needham (eds.), *Romantic Traditions and British Romantic Literature* (Bloomington, 1995).

10 For the Elgin Marbles and pertinent nineteenth-century essays, see Timothy Webb, *English Romantic Hellenism* (New York, 1982), 220; see also William St Clair, *Lord Elgin and the Marbles* (London, 1967), 127–43, 249–60. For Keats and the marbles see *Letters*, i. 122 n.; William Sharp, *Life and Letters of Joseph Severn* (London, 1892), 32, cited in *AP*, 104.

11 The *Annals*, first published 1816, was dedicated to defending the Marbles as the highest expression of Greek art, and to advancing Haydon's career as historical painter. See also A. W. Phinney, 'Keats in the Museum: Between Aesthetics and History', *JEGP* 90 (1991), 213–15, and Jack, *Keats and the Mirror of Art*, 46–57.

12 See St Clair, *Lord Elgin*, 191 n.; Webb, *English Romantic Hellenism*; J. J. McGann (ed.), *Lord Byron: The Complete Poetical Works* (7 vols., Oxford, 1980–93) i. 323–4, esp. lines 89–122. See also Hazlitt, 'On the Ideal', *Champion*, 8 Jan. 1815; 'The Elgin Marbles', *Examiner*, 16 June 1816; 'Fine Arts', *Encyclopaedia Britannica*, 1817; 'On the Elgin Marbles' and 'The Same Subject Continued', *London Magazine*, Feb. and May 1822; all rpt. *HW*, xviii.

13 Winckelmann was translated into English by the painter Henri Fuseli, and was widely read. See *Reflections on the Painting and the Sculpture of the Greeks* (London, 1765). For Winckelmann's praise of the Apollo Belvedere, see Phinney, 'Keats in the Museum', 211.

14 Hazlitt, 'On the Ideal', *HW*, xviii. 81. J. Scott, 'The Elgin Marbles', *Champion* 155 (24 Dec. 1815), 390, in Grant Scott, 'Beautiful Ruins', 129 n.

15 'Letter from a Foreign Gentleman', 16 (1803), 15. St Clair, *Lord Elgin*, 99–103 summarises responses to news of Elgin's removal of the marbles and other excavated pieces.

16 J. Greig (ed.), *Diary of Joseph Farington* (8 vols., London, 1923–8) iv. 145 and v. 46. For Beaumont, see Grant Scott, 'Beautiful Ruins', 125–6. *Byron: Complete Poetical Works*, i. 261, lines 1029–30. Hazlitt, *HW*, xviii. 115; for Hemans, see sonnet 91 in *Modern Greece* (1817); rpt. D. Reiman

(ed.), *'Poems'*, *'England and Spain'*, *'Modern Greece'* (New York, 1978).

17 My discussion of the Elgin Marbles and Keats's early sonnet is indebted to Grant Scott, 'Beautiful Ruins', 133, 125–7.

18 'Elgin Marbles', *HW*, xviii. 101.

19 Haydon to Keats, in *Letters*, i. 122, and Grant Scott, 'Beautiful Ruins', 137, on how Haydon misconstrues Keats's eagle image.

20 The House of Commons heard testimony in February and March 1816; its report was published early April and widely discussed in periodicals. Parliament debated the marbles in June; Hazlitt's *Examiner* essay appeared 16 June (see n. 12 above). In the end, Parliament voted to transfer ownership of the marbles from Elgin to England.

21 *KL*, 12–14.

22 Keats may have reread Robertson (6th edn, 3 vols., London, 1792, esp. i. 284–91, iii. 19–49) in 1818 and certainly did in spring 1819, when he mentions reading about 'Piziaro' in a letter to the George Keatses; *Letters*, i. 255 n., 263 n.; ii. 100, 156 n. Although Keats makes no mention of reading Williams's *Peru*, its critique of Spanish conquest in the New World illustrates a liberal English view already well established at the beginning of the Peruvian war for independence from Spain in 1813. Williams quotes extensively from Robertson in documentary notes, and makes a special point (via Robertson) of Pizzaro's pillage of Peru. See *Peru* (London, 1784), 77, quoting Robertson, iii. 36–7.

23 For Keats's politics, see *KP* and Carl Woodring, *Politics in English Romantic Poetry* (Cambridge, 1970), 77–83.

24 See for example Alan J. Bewell, 'The Political Implication of Keats's Classicist Aesthetics', *KP*, 220–30.

25 Bewell, 'Political Implication', 224–5, quoting *Quarterly Review*. For a recent account of the residual power of this evolutionary model, see Martin Bernal, *Black Athena* (New Brunswick, N.J., 1987).

26 For scholarly works and public interest prompted by Napoleon's Egyptian campaign, see Bewell, 'Political Implication', 225.

27 *Annals* 3 (1818), 494 and 4 (1819), 183.

28 *AP*, 434 n. notes that, among other sources Keats had read, Lemprière's *Classical Dictionary* describes the sound of Memnon's statue.

29 *Keats and Hellenism*, 113.

30 Hazlitt was inconsistent on this point. In 1815 he writes that the marbles are supposed to be the work of Phidias; the next year he says they are not by him, but probably 'done by persons under his direction'. In later essays, including his *Encyclopaedia Britannica* article, Hazlitt again presents the marbles as the work of Phidias.

31 *The Sister Arts* (Chicago, 1958), 18 n. See too Murray Krieger, 'The Ekphrastic Principle and the Still Movement of Poetry', in *The Play and Place of Criticism* (Baltimore, 1959), 127 and *Ekphrasis: The Illusion of Natural Sign* (Baltimore, 1992); and James O'Rourke, 'Persona and Voice in the "Ode on a Grecian Urn"', *SIR* 26 (1987), 27–48. Krieger

and O'Rourke assume that the speaker's ekphrastic gesture ratifies the urn's claims, as does Kenneth Burke, *A Grammar of Motives* (Berkeley, 1962), 457–8.

32 See Spitzer, 'The "Ode on a Grecian Urn"', or Content vs. Metagrammar', in *Essays on English and American Literature* (Princeton, 1962), 72; K. S. Calhoon, 'The Urn and the Lamp', *SIR* 26 (1987), 8–10; Bruce Thornton, 'Cold Pastoral: Theocritus' Cup and Keats's Urn', *Classical and Modern Literature* 7 (Winter 1987), 11–18.

33 Cf. Keats writing to George and Georgiana Keats, October 1818, of being 'with Achilles shouting in the Trenches' or 'with Theocritus in the Vales of Sicily'; *Letters*, i. 404. Because his description of Achilles echoes Pope's translation of the *Iliad*, he may also have read Pope's *Discourse on Pastoral Poetry*; see E. Audra and A. Williams (eds.), *Pastoral Poetry and an Essay on Criticism* (New Haven, 1961), 29.

34 *The Idylls, Epigrams, Fragments of Theocritus, Bion and Moschus*, trans. Richard Polwhele (Exeter, 1786), 19. This translation was reprinted six times before 1822.

35 Jack, *Keats and the Mirror of Art*, 216; *KHM*, 44–5. Moses, *A Collection of Antique Vases* (London, 1814), 1–14, quoted by *AP*, 534 n.

36 Keats uses the term 'laconiscism' (*sic*) to describe Hazlitt's style in a letter of 2 Jan. 1819, *Letters*, ii. 24. Benjamin, 'The Storyteller', in *Illuminations* (New York, 1968), 91.

37 Thornton, 'Cold Pastoral', 118. Calhoon, 'The Urn and the Lamp', 5–8 and Tilottama Rajan, *Dark Interpreter* (Ithaca, N.Y., 1980), 133–5, remark that the ode is careful not to mention the urn's funerary purpose.

38 'The "Ode on a Grecian Urn"', 74–5.

39 *Keats and the Mirror of Art*, 217.

40 For the ode's sexual violence as indictment of Keats's historical amnesia or silencing of women, see Daniel P. Watkins, 'Historical Amnesia and Patriarchal Morality in Keats's *Ode on a Grecian Urn*', in G. A. Rosso and D. Watkins (eds.), *Spirits of Fire: English Romantic Writers and Contemporary Historical Methods* (London and Toronto, 1990), 240–59. Other feminist readings suggest that what Keats ascribes to women is a version of what he fears himself; in this instance, fear of being silenced. See for example Susan Wolfson, 'Feminizing Keats', in H. de Almeida (ed.), *Critical Essays on John Keats* (Boston, 1990), 317–57 and Margaret Homans, 'Keats Reading Women, Women Reading Keats', *SIR* 29 (1990), 341–70.

41 Richard Brilliant, *Visual Narratives* (Ithaca, N.Y., 1984), 23, 21.

42 G. H. Lessing, *Laocoön: An Essay on the Limits of Painting and Poetry*, trans. E. A. McCormick (Baltimore, 1984), 19–20.

43 See Susan Wolfson, *The Questioning Presence* (Ithaca, N.Y., 1986), 321, and, for a counter-argument, Douglas Wilson, 'Reading the Urn: Death in Keats's Arcadia', *SEL* 25 (1985), 834–6. See also Hazlitt, 'On Gusto', *HW*, iv. 79, quoted by *AP*, 535 n.

44 *HW*, xviii. 83.

45 See *Keats and the Mirror of Art*, 219.
46 Phinney, 'Keats in the Museum', 223. Wolfson, *Questioning Presence*, 319.
47 For thoughtful analysis of how the ode and the Elgin Marbles sonnet reflect this tension, see Phinney, 'Keats in the Museum', 216–17, 221–3.
48 See for example Marshall Brown, 'Unheard Melodies: The Force of Form', *PMLA* 107 (May 1992), 465–81.
49 'The Exhibition of the Cartoons', 258, quoted by Jack, *Keats and the Mirror of Art*, 51.
50 See Stillinger, 'Who Says What to Whom at the End of "Ode on a Grecian Urn"?', *The Hoodwinking of Madeline* (Chicago, 1971), 167–73; Phinney, 'Keats in the Museum', 227; O'Rourke, 'Persona and Voice', 48; Helen Vendler, *The Odes of John Keats* (Cambridge, Mass., and London, 1983), 149. Stuart Peterfreund queries the sufficiency of the urn's dictum in 'The Truth about "Beauty" and "Truth" in Keats's "Ode on a Grecian Urn"', *K–SJ* 35 (1986), 71–2.
51 'Theses on the Philosophy of History', in *Illuminations*, 257.
52 See Richard Woodhouse's account in a letter to Taylor, 19–20 Sept. 1819, *Letters*, ii. 162–3.
53 *Poetry and Pragmatism* (London, 1992), 57–8.
54 On the liabilities of this kind of materialism see Garrett Stewart, 'Staying Powers', *Modern Language Quarterly* 54 (June 1993), 306; for attentive description of how the theoretical disposition of Romantic studies has shifted away from this kind of materialism see Levinson, 'Romantic Poetry: The State of the Art', *ibid.*, 183–214.
55 *Is Literary History Possible?* (Baltimore, 1992), 16–27, 185.

CHAPTER 12

Keats's literary tradition and the politics of historiographical invention

Greg Kucich

William Mavor, one of Keats's favourite historians, crowns history in 1802 the 'master science' of his epoch, a comprehensive structure of knowledge displacing the traditional role of religion in rendering the ultimate truths of experience.[1] Yet, like religion, historiography could assume many different modes for representing truth, and its shifting methods of knowledge formation could perform crucial ideological functions in the power dynamics of its material contexts. The competition for epistemological and political authority among vying interpretations of the past preoccupied European historians, politicians, and poets throughout the turbulent revolutionary period of the late eighteenth and early nineteenth centuries. Keats entered wholeheartedly into this arena of contention, fully aware of the inventive nature of historical writing and the significance of fashioning such an important discourse of truth toward redemptive political ends. He consumed an impressive range of historical texts from an early age and maintained a steady reading of historical writers like Gibbon, Voltaire, Robertson, Xenophon, Livy, Vertot, Raleigh, Holinshed, and Davies throughout his mature years.[2] The burning question of how to reconstruct the 'mouldering scrolls' of a volatile historical field (*Endymion*, III. 129), and the political challenges of such interpretive acts, drive much of his own poetic enterprise, from the early vision of British political retrenchment in *Lines Written on 29 May, the Anniversary of Charles's Restoration*, to the chronicle of political tyranny in Book III of *Endymion*, through the monarchical struggles of the Hyperion narratives and the late historical dramas, *Otho the Great* and *King Stephen*.[3] If Apollo is the presiding deity of Keats's poetry, Clio (Muse of History) and the political imperative of 'the patriot's stern duty' also play a central role in the development of his creative imagination (*To Charles Cowden Clarke*, 68–9).

J. Philip Eggers and, more recently, Thomas A. Reed have argued for the centrality of Keats's historical consciousness in his poetic productions. But we still need, as Daniel P. Watkins suggests in his study of Keats's politics, a more comprehensive account of Keats's historiographical procedures, their relation to his era's prominent historical texts, and their complicated interventions in the politics of his day.[4] These themes converge most strikingly in Keats's reliance on historiography, particularly eighteenth-century historical writings, to formulate one of his most urgent creative concerns – his vision of his own poetic identity and development within the contexts of British literary and political history. To investigate the historiographical contexts of Keats's creative autobiography is to deepen considerably our understanding of the fundamental, often puzzling divisions in his sense of relation to the literary past, conflicts that left him simultaneously confident of ranking 'among the English Poets' (*Letters*, i. 394) and convinced that 'the scroll . . . of mighty Poets' is filled, eternally 'folded by the Muses' (*Endymion*, II. 724–5). Still more broadly, such an inquiry can also reveal in his struggle with those divisions the degree to which his overall creative endeavour both conforms to and challenges the politics of his era's dominant gender codes and structures of understanding.[5]

Ever since Harold Bloom labelled Keats's memorable outcry against Milton – 'Life to him would be death to me' (*Letters*, ii. 212) – the motto of British poetic history and its influence anxieties, we have come to think of Keats and his Romantic contemporaries as poets conditioned and sometimes irreparably crippled by an agonistic relation to their cultural inheritance. Stuart Curran has more recently argued for a more confident Romantic attitude toward the past, citing Keats as a representative example: 'obsessed with poetic fame, just twenty-one and a spokesman for his culture: "Great spirits now on earth are sojourning . . . Listen awhile ye nations, and be dumb"'.[6] The evidence of Keats's efforts to forge his own poetic identity in relation to the past would seem to bear out both readings. His anxious expressions of cultural belatedness rank among the most memorable passages in his poetry and letters. '[T]ruth is', he confesses to Haydon at the outset of his first major poetic venture, *Endymion*, 'I have been in such a state of Mind as to read over my Lines and hate them . . . the Cliff of Poesy Towers above me'. The one great obstacle to his creative development, he admits to Taylor, lies in his inclination toward 'cowering under the Wings of great Poets' (*Letters*, i. 141, 239). Although Keats may have stooped under the burden of the past, however, he could also derive great inspiration and confidence from his predecessors. Shakespeare could seem like a 'good Genius' presiding over his creative maturation (*Letters*, i. 142), and Spenser could encourage his 'daring steps' toward the pantheon of immortal poets (*Specimen of an Induction to a Poem*, 57). If Bloom is right to find the ghosts of antiquity paralysing Keats, Curran is equally justified in arguing for their enabling tendency to spring his imagination free, just as 'the Remembrance of Chaucer' sets him 'forward like a Billiard-Ball' (*Letters*, i. 142, 147).

Part of the continuing difficulty in resolving these contradictions lies in our tendency to dehistoricise literary influence by investigating the dynamics of poetic relations on exclusively psychoanalytic and textual levels. Bloom's agonistic tale depicts literary tradition as a completed, essential monument of its own making, which Keats and the Romantics passively received in the troubled regions of their private psyches. Even those who challenge Bloom's influence theory, like Curran, tend to ground their arguments in the same psychological category, stressing the moods of mind Keats brought to his encounters with the past. Critics seeking to negotiate between these two influence models, such as Geoffrey Hartman, similarly focus on the 'literary mind' of belated poets 'haunt[ed]' by a monolithically 'grand' past that is 'now inspiring and now depressive'.[7] Much as these investigations have taught us about the psychodynamics of poetic relations, we may gain a deeper understanding of the contrariety of Keats's encounter with the literary past if we situate it within the socio-historical contexts of his time. For the literary history he confronted was not so much a monumental accomplishment, but rather an ever-shifting invention of the present whose protean configurations and reshapings were driven by the competing ideological forces of the day.

Keats was aware of this relation between literary history and material politics, frequently aligning his intense preoccupation with poetic influence and his responses to the political crises developing around him.[8] Thus one of his earliest meditations on the literary past, *Written on the Day That Mr. Leigh Hunt Left Prison*, celebrates achievements of Spenser and Milton while attacking the 'wretched crew' responsible for Hunt's prosecution and imprisonment (14). Conversely, his apprehensions about cultural belatedness are frequently shaded by his worries about the failure of contemporary political reform. In *Sleep and Poetry*, for instance, Keats's reflections on the 'desperate turmoil' of literary ambition and possible defeat were for the most part composed in Hunt's library under the 'mightily forlorn' gaze of Kosciusko, the Polish patriot (308, 387–8). His apprehensions of inferiority to Boccaccio in *Isabella* immediately follow his sustained critique of the mercantile savagery of Isabella's brothers, those 'ledger-men' and 'money-bags' whose predatory economic practices are generally associated with the ever-widening depredations of nineteenth-century industrial capitalism (137, 142). The 'Cliff of Poesy' towers above Keats in a letter to Haydon that is also preoccupied with Southey's reactionary politics, the fall of Napoleon, and the restoration of European monarchy (*Letters*, i. 141–5). On the other hand, the mountainous landscape of poetic tradition usually becomes more accessible when Keats considers the political advances in progress around him. His 'wild surmises' about joining 'the elder Bards' in *On Receiving a Laurel Crown from Leigh Hunt* (13) (recalling the 'wild surmise' arising from spectacular poetic discovery in *On First Looking into Chapman's Homer*, 13) closely follow his prophecy of the impending demise of monarchy – 'A trampling down of what the world most prizes,/Turbans and crowns, and blank regality' (11–12).[9]

Much as these political inflections should alert us to the material contexts of Keats's influence theory, we should not conclude that his conflicting ideas of literary tradition arise solely from his various political attitudes. The full relation between these categories actually depends on a third level of discourse that conditions his views of both political and literary development – that is, the historical work that informs his meditations on cultural progress and decline. When Keats turns his attention to the 'Cliff of Poesy', he habitually draws upon eighteenth-century historiography to formulate his own position in the evolving patterns of literary tradition. At the beginning of his sustained consideration of the cultural progress from Milton to Wordsworth, for instance, he relies heavily on the topographical language of Robertson's *History of America* and Buffon's *Natural History* (Paris, 1749–89) to depict cultural improvement in terms of explorative journeys to vast, new continents (*Letters*, i. 255 and n. 6). He was also reading Voltaire and Gibbon at the time of that memorable confession 'to a cowering under the Wings of great Poets' (*Letters*, i. 237–9). These historiographical contexts are not only implicated in his divided responses to the cultural past, they also involve Keats's ambivalent literary historicism with his reactions to contemporary political events. The argument for Wordsworth's superiority over Milton, as Thomas Reed suggests, raises disturbing and unsettled questions about Britain's political improvement since the Reformation.[10] To see how this eighteenth-century historiographical background connects Keats's views of politics and literary tradition, we may turn to one of his earliest and most dramatic encounters with 'the elder Bards', *On First Looking into Chapman's Homer*.

Until recently, Keats's critics have read this sonnet as a joyous discovery of 'the great poetry of the past', which inspires a 'new confidence' about creative possibilities in the present. Marjorie Levinson, however, has stressed the poem's uneasy and highly politicised relation to the traditions of high culture in its parodic acknowledgement of Keats's own class-inflected exclusion from the languages and literatures of antiquity.[11] His enthusiasm about joining that tradition may be traced in the way he associates the 'wild surmise' of discovery in the Chapman sonnet with his own 'wild surmises' about impending creative achievement in the sonnet on Hunt's laurel crown. The apprehension Levinson notes in the Chapman sonnet, and its political implications, may be discerned as well through intertextual relations with other Keats poems of the same period. His figure of literary tradition as a 'new planet' (10) assumes a threatening dimension in *Sleep and Poetry*, where the achievement of Renaissance poetry is represented as a 'Huge . . . planet' that 'roll[s] round,/ Eternally around a dizzy void' (176–7). Keats's other prominent metaphor for literary tradition in the Chapman sonnet, a vast ocean dotted with 'many western islands' (3), grows similarly disturbing in *Sleep and Poetry* when it reappears as 'An ocean dim, sprinkled with many an isle', that 'Spreads awfully' before the modern poet who, like Icarus, plummets 'Convuls'd and headlong!' into its whelming depths (303–12). Keats's sonnet *On the Sea* hints at the political turmoil behind these literary anxieties. Written as Keats began *Endymion*, the sonnet contrasts the 'uproar rude' of social life (associated in *Endymion*, III. 19 with the 'uproar past' of political tyranny) and the 'eternal whisperings' of the sea (11, 1). In this 'gentle temper' (5), the sea offers a temporary lyrical respite from political and literary anxieties alike (*Letters*, i. 374, 132).

The historiographical context linking these political and creative apprehensions appears in William Robertson's *History of America* and its particular accounts of famous discoveries by Cortez and Balboa, widely recognised as Keats's principal sources for the conception and imagery of the Chapman sonnet. It is the contradictory and highly politicised nature of Robertson's discovery narratives that most specifically conditions the divided attitudes of Keats's sonnet. Robertson represents Balboa's search for the Pacific Ocean as the voyage of a belated explorer seeking to rival the discoveries of his great predecessor, Columbus. 'Elated with the idea of performing what so great a man [Columbus] had attempted in vain', Balboa conducts a personal quest for glory that results in 'his transports of joy' when he becomes the first European to behold the South Sea. That spirit of exaltation at surpassing one's precursors clearly informs Keats's enthusiasm about discovering and extending the great literary tradition commemorated in the Chapman sonnet. But Robertson's story of achievement is severely qualified by his attention to the brutal greed of the Spanish explorers. Balboa's expeditionary force is primarily motivated, in fact, by desire for gold, reputed to be abundant in a 'wealthy kingdom' near the South Sea.[12] Similarly, Cortez's men drive on to Mexico City preoccupied with the 'ample recompense' of booty they expect to receive 'for all their service and sufferings'. Along the way toward their destinations, both parties abuse and 'slaughter' the native populations that oppose them, demonstrating the vicious imperialism that Robertson identifies with the Spanish experience in America.[13] Discovery, in Robertson's narrative, is both magnificent and ghastly.

Daniel Watkins has noted that Keats largely elides these grim political realities from his own portrait of imaginative discovery in the Chapman sonnet.[14] However, Keats's opening address to those 'realms of gold' does call attention to the principal aspect of the Spanish colonial institution that Robertson deplores – its murderous greed in the pursuit of commercial gain, overwhelmingly symbolised by its lust for gold. Columbus is fascinated by the gold ornaments of the first natives he encounters and directs his explorations in pursuit of that 'precious metal'. The natives are 'astonished at his eagerness in quest of gold', and disgusted by the way Balboa's men are 'so passionately fond of gold'. Everywhere the Spaniards travel, the rapacious desire 'to penetrate the bowels of the earth' in search of 'gold' controls their behaviour and drives them to decimate the lands and peoples they encounter.[15] Marjorie Levinson and K. K. Ruthven have shown how Keats often uses images of gold – in the Nebuchad-nezzar sonnet, in the tirade against Isabella's brothers, in Lamia's palace, and elsewhere – to depict the cultural 'impoverishment' of nineteenth-century industrial capitalism.[16] Keats's historical reading would have taught him, of course, that the economic and political conditions of colonial America were different from those governing his own era. Still, he tended to invoke the predatory commercialism of earlier periods, as many critics have noted of *Isabella*, for the purpose of condemning the dehumanising forms of capitalism also pervasive in modern life. He may have drawn upon Robertson's reference to Balboa's violent acquisition of 'a considerable quantity of pearls', in fact, for his portrait of the 'Ceylon diver' in *Isabella* as a victim of modern commercial greed (113).[17] To begin the Chapman sonnet with a striking image of gold (drawn from the violent, colonial history in Robertson) might also reflect upon and provoke questions about the cultural and political impoverishment of his own commercial 'realm', even as Keats celebrates the wealth and amplitude of an earlier 'Golden Age' of poetry.[18] From Robertson's historical narrative of ambiguous discovery in early America, Keats thus began to develop his own views of a literary history inflected by the troubled social conditions of nineteenth-century Europe.

Interdisciplinarity, especially in relation to politics and the arts, forms one of the key methodological principles of historiography in the eighteenth century. Although specialised histories of economics, biology, geology, politics, and literature appear in abundance, the most compelling form of historical inquiry remains one grounded in what James Granger terms in 1769 'synchronism'.[19] That interdisciplinary 'synchronism', announced in sweeping titles like Goldsmith's *A General History of the World*, or Mavor's *Universal History, Ancient and Modern*, often focuses on the complex relation between political and artistic developments. Voltaire's *Siècle de Louis XIV* stresses the interrelated revolution in 'nos arts, dans nos esprits, dans nos moeurs, comme dans notre gouvernement' that distinguishes the reign of Louis XIV. Robertson makes a similar claim for a different period in *The History of Scotland*, arguing that the interconnected artistic, intellectual, and political innovations of the Reformation make it 'one of the greatest events in the history of mankind'. Mavor claims that classical Greece excelled so spectacularly in the arts because of its political 'freedom'.[20] The impact of these arguments on the historical consciousness of Keats's generation can be measured by their frequent recurrence in the writings of his intellectual associates. Hazlitt, for instance, rehearses Robertson's account of the Reformation in his *Lectures on the Dramatic Literature of the Age of Elizabeth*, and Shelley memorably expands Mavor's reading of classical Greece in the preface to *Prometheus Unbound*.[21] If some of the Romantics wish to evade political reality through their art, as recent theories of Romantic ideology would suggest, that desire is mediated for most of them by a strong consciousness of the inextricable relation between the histories of art and politics.

The issue at the centre of this interdisciplinary historicism is whether cultural and social conditions are progressing or degenerating from earlier periods – a major preoccupation of such giants of historiography as Bacon, Hume, and Gibbon in England, and Voltaire, Condorcet, Volney, Kant, Schiller, and Hegel on the continent. This question of progress or decline becomes increasingly urgent in the developing arguments about the history of the French Revolution, with supporters of political reform like Paine, Priestley, Godwin, Hazlitt, and Shelley stressing cultural progress and defenders of tradition like Burke, Barruel, and Southey apprehending, often in apocalyptic terms, the collapse of civilised life. This dispute about historical progress, moreover, does not simply break down along party lines. Those who champion the liberal cause find their visions of progress regularly qualified by setbacks like the Reign of Terror, the fall of Napoleon, and the Bourbon restoration, all of which contribute to apprehensions of retrenchment among those historical writers most deeply committed to the progress of reform. Mary Wollstonecraft, for instance, passionately insists on the 'progressive state of improvement' in world politics; but as she writes her *Historical View of the French Revolution* in 1794, the atrocities of the Reign of Terror make her take a 'most melancholy . . . retrospective glance' over the degenerating motions of recent European history. Hazlitt, who keeps stoking the fires of reform through the dark years following Waterloo, has to admit in characterising the 'spirit of the age' that 'scarce a shadow . . . remains' of Godwin's *Political Justice* and all the hopes for political progress that it embodies.[22] These conflicting visions of political history would have made it difficult for a writer like Keats, committed to the liberal side of the question and convinced of the intertwined fates of art and politics, to feel anything but ambivalence about the status of modern poetry in relation to its lofty past.

Such divisions of historical outlook are further complicated by a more fundamental contrariety in the era's theoretical modes of conceptualising history as a 'master science' that explains the motion and meaning of all experience. Although eighteenth-century historians fully recognise variable rates of development among different cultures and fields of endeavour, they generally seek to produce totalising narratives, universal histories, that organise all of human experience within grand patterns of development. In *Siècle de Louis XIV*, Voltaire divides the history of cultural achievement into four epochs, the eras dominated by classical Greece, Augustan Rome, Renaissance Italy, and enlightenment France. Mavor, seeking to define the 'general laws [that] regulate the development' of all human experience, presents 'a sort of historic map' partitioning world history into eleven categories.[23] To formulate these divisions into the meaningful patterns of a 'master science', the makers of universal history rely on linear narrative structures of progress and decline. The structuring of these narratives along such lines is frequently informed, as Rene Wellek has argued, by scientific models of biological evolution and theological paradigms of Christian apocalyptic history.[24] Most significant for the divided historical consciousness of Keats's generation is the tendency in these linear narratives to conflate the lines of progress and decline as essential components of a single pattern of contrary motion.

To champion either the prolific or the devouring energies of this linear narrative is to embrace or at least to acknowledge the pressure of its contrary. The biological model, for instance, fosters a view of human civilisation's movement, like that of a plant, along a double bias of growth and decay, with each stage of maturation also representing the encroachment of decline. Hence Goldsmith compares the permutations of human history to 'the vicissitudes of the seasons' and the 'revolutions of the vegetable world'. Depending on how one views one's own position amid these cycles of change, civilisation can seem either progressing toward enlightenment or 'relaps[ing] into pristine barbarity'.[25] The Christian pattern of apocalyptic history provides many eighteenth-century historical writers with a more complex version of linear contrariety. Its doubling motion, down from a fall and upward toward the millennium, could offer a circuitous pathway out of history into transcendental redemption – a model of apocalyptic progress enthusiastically secularised, as M. H. Abrams has argued, in the political philosophy of revolutionary France and the universal histories of Kant and Schiller.[26] But from the time-bound perspective of many eighteenth-century historians, the temporal present could seem trapped in a steady decline from innocence into multiplying layers of corruption. Thus William Duff, attributing 'the revolutions in the works of art' to the consequences of original sin, envisages nature and human civilisation travelling downward toward 'corruption and degeneracy'.[27] If Joseph Priestley could see revolutionary France marching forward to the brink of the New Jerusalem, Edmund Burke could draw upon the same Christian paradigm to envision the social fabric of the world collapsing amid the flames of the Antichrist's apocalypse. These histories were thus adopted by both parties, helping to foster that inclination in eighteenth-century historical writing to conceptualise the motion of humanity through time as an ongoing tension between linear contraries.

If we keep in mind the models of contrariety that inform these master narratives of universal history, we may find them not simply presenting contested models of progress and decline – the retrograde scenario of Gibbon's history of Rome, for instance, versus the progressive structure of Walpole's steady 'improvements in arts and sciences' – but rather articulating complex theories of perpetual tension between these two inclinations.[28] Hume, for instance, argues for a progressive refinement in British arts and government at the same time that he finds 'the arts and sciences' subject to a 'natural' and 'necessary' process of 'decline'. He characterises this paradox in terms of an ongoing tension between 'progress' *and* 'decline', emphasising the 'contrary direction' toward which all human activity coalesces.[29] Malthus offers one of the most striking paradigms of narrative contrariety in eighteenth-century historical writing, presenting human history as an 'oscillation' or 'vibration' between endlessly repetitive cycles of population growth and decline. That characterisation of historical process as a dynamic of 'retrograde and progressive movements' exerted a tremendous influence, mostly of a discouraging nature in Shelley's view, over the historical consciousness of generations to come.[30] Several decades later, Southey was still conceptualising history as a linear conflict between the energies of 'general improvement' and the encroaching disintegration of 'every thing which has hitherto been held sacred' in literature and government.[31]

The major impact of these contrariety models on Keats's historical thinking may be gauged by their centrality in the historical writings that interested him the most – those works by Voltaire, Robertson, Goldsmith, Godwin, Gibbon, Burnet, and Mavor. Voltaire begins *Siècle de Louis XIV* with a dramatic claim that European civilisation is progressing toward its highest forms of 'perfection' in the modern age. Yet, as Keats was keen to notice, *Siècle de Louis XIV* and Rousseau's *Essai sur les moeurs et l'esprit des nations* also highlight the crimes and miseries that have continued to depress civilisation throughout world history (*Letters*, ii. 100–1; *KC*, i. 259). Burnet calls history 'crooked', in his delineation of the contrary 'turns' of progress and decline that shape the uneven contours of Scottish history.[32] Robertson is a strong proponent of linear progress, arguing in *The History of the Reign of the Emperor Charles V* for the steady 'improvements' and 'progress of society' in European history. But his *History of America*, as we have seen, specifically contrasts such European 'progress' with the concomitant decimation of the indigenous American cultures. Robertson even supplies a succinct theory of linear contrariety with his biological metaphor of Roman society as a human body, representative generally of social development, maturing but simultaneously declining into old age.[33] Goldsmith employs a different, even more provocative scientific metaphor to conceptualise the warfare of linear contraries that he finds driving all human and elemental motion. 'The heavenly bodies of our system', he concludes, are 'acted upon by two opposing powers; namely, by that of *attraction*; which draws them toward the sun; and that of *impulsion*, which drives them straight forward into the great void of space; they pursue a track between these contrary directions.' Such theories of competing trajectories clearly inform the historical consciousness of Hazlitt, one of Keats's most important intellectual guides, who dismisses progress models in formulating his own vision of historical contrariety. 'All things move', he claims in a review of *The Excursion*, 'not in progress, but in a ceaseless round; our strength lies in our weakness; our virtues are built in our vices.'[34]

If we consider the integration of artistic and socio-political history in these master narratives of divided motion, it should not be surprising to find their contrary linear structures conditioning the more specialised literary histories that appear in the later eighteenth century. Among the many competing, often contradictory narratives of cultural development in eighteenth-century British literary historiography, such writers as Young, Duff, Goldsmith, Percy, Johnson, and the Wartons offer widely varying opinions of ancient versus modern literature, the relative achievements of different national cultures, and the shifting rates of improvement in different artistic disciplines. But the one conceptual outlook they share to varying degrees is their inclination to organise literary history along linear tracks that swerve in 'contrary directions'. Thus, Thomas Warton fashions his highly influential *History of English Poetry* as a progressive narrative of 'the great lines of the history of poetry' while also regretting the modern period's decline from 'the golden age of

English poetry' in the Elizabethan period.[35]

This vision of contrariety in recent literary and socio-political historiography exerted a strong influence on Keats's divided view of cultural tradition. But we may find its deepest impact on his historical outlook deriving from its negative political implications and their particular tendency to enforce apprehensions of cultural belatedness. For Keats knew, along with Shelley, that the retrograde motion in such a paradigm of history's contrary motions could seem to assert a perpetual condition of political tyranny and suffering – a problem recognised by Voltaire, Godwin, and other reformers who try, without complete success, to explain recurrent historical episodes of despotism as temporary setbacks in a general progression of liberty. Moreover, Malthus indicates that historical 'oscillations' always increase the prosperity of the elite while subjecting the lower classes to repetitive cycles of woe. To find the movements of literary tradition implicated in the disturbing contrariety of this socio-political history was thus not only to gain a deeper sense of literature's material base. It could also mean locating the history of poetry in an iron cycle of endless suffering that could prompt despair of any form of political or cultural renewal.

It is this problematic dimension of eighteenth-century historical contrariety that most profoundly controls Keats's own historiographical project. Those critics who discuss his theory of history usually stress its linear framework and the 'unfaltering belief in progress' that underpins it, most obviously evident in his famous formulation of Wordsworth's superiority over Milton as a representative example and natural consequence of 'the general and gregarious advance of intellect'.[36] That 'grand march of intellect' (*Letters*, i. 282) sweeps history along in a continual process of creative and political improvement that guarantees the cultural advances of each successive generation. Yet some recent critics have noticed uncertainties in Keats's arguments for linear progress, such as his paradoxical portrait of Milton's achievement as fixed, unassailable, yet simultaneously part of an ever-developing historical process.[37] These qualifications frequently assume the form of those models of linear contrariety informing the historical consciousness of Keats's era. If he often finds Britain's political history since Milton moving along progressive lines, he can also see it travelling in a contrary, retrograde direction. 'We have no Milton, no Algernon Sidney,' he laments, 'All the departments of Government have strayed far from Spimpicity [*sic*] which is the greatest of Strength – there is as much difference in this respect between the present Government and oliver Cromwell's, as there is between the 12 Tables of Rome and the volumes of Civil Law which were digested by Justinian' (*Letters*, i. 396–7). Such an apprehension certainly reveals Keats's dissatisfaction with any simplistic accounts of Godwinian 'perfectibility' that posit unswerving lines of cultural improvement. Yet it does not, on the other hand, represent a thorough conviction of inexorable decline. Instead Keats embraces the broader, intersecting movements of progress and regression, reform and reaction in narratives like Godwin's, incorporating the contrariety models of eighteenth-century historiography into his own complex vision of history's oscillating patterns.

The linear contrariety of that outlook, its specific origins in eighteenth-century historiography, and its potentially disturbing political implications are all apparent in Keats's evocative representation of historical experience as a 'vale of Soul-making'. It is his reading of Robertson's *History of America* and Voltaire's *Siècle de Louis XIV* that inspires this memorable formulation. The powerful emphasis of both works on the intense human suffering that pervades modern and primitive life confirms Keats's distrust of any singularly progressive linear history. 'But in truth,' he concludes, 'I do not at all believe in this sort of perfectibility – the nature of the world will not admit of it'. At the same time, however, Keats resists an exclusively degenerative line of historical motion, striving to 'imagine' human improvement 'carried to an extreme'. To do so, he draws upon the contrariety scenarios of his eighteenth-century predecessors, even using one of their central biological metaphors to depict human experience as a movement along contrary trajectories like the maturation of a rose that 'blooms' into decay. We may gauge how deeply that image of history gripped Keats's imagination by its poignant recurrence in his last great poem, *To Autumn*, where 'barred clouds bloom the soft-dying day' (25). The highly problematic political implications of this historicism emerge in Keats's apprehension of its tendency to affirm the perpetual existence of political tyranny. Those 'hardships and disquietude[s]' of the reign of Louis XIV, which Keats condemns several months later as the burdens of 'abject slave[ry]', can seem to make up an essential component of human 'destiny' within the contrariety model of linear history (*Letters*, ii. 100–2, 193).

Such a concern, in fact, becomes central to his later situation of Louis's era within the dynamic of history's linear contraries. Provoked in mid-September 1819 by the Peterloo catastrophe and the crisis it precipitated, Keats seeks to account for these political setbacks by adopting Godwin's strategy in *Political Justice* of conceptualising historical contrariety as a cyclical motion of progress interrupted by temporary lapses into reaction. Keats's version of this cyclical form of cultural renewal describes a gradual movement toward enlightenment in European history consisting of 'Three great changes ... in progress – First for the better, next for the worse, and a third time for the better once more.' He associates these three epochs with the annihilation of aristocratic feudal tyranny, the subsequent fall into monarchical despotism, and the recent progression of democratic movements sweeping across Europe. His desire to find a general 'improvement' in these cycles is qualified, however, by his recognition that the third movement's return to progress, embodied in the political breakthroughs of the French Revolution, has been disrupted by the 'horrid' atrocities of the Revolution and the reactionary movements they have engendered. Although Keats strives to interpret this last setback as only a 'tempor[a]ry stop' to progress, he cannot fully dismiss apprehensions of the continuous presence of tyranny as an essential contrary in his model of historical 'oscillation'. Vincent Newey senses this apprehension in the 'tentativeness' of Keats's rhetoric of progress – 'there *should be* a continual change for the better'; 'Perpaps [*sic*] on this account the pres'ent distresses of this nation are a fortunate thing'; 'Now it is in progress again and I thing [*sic*] in an effectual one' (*Letters*, ii. 192–4).[38] The spelling slips here – 'Perpaps', 'thing' – though common enough in Keats's letters, may very well punctuate his continuing uneasiness with the politics of the contrariety scenarios that so deeply inform his understanding of experience. Even cyclical models of improvement, like Godwin's, rely on alternating linear narratives of progress and decline that reinforce the ongoing agency of both contraries. Although such modes of historical interpretation could support visions of political improvement, they could also confirm, as Voltaire and Robertson would seem to imply, a perennial condition of political degeneration.

If we consider how the politics of Keats's historiography inform his ideas of literary tradition, we might well expect, at this point, to find his poetic inventions of literary history duplicating these same contrary lines of development and their disturbing political implications of constant decline. His first substantial poetic narrative of literary history, the sketch in *Sleep and Poetry* of Britain's creative development

from the Renaissance to the present, specifically anticipates the
Godwinian cyclical structure of his 1819 portrait of European history.
From its early Renaissance glory, Britain's poetic tradition lapses
temporarily into the 'musty laws' and 'wretched rule' of neo-classicism
(195), which give way before a new creative renewal, 'a fairer season'
(221), in Keats's own day. Much as Keats draws confidence from this
redemptive vision of a generally progressive tendency, he comes at the
end of *Sleep and Poetry*, as we have seen, to focus on the historical
persistence of political despotism and his related apprehensions of
creative decline in the modern age. This scenario of simultaneous
linear progress and degeneration continues to govern Keats's poetic
constructions of cultural history, from *Endymion* and its opposing
visions of Helicon's exhausted and perpetually flowing springs of
inspiration (I. 23; II. 716–23) to the rise and fall of competing
heavenly orders in the Hyperion poems. To see how deeply the
historiographical structures of linear contrariety, and their political
limitations, inform these models of literary tradition is to understand
more fully why Keats could simultaneously feel so enthusiastic and
demoralised about his prospects of ranking 'among the English
Poets'. It is also to recognise how his darkest apprehensions of being
overpowered by the 'idea of our dead poets' also respond to the
political crises of his immediate historical moment. Milton threatens
his life as a poet in the same journal letter that struggles with the
political history of Europe and all its recent 'horrid . . . experience'
(*Letters*, ii. 193, 212).

   Although the historiographical procedures of Keats's time may
have thus shaped his attitudes toward politics, literary tradition, and
the anxiety of influence, we should not conclude that he subscribes
unconditionally to those dominant structures of understanding and
the problematic forms of knowledge they can produce. Even as he
draws upon them, he seeks to resist and transform the historical
patterns of linear contrariety that can seem to validate political and
cultural retrenchment. His rejection of 'pageant history' in Book II of
Endymion, for instance, does not so much betray his alienation from
material reality as it suggests his movement towards a historicism that
differs from his era's master renditions of progress and decline. Where
those totalising narratives focus on the rise and fall of empires – the
grand, impersonal, and ceaselessly violent sweep of historical
'Struggling' (*Endymion*, II. 10) – Keats turns instead to the more
personalised history of love embodied in the emotional situations of

women like Cressid, Juliet, Hero, Imogen, and Pastorella. Keats's emphasis on the literary character of these alternative narratives does not imply his abandonment of purportedly 'real' history, which he clearly recognises as another form of fictive invention containing at once the activities of Themistocles, Alexander, and Ulysses (II. 22–7). Rather, his turn to an openly symbolic order of experience calls attention to the capacity of the imagination to select and develop alternative models of history. In this imaginative swerve, Keats jettisons the universal paradigms of linear history to emphasise the specific conditions of suffering individuals, particularly those beleaguered female subjects generally elided from history's master narratives. That gesture toward a revisionary history of human subjectivity and, more particularly, female experience takes on a broader form in Book III of *Endymion*, which moves from the pageantry of war to the 'gorgeous pageantry' of love (III. 36). Its fullest elaboration appears in the titanic sufferings of *Hyperion*, usually read as the consummate poetic embodiment of Keats's historical imagination.

Where most critics find a straightforward division between theory and practice in the historical consciousness of *Hyperion*, a conflict that supposedly drives Keats to abandon the poem, we may find his developing historicism shaping a much more complicated, and ultimately productive tension between his investment in the master narratives of linear contrariety and his revisionary efforts to humanise them.[39] Critics of *Hyperion* have frequently read its narrative of transitions among the gods as a sustained dramatisation of Keats's 'linear, progressive . . . optimistic' view of history, with the passage from the Titans to the Olympian gods representing variously the political progression from the seventeenth-century Restoration to the present age of revolution, the fading of Europe's *ancien régime* before Napoleon's democratic innovations, the development of world culture from the ancient East to the modern West, the advance of poetry from the past to the present. Oceanus's speech about the evolutionary progress of 'Nature's law' (II. 181) has seemed the succinct encapsulation of these various scenarios of historical improvement.[40] More recently, however, the poem's critics have become less comfortable with its abstract theories of progress, noticing their incompatibility with the Titans' degenerative suffering and the historical reality of Napoleon's destructive quests for imperial dominion.[41] These clashing inclinations toward progress and decline, optimism and grief, may seem to arise from Keats's distrust of abstract historical theory. We may better comprehend the full complexity of the poem's historical consciousness, however, by recognising how such 'contrary directions' map out the very structures of linear contrariety in those eighteenth-century historical writings that so profoundly influenced Keats. It should come as no surprise that his continuing engagement with that historiographical tradition in *Hyperion* inspired him in April 1819 to reread two of its practitioners who influenced him most, Robertson and Voltaire.

If we bear in mind Keats's growing interests in transforming those models, we can see *Hyperion* also developing the kind of alternative history of the suffering subject introduced in *Endymion*. Indeed, the poem's increasing attention to the 'big hearts' of the anguished Titans, 'Heaving in pain' (II. 26–7), and its eventual turn to Apollo's 'fierce convulse' (III. 129) discloses a new preoccupation with the plight of the individual subject rather than the sublime trajectories of universal progress and decline. The drama of consciousness in *Hyperion* is not so much between abstract theory and material experience as between contending modes of historical understanding.

Christina Crosby has characterised the discourse of mainstream historiography (that 'master science') as a gendered structure of masculine knowledge, 'man's truth', strategically constructed to elide women and other marginal groups from 'historical and political life'.[42] It is the totalising modes of this historiographical tradition, those very paradigms of universal contrariety adopted and eventually questioned by Keats, that perform such effacements of individual, particularly female, experience. British women historians of the late eighteenth century, like Catharine Macaulay and Mary Wollstonecraft, were acutely sensitive to the gender dynamics of such totalising procedures, which they sought to reformulate by displacing man's universal history with a sustained emphasis on the emotional life of the oppressed subject, something more like 'herstory'. Wollstonecraft maintains a comprehensive vision of political progress throughout her *Historical View of the French Revolution*, but she pauses in her description of the abandoned Versailles of 1794 to pity the sufferings of unjustly oppressed aristocrats during the Reign of Terror: 'I tremble, lest I should meet some unfortunate being, fleeing from the despotism of licentious freedom, hearing the snap of the *guillotine* at his heels; merely because he was once noble, or has afforded an asylum to those, whose only crime is their name.'[43] This emphasis on individual grief rather than the abstractions of partisan politics often focuses on the particular 'misery' of 'wom[e]n of low birth', as is apparent in the *Historical View of the French Revolution* and, more emphatically so, in *A Vindication of the Rights of Woman*. Such a revisionary approach to the subject among British women historians, which I have termed 'feminist historiography' in another context, had an influential though as yet little recognised function in transforming the historical consciousness of Keats's generation.[44] Shelley's readings in Macaulay and Wollstonecraft helped inspire his own subversion of the totalising linear structures of historical contrariety. Wollstonecraft's impact on Keats's revisionary historicism in *Hyperion* is a tantalising possibility.

There is no direct evidence that Keats read Wollstonecraft's *Historical View of the French Revolution*. But the book was well known to most members of his circle, and its descriptions of the emptied Versailles, site of a fallen order of ancient rulers, are so remarkably similar to Keats's own portrait of the Titans' frozen condition in their 'nest of woe' (II. 14) as to make it a likely source for *Hyperion*. Struck by the icy silence of Versailles during her visit in 1794, Wollstonecraft writes:

How silent is now Versailles! – The solitary foot, that mounts the sumptuous staircase, rests on each landing-place, whilst the eye traverses the void, almost expecting to see the strong images of fancy burst into life. – The train of the Louises, like the posterity of the Banquos, pass in solemn sadness, pointing at the nothingness of grandeur, fading away on the cold canvas, which covers the nakedness of the spacious walls – whilst the gloominess of the atmosphere gives a deeper shade to the gigantic figures, that seem to be sinking into the embraces of death.

The very air is chill, seeming to clog the breath; and the wasting dampness of destruction appears to be stealing into the vast pile, on every side . . . [A]ll is fearfully still; and, if a little rill creeping through the gathering moss down the cascade, over which it used to rush, bring to mind the description of the grand water works, it is only to excite a languid smile at the futile attempt to equal nature.[45]

The stillness, silence, and cold evoke an atmosphere remarkably similar to that at the opening of *Hyperion*. And the description of 'gigantic figures' gloomily casting a 'deeper shade' over a diminished 'rill' in this seat of deposed aristocracy outlines the precise details of Saturn's vale: 'Deep in the shady sadness of a vale . . . Sat gray-hair'd Saturn, quiet as a stone,/ Still as the silence round about his lair; . . . No stir of air was there . . . A stream went voiceless by' (I. 1–11). If

Keats did, indeed, draw upon Wollstonecraft for this portrait of sorrow, he would have also learned how such a humanised vision of history could challenge those exclusionary modes of understanding sanctioned by the totalising linear structures of masculine historiography. That education in 'feminist historiography' may help explain his shift to what so many readers of *Hyperion* since Leigh Hunt have characterised, often in a puzzled way, as the 'human' and 'feminine' qualities of Apollo's story in Book III of the poem.[46]

Such an alternative concentration on the pathos of the historical subject could free Keats from the burden of conceptualising literary history in terms of progress, decline, and the Oedipal struggle of sons against fathers. He could now 'look upon' his great predecessors 'like a Lover', with sympathy for their individual situations and, as in Shakespeare's case, their 'miserable' sufferings (*Letters*, ii. 139, 115). It could also provide a new, more enabling mode of inquiry that contends against the oppressions of the time, instead of submitting to them, by recovering the experience and the voices of those individuals marginalised from political and historical life.

Recognising Keats's movement toward this new type of historicism may lead us to reformulate the questions that so many critics have posed about his reasons for abandoning *Hyperion*. Why did he break off a narrative that was apparently moving toward a more constructive historicism? The answer may lie with the very questions that so many eighteenth-century historians consciously raise about how to interpret the past, queries that call attention to history's multivalency, its infinitely varied modes of representation. Keats's growing awareness of the chameleon nature of historical inquiry may be traced in his eventual resistance to any fixed points of historical reasoning, even the humanised alternative to linear history. For the end of *Hyperion* does not so much embrace a new, singular historiographical mode (which might have seemed like replacing one limited model with another) as throw open the fundamental question of interpretation issuing from the variety of alternative, often competing forms of historicism. Awareness of historical process as the 'master science' of signification may lead Apollo to godlike insight. But he does not simply receive a monolithic 'history' into 'the wide hollows of [his] brain' at the moment of his deification. Rather the 'Knowledge enormous' that makes him a god consists of the multiple 'histories' rendered by alternative structures of understanding. One set of opposing terms – 'Creations and destroyings' – implies the linear contrariety of eighteenth-century historiography. Another list of referents – 'rebellions/ Majesties, sovran voices' – suggests the impersonality and patriarchal coding of that universal historicism. Still another pattern of details – 'Names . . . agonies' – gestures at the personalised history of the suffering subject. And 'gray legends' calls attention to the fictive quality of all historical methods (III. 113–18). If Keats was moving towards a non-totalising history in *Hyperion*, he was also moving toward an even more comprehensively open-ended hermeneutic that embraces all forms of historicism in calling attention to the indeterminate process, itself, of how we look upon the 'illimitable gulph/ Of times past' (*Otho the Great*, III. i. 5–6).

This new kind of meta-history called for a different kind of narrative, one that would foreground such questions about the act of historical interpretation. *The Fall of Hyperion* provides this framework by embedding the Hyperion narrative, and its various types of historicism, within the dramatic structure of the poet figure's struggle to comprehend their significance. His difficult journey toward knowledge leads him to confront, in the 'blank splendor' of Moneta's 'visionless' eyes (I. 267–9), not so much the truth of history as the arabesque of interpretation figured in the various historiographical procedures of the original Hyperion narrative. Moneta's enigmatic nature, at once sympathetic and impersonal, associated with abstract wisdom and the material contexts of the Roman mint, itself represents the multivalency of the historical methods over which she presides. The interpretation of such a protean form of understanding constitutes the dramatic substance of Keats's historical consciousness in his later poems – from the intense effort to interrogate that cryptic, 'Sylvan historian', the Grecian urn, to the charged encounter with 'the silent pages of our chroniclers' in *King Stephen* (I. ii. 5), to what Levinson has characterised as the consuming 'reflections' about 'reinvent[ing] history' in *Lamia*.[47] This passionately quizzical mode of historicism may have offered Keats, in the end, the richest possibilities of integrating his hopes for creative and political renewal. For its resistance to fixed structures of understanding works against dominant and exclusive codes of Knowledge – historical, literary, political – through a process of invention and reformulation that continually opens up the past for new conversations with the present.

We may thus find that Keats's views of literary tradition derive not simply from his investments in the politics of historical contrariety, but rather from his incorporation of that interpretive mode (with its threat of cultural decline) as part of a more redemptive hermeneutics of historical indeterminacy. If eighteenth-century historiography encouraged his complicity in his era's dominant ideologies of knowledge, and the anxieties of cultural belatedness they imposed, it could also provoke him to challenge those structures of understanding in ways that inspired his confidence about cultural renewal. The many-sided, shifting structure of his mansion of 'history' would always make the past, or the 'pasts', seem at once threatening and inviting, close and open-ended. Keats's struggle with the problems of historiographical tradition showed him, in the end, how questioning its basic procedures could best situate him, however tentatively, amid the political struggles of the present and 'among' the Poets of the past.

NOTES

1 *Universal History, Ancient and Modern* (25 vols., London, 1802) i. viii.
2 Charles Cowden Clarke records Keats's adolescent reading of Robertson, Mavor, and Burnet, in Charles and Mary Cowden Clarke, *Recollections of Writers* (London, 1878), 123–4.
3 The role of this historiographical consciousness in Keats's emergence as a poet can be measured by the preoccupation with historical figures throughout his first poetic efforts, which feature Alfred, Brutus, Dido, Lear, Tell, Cortez, Wallace, Charles II, Sydney, Russell, Vane, and Milton.
4 Eggers, 'Memory in Mankind: Keats's Historical Imagination', *PMLA* 86 (1971), 990–7; Reed, 'Keats and the Gregarious Advance of Intellect in *Hyperion*', *ELH* 55 (1988), 195–232. *KPP*, 27, 65.
5 Critical dispute over whether Keats's poetry reinforces or subverts his era's dominant ideological structures continues to shape studies of the historicity of his poetry. In addition to recent studies noticed in the introduction to this volume, see also Theresa M. Kelley, 'Poetics and the Politics of Reception: Keats's "La Belle Dame sans Merci"', *ELH* 54 (1987), 333–58, and Terence Hoagwood, 'Keats and Social Context: *Lamia*', *SEL* 29 (1989), 675–97. Keats's divided complicity and oppositionality is also central to feminist criticism of his poetry's gender codes; see Susan Wolfson, 'Feminizing Keats', in H. de Almeida (ed.), *Critical Essays on John Keats* (Boston, 1990), 217–57; Margaret Homans, 'Keats Reading Women, Women Reading Keats', *SIR* 29 (1990), 341–70; Karen Swann, 'Harassing the Muse', in Anne K. Mellor (ed.), *Romanticism and Feminism* (Bloomington and Indianapolis, 1988), 81–92; Marlon Ross, *The Contours of Masculine Desire: Romanticism and the Rise of Women's Poetry* (New York and Oxford, 1989). My argument suggests that Keats's investments in eighteenth-century historiography reinforce these divisions on a fundamental level of consciousness.

6 Bloom, *The Anxiety of Influence: A Theory of Poetry* (London, 1973), 32. Curran, *Poetic Form and British Romanticism* (New York, 1986), 17.
7 *The Fate of Reading and Other Essays* (Chicago and London, 1975), xiii.
8 Recent Keats critics have been attentive to the political inflections of his literary historicism. David Bromwich, 'Keats's Radicalism', notes how Keats's model of 'three stages of political liberation' coincides with his theories about 'the progress of poetry'; Alan J. Bewell, 'The Political Implication of Keats's Classicist Aesthetics', finds Keats's development of an 'ideology of [poetic] progress' converging with his 'assumption of a political voice'; see *KP*, 209, 222. Marjorie Levinson associates Keats's responses to literary tradition with nineteenth-century class struggle, *KL*, 26; Vincent Newey, in '"Alternate uproar and sad peace": Keats, Politics, and the Idea of Revolution', in J. R. Watson (ed.), 'The French Revolution in English Literature and Art', MHRA *Yearbook of English Studies* 19 (1989), 274, links Keats's 'view of supersession in the kingdom of letters' with his 'reflections upon change in the kingdom of England'. Watkins, *KPP*, 42, argues that 'Bloom does not adequately emphasize or explore . . . the extent to which . . . [Keats's poetic experience] is determined by sociohistorical context . . .' Despite these claims for the intersection of politics and literary influence, Keats studies still display a tendency to relegate influence concerns to a separate, psychological sphere. Kurt Heinzelman, for instance, distinguishes 'the anxieties of merely aesthetic influence' from 'sociological' concerns, 'Self-Interest and the Politics of Composition in Keats's *Isabella*', *ELH* 55 (1988), 162.
9 The reference to 'the elder Bards' is from Richard Woodhouse's commentary on the Hunt sonnet, cited by *AP*, 109.
10 'Keats and the Gregarious Advance', 207.
11 Walter Jackson Bate, *John Keats* (Cambridge, Mass., 1963), 89. *KL*, 12–14.
12 (6th edn, 3 vols., London, 1792) i. 283–90.
13 Ibid., ii. 294; i. 289.
14 *KPP*, 31.
15 Robertson, *History of America*, i. 135, 138, 284, 172.
16 *KL*, 257; Ruthven, 'Keats and *Dea Moneta*', *SIR* 15 (1975), 458.
17 *History of America*, i. 270.
18 The publishing context of Keats's poem, Leigh Hunt's oppositional *Examiner*, would have reinforced such implied reservations about modern commercial and imperial practices.
19 *Biographical History of England* (2 vols., London, 1769) i. v.
20 Voltaire, François-Marie Arouet (2 vols., Paris, 1826) i. 3. Mavor, *Universal History*, i. 44. Robertson (11th edn, 2 vols., London, 1787) i. 143. Hume qualifies this theory by arguing, as Rene Wellek puts it, that 'learning flourishes better in republics, the arts in monarchies', *The Rise of English Literary History* (New York, 1966), 59.
21 *HW*, vi. 181–6; Thomas Hutchinson (ed.), *Shelley: Poetical Works*, corrected by G. M. Matthews (Oxford, 1970), 204–7.

22 Wollstonecraft, *An Historical and Moral View of the Origin and Progress of the French Revolution and the Effect It Has Produced in Europe* (New York, 1975), 515. *HW*, xi. 18.

23 *Universal History*, i. 1–3.

24 *Rise of English Literary History*, 72–3.

25 Oliver Goldsmith, *Letters from a Citizen of the World*, in *The Miscellaneous Works of Oliver Goldsmith* (4 vols., London, 1820) iii. 250.

26 *Natural Supernaturalism* (New York, 1971), 63, 210–13.

27 *Sermons on several Occasions* (2 vols., Aberdeen, 1786) i. 43, 20.

28 Horace Walpole, *Anecdotes of Painting in England* (4 vols., London, 1762) i. ix.

29 David Hume, *The History of England, from the Invasion of Julius Caesar to the Accession of Henry VII* (6 vols., London, 1762) ii. 440–1; quoted by Wellek, *Rise of English Literary History*.

30 Thomas Malthus, *An Essay on the Principle of Population* (London, 1798), 13; Hutchinson, *Shelley: Poetical Works*, 34, 207.

31 Robert Southey, *Sir Thomas More: or, Colloquies on the Progress and Prospects of Society* (2 vols., London, 1829) i. 130.

32 Voltaire, *Siècle de Louis XIV*, i. 3. J.-J. Rousseau (Paris, 1804, 1805). Gilbert Burnet, *Bishop Burnet's History of His own Time* (London, 1850) i. 294.

33 *The History of the Reign of the Emperor Charles V* (3 vols., London, 1769) i. xii. *History of America*, i. 35. In the latter, Robertson provides this account of such contrary lines of development: '[The first Spanish explorers,] enlightened and ambitious, formed already vast ideas with respect to the advantages which they might derive from the regions that began to open to their view. The . . . [native peoples], simple and undiscerning, had no foresight of the calamities and desolation which were approaching their country', i. 133–4.

34 Goldsmith, *An History of the Earth* (8 vols., London, 1774) i. 4. *HW*, xix. 18.

35 Warton, *An Enquiry into the Authenticity of the Poems Attributed to Thomas Rowley* (London, 1782), 7. *The History of English Poetry* (4 vols., London, 1824) iv. 321.

36 Bromwich, 'Keats's Radicalism', 202.

37 See Reed, 'Keats and the Gregarious Advance', 207.

38 Newey, '"Alternate uproar and sad peace"', 282. Eggers, 'Memory in Mankind', 991, similarly notes the ambivalence of Keats's arguments for progress.

39 Bate, *John Keats*, 402–8; Reed, 'Keats and the Gregarious Advance', 217; Newey, '"Alternate uproar and sad peace"', 271.

40 Newey, '"Alternate uproar and sad peace"', 280; Bate, *John Keats*, 388–417; Stuart M. Sperry, *Keats the Poet* (Princeton, 1973), 155–97; *KL*, 197. This line of interpretation informs most of the arguments in *KP*.

41 See Reed, 'Keats and the Gregarious Advance', 213–26; Newey, '"Alternate uproar and sad peace"', 278; Marilyn Butler, *Romantics, Rebels, and Reactionaries. English Literature and its Background 1760–1830* (Oxford and New York, 1981), 151–4.

42 *The Ends of History* (New York, 1991), 1.
43 p. 163.
44 Wollstonecraft, *Historical View*, 139. See my 'Romanticism and Feminist Historiography', *Wordsworth Circle* 24 (Spring 1993), 133–40.
45 *Historical View*, 161–2.
46 Wolfson discussed Keats's fascination with exploring 'the permeable boundary between masculine and feminine' ('Feminizing Keats', 318). That 'fascination', I may suggest, derives in part from his interrogation of the gendering of historical discourse in the 'master science' of his era. See also Marlon Ross's discussion of gendered language in *Hyperion*, 'Beyond the Fragmented Word: Keats at the Limit of Patrilineal Language', in Laura Claridge and Elizabeth Langland (eds.), *Out of Bounds: Male Writers and Gender(ed) Criticism* (Amherst, Mass., 1990), 110–31.
47 *KL*, 287, 293.

CHAPTER 13

Keats and the prison house of history

Nicola Trott

'IN THE . . . PRISON-HOUSE'

> The poetry is for the most part ironed and manacled with a chain
> of facts, and cannot get free; it cannot escape from the prison
> house of history . . . Poetry must be free!

These remarks, from an unfavourable notice of *Richard Duke of York*, a
compilation of the three parts of *Henry VI*, appeared in the *Champion*
for 28 December 1817. Scholarly fact has now chained the authorship
to John Hamilton Reynolds, dramatic editor of the *Champion*, but it
was for many years thought to be by Keats, who had produced the
previous week's review, of Kean's performance in *Richard III*.[1] And,
indeed, the sentiments expressed tally with Keats's posthumous
reputation as an aesthete who had nothing to do with 'passing
events':[2] Shakespeare is properly an Ariel, his poetry 'generally free as
the wind – a perfect thing of the elements, winged and sweetly coloured'.

Keats was entranced by Ariel as a figure of imaginative liberty, and
markings in his copy of *The Tempest* reveal a special interest in
Prospero's words of parting to his spirit: 'then to the elements/ Be free,
and fare thou well!'[3] But this is spoken as a master honouring his
pledge to release his servant; however free by nature, Ariel is not, in
fact, a free agent until the end of the play. He is, paradoxically, a
spirit-slave. And this tension between the idea of imagination as
ecstatic escape-artist, and the constraining conditions under which it
operates, is fundamental in Keats. The imagination is ambiguously
both enthraller and enthralled.[4]

Keats is neither able nor willing to keep to so conventional a
separation of discourses – fact and history, imagination and poetry –
as is maintained by the review I quoted at the start of this essay. Yet
this separation has bedevilled Keats criticism. Aesthetes, formalists,
and historicists have, in their turn, sought to claim him for their own,

the last of these on materialist grounds.[5] Whatever his own will to apartheid, Keats understands it to be as fallacious as the wish 'To unperplex bliss from its neighbour pain' (*Lamia*, I. 192). This seemingly paradisal knowledge is offered to the inexperienced Lycius by Keats's Lamia, 'a lady bright' who, moments earlier, had herself been 'touch'd with miseries', 'convuls'd with scarlet pain' (I. 171, 54, 154). What is more, her suffering was caused by longing for a human shape while being locked in a 'serpent prison-house' (I. 203). This serpentine form is one of Keats's governing devices for describing the limits of desire as he sees them – limits which, I suggest, are instituted partly by the 'prison house of history' within which the imaginary is necessarily, if reluctantly, enclosed.

One of Keats's marginalia to *Paradise Lost*, made probably in 1818, seizes on the occasion in Book IX when Satan is 'constrained' to 'imbrute' his 'essence' in the body of the serpent. Keats notes that

Satan having entered the Serpent, and inform'd his brutal sense – might seem sufficient – but Milton goes on '*but his sleep disturb'd not.*' Whose spirit does not ache at the smothering and confinement – the unwilling stillness – the '*waiting close*'? Whose head is not dizzy at the prosaible speculations of satan in the serpent prison – no passage of poetry ever can give a greater pain of suffocation.[6]

In paraphrasing Satan's transference of intelligence to the brute sense of the snake, Keats has substituted his own verb ('inform'd') for Milton's ('inspired'). Satan has performed the chameleonic act of 'in for[ming] . . . and filling some other Body' (*Letters*, i. 387). But, as Keats's further 'speculations' disclose, the merging of identities is monstrously incomplete: the informing mind remains Satan's own, condemned to endure the suffocating closeness of the host organism.

What may be deduced from Keats's impassioned commentary on Milton's lines? There is the identification: we find Satan immersed in his familiar role of surrogate Romantic ego. More troublingly, his invasion of the serpent diabolically parodies the Keatsian poet who 'has no self' (*Letters*, i. 387). His predicament marks an ethical indecision between the chameleon, who renounces his identity for those of others, and the egotist, who is tormented by its suppression. Yet if Satan-in-the-serpent suggests an egotistical poet in chameleon's clothing, the hybrid also implies Keats's awareness that the two are not strict antitheses, but that a poetic persona is at work in each. By extension, this persona is the animating force behind all forms, whether identifiably separate from, or inextricably identified with, the creatures of its imagining.[7] Satan thus insinuates a lurking egotism in Keats's poetics and, consequently, their partial compliance with the idealist philosophies of Romanticism.[8] To be more precise, the strength of Satan's identity, and the fascinated horror evoked by his smothering, are recognisably a gloss upon the 'egotistical sublime', the coinage supplied by Keats, in October 1818, for effects that similarly attract and repel him in Wordsworth (*Letters*, i. 386–7).

Keats's satanised serpent is analogous to the Romantic consciousness, his own or Wordsworth's, brilliantly 'speculating' upon the supine corpus of Milton's text. But it also places the free-thinking mind in a 'prison-house'. What might be termed the Satanic consciousness emerges from a 'serpent prison' of brutal and stubborn materiality. Keats is invariably troubled by the growth of consciousness, and as invariably associates it with the recognition of harsh realities and frustrating limitations. The poet to whom he looks for exactly this interinvolvement of mind with recalcitrant matter is Wordsworth. It is 'the "burden of the Mystery"', a weight drawn equally from what is to be borne and from consciousness itself, which Keats's elects to carry, from 'Tintern Abbey', to his own 'dark Passages' of poetry on the suffering mind (*Letters*, i. 281). And it is these necessary facts that Keats sets himself to explore and accommodate, in the idealised history of his development he calls the 'life of Allegory'.

ALLEGORICAL LIVES

'[T]hey are very shallow people who take every thing literal', Keats tells his brother and sister-in-law in early 1819, turning as he does so from some gossip about Benjamin Bailey's amorous deceptions, to a spectacular lift out of the literal:

A Man's life of any worth is a continual allegory – and very few eyes can see the Mystery of his life – a life like the scriptures, figurative . . . Lord Byron cuts a figure – but he is not figurative – Shakespeare led a life of Allegory; his works are the comments on it –   (*Letters*, ii. 67)

The procedure is by turns antithetical and synthetic. As usual, Keats is setting one author against another (Byron and Shakespeare in this instance). Less explicitly, he favours the poet who elides opposing categories – here, of the life and the work. Life, if it is 'of any worth', is always already allegorical, scriptural, figurative. Like writing, it is inherently purposive, and therefore interpretable to those whose 'eyes can see' to read.

Marjorie Levinson shrewdly points to allegory as the site of idealisation in Keats and, in an ingenious critique, interprets Keats's life as 'the allegory of a man belonging to a certain class and aspiring . . . to another'.[9] It is this – often conflictual – relation between the 'literal' and 'allegorical' that I wish to take up. But I shall do so by understanding it as part of an internal debate about the liberty or duress with which the poetic personality and its cognates, the chameleon and the serpent, are felt to act.

Levinson's counter-allegory tends to evacuate the life to which it alludes: 'The accomplished poetry may be considered the negative knowledge of Keats's actual life: the production of his freedom by the figured negation of his given being, natural and social.'[10] Under these conditions, Keats's poetry has a purely negative capability. To speak positively, one might observe that, in its inquisition of its own escapism, his 'accomplished poetry' is emphatically engaged with 'actual life', and its 'freedom' produced by exact acknowledgements of constraint.

In prefacing his *Characters of Shakespear's Plays*, Hazlitt quotes from Schlegel the dictum that Shakespeare 'gives us the history of minds', in that his drama 'lays open to us, in a single word, a whole series of preceding conditions'.[11] Keats's Shakespeare, on the other hand, offers a biographical model, in that he applies the form of art to the flux of experience. To lead a 'life of Allegory' is to exemplify a coherent existence, as opposed to a contingent one. Yet the strictness of form reflects a need to impute an order to the random forces of the 'literal'. The peculiarly intrusive sympathy of Keats's art – its power of entering alternative lives – also renders him permeable by life, sometimes painfully so. In his letter describing the chameleon poet, for instance, the capacity of losing himself in the imagining of other identities is disturbingly inverted among real people: 'the identity of every one in the room begins [so] to press upon me that, I am in a very little time annihilated' (*Letters*, i. 387). A year earlier, in autumn 1817, Keats writes to commiserate with Bailey over a delay in his ordination: 'Such is this World – and we live . . . in a continual struggle against the suffocation of accidents'.[12]

Already, notably, there is the 'pain of suffocation' under constraint. Yet the strong paradox of Keats's 'life of Allegory' is that it undertakes the struggle against accidents. The good life is allegorical as much because of its proximity to experience as its resemblance to art. On the day after he chooses to 'burn through' *King Lear* once again, Keats is reminding Bailey that 'The best of Men have but a portion of good in them – a kind of spiritual yeast in their frames which creates the ferment of existence – by which a Man is propell'd to act and strive and buffet with Circumstance' (*Letters*, i. 210; see also i. 270).

That circumstance may be a source of resistance as well as suffocation makes it somewhat less perplexing that Keats should think of it as defining a personal identity. Moreover, this is where the countervailing form of allegory is most categorically imposed. In May 1818, Keats associates a world 'full of Misery and Heartbreak, Pain, Sickness and oppression', with an allegorical rite of passage: 'human life' is 'a large Mansion of Many Apartments' leading from thoughtlessness to the burdensome consciousness of such realities (*Letters*, i. 280–1). In April 1819, he repudiates the Christian allegory of the world as 'a vale of tears' redeemable only by divine intervention, and substitutes his own term, 'The vale of Soul-making', to designate a 'system of salvation' within 'a World of Pains and troubles' (*Letters*, ii. 101–2).[13] Keats adopts a progressive 'medium', in which the contingent and literal may acquire the idealised form of allegory.

The 'life of Allegory' seeks to place the accidental within an aesthetic order. In addition to a local history of malign or awkward circumstances, there is a grand narrative of the meliorative and meaningful developments that take place in individuals and cultures alike. Each is continuously and ambiguously present in the hybrid form of Keatsian allegory. Levinson describes Keats's social position 'not as a healthy both/and but as the monstrous neither/nor constructed in the reviews'.[14] Such hybridisation is endemic in Keats himself, not least because he recognises his own aesthetic ambivalence, and the connection it has with the conflicting perspectives of the compassionate and progressive imaginations: the one demanding a subjective and sympathetic, the other a general and gregarious, evaluation of experience.

PROGRESS AND STASIS

The progress of the self naturally lends itself to a progressive theory of history.[15] Not surprisingly, it is in his letter on the chambers of thought that Keats first develops the notion of a 'general and gregarious advice of intellect'. More startling, perhaps, is the extent to which he is prepared to think of this advance as historically determined. He vividly excuses Milton his jejune philosophy on the grounds that the 'ideas on virtue, vice, and Chastity in Comus' occur 'just at the time of the dismissal of Cod-pieces and a hundred other disgraces'; while the 'hintings at good and evil in the Paradise Lost' are made 'when just free from the inquisition and burrning in Smithfield'. History gives evidence of the advancement of learning beyond certain types of oppression and, equally, of the limits imposed by the context in which it occurs. That 'Wordsworth is deeper than Milton' is doubly corroborative: it 'proves there is really a grand march of intellect'; conversely, it 'proves that a mighty providence subdues the mightiest Minds to the service of the time being' (*Letters*, i. 281–2). The intellect's effectiveness depends upon its incarceration in the historical prison house.

On an enlarged scale, Keats's life of allegory becomes an allegory of life. Both these forms, the poetic and the historical, are compelled by an ideology of progress. Keats's interest in his own forwardness is transparent. The pattern of his work is, as de Man remarks, 'prospective': hopes for the future govern the way he conceives of his development and, from *Sleep and Poetry* onwards, his poetic ambitions are gathered under the topos of a 'progress of poetry'.[16] If this is Keats's way of encouraging himself, it does not stop here, but widens to embrace all humanity in the massed ranks of a 'march of intellect'. Such idealisations – what he calls 'ethereal finger-pointings' (*Letters*, i. 231) – are deliberately flying in the face of the available evidence, from the restoration of monarchical Legitimacy in 1815 to the Peterloo massacre four years later.[17] It is indicative that, a month after Peterloo, as Shelley is finishing *The Mask of Anarchy* in a 'torrent of indignation', Keats is sanguine enough to tell his brother and sister-in-law: 'All civiled countries become gradually more enlighten'd and there should be a continual change for the better.'[18]

This is a history told by the Enlightenment and endowed with predictive force. But its projection into the future is prompted by the special intimacy in Keats between his personal aspirations and a more general wish for improvement. His conflation of poetic and historical progress begins to have a defining effect in early 1818. Contemplating the writing of *Hyperion*, in January, Keats buoyantly assures Haydon that 'the march of passion and endeavour will be undeviating', since Apollo 'being a fore-seeing God will shape his actions like one'

(*Letters*, i. 207). The god of poetry will lead an allegorical life as a matter of course, his own empowerment conferring on the myth of the Olympian succession the form of a progress poem.[19]

Yet although *Hyperion* is conceived as an allegory of historical progress, the fragment as it stands is caught up by states of fixity and paralysis. Superseded by a more 'beautiful mythology' (*PJK*, 103), the Titans fall from the sky to find themselves 'pent in regions of laborious breath' (*Hyperion*, II. 22). Their defeat, whose analogy with that of the *ancien régime* hovers within the poem's interpretative horizons, should on the face of it have appealed to Keats, wholeheartedly on 'the Liberal side of the question' as he was.[20] Far from being triumphalist, however, the work generates sympathy for the predicament of the Titans, who feature as benign, traditionary gods, cast out from bliss into anthropomorphic torments.[21] To Keats's imagining, their mountain-prison is emotive precisely because it is conceived as an imprisonment. The Titans are literally 'Lock'd up' (II. 25) in sign of their figurative incarceration by historical events. These events take the 'sky-children' (I. 133), once untouched by passion and pain, into the 'world of Circumstances' (*Letters*, ii. 104). Hyperion, the doomed precursor of Apollo, is initiated into this world through the central Keatsian image of psychic and physical suffering:

> . . . through all his bulk an agony
> Crept gradual, from the feet unto the crown,
> Like a lithe serpent vast and muscular
> Making slow way, with head and neck convuls'd
> From over-strained might.   (I. 259–63)

In a powerful reversal of *Paradise Lost*, the Satanic act of invading the serpent becomes the subjective experience of being invaded by it.[22] The knowledge of pain and weakness enters Hyperion with a perverse intimacy and alien strength. The poet Apollo, by contrast, readily imbibes a 'Knowledge enormous', and the corresponding enlargement of mental space 'makes a God of [him]'. In this further reversal of Milton, knowledge confers the godhead that was denied to Adam and Eve. But it does so by relating to the power struggles of human history:

> Names, deeds, gray legends, dire events, rebellions,
> Majesties, sovran voices, agonies,
> Creations and destroyings, all at once
> Pour into the wide hollows of my brain,
> And deify me . . .   (III. 114–18)

Keats's myth requires a history of crisis, of the birth and death of cultures. Yet the Titans and Olympians represent stages in development as well as warring dynasties. As the poem stands, Apollo barely emerges into godhead, but his change marks a point of regeneration. The Apollonian poet is able to generalise what would otherwise remain an inarticulate horror. Through him, the poetry moves from circumstantial to providential awareness, from the victim to the interpreter of historical change.

Hyperion reflects the suffocated, accidental side of Keats, Apollo his (trans)figurative alter ego. They are, to adapt Hazlitt on the egotistical Wordsworth, two persons in one poet.[23] If *Hyperion* reads allegorically, it does so by inserting a continuous experience of self within the overtly catastrophic history supplied by the myth. During its composition, Keats was living through the death of his brother Tom; in the months before its writing, he enunciated a progress of poetry, whose tendency was to 'think into the human heart' (*Letters*, i. 282).[24] *Hyperion* daringly mythologises the passage, initiated in Keats's letters, from preconscious bliss, to mortal experience, and thence to a saving knowledge. That the structure is as much developmental as revolutionary is confirmed by the verbal repetitions of the poem: the Titans, Hyperion, and Apollo alike undergo an agonising metamorphosis, culminating in the 'fierce convulse' with which the poet is said to 'Die into life' (*Hyperion*, I. 262; II. 27; III. 129–30).

Keats is notoriously a young poet, and is never more so than when trying to be an old one. The urgency of his growing up is measured by his growth pains – from the poet who anticipates passing the joys of 'sleep and poetry' in quest of the 'agonies, the strife/ Of human hearts' (*Sleep and Poetry*, 124–5), to the dreamer who yearns to comprehend suffering as one 'to whom the miseries of the world/ Are misery' (*The Fall of Hyperion*, I. 148–9).[25] In the antithetical terms preferred by Keats, pleasure is overtaken by philosophy, sensation yields to thought. However negatively capable his 'hovering . . . between' such categories, the life of allegory insists on a progress from one to the other (see *Letters*, i. 271). The Hyperion poems are so inescapably Miltonic, it seems, because this hard task of relinquishment is especially associated with Milton. Keats's marginale on *Paradise Lost* argues that

he had an exquisite passion for what is properly, in the sense of ease and pleasure, poetical Luxury; and with that it appears to me he would fain have

been content . . . but there was working in him as it were that same sort of
thing as operates in the great world to the end of a Prophecy's being
accomplished: therefore he devoted himself rather to the Ardours than the
pleasures of Song . . .

Milton's life of allegory is plainly an allegory of Keats's. As a result,
both censor and libido are at work: an arduous poetry is conscientiously
in touch with the 'great world'; the self-pleasuring is wistful for a
refuge of its own. Thus, while *Paradise Lost* exists because Milton
'committed himself to the Extreme', the 'finest parts of the Poem' are
produced by his occasional bouts of self-indulgence – his 'solacing
himself at intervals with cups of old wine'.[26]

Keats requires a transition from original pleasure to painful
knowledge, yet intuits the incompatibility of the Miltonic 'Extreme'
with the aesthetic effects he cherishes. It is partly that the epic makes
him acutely conscious of the canon he is seeking to enter. These formal
conditions are both paralysing to and parodied by the Hyperion
poems. Keats's epic allows for a visceral enjoyment of imitation, in
Miltonisms that verge on pastiche; and a moral sympathy with pain,
in divinities that are not symbiotic with, but excruciatingly trapped
within, the forms they inhabit. As Keats is uncannily aware, on giving
up *The Fall* in September 1819, the epic threatens his death-by-Milton:
'Life to him would be death to me' (*Letters*, ii. 212).[27]

The Titans are 'Dungeoned' by historical events; the mobile Keats
is threatened with the prison house of literary history – in Harold
Bloom's terms, by the corpus of the precursor: 'yet the past doth
prison me' (*Endymion*, IV. 691). But Keats is perpetually at risk of
confinement for reasons other than those of influence. He is haunted
by the threat of his own poetic stunting, and so defines a poetry of
alternate paralysis and movement. His narrative of entrapment and
escape goes back to *Endymion*, where a power of redemption vies with
death or dormancy, to the point of inducing a torture of 'renewed life'
(I. 919, and see also II. 457–533). Book III of the poem recounts the
legend of Glaucus and Circe, the enchantress to whom the sea-god is
sensually enslaved and from whom he escapes only to be cursed with a
lingering death, until Endymion appears as his 'deliverer':

>   . . . thou openest
> The prison gates that have so long opprest
> My weary watching. Though thou know'st it not,
> Thou art commission'd to this fated spot
> For great enfranchisement.   (III. 295–9)

The story of Glaucus and Circe has an explicitly political frame, since Book III begins with an attack on the Legitimacy in the manner of the *Examiner*. If *Hyperion* is written for an era of revolutionary shifts in power, *Endymion* speaks to its ideological enslavements and liberations.[28] But the romance also indicates how seamlessly (and, until recent criticism, invisibly) Keats's poetry joins the stuff of history to what it is always doing of itself – that is, acting out its own compulsive movements of feeling and empathy, fixation and flight.

'History' here is an enlargement of an existing scale. One way of measuring the enlargement is to be found in Hazlitt. As a republican, Hazlitt is notoriously the enemy of Legitimacy; as a realist, he is hard-headed about the prospects for reform. Reviewing *The Excursion* in August 1814, he answers Wordsworth's 'fond conclusion' as to the eventual 'triumph of virtue and liberty' with the brutal contradiction: 'All things move not in progress, but in a ceaseless round.'[29] In the final collapse of revolutionary ideals before the downfall of Napoleon (the French monarchy had been restored in May), Hazlitt disabusingly insists that history is circular, and 'progress' a purely ideological illusion.

A sense of futility enters Keats's poetry as the fearful contrary of his progressive 'endeavour'. In the *Ode to a Nightingale*, the poet's envious cry, 'No hungry generations tread thee down' (62), tacitly echoes *The Excursion*, this time in its sceptical questioning of Enlightenment historiography: 'Do generations press/ On generations, without progress made?' (V. 466–7). Similarly, Apollo is envisaged as 'a fore-seeing God', but his power of divination arises from his not being 'led on, like Buonaparte, by circumstance' (*Letters*, i. 207).[30] Keats is seemingly unable to think of a providential and poetic history without invoking the antithetical world of circumstantial and circumscribed action: in de Man's words, 'History can only move by becoming aware of its own contingency.'[31]

'Even here, into my centre of repose', says Hyperion, 'The shady visions come to domineer' (I. 243–4). The poetry of refuge is overtaken by the allegory of life, and its complex assimilation of realities. Keats is deeply indebted to Hazlitt for his development and the turn to 'philosophy' with which it is associated. But the turn is problematic in that it fosters the distrust Keats feels for his own aesthetic, as the sign of an immaturity that must be overcome. What is more, Hazlitt makes knowledge inimical to poetry. His essay on 'Why the Arts are not progressive' defines the 'stationary' history of art by its antithesis to the mobile history of science and thought.[32] A theory of social progress is brought into ironic alignment with a theory of artistic decline. Having been perfected in a primitive state of society, the argument goes, art is an anachronism in the present. Indeed, Hazlitt's ancients barely allow the moderns to enter the lists: 'in grace and beauty they have never been surpassed.'[33]

Hyperion, of course, attempts to found a modern poetry of knowledge. It envisages a progression that is led by the poet, and which dictates that beauty supersede strength. Yet the threat of stasis remains. In taking Hazlitt's mischievousness to heart, Keats also sets its ironies to work. The Titans are immobilised by the very poetics of progression which the superior beauty and changeable form of Apollo represent, and their sculptural forms rigidly correspond to the notion of a 'stationary' art. The pressure of Hazlitt's thinking is more directly felt in the poems of summer 1819, *The Fall of Hyperion* and, especially, *Lamia*, which subscribes to the antagonism that Hazlitt perceived between the discoveries of science and the *terra incognita* of art: 'the progress of knowledge and refinement has a tendency to circumscribe the limits of the imagination, and to clip the wings of poetry . . . There can never be another Jacob's dream. Since that time, the heavens have gone farther off, and grown astronomical . . .'[34] Pegasus is brought down to earth, and the heavens estranged. It is to this sort of nostalgia that Keats gives way in his lament for the 'awful rainbow once in heaven' (*Lamia*, II. 231). As in Hazlitt, though, the idealist aesthetic is subject to critique. *Lamia* conducts an ironic progress of knowledge. And its heroine is certainly no Ariel.

The poem has an explicitly evolutionary setting: in the opening lines, the narrator casts back to the era before the 'faery broods' drove out the deities of Greek mythology. Keats returns to the scenes of his earliest poetic infatuation, but to very different ends: the destruction of the imaginary by science, and the slaying of Lamia by her philosopher–antagonist. *Lamia* is peculiarly sensitive to Keats's ambivalent understanding that 'truth' is at once the enemy of imagination, and the standard to which art should conform. In its use of the lamia legend, the poem is comparable to other applications of literary history in Keats. The archaisms, medievalisms, and faery of *The Eve of St. Agnes, La Belle Dame sans Merci*, and *Ode to a Nightingale*, seek to uphold the imaginary by their distance from the 'real'. But they also risk its being unmasked as a 'cheat', an anachronism, or evasion. Hence the opposite tendency in Keats, of bringing his mythologies to the test of modernity or 'reality', and to the production (first glimpsed at the end of *The Eve of St. Agnes*) of an 'unsmokeable' art.

Lamia escapes from her serpent prison, only to enter the prison house of history. Under Apollonius's coldly philosophical gaze, she is exposed as a 'deceiving elf' (*Ode to a Nightingale*, 74). Keats is apparently writing against the evolutionary structure of *Hyperion*, where the progressive force is personified as the god of poetry, in whom beauty and knowledge are made one. In *Lamia*, the imaginary is not only incompatible with knowledge, but is itself deceptive. To Hazlitt's prescription of imaginative limits, Keats adds the Platonic stigma of the lie: the 'virtuous philosopher', to whom the lamia is an acknowledged fake from the start, makes the imaginings of the chameleon poet look like a serpent-prison.[35]

STILL LIVES AND CHAMELEON FORMS

The serpent denotes Keats's fear of fixity; the chameleon his compulsion to change. They are two beasts in one poet. While the Satanic consciousness is invaded by, or insufficiently subdued to, a bodily existence, the chameleon is 'continually in for[ming] and filling some other Body'. It is perhaps not surprising that Keats has been the object of formalist scrutiny. In his own recognition, the chameleon is a formative principle, at once imparting itself to, and taking on the identity of, its creations. The poetry craves existences that it may enter, in satisfaction of its own avid hunger for form. Its characteristic movement is from one entity to another (rather than 'hovering between images', as in a Coleridgean poetry of indeterminacy): in *Endymion*, the pleasure-thermometer measures palpable objects of desire; the relentless succession of its pageant-forms, the endearing literalness of its mythologies, seek to embody forces of love and nature. Keats's 'fellowship with essence' must have substance (*Endymion*, I. 779); his way of feeling is transitive – it takes an object.

The dramatic persona of Hazlitt's Shakespeare, from which the idea of the chameleon poet derives, becomes a formal premise in Keats. The imagination's dual capacity, to be submerged in parallel lives, and be drawn by fresh objects, means that it has both a freedom to change and a formal fetish – as in the ravenous lines from the *Ode on Melancholy*: 'Or if thy mistress some rich anger shows,/ Emprison her soft hand, and let her rave,/ And feed deep, deep upon her peerless eyes' (18–20). Since Keats's imagination requires form, it is to that extent a prey to fixation and fixity. The chameleon moves between

points of stasis, adopting other identities in recognition of their formal
constraints. It has, then, a kinship to its reptilian other, the serpent,
and to the gamut of imprisoned figures which fall under the heading
of Keats's commentary on Satan: Circe, with her 'serpenting'
captives and piteous elephant-man, and Glaucus, cursed with age
and the 'serpent-skin of woe' (*Endymion*, III. 501, 240); the impotent
Titans – Saturn, his arm 'nerveless, listless, dead', Hyperion, overcome
by the 'lithe serpent' of his own frailty, and Iäpetus gripping a
'serpent's plashy neck' (*Hyperion*, I. 18, 261; II. 45); finally, Lamia,
trapped in her weird serpentine beauty, and desiring human form.

All these figures render states of circumstantial entrapment, and
their 'pain of suffocation' testifies to Keats's fascinated horror of stasis.
His mind is continually driven to imagine its own death, or, less
catastrophically, the cessation of its development: 'When I have fears
that I may cease to be/ Before my pen has glean'd my teeming brain
. . .' (*When I have fears that I may cease to be*, 1–2). The poet of progress
conceives an art-form whose age and stillness are a final apotheosis,
transcending the erotic instability of his own 'rhyme': 'Thou still
unravish'd bride of quietness,/ Thou foster-child of silence and slow
time,/ Sylvan historian . . .' (*Ode on a Grecian Urn*, 1–2). Such
inviolability is the condition of an art that is purely historical. It is the
living poet whose desire endows the urn with a future in the image of
'breathing human passion', 'For ever warm and still to be enjoy'd'
(28, 26). For ever 'Cold' and static, the urn excludes all contingency,
so that its closure may 'tease' the interpretative impulse (44–5), and
provoke the 'struggle to escape' of the poem.

By over-identifying with his own method, the chameleon poet ends
up in a serpent-prison.[36] Nevertheless, a distinction is drawn between
them, which may also be tied to the larger question of Keats's relation
to history. The chameleon is associated with Shakespeare, with
freedom, and with the life of allegory – the self effortlessly elided by a
life lived at the level of art. The serpent-prison is associated with
Milton, confinement, and the allegorising of life – the drama of
self-overcoming necessitated by circumstance. In either case, it is the
accidental which enforces the larger shapes of an ideal history in
Keats. But the relation between the two is by no means axiomatic.
One way of thinking about this is to say that the effects of his poetry
escape and exceed the totalising structures within which they are
placed. His poems resist the allegorical interpretations for which they
are intended, owing in part to what Barbara Everett has called the

role of the 'haphazard' in his work.[37] The official design of *Endymion* is to achieve a 'fellowship with essence', but it is also consumed by a wayward and excitable observation. In what is surely a metaphor for his own art – a catalogue-epic of extreme fluidity and inclusiveness – Keats describes the 'ambitious magic' of Glaucus's embroidered cloak:

> The gulphing whale was like a dot in the spell,
> Yet look upon it, and 'twould size and swell
> To its huge self, and the minutest fish
> Would pass the very hardest gazer's wish,
> And shew his little eye's anatomy.   (III. 205–9)

The chameleon opposes a determining fixity with freedom within formal bounds – as in the roomy manoeuvre of 'Obstinate silence', in Book II, 'Feeling about for its old couch of space/ And airy cradle' (II. 335–7). And a similar combination of definiteness and changeability informs Keats's allegorical interpretations of history, in a fortuitous and unrigorous mix of necessity and contingency. The same chancy assurance that allows him to 'do half at Random' things that 'are afterwards confirmed by [his] judgment in a dozen features of Propriety', governs the meta-narratives of soul-making and the march of intellect (*Letters*, i. 142).

Keats's ideal is both determined and open-ended, a progress of poetry that is free at the point of writing. As Bloom remarks of the *Ode to Psyche*, which addresses the 'latest born' of the Olympians, he hopes for 'a map with blanks' in it. Literary history would petrify were not the poet an explorer of its formal possibilities.[38] The odes are the fullest example of how Keats's promiscuous identity (the erotic impulse uncoercively at play) is also generically innovative and enabling. Similarly, they reveal how poetry may, as Hartman suggests, 'tell the time of history – without accepting a historical determinism'.[39]

To Autumn is a progress-poem, in the sense that it does not seek a return. Though it ends with antiphonal thoughts of spring, its seasonal form is not cyclical but linear (the 'full-grown lambs' (30) refer to a completed temporal sequence rather than to a possible recurrence). Much of the ode's greatness derives from this oblique morbidity: time is not stopped but stayed, as though death had become implicit, and so made room for a triumph of life or fruitfulness. The suspension of the inevitable allows for both the extraordinary glutting of the first stanza (where the season conspires, by an illusion of permanence, 'to set budding more,/ And still more, later flowers'), and the satiated ease of the second (where Autumn gathers to herself the products of human labour). At the centre of the poem, the activity of harvesting is replaced by still lives of the season, in which work is an achievement of rest, and productivity a reward of contemplation. The drive to progress has been overtaken by organic processes and their 'patient' evolution. These 'last oozings' are as slow as you can go while still sustaining motion (21, 22). By taking out the evolutionary dilemmas that had so beset *Hyperion* and *Lamia*, *To Autumn* evades the accusation of fixity – both formal (the figure of Autumn fluently metamorphoses everywhere you look), and temporal (the problem of anachronism does not occur in 'nature').[40] The forms of the harvest – winnowing, reaping, gleaning, apple pressing – succeed one another in the finer tone of Autumn's unwilled fertility, as if in final reconciliation of the conflicting impulses of indolence and urgency, stasis and momentum.

As a model of history, Keats's 'gregarious advance of intellect' is evidently problematic. Yet in his astonishing development we find the ocular proof, as it were, of his faith that time itself is progressive, or the 'maturing' element in which we inevitably move and grow. Standing 'tip-toe', eager for the unfolding of futurity, Keats projects his own life of allegory, and equates it with a 'general' progress. Yet although the literal is put on terms with the allegorical, the convergence is not achieved in any final sense. There remains a sharp and contradictory awareness, both of the absolute nature of individual suffering, and the ineradicable subjectivity of experience. The conditions of the literal life are not to be denied – hence the destabilising weight of the satire Keats brings to the romance, and the burdensome knowledge that the 'march of intellect' occurs only through a progressive entanglement in circumstances. There are many confines, in life and art, as well as history; Keats's rich and risky amplitude is to move between them, threatened with imprisonment by each.

NOTES

1 See Caroline Spurgeon, *Keats's Shakespeare. A Descriptive Study Based on New Material* (London, 1928), 6. Leonidas M. Jones, 'Keats's Theatrical Reviews in *The Champion*', *K–SJ* 3 (1954), 55–65, traces the erroneous attribution to *L&L*, and makes a convincing attribution to Reynolds.

2 W. J. Courthope, 'The Latest Development of Literary Poetry', *Quarterly Review* (Jan. 1872); *KCH*, 33.

3 See Spurgeon, *Keats's Shakespeare*, 86. Cf. Hazlitt's *Characters of Shakespear's Plays*: 'Ariel is imaginary power, the swiftness of thought personified'; *HW*, iv. 241.

4 See Lucy Newlyn, *'Paradise Lost' and the Romantic Reader* (Oxford, 1993), 250–5.

5 See *KHM*, 61, for the definition of 'Romanticism' as both 'a reactionary and "escapist" art movement', and 'an intense expression of critique'.

6 John Barnard (ed.), *John Keats. The Complete Poems* (Harmondsworth, 1973), 526; for the very free 'speculations' given to Lamia in her 'serpent prison', see *Lamia*, I. 202–19.

7 Keats's understanding of the egotistical and dramatic impulses is comparable to Coleridge's of Milton and Shakespeare, the latter being able 'to become by power of Imagination another Thing . . . yet still the God felt to be there', R. A. Foakes (ed.), *Collected Works of Samuel Taylor Coleridge. Lectures 1808–1819 On Literature* (2 vols., London and Princeton, 1987) i. 69. See John Bayley, *The Characters of Love* (London, 1960), 19.

8 On idealism, see Paul Hamilton, 'Kant and Critique', in Marjorie Levinson et al., *Rethinking Historicism: Critical Readings in Romantic History* (Oxford, 1989), 108–42.

9 *KL*, 5.

10 Ibid., 6.

11 *HW*, iv. 172; cf. *Measure for Measure*, 1.1.26 ff., a passage underlined by Keats: 'There is a kind of character in thy life,/ That, to the observer, doth thy history/ Fully unfold'.

12 *Letters*, i. 179 where Keats simultaneously wishes to reform the world and remain untouched by it.

13 Keats refuses the pessimism of a Christian theology, which postpones salvation until the next world, and the optimism of a rationalist teleology which assumes perfectibility in this (for his anti-Godwinism, see *Letters*, i. 397; ii. 101).

14 That is, 'sandwiched between the Truth of the working class and the Beauty of the leisure class', *KL*, 5.

15 For various permutations of this theory, see Isaiah Berlin, 'Historical Inevitability', *Four Essays on Liberty* (Oxford, 1969).

16 See Paul de Man (ed.), *Selected Poetry of John Keats* (New York, 1966), xi. For Keats's use of the 'progress' topos, see the opening of *Endymion* IV.

17 Keats's hopefulness was far from the post-Napoleonic triumphalism of Leigh Hunt's *Descent of Liberty*, and the sequence of thunderous odes Wordsworth wrote between 1814 and 1816. For Keats's awareness of the prosecutions of liberal publishers, see *Letters*, i. 191; ii. 62, 194.

18 *Letters*, ii. 193 ff.; see also the political allegory of i. 232 and, for a contrasting sense of the degeneracy of modern political life, i. 396.

19 On the progress poem, see Alan J. Bewell, 'The Political Implication of

Keats's Classicist Aesthetics', in *KP*. According to *AP*, 395, 'the affirmation of the law of progress' in *Hyperion* is Keats's own invention.

20 See Kenneth Muir, 'The Meaning of *Hyperion*', in K. Muir (ed.), *John Keats. A Reassessment* (Liverpool, 1969), 102–3, and *Letters*, ii. 180. See also David Bromwich, 'Keats's Politics', *A Choice of Inheritance* (Cambridge, Mass., and London, 1989), 92–105.

21 See *Hyperion*, I. 328–35, II. 92–5. Marilyn Butler points out that the poem is a narrative of liberal 'progress' and of 'the individual victims of the historical process', *Romantics, Rebels, and Reactionaries. English Literature and its Background 1760–1830* (Oxford and New York, 1981), 151–4. See also Laurence S. Lockridge, 'Keats: The Ethics of Imagination', in J. R. Barth and J. L. Mahoney (eds.), *Coleridge, Keats, and the Imagination* (Columbia, Mo., and London, 1990), 143–73.

22 Keats inserts into the text his own moral empathy with suffering, finding a Milton who is 'godlike in the sublime pathetic' (Barnard, *Complete Poems*, 522). See also Susan Wolfson, *The Questioning Presence* (Ithaca, N.Y., 1986), 262.

23 'The recluse, the pastor, and the pedlar, are three persons in one poet' – Hazlitt's verdict on *The Excursion*, *HW*, xix. 11.

24 On the day *Hyperion* was abandoned, 21 April 1819, Keats wrote to his brother and sister-in-law about making the soul by the 'medium of the heart'; *Letters*, ii. 104.

25 The notion of a graduation in genre, from pastoral to epic, is established from classical times; see Geoffrey Hartman, *Minor Prophecies* (Cambridge, Mass., and London, 1991), 57.

26 Barnard, *Complete Poems*, 517. It seems likely that this commentary is contemporaneous with the letter written 24 April 1818.

27 See Jonathan Bate, 'Keats's two *Hyperions* and the problem of Milton', in K. Hanley and R. Brinkley (eds.), *Romantic Revisions* (Cambridge, 1992, 321–38.

28 Bloom, *The Anxiety of Influence: A Theory of Poetry* (London, 1973). In Book I, the serpent image is politicized in a fantasy of 'wip[ing] away all slime/ Left by men-slugs and human serpentry' (I. 820–1).

29 See 'What is the People?', *HW*, vii. 259–81, and *HW*, xix. 17–18 (referring to the Wanderer, *Excursion*, IV). For Hazlitt's similar awareness that 'friends of liberty' are doomed by their inability to combat tyranny, see 'Julius Caesar', *HW*, iv. 198.

30 Cf. *Letters*, i. 144, on Haydon's review of a manuscript said to be sent by Napoleon from St Helena, and *KPP*, 93.

31 *John Keats*, xxi.

32 'What is mechanical, reducible to rule, or capable of demonstration, is progressive . . . what is not mechanical or definite, but depends on genius, taste, and feeling, very soon becomes stationary or retrograde'; *HW*, iv. 161. Hazlitt's thesis is taken up in Peacock's 'Four Ages of Poetry' (1820), 'The march of [the poet's] intellect is like that of a crab, backward'; see

H. F. B. Brett-Smith and C. E. Jones (eds.), *The Halliford Edition of the Works of Thomas Love Peacock* (10 vols., London and New York, 1924–34) viii. 20–1. Contrast Coleridge's view of man 'as a progressive being', Foakes, *Lectures 1808–1819*, ii. 193.

33 'Why the Arts are not Progressive', *HW*, iv. 162. For the battle of Ancients and Moderns, and its relation to ideas of progress, see Murray Krieger, 'The Arts and the Idea of Progress', in G. A. Almond et al. (eds.), *Progress and its Discontents* (Berkeley and London, 1982), 449–69; and David Spadafora, *The Idea of Progress in Eighteenth-Century Britain* (New Haven and London, 1990), chap. 2.

34 *HW*, v. 9.

35 For Lamia as 'a perverted form of negative capability', for Lycius and Apollonius as forms of the serpentine, and the role of snakes in pharmacy and mythology, see H. de Almeida, *Romantic Medicine and John Keats* (New York and Oxford, 1991), 182–96.

36 For Geoffrey Hartman, 'In-feeling, in Keats, is always on the point of overidentifying'; 'Poem and Ideology: A Study of Keats's "To Autumn"', in *The Fate of Reading and Other Essays* (Chicago and London, 1975), 131.

37 'Keats: Somebody Reading', *London Review of Books* (1984), quoted in *KL*, 31.

38 See Harold Bloom, *A Map of Misreading* (Oxford and New York, 1975), 152, and Keats's sonnet *If by dull rhymes our English must be chain'd*.

39 *The Fate of Reading*, 126, and see p. 143.

40 Even so, an aesthetic primitivism is being invoked; Ian Jack points to the influence of Hazlitt, who remarks of Poussin, one of Keats's pictorial models in *To Autumn*: 'his implements of husbandry are such as would belong to the first rude stages of civilization; his harvests are such . . . as would yield to no modern sickle'; *Keats and the Mirror of Art* (Oxford, 1967), 69.

CHAPTER 14

Writing numbers: Keats, Hopkins, and the history of chance

John Kerrigan

The publication, in 1878, of *Letters of John Keats to Fanny Brawne* sent shock waves through the poet's high Victorian readership. An author whose sensuality had seemed redeemable by virtue of his dying 'Like a pale flower'[1] was found to have spent his final days in an all-too-human confusion of desire, despair, and bitterness. Even so sympathetic a Keatsian as Swinburne was moved to protest 'that a manful kind of man or even a manly sort of boy . . . will not howl and snivel after such a lamentable fashion'.[2] Matthew Arnold, more intelligently ambivalent, conceded the charge of effeminacy but sought ways of discounting the crime.[3] According to George Keats, he pointed out, 'John was the very soul of manliness and courage.' Many of the letters were written 'under the . . . unmanning grasp of mortal disease'. Though ill-educated and 'sensuous', he was eager to 'study' and loved 'the Principle of Beauty' more than 'pleasure'. Two considerations above all strike Arnold. First, Keats's growth was 'cut short by misfortune'. In an essay notably sceptical about the poet's use of capital letters (as in 'Principle' and 'Beauty'), Arnold insists that Keats 'had against him the blind power which we call Fortune'. Moreover, Keats had reserves of 'flint and iron'. How else, Arnold wonders, can we explain the poet's impulse towards 'high work' and 'the best kind of poetry'. 'This severe addiction of his to the best sort of poetry', Arnold claims, 'affects him with a certain coldness, as if the addiction had been towards mathematics, towards those prime objects of a sensuous and passionate poet's regard, love and women.'

It is with a calculating Keats, as well as an unfortunate one, that this essay will be concerned. Arnold is not always an easy critic to agree with, but the language of his 1880 preface responds to key elements in Keatsian writing which interact with developments across a whole field of social and intellectual history. Certainly it is a sign of Arnold's empathy that Keats's first surviving letter to Fanny

Brawne – not published until 1883 – should devolve to an idiom of
luck: 'I will never return to London if my Fate does not turn up Pam
or at least a Court-card . . . I must live upon hope and Chance'
(*Letters*, ii. 123).[4] Language of this sort recurs, often to poignant effect.
When Keats tells Miss Brawne that 'The utmost stretch my mind has
been capable of was to endeavour to forget you for your own sake
seeing what a change [*for* chance] there was of my remaining in a
precarious state of health', he lets 'slip' a longing which can be
confirmed as 'Freudian' by a missive sent shortly afterwards to his
sister: 'We have been so unfortunate for so long a time . . . that I must
persuade myself to think some change will take place in the aspect of
our affairs. I shall be upon the look out for a trump card –' (*Letters*, ii.
258, 309). This idiom is not confined to the letters. A late sonnet such
as *Bright star, would I were stedfast as thou art* has a figurative texture
enriched by the presence in the prose of 'To be happy with you seems
such an impossibility! it requires a luckier Star than mine!' (*Letters*, ii.
312). Yet there are deeper and more immediate links than those of
imagery between being, or not being, 'happy' and the rhythm of those
'tuneless numbers' (*Ode to Psyche*, 1) – as Keats modestly put it – the
late odes. When the poet describes a 'numbness' compacted not of
'envy of' the nightingale's 'happy lot,/ But being too happy in thine
happiness' (5–6), we are reading verse embedded not only in an
'unfortunate' life but in a longer history of 'lots' to which it matters
that these lines should celebrate a bird who, among 'shadows
numberless' (uncountably full of numbers), sings.

The idea of numerical structuring in poetry is, of course, ancient.
Measure itself, *rhuthmos* in Greek, is often called *numerus* by Latin
rhetoricians. In English verse, from *Pearl* to *Paradise Lost*, numerological
patterns count.[5] Even a writer as rumbustious as Skelton is capable,
as Geoffrey Hill points out, of using metrical 'Nomber' and 'Measure'
to 'embody and enact his ethical priorities'.[6] From the late seventeenth
century through to that crucial decade of Keats's reception, the
1880s, there were changes in the context and significance of numbering,
an 'emergence of probability' and 'taming of chance', which affected
the way in which 'Measure' was figured.[7] When Pope writes to Dr
Arbuthnot, 'I lisp'd in Numbers, for the Numbers came', he does so in
the knowledge that his correspondent has translated Christian
Huygens's *De ratiociniis in aleae ludo* (1657), 'the first published work in
mathematical probability',[8] and is the author of a celebrated paper
maintaining that the division of sexes in birth statistics (which show a

constant tendency to surplus males) was providentially determined.[9] The early eighteenth-century poet is open to Lucretian and Epicurean influences, but, following the example of such authors as Glanvill and Charleton, he accommodates classical ideas of randomness to the growing confidence of his age that chance is ruled by laws, imperfectly understood, that 'All Nature is but Art, unknown to thee;/ All Chance, Direction, which thou canst not see'.[10] Even when lisped, Popean 'Art' is itself governed by rules which reflect what is known of the laws of 'Nature', as surely as Augustan 'Chance' is the product of gaps in knowledge not ingrained randomness. By the end of the nineteenth century, philosophers like Nietzsche and C. S. Peirce were adopting a different view, in which chance was the world's necessity. Heaven became (as Zarathustra put it) 'a divine table for divine dice and dice players'.[11] These intellectually complex changes produced surprising affinities. The young nominalist Peirce, for instance, argued his way into admiration for Hopkins's 'rarest-veinèd unraveller', the scholastic realist Duns Scotus.[12] More importantly for this essay, when Hopkins praised Arnold's account of Keats, insisting on the young poet's 'powerful and active thought' and 'distinctively masculine powers', he was writing from a body of creative work which not only drew deeply on Keats's example but which had itself been forced into quasi-mathematical self-consciousness by anxiety about statistical determinism and a crypto-psychoanalytic concern with the contribution made by numbers to the organisation of experience in mental space.[13]

That Keats was a numbering writer is evident. His verse is full of references to 'the Nine', 'the Olympian twelve', and those 'seven' stars (the Pleiades) which so conveniently rhyme with 'heaven'. That late, satirical work *The Jealousies* is as prompt to demonstrate the specificity of objects by enumeration as is *The Eve of St. Mark*. In Keats's letters casual phrasing about 'two or three sensible people' will blossom into metre –

> Two or three Posies
> With two or three simples
> Two or three Noses
> With two or three pimples –

and continue in this vein for twenty-eight lines before breaking off, 'Good bye I've an appoantment' (*Letters*, ii. 56–7). Long sequences number the tactics of 'Miss M's ten Suitors' or the capacities of 'three witty people' and 'three people of no wit at all' (*Letters*, ii. 29, 245–6).

With sphinx-like oddness Keats will riddle a rambling syntax to enact his ascent of Ben Nevis: 'sometimes one two sometimes on three, sometimes four legs – sometimes two and stick, sometimes three and stick, then four again, then two . . . foot, hand, Stick, jump boggle, stumble, foot, hand, foot, (very gingerly) stick again, and then again a game at all fours' (*Letters*, i. 354). But his numbers (and feet) can more subtly run with and against our sense of 'Measure'. A gadfly provokes the thought,

> Has any here a Lawyer suit
> Of 17, 43
> Take Lawyer's nose and put it to 't
> And you the end will see   (*Letters*, i. 335)

and the joke is not just that '3' must be heard and seen as 'three' for the stanza fully to rhyme, but that the digits need a comma to show their conformity to a 'Measure' which 'one seven four three' will no more fit than 'seventeen hundred and . . .' or 'one thousand seven hundred and . . .'

Among Keats's correspondents, numerical wit was most appreciated by John Hamilton Reynolds. This is hardly surprising, given that a decade of his life was spent among figures in the Amicable Insurance office. When Keats tells Reynolds about the guide at Burns's cottage, who 'drinks glasses five for the Quarter and twelve for the hour' (*Letters*, i. 324), his mischievous improvement on 'Christabel' – 'Four for the quarters, and twelve for the hour' – is calculated to appeal to a man who had mocked that very line in an essay called 'The Arithmetic of Poetry'.[14] Reynolds's purpose there was to show that 'A poet now-a-days turns cocker[15] when he writes, and ingeniously hangs the fetters of rhymes over the addition table.' Leading with the Popean epigraph, 'I lisp'd in numbers, for the numbers came', he sketches 'the whole course of studies which a modern poet pursues. He reads the Tutor's Assistant all the week and *muses* over that book of the Bible called "Numbers," on Sundays: – thus, – and we can account for his being so deeply *versed* in arithmetic . . .' After a page of similarly execrable puns, typical of the Keats circle, Reynolds quotes Wordsworth,[16] Byron, Campbell, and some apocryphal ('I'll take care of number one') as well as actual lines of Southey to prove that numbers are running riot in contemporary verse. His essay is the more amusing for being the work of a writer who, in 1819, would publish a farce called *One, Two, Three, Four. By Advertisement*. That Reynolds was not

Figure 14.1   Frontispiece of W. Sketchley, *The Cocker* (London, 1814)

just satirically drawn to 'cockering' is shown by the return of that
term, and related accountant's quibbles, in 'The Cockpit Royal'.[17]
This piece excerpts a treatise on 'breeding Game Cocks, with
Calculations for Betting' and describes, in attentive detail, the
methods of gambling employed at the pit. The spectacle (Fig. 14.1)
and mathematics (Fig. 14.2) of cockfighting were familiar to Londoners
during Keats's lifetime. Betting on probabilities and games of chance
was a stock amusement for the poet and his friends. He tells his
brothers, 'I was at a Dance at Redhall's . . . drank deep and won 10.6
at cutting for Half Guinies' (*Letters*, i. 200), and reports, 'There were
Taylor Woodhouse, Reynolds – we began cards at about 9 o'Clock . . .
played at Cards till very daylight – and yesterday I was not worth a
sixpence'   (*Letters*, ii. 93).

Does the eagerly numbering Keats fall under the bludgeon of 'The
Arithmetic of Poetry'? Up to a point, it would appear so. Yet it is apt
that the news of his all night card-game should belong to the same
letter as his comments on *La Belle Dame sans Merci*:

> She took me to her elfin grot
>   And there she wept and sigh'd full sore
> And there I shut her wild wild eyes
>   With kisses four . . .

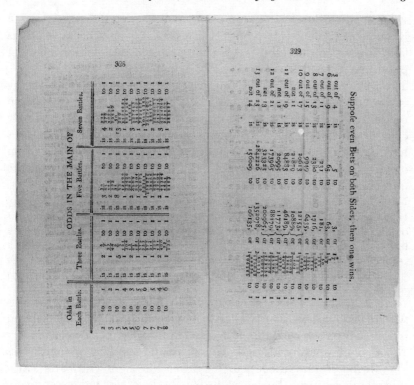

Figure 14.2 *How to Calculate Bets in Cock-Fighting*, from Edmond Hoyle, revised and corrected by Charles Jones, *Hoyle's Games Improved . . . With an Essay on Game Cocks* (London, 1800)

Why four kisses – you will say – why four because I wish to restrain the headlong impetuosity of my Muse – she would have fain said 'score' without hurting the rhyme – but we must temper the Imagination as the Critics say with Judgment. I was obliged to choose an even number that both eyes might have fair play: and to speak truly I think two a piece quite sufficient – Suppose I had said seven; there would have been three and a half a piece – a very awkward affair . . .   (*Letters*, ii. 96–7)

This shows more than an amused awareness of what kisses share with gambling – you go ahead at random but expect the hazards to end up even ('that both eyes might have fair play'). It reveals the self-awareness of a Keats who knows that, in his poetic arithmetic, 'seven' comes straight after 'four'. It is tempting to interpret the passage as a Reynoldsian joke made at the poet's own expense, because 'kisses four' is what (quite rightly) gets printed in the anthologies. The text published in 1820, however, reads: 'sighed deep . . . kissed to sleep'. The four/score passage is thus not only followed (in the letter) by the variant, 'Chorus of Faries <three> 4', but by disabling numerical revision in one of the loveliest poems in the language. Keats is so finely capable of exploring such scruples humorously that his number jokes have a texture quite different from those of Reynolds. His description of Mrs Wylie's cook, for example, is a brief Shandean essay on the uncertainty of memory and report:

When I ask'd 'Is Mrs Wylie within' she gave such a large, five-and-thirty-year-old smile, it made me look round upon the forth stair – it might have been the fifth – but that's a puzzle. I shall never be able if I were to set myself a recollecting for a year, to recollect that – I think I remember two or three specks in her teeth but I really cant say exactly.   (*Letters*, ii. 207)

That Reynolds was interested in cards and cockfighting squares with his occupation. The similarity between insurance and gambling is now so deeply buried that it takes a scandal like the one of the early 1990s – with wealthy Lloyd's 'names' seeking tax relief on their losses – to bring it into the open.[18] During the eighteenth and early nineteenth centuries, however, the two modes of risk-judgement were thought ethically as well as mathematically continuous. The idea of life insurance as a form of prudence, rather than a bet against the future, was only developing during this period.[19] Keats shrewdly recognises that Reynolds's employment is a source of comedy. Writing to Haydon about the likelihood of getting together 'for one of our right Sort meetings', he notes (with an upper-case jab at insurer's language), 'I was at Reynolds's when he received your Letter and am therefore up to Probabilities' (*Letters*, i. 148). More ponderably, Reynolds's occupation helps sharpen Keats's conscience into recognising the incalculability of persons. In the magnificent letter of 19 February 1818 (*Letters*, i. 231–3), he shows that there can be no calculus to average the possibilities of human lives because 'almost any Man may like the Spider spin from his own inwards his own airy Citadel'. Rebutting the Augustan dismissal (as, for instance, in Swift) of a spider's self-wrought futility, Keats celebrates the soft errancy of gossamer-threads. Where does such insistent, though delicate, individuation leave the concept of society? '[T]he Minds of Mortals are so different and bent on such diverse Journeys', he tells Reynolds, 'that it may at first appear impossible for any common taste and fellowship to exist between two or three under these suppositions – It is however quite the contrary – Minds would leave each other in contrary directions, traverse each other in Numberless points, and all [*for* at] last greet each other at the Journeys end . . .' It is by means of the incalculable, 'all'-inducing plenitude of that upper-case ode-word, 'Numberless', that Keats arrives at his equivalencing declaration, 'Humanity instead of being a wide heath of Furse and Briars with here and there a remote Oak or Pine, would become a grand democracy of Forest Trees.'

Few Keatsian utterances did more damage in Victorian eyes than the one quoted at the start of Arnold's preface, and deplored in turn by Hopkins: 'O for a Life of Sensations rather than of Thoughts!' (*Letters*, i. 185). That this was the cry of a poet intensely burdened with 'Thoughts', who could not expect to escape them, did not sufficiently register. More characteristic of Keats, in any event, is his return to the topic in a letter sent to Reynolds when the latter was abandoning insurance for a position in the law (3 May 1818). 'An extensive knowledge is needful to thinking people', he writes,

it . . . helps, by widening speculation, to ease the Burden of the Mystery: a thing I begin to understand a little, and which weighed upon you in the most gloomy and true sentence in your Letter. The difference of high Sensations with and without knowledge appears to me this – in the latter case we are falling continually ten thousand fathoms deep and being blown up again without wings and with all [the] horror of a <Case> bare shoulderd Creature – in the former case, our shoulders are fledge <d>, and we go thro' the same <Fir> air and space without fear. This is running one's rigs on the score of abstracted benefit – when we come to human Life and the affections it is impossible how a parallel of breast and head can be drawn . . . (*Letters*, i. 277)

This is a complicated passage, enriched rather than confused by Derrida's reminder that 'the words "chance" and "case" descend, as it were, according to the same Latin filiation, from *cadere*, which – to indicate the sense of the fall – still resounds in "cadence," "fall" (*choir*) . . . as well as in "accident" and "incident"'.[20] Keats's prose echoes *Paradise Lost* II. 883–942, recalling a region of 'embryon atoms' where 'Chaos umpire sits' with 'high arbiter/ Chance', and where fallen Lucifer 'drops/ Ten thousand fathom deep' until, 'by ill chance/ The strong rebuff of some tumultuous cloud . . . hurried him/ As many miles aloft'.[21] In this linguistic environment it seems natural for

'<Case>' – like 'change' in that letter to Fanny Brawne – to 'slip' or 'chance' into writing (the Freudian *lapsus*, 'fall'), much as it comes as no surprise to learn that 'the most gloomy and true sentence' of Reynolds's letter described the unhappiness of his 'lot': 'I fear there is little chance of any thing else in this life' (*Letters*, i. 278). 'Knowledge' might be consoling because it curbs the 'fear' of falling at 'chance''s whim, but it cannot abolish that force since we are subject to one 'case' or another. And could even an insurance man credit (Keats goes on to wonder) such high-handed play with 'the score of abstracted benefit' – 'the calculus of future rewards' among other things? To measure the 'benefit' of 'knowledge', as it stabilises an individual 'case', lies beyond our ken.

The presence in this letter of that 'Chief of organic numbers', Milton,[22] becomes explicit in a comparison with Wordsworth (*Letters*, i. 281–2) but reaches its climax in the claim that 'there is really a grand march of intellect . . . a mighty providence subdues the mightiest Minds to the service of the time being' (*Letters*, i. 282). This assertion, which rings the stronger for recalling the works of Milton's left hand, is often, and with justice, referred to Oceanus's speech in *Hyperion* (II. 173–243). What tends to be overlooked is that the proto-Hegelian deity retains an allegiance to 'the atom-universe' (II. 183) which leaves his world – and the 'forest-trees' which inhabit it (II. 224) – open to 'chance'. In far-reaching but immediate ways (signalled by the revised title), but also through their relations with political theory, *Hyperion* and *The Fall of Hyperion* are concerned with what will 'befall' in history by virtue of what 'falls' through time. We should not miss the radical associations of 'atom-universe': words which invoke a conception of nature often associated at this date with republican theories of progress.[23] More than historical 'chance' makes Marx's Jena dissertation, *The Difference between the Democritean and the Epicurean Philosophies of Nature*, begin his materialist critique of Hegel by arguing that the deflection of falling atoms in Epicurus resembles the swerve of persons into social units by individualistic turnings. Yet there are other, equally anti-Popean but conservatively sceptical resonances to Oceanus's phrase which make it difficult to share the often-aired idea that the god demonstrates Keats's belief in evolution towards perfection. That the poet had doubts about human perfectibility cannot be disputed; he says as much in the letter which discusses 'kisses four' (*Letters*, ii. 101–2). As tellingly, his note to Rice about Milton's nose, marking the turf 'at equidistances' while the

'Chief of . . . numbers' rolled around 'a certain meadow' (*Letters*, i. 254–7), is as relevant to *Hyperion* as any epistle about the 'march of intellect'.[24] Giving a paradoxical twist to eighteenth-century atomism, Keats suggests that the world 'still is made up of the same bulk – nor ever varies the number of its Atoms'. In such an 'atom-universe', 'that which was in Miltons head could not find Room in Charles the seconds – he like a Moon attracted Intellect to its flow', leaving all the 'Bucks Authors of Hengist and Castlereaghs of the present day' short of matter in their pates. Far from an evolving world destined to move onward and upward, we live in a steady state swayed by irony and the tug of the moon.

Byron quipped in 1823 that, though he could think 'The World . . . a glorious blunder –/ If it be Chance', he was 'grown lately rather phthisical' and found that, 'as I suffer from the shocks/ Of illness, I grow much more orthodox'.[25] As Keats's faith in 'providence' was sapped by Tom's and his own 'misfortune', he became, on the contrary, less 'orthodox' and more convinced of the power of 'Chance'. It is true that when comforting the George Keatses about money trouble he does not just ask, 'who can avoid these chances', but declares 'the whole is with Providence' (*Letters*, ii. 186, 211). The language applied to himself, however, modulates from gambling to loss, from "T is at present the cast of a die with me' to 'O, that something fortunate had ever happened to me or my brothers!' (*Letters*, ii. 210, 352). Late Keats can be archly bombastic about 'the fortunate star/ Of boisterous Chester' who holds 'vile odds' against his foe (*King Stephen*, I. i. 21–5), and bleakly jest with Brown over a missed meeting, 'There was my star predominant!' (*Letters*, ii. 359). But fate did seem to 'cast . . . a die' which ended 'hope and Chance' before the poet was well finished with his game. This would not have been so painful had the operation of 'Chance' been limited to the realm of 'Circumstances'. As he dragged out a 'posthumous' existence, however, Keats felt the zest, the surprisingness of his mind, close up like a pack of cards tidied by suit and number. The poet who had once mocked 'Miss H.' as 'fit for nothing but to cut up into Cribbage pins, to the tune of 15.2' was moved to write, 'is not this extraordinary talk for the writer of Endymion? whose mind was like a pack of scattered cards – I am pick'd up and sorted to a pip' (*Letters*, ii. 68, 323).

Hopkins thought it a sign of 'manly' excellence that Keats's 'fine judgement . . . kept him from flinging himself blindly on the specious

Liberal stuff that crazed Shelley' (*FL* 386). Allowances have to be made for the conservatism of his correspondent, Coventry Patmore – so confident a traditionalist that he excluded Keats from the 'first class' on grounds of 'femininity', then added that his was a 'gift, such as no mortal lady has ever attained or ever will attain'.[26] Even so, Hopkins's words are not those of someone eager to identify the object of his admiration with Oceanus's evolutionary radicalism. The course of history, for the Catholic poet, was a manifestation of divine purpose in which the very dates might be coded. From his earliest diary entries Hopkins can be found looking for patterns in number: a vision of Edward the Confessor's suggests that, 'Taking 1525 as the date of the Reformation and a furlong as 125 years . . . three furlongs would $= 375$ years and bring the date of reunion to 1900';[27] bizarre calculations, found in the *Pall Mall Gazette*, predict the end of Louis Napoleon's reign in 1869 (*J* 73). Though superficially eccentric, such jottings show a form-seeking impulse consistent with the Platonism which remained integral to Hopkins's make-up. At Oxford he studied Lucretius, Bacon, and Hobbes; 'atomistic' science was dominant;[28] Walter Pater, Hopkins's tutor, was partly 'Epicurean' in his aesthetics. But in 'The Probable Future of Metaphysics' (*J* 118–21) the young poet rejects 'atomism' as 'a stiffness or sprain . . . a disproportioned sense of personality'. In place of Romantic 'atomism', with its emphasis on the rights of particles to swerve and congregate at will, he urges a 'new Realism' which 'will maintain that in musical strings' – for instance – 'the roots of chords . . . are mathematically fixed'. Hopkins lists 'forms which have a great hold on the mind . . . such as the designs of Greek vases and lyres, the cone upon Indian shawls' and claims for them 'an absolute existence'. It should be 'one work' of metaphysics, he says, to demonstrate that such 'forms' are realised only when 'precise conditions are fulfilled . . . to point out how they are to be mathematically or *quasi*-mathematically expressed'.

Though he once jokingly pretended to have failed a maths exam (*FL* 84) and was, much later, implicitly discouraged by Dixon from devoting time to the subject,[29] Hopkins remained competent in and fascinated by the art of numbers. 'They tell me I must study lines and tangents and squares and circles', Keats drily informed his sister, 'to put a little Ballast into my mind' (*Letters*, ii. 287). Even as an undergraduate Hopkins was acquainted with far more advanced, non-Euclidean geometry,[30] and as late as 1886 he was drafting a 'sort of popular account of Light and Ether' (*LD* 139). Written with 'no mathematics' on show, for the sake of the general reader, this was still 'not . . . easy reading' – and hardly could be, given that the topic cut across contentious questions in science (e.g., how did light pass through massed atoms of water?) and led into problems of 'elasticity' in mathematical theory. Between Keats and Hopkins falls more than an Oxford education: the 1820s and 30s saw a growing sense that calculation was approaching the hiding places of divinity. When Keats writes to Reynolds, 'I have not time to elucidate the forms and shapes of the grass and trees; for, rot it! I forgot to bring my mathematical case with me; which unfortunately contained my triangular Prism so that the hues of the grass cannot be dissected for you' (*Letters*, i. 162), the banter has undercurrents of anxiety which surface in the passage in *Lamia* about the dispersal of the 'awful rainbow':

> Philosophy will clip an Angel's wings,
> Conquer all mysteries by rule and line,
> Empty the haunted air, and gnomed mine –
> Unweave a rainbow . . .   (II. 234–7)

Science and poetry are enemies here, though both use 'rule and line'. In Hopkins, by contrast, 'Philosophy' is valuably 'mathematical' if it educes 'form' from nature. For science can lead to God. When he writes in the 1873 Journal, 'I counted in a bright rainbow two, perhaps three/ complete octaves, that is/ three, perhaps four/ strikings of the keynote or nethermost red' (*J* 237) there is no dread of unweaving, no Reynolds-like awkwardness about 'arithmetic'. The neutral accuracy of numbers allows them to 'express' the 'form' of the sublime, to prism the transparency of air into lines which almost measure their length by counting:

> . . . this blue heaven
> The seven or seven times seven
> Hued sunbeam will transmit
> Perfect, not alter it.[31]

For readers not given to Mariolatry, 'seven or seven times seven' risks bathos. That the numbers allude to the Virgin's joys and sorrows is hardly enough – even in these exquisitely enjambed trimeters – to sustain them. At times excessively trusting in numbers to communicate mysterious truth, Hopkins lapses into brittle piety. The letter to his Anglican father justifying conversion to Rome, for instance, adopts an ardently formulaic, counter-reformation simplicity almost calculated to cause distress: 'ask the Mother of sorrows to remember her three hours' compassion at the cross . . . and her seven dolours . . . casting yourselves into . . . His five adorable Wounds' (*FL* 94–5). Yet without these cinquefoil tokens, or those of 'Rosa Mystica' and 'In S. Winefridam', we should not have the glorious exclamation, 'Five! the finding and sake/ And cipher of suffering Christ' (169–70), in

> The Wreck of the Deutschland
> December 6. 7. 1875.
> *to the*
> *happy memory of five Franciscan nuns,*
> *exiles by the Falck Laws,*
> *drowned between midnight and morning of*
> *December 7*

This mark and signal suggests the 'form' of what will follow. The date below the (five-word) title is not that of composition but of the events described. We look at it for a meaning. Though the (five-line) dedication to '*five . . . nuns*' does clarify '6. 7.', the difference between those numbers and '*midnight and morning of/ December 7*' could hardly less resemble Keats's play between numeral and word. Each account of time shows inexactness in the other, yet adumbrates respect for such accuracy as can be had. These discreetly laboured details make the more moving the approximations prompted by the insignificance of individuals against the storm: 'Take settler and seamen, tell men with women,/ Two hundred souls in the round . . . of a fourth the doom to be drowned' (91–4). They also point to the difficulty of answering what is perhaps the pivotal question of the poem: 'What bý your méasure is the héaven of desíre . . .?' (207).

Hopkins's diacritical markings at this, the only point in 'The Wreck of the Deutschland' where the reader is addressed as 'you' (stanza 26), insist that the drift to syntactical dislocation at the arrival of '*Ípse*, the ónly one' (221) is not bound up with merely subjective failure (which would be 'yóur measure') but the inadequacy of all human calculation. Editors cite Jeremiah 31: 'If the heavens above can be measured.' Yet, another text is relevant – one important to Hopkins because taken from St Augustine by Duns Scotus in a key discussion of the will:[32] 'omnia in mensura et numero et pondere disposuisti' (Wisdom 11). That less than complete failure comes from the shortfall of 'your méasure' is registered in the justice with which Hopkins's numbers stress 'méasure' in ways commensurate with his 'cockering' note: 'Be pleased, reader . . . strongly to *mark the beats of the measure*, according to the number belonging to each of the eight lines of the stanza . . . namely two and three and four and three and five and five and four and six' (my italics). An assurance of proportion, of *mensura* and *numerus*, underwrites the poet's turn from whatever might have faithlessly struck us as the leading nun's 'méasure' of 'héaven' ('Nó, but it was nót thése') to the declaration, 'Other, I gather, in measure her mind's/ Búrden, in wínd's búrly and béat of endrágonèd séas' (209–16). In 'extremity' a believer's mind finds its *pondus*, the 'Burden' or 'bias' which weighs it towards God and grants it an intimation of true 'measure' even though (as the broken syntax of stanza 28 shows) Christ's advent is scarcely expressible. It is not for Him with simple majesty 'to cure the extremity where he had cast her' – 'cast' like dice, or down a chasm, into *'happy'* (i.e., 'fortunate') remembrance. The nun is saved by choosing the death which God has chosen for her. 'There must be something which shall be truly the creature's in the work of corresponding with grace', Hopkins wrote: 'this is the *arbitrium*, the verdict on God's side, the saying Yes' which does not deny necessity (*S* 154). The word *arbitrium* first appears in Hopkins's discussion of 'The fall from heaven [of] the rebel angels' (*S* 137). At a similar crux, Duns Scotus instanced a man who cast himself from a precipice: falling by natural necessity, he continued to choose freely to fall (*S* 348). Even Keats, feathering his shoulders to soar and plummet like the Satan of *Paradise Lost* II, had envisaged a broader margin of freedom than the one in which Hopkins locates the 'infinitesimal act' (*S* 155) of assenting to grace. In doing this the later poet develops and warps Scotian arguments (*S* 291 n. 4, App. II), yet we misrepresent his creative predicament if the debt to scholasticism is used to abstract him from particular, Victorian features of 'the history of chance'.

For accidents at sea not only roused Hopkins to poetry, they prompted his father, Manley Hopkins, to write *A Handbook of Average* (1857), *A Manual of Marine Insurance* (1867), and *The Port of Refuge, or Advice and Instructions to the Master-Mariner in Situations of Doubt, Difficulty, and Danger* (1873). These competent, widely read volumes show how matter-of-fact a Victorian marine insurer could be about the chances of appalling loss. Such analytic coolness is of its age. The early nineteenth century saw an explosion in the gathering of statistics. By the 1850s and 60s so many numbers were being sifted that predictions became accurate enough not only to put insurance on a fully prudential footing but to appear to endanger free will. Since our own assumptions are those of another chapter in 'the history of chance', the anxiety strikes us as naive. Yet it is with elaborate caution that John Venn explains, in his account of statistics and chance, 'It should be clearly understood that we need not be under any apprehension of getting involved in any Fate and Free-will controversy here; the difficulty before us does not arise out of the *foreknowledge*, but out of the *foretelling*, of what the agents are going to do.'[33] The popular misconception was: if it could be predicted that a certain number of persons were going to commit suicide in a given year, must not a deterministic hand be pushing them out of windows? As Tom Gradgrind reminded his father, on being exposed as a thief: 'So many people are employed in situations of trust; so many people, out of so many, will be dishonest. I have heard you talk, a hundred times, of its being a law. How can *I* help laws?'[34] Hopkins's insistence on the 'saying Yes' which preserves free will should be seen as giving faith some purchase on what 'befalls' in an epoch more insidiously subject to determinism than that of Duns Scotus, Pope, or Keats. That his writings on the *arbitrium* may be related to his father's insurance calculations and the statistical 'laws' of Mr Gradgrind is evident from a letter to Bridges of 1888: 'I have written a paper for an Irish magazine . . . I was asked and I rewrote something I had by me and it is to appear next month. And yet I bet you it will not: my luck will not allow it. But if it does, I then bet you it is intelligible, though on an obstruse subject, Statistics and Free Will.'[35] A later missive reports: 'My little Paper on *Statistics and Free Will* obeyed the general law and did not appear; so I win that wager, if you remember' (*LB* 294).

The manuscript of this essay seems to be lost,[36] but Hopkins's jokes give an indication of its likely argument. There is 'general law' in a statistical sense, but room remains for uncertainty, for making wagers and winning. The 'laws' invoked by Tom Gradgrind do not apply at those depths where, as 'Duns Scotus . . . shews', 'freedom is compatible with necessity' (*LB* 169). Even so, Hopkins does find a 'deep' role for numbers when he says that the 'bare self, to which no nature has yet been added . . . is indeed nothing, a zero, in the score or account of existence, but as possible it is positive, like a positive infinitesimal' (*S* 146). And it is not irrelevant that the word used to describe the temper of this self, 'pitch', belongs to a game of hazard (cf. 'toss'). The available 'pitches' are ordered, like notes in music or the colours of a rainbow, yet a 'pitch' is what one 'happens' to have, and what dragonflies and bells 'fling out'.[37] Similar imagery recurs in the journals. Snowdrifts, for instance, show that 'chance left free to act falls into an order as well as purpose' (*J* 230). Since 'chance' is not itself an organising force, it is not inconsistent for the poet to say that 'Chance . . . is the ἐνέργεια, the stress, of the intrinsic possibility which things have' yet (in a passage continuous with his Oxford attack on atomism) deny it power to achieve or maintain identity (*S* 123–4). Of course the despondent poet of 1888 would not have diverted his own *energeia* into 'Statistics and Free Will' did popular anxieties not bear on his own predicament. Significantly, during the last decade of his life, Hopkins's letters repeatedly invoke 'the hand of providence' (*FL* 63), 'special guidance, a more particular providence' (*LD* 93). Such appeals were sharply at odds with the 'laws' established by probabilists and statisticians from Laplace to Francis Galton. Within 'the history of chance', it was a far bolder gesture in the 1880s than it had been for the Miltonic Keats. In the almost suicidally dark phases of his Irish period, however, Hopkins needed to think of God as a benign statistician who dealt in selves, who 'counts all our steps', as a Liverpool sermon put it (*S* 91). 'You should know that *there is a special providence over death*', he assured himself: '*You*, [God] says, *are worth more than . . . any* number of *sparrows . . . the hairs of your head*, Christ says, are *numbered*' (*S* 252).

Part of Hopkins's problem was that, during the mid-nineteenth century, Epicurean atomism combined with new hypotheses of randomness – notably in the work of Clerk Maxwell – to reinforce (not unparadoxically) the ancient idea of chance as fate:

> One better backed comes crowding by: –
> That level power whose word is Must
> Dances the balls for low or high:
> Her urn takes all, her deal is just . . .

Hopkins's translation of Horace's 'Odi profanum volgus . . .' has been called 'forced and arbitrary' for having '*balls* where "dice" would be clearer'.[38] In fact, it renders a 'forced and arbitrary' world by echoing those treatises on probability which instance 'balls' drawn from an 'urn', rather than dice-play, because that model of chance resembles an atomistic universe. When Keats, in 1819, called his life 'the cast of a die', he was being far from 'orthodox'. By the 1860s many poets were saying, with Fitzgerald's Omar Khayyám, 'The Ball no Question makes of Ayes and Noes,/ But Right or Left as strikes the Player goes'.[39] In 'The Card-dealer', for instance, Dante Gabriel Rossetti describes a mystic figure whose cards 'fall . . . on the bright board' to 'play' all men their chances.[40] Though he claimed to be a Christian, Rossetti's lyric is bereft of providential (or any other, beyond a card-deck's) design, and the only purchase of understanding lies in the dealer's foreknowledge of what she absolutely casts: 'Thou seest the card that falls, – she knows/ The card that followeth'. Like the 'Rubáiyát', and much high Victorian poetry, Rossetti's verse is consequently memorable when caught in a moment from which the past appears 'a clanging swarm' ('Rose Mary') and the future 'a sealed seed plot' ('The Cloud Confines'). His memory is haunted by missed chances, by the 'Might-have-been'. Keatsian phrasing may persist, as when Rossetti describes 'the dying day':

> And now the mustering rooks innumerable
> Together sail and soar,
> While for the day's death, like a tolling knell,
> Unto the heart they seem to cry, Farewell,
> No more, farewell, no more!

Yet this 'innumerable' host is more alarming than the 'gathering swallows' of *To Autumn* (33). Keats's birds have somewhere warm and sunny to go; 'Hope' in Rossetti's 'Sunset Wings' is pointedly 'not plumed'. The 'shadows numberless' of *Ode to a Nightingale* are signs of creative possibility; they show that the game can still be won by a 'happy . . . lot' (9, 5). As Rossetti's dark birds 'wing to the rooky wood', their very thronging seems fatal.

The statistical speculations of scientists like Galton had such an extensive impact that it would be possible, given time and space, to trace their effect upon even so withdrawn a poet as Rossetti. With Hopkins the task is easier. Despite his commitment to a religion regarded by many as hostile to science, he was demonstrably acquainted with up-to-the-minute research. After announcing the rejection of 'Statistics and Free Will', he told Bridges: 'meantime I get into print in a way I would not. My father wrote a little book on Numbers, the numbers one to ten, a sketchy thing, raising points of interest in a vast, an infinite subject' (*LB* 294). Galton's *Inquiries into Human Faculty and its Development* (1883) had illustrated with engravings the spatial and synaesthetic sense of number of various persons (e.g., Fig. 14.3). An unnamed 'relation' of Manley Hopkins – i.e., the poet – is reported in the 'little book', *Cardinal Numbers*, as finding these diagrams 'very fantastic and interesting':

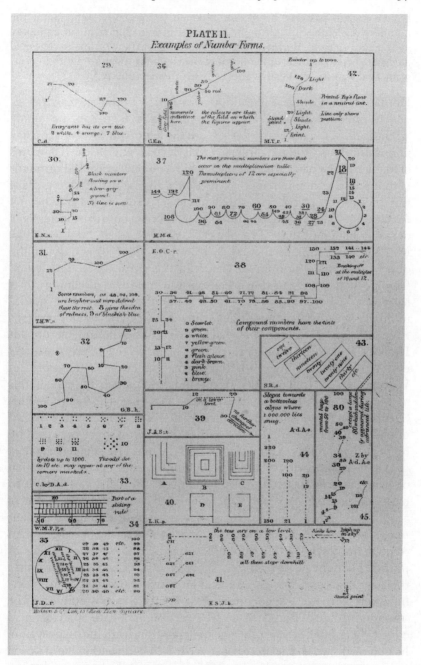

Figure 14.3   *Examples of Number Forms*, Plate II of Francis Galton, *Inquiries into Human Faculty and its Development* (London, 1883)

I have such a pattern. From No. 1 which [is] scarcely seen, to 12, the numbers rise either uprightly, or leaning a little to the right, in a gloomy light. From 12 to 20, they run to the right, rising a little, and are in a cheerful daylight. From 20 to 100, the numbers are as if far away to my right, and seem as if I must go towards them, to see them properly.[41]

Hopkins drew Bridges's attention to a notice in the *Saturday Review* which, under the remorseless title '1, 2, 3, 4, 5, 6, 7, 8, 9, 10', made 'great game' of *Cardinal Numbers*.[42] 'On the left of number *one* are a few minus numbers,' the poet informed his father: 'and below it, swarms of fractions. The place where these appear is gloomy grass. Backgrounds of rooms and remembered open-air scenes appear in different parts of this picture or world' (21). The reviewer sank in his hatchet by remarking: 'The language contains few more accurate or impressive decasyllabic lines' than 'The place . . . gloomy grass', 'and we invite Mr. Manley Hopkins to a sympathetic shudder of ecstasy at the observation that the number of feet in this decasyllabic line is *ten*.' Clumsy though the put-down is, it must have caused discomfort to at least one 'Mr. Manley Hopkins'. Galton was drawn to spatial numbers because they might help show how far conceptual patterns were inherited, how far influenced by private associations. Gerard M. Hopkins will have wanted to reconcile the selved instress of these patterns with his respect for the 'forms' which gave the world of Wisdom 11, as well as the conceptual field which he called 'this picture or world', mathematical shape. The poet who numbered his 'Deutschland' stanza towards, then away from, 'five and five' would not have been indifferent to learn that the mental space occupied by his negative numbers and fractions had the measure of a pentameter.

Whether numbering syllables or counting trees, dividing a meditation or using figures to structure mnemonics,[43] Hopkins was drawn to mathematical order in ways which provided an antidote to theories of atomistic 'chance' and fateful statistics. For historical as well as temperamental reasons, Keats's impulses were different. When Arnold quotes his letter about 'writing at random – straining at particles of light' (*Letters*, ii. 80), he does so to enforce the claim that the poet regretted his ignorance. The words cannot resonate fully, however, without a recognition that Keats was hospitable to the 'random'. John Wilson Croker observed as much, with an ideological edge, when, after turning the cockney poet's arithmetic against him, he objected that 'He seems to us to write a line at random' and be led to his next thought 'by the *rhyme*'.[44] It is historically unguarded to say (as Barbara Everett does, in her perceptive 'Keats: Somebody Reading') that 'the "haphazard" . . . is one of the faces of the natural . . . part of the literary'.[45] Yet there is no doubt that Keats absorbed from the Reynolds/Taylor/Woodhouse milieu of wagering, playful numbers and liberal individualism, and more broadly from a late-Enlightenment belief that 'chance' was a shadowy field ('straining at particles of light') which fell short of full knowledge but was not alien to it, a love of creative 'hap': a sense that there could be (in Pope's word) 'Direction' within the random, if only for chosen spirits. His delight in 'happiness' of this sort is shown in a letter to Haydon: 'I remember your saying that you had notions of a good Genius presiding over you – I have of late had the same thought. for things which I do half at Random are afterwards confirmed by my judgment in a dozen features of Propriety' (*Letters*, i. 141–2). That Keats adds, 'Is it too daring to Fancy Shakspeare this Presider?' returns us firmly to life as 'the cast of a die' and Reynolds on cockfighting, for two pages later Keats quotes *Antony and Cleopatra*, a play which he had just read. 'Genius' is a rare word in Shakespeare, but Macbeth says 'My Genius is rebuk'd, as it is said/ Mark Antony's was by Caesar'[46] and, in a scene marked in Keats's copy,[47] Antony attributes Caesar's 'luck' to a presiding daemon: 'The very dice obey him . . . If we draw lots, he speeds;/ His cocks do win the battle still of mine' (II. iii. 34–7).

Inspired randomness was so integral for Keats that he described composition as 'trac[ing] . . . shadows with the magic hand of Chance' (*Letters*, i. 222). As a result, there is nothing in him like Hopkins's comparison of rhythmic variety to 'the ratio of . . . circumference to . . . diameter' in 'the circle and ellipse' (*J* 283). Keats was prepared to entertain the fancy that 'some . . . letters are good squares others handsome ovals, and others some orbicular, others spheroid' (*Letters*, i. 279). But the missive which raises this is said to be shaped 'like a Rat-trap'; and anyway, 'If I scribble long letters I must play my vagaries . . . I must play my draughts as I please, and for my advantage and your erudition, crown a white with a black, or a black with a white, and move into black or white, far or near'. When not ranging haphazardly across an imaginary draughtboard Keats takes a perverse delight in underplaying his hand. Deciding to write an exactly sheet-long epistle to Dilke, he is struck by the absurdity of calculating language in this way, and puts on the naivety of a person who thinks that logic means always starting with *one*, the least chancy card: 'in the Game of Whist if I have an ace I constantly play it first'

(*Letters*, i. 367).[48] Because of his allegiance to 'mathematically . . . expressed' forms, Hopkins has a far less ludic feel for the disposition of texts. He is not just concerned to analyse the 'numbers' of prosody (e.g., *J* 267ff., *LB* 119–20, 203); the mathematics of verse lie near the root of larger orders. Planning a book on Dorian Measure ('it needs mathematics'), he says that his 'purpose' is, in practice, 'to write almost a philosophy of art' (*LB* 246–7). Consider the generation of his most characteristic form. The doubleness of blue and white when the 'sky is two and two';[49] the threeness of a 'triple *cuckoo*' and 'holy Three in One';[50] the fourness of the architecture of Netley Abbey (*J* 216); the sevenness of music ('a sort of rhyming on seven rhymes') and 'Charles's Wain':[51] when taken with Hopkins's conviction that art-objects should have the μορφὴ μία or 'one form' possessed by the elm seen near Bullaton Rocks (*J* 153), these recurrent numbers converge on a structure capable of accommodating other 'forms': the fourteen-line, rhymed sonnet. To explain Hopkins's attraction to the sonnet in this way is not to exaggerate his mathematical self-consciousness. 'The equation of the best sonnet', he told Dixon, 'is $(4+4)+(3+3)=2.4+2.3=2(4+3)=2.7=14$' (*LD* 71).[52]

It might be wondered how the poet could sustain these 'Platonic' inclinations in the age of Galton. Significantly, in that essay which is itself a calculation of chances, 'The Probable Future of Metaphysics', the words 'type or species' are used interchangeably with 'form'. The claims of evolutionary science were so much more pressingly disruptive for Hopkins than the author of *Hyperion* that he could hardly use 'Platonic' language without a Darwinian accent. At this date, questions of number and chance were urgently related to natural selection. Venn's *Logic of Chance* has on its title page: 'So careful of the type she seems,/ So careless of the single life'.[53] *On the Origin of Species* raised for many the thought that 'species' could not develop without chance. Galton considered it a major discovery that apparently random variables between generations could be reduced to a 'curve'. Nature had a 'law of error' which 'would have been personified by the Greeks and deified, if they had known of it'.[54] From this perspective a 'type or species' was a 'form' with 'real' existence in the statistically varied relations of things through time. Partly to help readers visualise such entities, Galton reproduced on the frontispiece of *Inquiries into Human Faculty* superimposed photographs of people with 'Tubercular Diseases' (Fig. 14.4). Keats knew that his death was, in the Latin sense, probable ('evident from tokens and medical

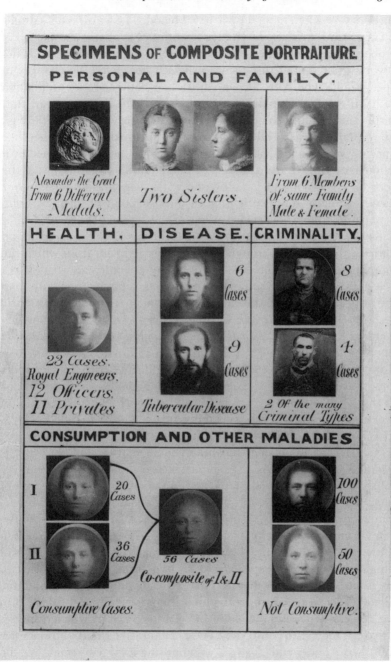

Figure 14.4 *Specimens of Composite Portraiture*, Frontispiece of Francis Galton, *Inquiries into Human Faculty and its Development* (London, 1883)

authority')[55] when he spat up arterial blood. The features of Galton's '6 Cases' and '9 Cases' (etymology continues to speak) show a fall of probabilities which allow the 'type' of consumption to appear. It lies beyond the scope of this essay to suggest how semantic changes in 'species' and 'type' correlate with differences between Keats's affiliation with Milton and Hopkins's awareness of Keats. But it is clear that, despite his hostility to crude evolutionary theory in aesthetics (e.g., *LB* 171–2), there is a Galtonesque timbre in Hopkins's claim that, like 'species' which are 'distinct' but 'grouped', 'the modern medieval school is descended from . . . Keats, Leigh Hunt', and that, just as the poor of Liverpool and Glasgow show 'the degradation even of our race', so 'many sonnets in English may in point of form be great departures from and degenerations of the type' (*LD* 97).

Keats, 'in point of form', wrote Miltonic then Shakespearean sonnets, then passed through a phase of experiment from which the 'numbers' of the odes emerged. Hopkins wrote tailed and truncated, as well as large-scale sprung-rhythm sonnets, but remained faithful to the Miltonic 'type'. That Keats thought sonnet-rhyming problematic is shown by a letter to the George Keatses (*Letters*, ii. 108) which includes the sonnet, *If by dull rhymes our English must be chain'd*. While 'the chances of rhyme'[56] seem to have stimulated his 'half . . . Random' flow in couplets, the complex regularities of the fourteen-line form shackled 'the magic hand of Chance' (a sonnet-word itself forced to rhyme). Consonance was less intuitive for Hopkins. His notes on 'Poetry and Verse' suggest a geometric view of word-sound: 'Poetry is speech framed . . . to be heard for its own sake and interest even over and above its interest of meaning. Some matter and meaning is essential to it but only as an element necessary to support and employ the shape which is contemplated for its own sake' (*J* 289). This love of 'shape' or *'figure'* (*J* 267) becomes visible as well as audible in manuscript, where an increasing tendency to subdivide sonnet octaves and sestets finally leads Hopkins to score them with 'braces in the left margin to identify the structural units'.[57] Indeed his division of 'single, sonnet-like inscape' (*J* 259) by two, three, four, and seven can be traced into verbal detail. Take two, again: 'The Sea and the Skylark' declares in its opening line (if not in its sibilant title) – 'On ear and ear two noises too old to end' – a stereophony which disperses ('two . . . too . . . to') into sub-verbal, alliterative ringing ('flood or a fall', 'wear and wend') as well as mounting a larger *'figure'*. Yet the strongest effect of rhyme and chime, in this sonnet as elsewhere, leaving nothing (it might be felt) to chance, is that '*oftening, over-and-overing, aftering* of the inscape' which, Hopkins said, 'must take place in order to detach it to the mind' (*J* 289). In 'Hopkins as a Decadent Critic', Donald Davie objects to his 'crammed, stimulated and knotted' language.[58] It is the simultaneous urge towards abstraction, however, which might earn the label 'decadent'. Comparison with Mallarmé is just, if by that we mean a writer for whom 'La syntaxe était . . . une algèbre', and who wrote the sonnet because it works 'contraindre l'esprit de considérer le *fond* et la *forme* comme des conditions égales entre elles . . . il nous enseigne à découvrir qu'une forme est féconde en *idées*, paradoxe apparent et principe profond d'où analyse mathématique a tiré quelque partie de sa prodigieuse puissance.'[59] A sonnet such as Mallarmé's 'Salut' has an inturned delicacy refined to 'Rien . . . À ne désigner que la coupe'.[60] White space is blank, and '*la forme*' is the champagne flute of occasion: a 'coupe' which, quibbling on 'coup', reminds us that the text is a throw hazarded, and that Mallarmé's great poem of shipwreck does not '*over-and-over*' fiveness or any other '*figure*' but scatters the message, 'Un Coup de Dés jamais n'abolira le Hasard'.[61]

Mallarméan randomness is swayed by forces which Hopkins registers but resists. The broken, drifting discourse of 'Un Coup de Dés' instantiates a 'haphazardness' more radical than anything insured or diced against by Reynolds. The post-Nietzschean chances of our own late century, coloured by quantum mechanics and chaos theory, by psychoanalytic contingency,[62] abstract expressionism, the aleatory works of John Cage and Jackson Mac Low, and the 'Lots, Sorts, and Futures' of postmodern fiction,[63] make the principles which motivate Keatsian and Victorian 'numbers' only superficially accessible. If the 'haphazard' in Keats looks like 'one of the faces of the natural', it is because historical rhyming – and no more – is possible between different periods' ideas of chance. Even those modern poets who adopt a Keatsian idiom have their language revealingly inflected. Wallace Stevens, for example, laureate of the Hartford Accident and Indemnity Company, once claimed that his employment could 'touch the imagination'. For 'Our prime instinct is to go on indefinitely like the wax flowers on the mantelpiece. Insurance is the most easily understood geometry for calculating how to bring the thing about.'[64] Against the thrust of Stevens's claim, the futility of attempting to arrest mutability is manifest in that stuffy image of sapless flowers on a bourgeois mantelpiece. The poet's vision of

Accident is too strong to credit insurers' 'geometry' with force. Thus, in 'Notes Toward a Supreme Fiction',

the constant

> Violets, doves, girls, bees and hyacinths
> Are inconstant objects of inconstant cause
> In a universe of inconstancy . . .[65]

The Keats of *To Autumn* does not doubt that the 'bees', for example, which gather their insurance against winter are subject to mutability.[66] Yet in his movingly poised description of that season then known (in England as well as America) as the 'fall',[67] the changes and chances through time of ageing ('full-grown lambs'), departure ('gathering swallows'), or simply being gusted ('as the light wind lives or dies') equally imply their opposites: spring 'lambs', the return of migrant birds, the undulatory movement of 'small gnats'. Those insects, indeed, 'borne aloft/ Or sinking' are a breath-quiet recollection of Satan, in the May 1818 letter to Reynolds, who 'drops' and soars 'aloft' (to a marked caesura) on the 'rebuff' of windy 'chance'.

Breathing matters because of what 'lives and dies' meant to a poet whose brother died of consumption, and who feared the same 'misfortune'. The 'wailful choir' of gnats are not the only musical voices in *To Autumn*, but they bring out with peculiar poignancy Keats's genius for taking a 'Direction' and participating in rhythms which were those of his body yet not his own. When John Aitken writes to the ailing poet, in 1820, 'I guessed . . . that I heard the parting beauty of the Swan's adieus in your numbers' (*Letters*, ii. 325), his commonplace is partly rescued by the epistle *To Charles Cowden Clarke*, where Keats compares himself to a 'swan' ruffled with 'diamond water drops'. These

> . . . drop like hours into eternity.
> Just like that bird am I in loss of time,
> Whene'er I venture on the stream of rhyme;
> With shatter'd boat, oar snapt, and canvass rent,
> I slowly sail, scarce knowing my intent . . .   (14–18)

More meets the ear in the chance of 'rhyme' than 'loss of time'; an acoustic blur with 'stream' helps make the 'loss' a gain, a 'losing track of' time along an 'eternal' drift of numbers. Aitken's clichéd image deepens into validity when we think of Keats being subject to a flow which he helps create. The poet who boasts, 'The patriot shall . . . in the senate thunder out my numbers/ To startle princes from their easy slumbers' (*To My Brother George* (epistle), 73–5) is more politically than creatively Keatsian because he neglects that resource of scarce-knowingness; similarly, though by contrast, the late, anguished cry, 'Physician Nature! let my spirit blood! ... till the flood/ Of stifling numbers ebbs from my full breast' (*To Fanny*, 1–4) has a claustrophobic self-awareness of inward flow which deadens the authentic note. As we have seen, beauty and truth are closest when Keats moves 'half at Random', stabilised by 'knowledge', gusted yet pinion-shouldered. In the earliest letter to Fanny Brawne, he dilates 'time' by saying, in defiance of number, 'I almost wish we were butterflies and liv'd but three summer days – three such days with you I could fill with more delight than fifty common years' (*Letters*, ii. 123). It was this kind of fragile, part-gusted yet winged passivity which encouraged Victorians to think him 'unmanly'. If the argument of this essay is correct, however, changes in 'the history of chance' made it hard for them to sympathise with Keats's trust in randomness. Such consonance as holds between our own ideas of chance and those of the early nineteenth century allows us to understand that his openness to what befell and might befall had less to do with 'effeminacy' than with feelings about uncertainty which, leading at worst to grim fatalism about life's lost wagers, at best made him uniquely sensitive to 'vagaries' and 'lots' in the world, in his own mind, in the 'numbers' of blood, and language.

NOTES

1 Percy Bysshe Shelley, *Adonais*, 48, T. Hutchinson (ed.), *Shelley: Poetical Works*, corrected by G. M. Matthews (Oxford, 1970).

2 Quoted by George H. Ford, *Keats and the Victorians* (New Haven, 1944), 71. For a full survey of gender-involved criticism see Susan Wolfson, 'Feminizing Keats', in H. de Almeida (ed.), *Critical Essays on John Keats* (Boston, 1990), 317–56.

3 Preface to Arnold's selection of Keats's poems in Ward's English Poets series; quotations from 'John Keats', in R. H. Super (ed.), *Complete Prose Works of Matthew Arnold* (11 vols., Ann Arbor, 1960–77) ix. 205–16.

4 In this essay errors and deletions in Keats's letters recorded by Rollins will only be reproduced when relevant.

5 The scholarly literature is extensive, but see, for some closely worked instances, Alastair Fowler, *Triumphal Forms: Structural Patterns in Elizabethan Poetry* (Cambridge, 1970) and, for larger fields of reference, Thomas

Crump, *The Anthropology of Numbers* (Cambridge, 1990), chaps. 3 and 9.

6 *The Enemy's Country: Words, Contexture, and other Circumstances of Language* (Oxford, 1991), 26.

7 See Ian Hacking, *The Emergence of Probability: A Philosophical Study of Early Ideas about Probability, Induction and Statistical Inference* (Cambridge, 1975) – despite its relative neglect of classical sources – and *The Taming of Chance* (Cambridge, 1990).

8 'An Epistle from Mr. Pope, to Dr. Arbuthnot', 128, J. Butt (ed.), *The Poems of Alexander Pope* (London, 1963); Lorraine Daston, *Classical Probability in the Enlightenment* (Princeton, 1988), 23.

9 'An Argument for Divine Providence, Taken from the Constant Regularity Observ'd in the Births of Both Sexes', *Philosophical Transactions of the Royal Society of London* 27 (1710), 186–90. On the paper's derivation and impact see Lester M. Beattie, *John Arbuthnot: Mathematician and Satirist* (Cambridge, Mass., 1935), 339–46.

10 Joseph Glanvill, *Philosophia Pia* (London, 1671); Walter Charleton, *Darkness of Atheism Dispelled by the Light of Nature* (London, 1652); 'An Essay on Man', I. 289–90 (Butt, *Poems of Pope*, 515).

11 *Thus Spake Zarathustra*, quoted by Hacking, *Taming*, 147.

12 'Duns Scotus's Oxford', 12, N. H. Mackenzie (ed.), *The Poetical Works of Gerard Manley Hopkins* (Oxford, 1990).

13 C. C. Abbott (ed.), *Further Letters of Gerard Manley Hopkins* (2nd edn, Oxford, 1956), 386; cf. 381–2, 384, 387; subsequent references (*FL*) in text.

14 'Christabel', 10, H. J. Jackson (ed.), *Samuel Taylor Coleridge*, The Oxford Authors (Oxford, 1985); for 'The Arithmetic of Poetry' see the *Champion*, 16 Feb. 1817; rpt. L. M. Jones (ed.), *Selected Prose of John Hamilton Reynolds* (Cambridge, Mass., 1966), 97–9.

15 From Edward Cocker (1631–75), author of mathematical handbooks.

16 Hugh Sykes Davies's account of 'seven', 'three', and (above all) 'one' deserves note; see J. Kerrigan and J. Wordsworth (eds.), *Wordsworth and the Worth of Words* (Cambridge, 1986), 103–18.

17 *London Magazine*, Nov. 1822; Jones, *Selected Prose*, 367–89.

18 See, e.g., the leader cartoon in the *Independent*, 19 June 1991, which shows a well-heeled lady at Ascot assuring her fashionable friends, 'I'm a member of Lloyd's, so if I lose, the government pays my debts.'

19 For useful summaries see Lorraine J. Daston, 'The Domestication of Risk: Mathematical Probability and Insurance 1650–1830', in L. Krüger et al. (eds.), *The Probabilistic Revolution* (2 vols., Cambridge, Mass., 1987) i. 237–60 and Gerd Gigerenzer et al., *The Empire of Chance: How Probability Changed Science and Everyday Life* (Cambridge, 1989), 19–26.

20 'My Chances/ *Mes Chances*: A Rendezvous with Some Epicurean Stereophonies', in J. H. Smith and W. Kerrigan (eds.), *Taking Chances: Derrida, Psychoanalysis, and Literature* (Baltimore, 1984), 5.

21 Cf. *Letters* i. 277 n. 4. Quotations from J. Carey and A. Fowler (eds.), *The Poems of John Milton* (London, 1968).

22 *Lines on Seeing a Lock of Milton's Hair*, 1.

23 See, e.g., Adrian Desmond, *The Politics of Evolution: Morphology, Medicine, and Reform in Radical London* (Chicago, 1989), esp. 236–7, 255–7, 264–7.

24 For valuable contexts and another emphasis see H. de Almeida, *Romantic Medicine and John Keats* (New York and Oxford, 1991), Pt IV, esp. 251 ff., 259–61.

25 *Don Juan* XI, 24–5, 37–40, J. McGann (ed.), *Lord Byron: The Complete Poetical Works* (7 vols., Oxford, 1980–93) v. 466.

26 The exchange was prompted by Patmore's review of Colvin's biography, rpt. in his *Principle in Art, Etc.* (London, 1912), 76–7, 80.

27 H. House and G. Storey (eds.), *The Journals and Papers of Gerard Manley Hopkins* (Oxford, 1959), 70; subsequent references (*J*) in text.

28 For accessible accounts of what 'atomism' came to mean, during Hopkins's years at Oxford, Roehampton, and Stoneyhurst, see William Kingdon Clifford, 'Atoms' (1874), collected in *Lectures and Essays*, ed. L. Stephen and F. Pollard (2 vols., London, 1879) i. 158–90, and the opening sections of John Tyndall, 'The Belfast Address' (1874), collected in his *Fragments of Science* (2 vols., London, 1899) ii. 135–201.

29 C. C. Abbott (ed.), *The Correspondence of Gerard Manley Hopkins and Richard Watson Dixon* (Oxford, 1935), 105; subsequent references (*LD*) in text.

30 Tom Zaniello, *Hopkins in the Age of Darwin* (Iowa City, 1988), 133–4.

31 'The Blessed Virgin compared to the Air we Breathe', 86–9.

32 See C. Devlin, S. J. (ed.), *The Sermons and Devotional Writings of Gerard Manley Hopkins* (Oxford, 1959), 343–4; subsequent references (*S*) in text.

33 *The Logic of Chance* (2nd edn, London, 1876), 466.

34 *Hard Times*, Book III, chap. 7; quoted by Hacking, *Taming*, 118.

35 C. C. Abbott (ed.), *The Letters of Gerard Manley Hopkins to Robert Bridges* (Oxford, 1935), 291–2; subsequent references (*LB*) in text.

36 Thanks are due to two Hopkins editors, Catherine Phillips and Graham Storey, and to Judith Priestman (Bodleian Library) and Fr Philip Endean (Campion Hall) for help in its pursuit.

37 *S* 151, 'As kingfishers catch fire . . .'

38 An opinion quoted by Mackenzie, *Poetical Works*, 299.

39 'The Rubáiyát of Omar Khayyám', 193–4, in C. Ricks (ed.), *The New Oxford Book of Victorian Verse* (Oxford, 1987).

40 Quotations from O. Doughty (ed.), *Poems* (London, 1961).

41 (London, 1887), 20.

42 22 Sept. 1888, 351–2.

43 On Hopkins's use of Loisette's system of 'physiological memory' see Alan Heuser, *The Shaping Vision of Gerard Manley Hopkins* (Oxford, 1958), 80.

44 '*Endymion: A Poetic Romance*. By John Keats', *Quarterly Review*, 19 (Sept. 1818), 206. On p. 205 Croker picks up Keats's prefatory apology for 'The two first books, and indeed the two last', scoffing 'two and two make four, and . . . that is the whole number of books', etc. See *KCH*, 112.

45 Rpt. *Poets in their Time: Essays on English Poetry from Donne to Larkin* (London, 1986), 150–2. Everett is rightly resisting Helen Vendler's overprotective insistence, in *The Odes of John Keats* (Cambridge, Mass.,

and London, 1983), 5, that 'an artist's choices are never haphazard'.

46 III. i. 55–6; quotations from G. Blakemore Evans (ed.), *The Riverside Shakespeare* (Boston, 1974).

47 See Caroline Spurgeon, *Keats's Shakespeare, A Descriptive Study Based on New Material* (London, 1928), 126–7.

48 For flexible handling of the ace in whist (and repeated advice to reserve it) see, e.g., Edmond Hoyle's oft-reprinted manual, rev. and corr. Charles Jones, *Hoyle's Games Improved . . . With an Essay on Game Cocks* (London, 1800), 4–8.

49 'The Woodlark'.

50 *J* 137, 'Summa'.

51 *LB* 169, 'Penmaen Pool'.

52 For an early (1865) version of such thinking see 'On the Origin of Beauty: A Platonic Dialogue' (*J* 86–114).

53 'In Memoriam', LV.7–8, C. Ricks (ed.), *The Poems of Tennyson* (2nd edn, 3 vols., London, 1987).

54 Hacking, *Taming*, 186; cf. Donald A. MacKenzie, *Statistics in Britain 1865–1930: The Social Construction of Scientific Knowledge* (Edinburgh, 1981), 56–63, 68–72.

55 For this semantic trail see Douglas Lane Patey, *Probability and Literary Form: Philosophic Theory and Literary Practice in the Augustan Age* (Cambridge, 1984), esp. 4–8, 36–45.

56 Cf. Charles Tomlinson's poem, under this title, in *The Way of a World* (Oxford, 1969), and the equivalently titled, but sadly uneven, critical study by Donald Wesling (California, 1980).

57 Mackenzie, *Poetical Works*, lxi.

58 *Purity of Diction in English Verse* (2nd edn, London, 1967), 175.

59 Paul Valéry, *Œuvres*, ed. Jean Hytier (2 vols., Paris, 1957–60), i. 685, ii. 1207.

60 *Oeuvres Complètes*, ed. Henri Mondor and G. Jean-Aubry (Paris, 1945).

61 On Mallarmé and chance see, e.g., Erich Köhler, *Der Literarische Zufall, Das Mögliche und Die Notwendigkeit* (Munich, 1973), chap. 2.

62 See, e.g., the conclusion of Freud's essay on Leonardo da Vinci (1910), as applied by Richard Rorty, *Contingency, Irony, and Solidarity* (Cambridge, 1989), 31.

63 See Gillian Beer's remarks on Pynchon, Peter Carey, and Julian Barnes in relation to the Victorian novel: 'The Reader's Wager: Lots, Sorts, and Futures', *EinC* 40 (1990), 99–123.

64 'Insurance and Social Change', in *Opus Posthumous*, rev. and enlarged edn by Milton J. Bates (London, 1990), 234.

65 *The Collected Poems of Wallace Stevens* (New York, 1955).

66 For a broader context see Helen Vendler, 'Stevens and Keats' "To Autumn"', in F. Doggett and R. Buttel (eds.), *Wallace Stevens: A Celebration* (Princeton, 1980), 171–95.

67 *OED* sb¹ 2.

Index